Studien zum ausländischen und internationalen Privatrecht

542

Herausgegeben vom

Max-Planck-Institut für ausländisches
und internationales Privatrecht

Direktorium:

Holger Fleischer, Ralf Michaels, Anne Röthel

Enforcing Private Regulation in the Platform Economy

Edited by

Federica Casarosa and Mateusz Grochowski

Mohr Siebeck

Federica Casarosa is Research Affiliate at the Sant'Anna School of Advanced Studies and part-time professor at the European University Institute in Florence, Italy.
orcid.org/0000-0002-5256-3505

Mateusz Grochowski is Affiliated Fellow at the Information Society Project, Yale Law School and Associate Professor of Law at Tulane University School of Law, New Orleans.
orcid.org/0000-0001-5013-4830

Open Access funding provided by Max Planck Society.

ISBN 978-3-16-163903-6 / eISBN 978-3-16-163904-3
DOI 10.1628/978-3-16-163904-3

ISSN 0720-1141 / eISSN 2568-7441
(Studien zum ausländischen und internationalen Privatrecht)

The Deutsche Nationalbibliothek lists this publication in the Deutsche Nationalbiblioraphie; detailed bibliographic data are available at *https://dnb.dnb.de.*

Published by Mohr Siebeck Tübingen 2025.

Printed on non-aging paper.

Mohr Siebeck GmbH & Co. KG, Wilhelmstraße 18, 72074 Tübingen, Germany
www.mohrsiebeck.com, info@mohrsiebeck.com

A Bianca, sensibile e volitiva
Federica Casarosa

To my Parents
Mateusz Grochowski

Preface

In recent years, online platforms have become some of the most powerful players in the global economy and have created entirely new models for organizing business activity and generating profit. These developments have had numerous social, economic, and legal ramifications. One of the most vivid and contentious among them is the inherent tendency of platform economies to produce self-regulatory schemes of varying nature, scope, and complexity.

This book considers these issues from three complementary perspectives. It begins with a general theoretical framework for private regulation in the platform economy; it then proceeds toward more specific aspects of platform-made private regulation; finally it offers insights on the interaction of platform- and state-produced rules in selected EU Member States. The book combines two key regulatory issues: rulemaking and enforcement, viewing them as inseparably linked aspects of the same phenomenon, their reflecting the shifting boundary between states and private entities as governors of the digital market and society.

This volume was made possible with the support of a grant from Villa Vigoni – the Italian-German Center for European Dialogue – which hosted the book's contributors at a meeting in the breathtaking setting of Lake Como. The event was the occasion for an in-depth discussion of the chapters and helped ensure coherence between them. The book project was co-sponsored by the Max Planck Institute for Comparative and International Private Law in Hamburg and the Robert Schuman Center for Advanced Studies at the European University Institute in Florence. The support of these three institutions was indispensable in bringing this book and the entire project to fruition.

We are also profoundly grateful to Professor Hans-Wolfgang Micklitz, who provided the introduction to this volume and who shared invaluable advice on the project's merits. And of course, no book would exist without its authors. We sincerely thank our colleagues who contributed to this project and submitted chapters for the volume. This includes Judge Dianora Poletti, whose premature passing cast a shadow over the final stages of our work. Last but certainly not least, we would like to express our heartfelt thanks to Professor Ralf Michaels for his generosity towards this project, as well as to Dr. Christian Eckl, Michael Friedman, and Janina Jentz of the Max Planck Institute for Comparative and International Private Law in Hamburg for their invaluable support in editing this volume and helping bring it to its final form.

Florence/New Orleans
February 2025

Federica Casarosa/
Mateusz Grochowski

Contents

Abbreviations

AcP	Archiv für die civilistische Praxis
ADR	alternative dispute resolution
AGCM	Autorità Garante per la concorrenza e il mercato – National Competition and Market Authority
AI Act	Artificial Intelligence Act
AJEE	Access to Justice in Eastern Europe
ALER	American Law and Economics Review
Am J Comp L	American Journal of Comparative Law
Am Bus LJ	American Business Law Journal
Am Pol Sci Rev	American Political Science Review
AmU LRev	American University Law Review
AmU Intl LRev	American University International Law Review
AP	Arbeitsrechtliche Praxis
API	Application Programming Interface
Ariz LRev	Arizona Law Review
AuR	Arbeit und Recht
AVMSD	Audiovisual Media Services Directive (Directive (EU) 2018/1808)
BAG	Bundesarbeitsgericht [Federal Labour Court, Germany]
Berkeley Tech LJ	Berkeley Technology Law Journal
BGH	Bundesgerichtshof [Federal Court of Justice, Germany]
BJS	Berliner Journal für Soziologie
BKartA	Bundeskartellamt [Federal Cartel Office, Germany]
CDA	Communications Decency Act
CJEU	Court of Justice of the European Union
CLLPJ	Comparative Labor Law & Policy Journal
CLS Rev	Computer Law & Security Review
CMLRev	Common Market Law Review
Colum LRev	Columbia Law Review
Comp Pol Stud	Comparative Political Studies
CPC	Consumer Protection Cooperation
CPC Regulation	Regulation (EU) 2017/2394 on cooperation between national authorities responsible for the enforcement of consumer protection laws
CPI	Competition Policy International
CSAM	child sexual abuse material
CT	Constitutional Tribunal
CUP	Cambridge University Press
CYELS	Cambridge Yearbook of European Legal Studies
DCC	Dutch Civil Code
DL	Decree-Law

DMA	Digital Markets Act
DMCA	Digital Millennium Copyright Act
DovenschmidtQ	The Dovenschmidt Quarterly
DPA	data protection authority
DPC	Data Protection Commission
DSA	Digital Services Act
DSC	digital services coordinator
DSM Copyright Directive	Directive (EU) 2019/790 on Copyright and Related Rights in the Digital Single Market
EBDS	European Board for Digital Services
ECD	E-Commerce Directive
ECJ	European Competition Journal
EDPL	European Data Protection Law Review
EJLS	European Journal of Legal Studies
EJLT	European Journal of Law and Technology
EJPLT	European Journal of Privacy Law & Technologies
EJRR	European Journal of Risk Regulation
ELJ	European Law Journal
ELLJ	European Labour Law Journal
ELRev	European Law Review
Environ Res	Environmental Research
ERCL	European Review of Contract Law
ERPL	European Review of Private Law
EuCML	Journal of European Consumer and Market Law
Eur JL Econ	European Journal of Law and Economics
Eur LJ	European Law Journal
EuZA	Europäische Zeitschrift für Arbeitsrecht
FCO	Federal Cartel Office (Germany)
GDPR	General Data Protection Regulation (Regulation (EU) 2016/679)
Geo LJ	Georgetown Law Journal
Geo Wash LRev	George Washington Law Review
Giur. comm.	Gurisprudenza commerciale
GLJ	German Law Journal
GLTR	Georgetown Law Technology Review
GTC	general terms and conditions
Harv ILJ	Harvard International Law Journal
Harv LRev	Harvard Law Review
HarvJoLT	Harvard Journal of Law & Technology
IDPL	International Data Privacy Law
IJ Media Cult Pol	International Journal of Media & Cultural Politics
IJC	International Journal of Communication
IJCL	International Journal of Constitutional Law
IJEC	International Journal of Electronic Commerce
IJGLS	Indiana Journal of Global Legal Studies

IJLIT	International Journal of Law and Information Technology
IJODR	International Journal of Online Dispute Resolution
ILJ	Industrial Law Journal
ILLeJ	Italian Labour Law e-Journal
IndBez	Industrielle Beziehungen
Intl Econ & Econ Pol	International Economics and Economic Policy
IPR	Internet Policy Review
IRLCT	International Review of Law, Computers & Technology
J Bus Ethics	Journal of Business Ethics
J BusRes	Journal of Business Research
J Eur Pub Pol	Journal of European Public Policy
J Serv Manag	Journal of Service Management
JCL&E	Journal of Competition Law & Economics
JCorpL	Journal of Corporation Law
JCP	Journal of Consumer Policy
JEBL	Journal of Business, Entrepreneurship & Law
JEEA	Journal of the European Economic Association
JIPITEC	Journal of Intellectual Property, Information Technology and E-Commerce Law
JITP	Journal of Information Technology & Politics
JLA	Journal of Legal Analysis
JLE	Journal of Law & Economic Regulation
JLS	Journal of Law and Society
JOR	Jurisprudentie Onderneming & Recht
JUS-online	JUS-online Rivista di Scienze Giuridiche
JZ	Juristenzeitung
KZfSS	Kölner Zeitschrift für Soziologie und Sozialpsychologie
Law Prac	Law Practice
LRev	Law Review
Md LRev	Maryland Law Review
Media L&Poly	Media Law & Policy
Mich LRev	Michigan Law Review
Minn LRev	Minnesota Law Review
MMR	Multimedia und Recht
Mod LRev	Modern Law Review
NCMEC	National Center for Missing & Exploited Children
NJ	Nederlandse Jurisprudentie
NJCL	Nordic Journal of Commercial Law
NJW	Neue Juristische Wochenschrift
NwU LRev	Northwestern University Law Review
NYU JLB	New York University Journal of Law & Business
NZA	Neue Zeitschrift für Arbeitsrecht
NZKart	Neue Zeitschrift für Kartellrecht

ODR	online dispute resolution
OECD	Organisation for Economic Cooperation and Development
Ohio St LJ	Ohio State Law Journal
OLG	Oberlandesgericht [Higher Regional Court, Germany]
OSJDR	Ohio State Journal on Dispute Resolution
OTK	Orzecznictwo Trybunału Konstytucyjnego [Case Law of the Constitutional Court, Poland]
OUP	Oxford University Press
ÖZS	Österreichische Zeitschrift für Soziologie
P2B	Platform to Business
P2B Regulation	Regulation (EU) 2019/1150 on promoting fairness and transparency for business users of online intermediation services
PDD	Personal Data Directive (Directive 95/46/EC)
Pol&Soc	Policy and Society
PPR	platform private regulation
PUP	Princeton University Press
QIL	Questions of International Law
RdA	Recht der Arbeit
Riv. Dir. Ind.	Rivista di Diritto Industriale
RJE	The RAND Journal of Economics
SCal Interdisc LJ	Southern California Interdisciplinary Law Journal
Secur J	Security Journal
SMU LRev	SMU Law Review/ Southern Methodist University Dedman School of Law
SoR	statement of reasons
SR	Soziales Recht
TEU	Treaty on European Union
Tex LRev	Texas Law Review
TFEU	Treaty on the Functioning of the European Union
TGI	Tribunal de Grande Instance de Paris
Theo Inq L	Theoretical Inquiries in Law
Theo Soc	Theory and Society
ToS	Terms of Service
TPR	transnational private regulation
TvC	Tijdschrift voor Consumentenrecht en handelspraktijken
UCDavis LRev	University of California Davis Law Review
UChi LRev	University of Chicago Law Review
UColo LRev	University of Colorado Law Review
UCPD	Unfair Commercial Practices Directive (Directive 2005/29/EC)
UCTD	Unfair Contract Terms Directive (Directive 93/13/EEC)
UIll LRev	University of Illinois Law Review
UNESCO	United Nations Educational, Scientific and Cultural Organization
UP	University Press

UPa LRev	University of Pennsylvania Law Review
UStThomas LJ	University of St. Thomas Law Journal
UTol LRev	University of Toledo Law Review
Vand LRev	Vanderbilt Law Review
VLOP	very large online platform
VLOSE	very large online search engine
VSP	video-sharing platform
VSSAR	Vierteljahresschrift für Sozial- und Arbeitsrecht
VuR	Verbraucher und Recht
Wash JL Tech & Arts	Washington Journal of Law, Technology & Arts
WashU LRev	Washington University Law Review
Wm&Mary LRev	William & Mary Law Review
Yale JLT	Yale Journal of Law & Technology
Yale LJ	Yale Law Journal
YEL	Yearbook of European Law
YLP Rev	Yale Law & Policy Review
YUP	Yale University Press
ZEuP	Zeitschrift für Europäisches Privatrecht
ZfA	Zeitschrift für Arbeitsrecht
ZfS	Zeitschrift für Soziologie
ZIAS	Zeitschrift für ausländisches und internationales Arbeits- und Sozialrecht
ZVglRWiss	Zeitschrift für Vergleichende Rechtswissenschaft

Prologue

Enforcing Digital Private Regulation Through Digital Private Regulation

Hans-W Micklitz

It all started in December 2020, when the European Commission published the Draft Digital Markets Act and the Draft Digital Services Act. The Draft Artificial Intelligence Act followed in April 2021. Since then, the EU legislative machinery has not stopped. Shortly before the end of the mandate in September 2024, the European Parliament, the Council, and the European Commission managed to adopt a whole series of regulations and directives, which I will call the EU Digital Policy Legislation. Depending on the counting criteria, one might quickly end up with more than 12 EU directives and regulations. Many, if not most, are not mere directives and regulations; they are comprehensive and detailed framework documents with extremely comprehensive recitals, detailed articles, and lengthy annexes, often reaching 100 pages or more in the Official Journal. Such an account is still incomplete, as the EU legislation requires the adoption of delegated and implementing acts, guidelines and recommendations, model contracts, codes of conduct and codes of practice, and last but not least a considerable amount of harmonized and non-harmonized technical standards, which still have to be elaborated by the European Standardisation Organisations (the ESOs) under participation of the four stakeholder organizations, SMEs, trade unions, and environmental and consumer organizations. It seems fair to assume that the binding laws, soft law rules, and technical standards arise from thousands of pages of documents.

The EU relies on co-regulation, on due diligence established in financial regulation, and on technical standards successfully promoted through the 1985 New Approach on Technical Standards and Specifications,[1] which combines public law – the adopted EU legislation – with private regulation, not to be equated with private law. Ex ante, the EU defines access rules that require private actors to respect binding EU law through private regulation. Post-market control, the monitoring and surveillance of many regulations and directives, is in the hands of the public national authorities and, to a limited

[1] Council Resolution of 7 May 1985 on a new approach to technical harmonization and standards [1985] OJ C136/1.

extent, those of the European Commission. More strongly than ever before, EU law obliges the Member States to provide their authorities with appropriate resources. The structure of the interaction between the European Commission, the European and national agencies and authorities, and the designated authorities – which for their part have to coordinate the national responsible bodies, not to mention the certification bodies and the auditing companies – is overtly complex. Post-market control is accomplished through the obligation imposed on economic operators – as they are now called – to develop and establish in-house complaint handling and online dispute resolution. The affected – another new term in the digital policy legislation – are now entitled to launch complaints to the public authorities. However, they do not have the right to put the public authorities into motion. Like the 1985 New Approach, the EU believes that a slightly amended Product Liability Directive[2] and national tort law are sufficient to protect end users against potential risks to their health and safety, and that no new rules on the contractual relationship are needed. This is the grand scenario.

With a few exceptions, most prominently in the Data Act, which defines requirements on standard terms in B2B relations, the EU digital policy legislation does not deal with private relations. The regulations and directives define binding legal requirements for the different economic operators in the form of due diligence obligations that the addressees must comply with and/or harmonized technical standards they may want to respect due to the presumption of conformity which grants them access to the Internal Market in the event of compliance. The EU digital policy legislation understands terms and conditions – contracting – as a tool through which the economic operators concretize their due diligence obligations. Here and there, the EU digital policy legislation limits commercial practices and advertising. This does not mean the EU digital policy legislation leaves private law relations untouched, nor that it does not affect contract or tort or the European private law acquis. The intense legislative debates within the European Parliament, within the European Commission and the Member States – inclusive of their ministries and Parliaments – and even within civil societies and among lobbyists focused on an appropriate regulatory regime to exercise and maintain control over potential risks to the economy and society. The risk-based approach, constituting the overall rationale behind the EU digital policy legislation, cuts across the different regulations and directives. The risks take various forms and require different safeguards depending on the type of economic operator and the potential use of the technology. Fundamental rights rhetoric played a prominent role during the law-making process and does so now, as well, in

[2] Philipp Hacker, 'The European AI Liability Directives – Critique of a Half-Hearted Approach and Lessons for the Future' (2023) 51 CLS Rev <https://www.sciencedirect.com/science/article/pii/S026736492300081X>.

the implementation process. The high-flying political debate on ethics, trustworthiness, and security might explain why private relations between different economic actors and between economic actors, citizens, and consumers largely fell by the wayside. There are exceptions, but the voices did not reach the European Parliament, the European Commission, or the Member States.

Private law scholarship has to fill the gap. True, the newly approved European Commission announced the elaboration of a 'digital fairness act',[3] which should address data privacy, consumer rights, and maybe more. In light of the Draghi report[4] and the already announced backpedaling not only, but also under the EU digital policy legislation,[5] one might wonder whether the envisaged digital fairness act will ever gain ground or whether minor revisions of the EU consumer law acquis are being sold to the public as digital fairness. The history behind the so-called 'Consumer Rights Directive' might be an uncomfortable precedent for a mismatch between a demanding title and poor content. The Directive does not deal with many rights, certainly not with the originally envisaged right to fair dealing, and the debates ended with a right to information and detailed rules on direct and distant selling.[6] The list of scholarly private law publications dealing with the potential impact of EU digital policy legislation is quickly growing. Single acts of the EU digital policy legislation are prominently dealt with through commentaries in the German legal tradition;[7] written in English by scholars from EU Member States, they address cross-cutting concepts

---

[3] 7 September 2024 – In the mission letter addressed to the Commissioner-designate for Democracy, Justice and the Rule of Law, President von der Leyen refers to the need to develop 'a Digital Fairness Act to tackle unethical techniques and commercial practices related to dark patterns, marketing by social media influencers, the addictive design of digital products and online profiling especially when consumer vulnerabilities are exploited for commercial purposes', <https://www.digital-fairness-act.com/>.

[4] The future of European competitiveness: Report by Mario Draghi <https://commission.europa.eu/topics/eu-competitiveness/draghi-report_en>.

[5] Initiatives on e-privacy and AI liability have already been withdrawn; see, more generally, Commission 2025 work programme <https://commission.europa.eu/strategy-and-policy/strategy-documents/commission-work-programme/commission-work-programme-2025_en>.

[6] Directive 2011/83/EU of the European Parliament and of the Council of 25 October 2011 on consumer rights, amending Council Directive 93/13/EEC and Directive 1999/44/EC of the European Parliament and of the Council and repealing Council Directive 85/577/EEC and Directive 97/7/EC of the European Parliament and of the Council Text with EEA relevance [2011] OJ L304/64 in comparison to the Brussels, 8 February 2007 COM/2006/744 final GREEN PAPER on the Review of the Consumer Acquis <https://eur-lex.europa.eu/LexUriServ/LexUriServ.do?uri=COM:2006:0744:FIN:en:PDF>.

[7] Reiner Schulze and Dirk Staudenmayer (eds), *EU Digital Law, Article-by-Article Commentary* (2nd edn, Beck, Hart, Nomos 2025); Tobias Mast and others (eds), *Digital Services Act/Digital Markets Act (DSA/DMA), Kommentar* (CH Beck 2024); Mario Martini and Christiane Wendehorst (eds), *Artificial Intelligence Act: AI Act, Brussels Commentary* (CH Beck 2026).

such as vulnerability[8] and occasionally the overall impact of digital concepts on private law relations and the emerging digital private law.[9]

Casarosa and Grochowski's edited book, Enforcing Private Regulation in the Platform Economy, puts *private regulation*, *enforcement*, and *online platforms* center stage. Each of the three pillars, but particularly in their combination, fills an essential gap in scholarly research, paving the way for rethinking the private law acquis, for strategic litigation, and for political action. The title of the book announces the message. Enforcement does not address the power and legitimacy of public authorities to monitor and survey private regulation in whatever form and design, or the appropriateness of collective private enforcement through consumer organizations. Instead, the editors' purpose is to deconstruct and concretize the meaning and relevance of private regulation in two key private law dimensions – in terms of their contractual and enforcement functions and, perhaps sharper and more concisely, in terms of the *enforcement of private regulation through private regulation*.

Private regulation in the EU digital policy legislation, this cannot be repeated often enough, is co-regulation. The online platforms, as the primary addressees of the book, are not entirely free to shape their business relationships. The EU digital policy legislation binds them and sets a compulsory framework. Private regulation is co-regulation in action. Co-regulation as governance allows us to rely on the established distinction between institutional, procedural, and substantive governance. The EU digital policy legislation interferes with all three levels of private regulation, at least if one adopts a broad understanding that includes outside terms and conditions and due diligence obligations, model codes, codes of conduct, codes of practices, and technical standards. Therefore, co-regulation reaches beyond bilateral relationships between two contract parties. The actors can be a single platform, a single business, or a single consumer, but they can also be business and consumer organizations that elaborate codes and technical standards. Conceptually, one might distinguish between private regulation as the result of collectivized private regulation (the actions or interactions of one or, respectively, multiple organizations) or as individualized private regulation between two parties. The EU digital policy legislation actively promotes the development of collectivized codes of conduct and practice. Still, EU law is much less outspoken on elaborating collectivized due diligence obligations or terms and conditions (except in respect of technical standards) where stakeholder organ-

---

[8] Camilla Crea and Alberto De Franceschi (eds), *The New Shapes of Digital Vulnerability in European Private Law* (Nomos 2024).

[9] Sebastian Lohsse, Reiner Schulze and Dirk Staudenmayer (eds), *Private Law and the Data Act. Münster Colloquia on EU Law and the Digital Economy VIII* (Nomos 2024); Irina Domurath and Hans-W Micklitz, 'EU Digital Private Law: Tattering or New Beginning?' (2024) 20 ERCL 263 <https://doi.org/10.1515/ercl-2024-2014>.

izations are involved. In the more theoretical analysis, institutional and procedural governance are dealt with under the catchword of process regulation, stressing the EU's incomplete open-ended approach.[10]

The other level of governance relates to substance, which is the prominent domain of private law and private law legal scholarship. Platforms provide all sorts of services. They may bring contracting parties together through mediation or by selling products themselves; through marketing mediation or purchase; and through monitoring and surveying their business strategies as well as the customers, businesses, or consumers. The E-Commerce Directive, adopted in 2000,[11] freed the platforms from the risk of being treated as contracting partners immediately and had far-reaching consequences regarding their liability towards the customers. Setting the exceptions aside, the platforms are mere intermediaries in business relations. The DSA, however, requires Very Large Online Platforms and Very Large Search Engines to moderate the content and to report to the European Commission properly. One may easily understand content moderation as a particular variant of private regulation. On the other hand, content moderation is the most far-reaching responsibility of the platforms, and it should not be confused with liability. Whether platforms are intermediaries or contracting partners, they use private regulation in data privacy policies, marketing and sales promotion, and contract terms. These three different formats – data privacy, advertising, and contract terms – follow different rules: the GDPR regulates data privacy; the various directives on advertising deal with unfair and misleading marketing practices; the Unfair Contract Terms Directive (Directive 93/13/EEC, UCTD) addresses standard terms in B2C relations and sector-specific or problem-specific directives address unfair terms imposed by tech companies on small and mediums-sized companies.[12]

The three levels of governance managed and implemented through private regulation are undoubtedly helpful for understanding the complexity of private regulation and identifying the mismatch between the various legal boxes – data privacy, advertising, and standard terms – which are all aimed at the substance of the three formats, setting aside the institutional and the procedural dimension of private regulation. The Court of Justice of the European Union seems ready to stretch the scope of application of standard terms to include the procedural and the institutional dimension of private regulation.[13]

---

[10] The EU is a constitution in constant making, and it is constantly evolving as a result of procedural change. There is a bulk of publications on the EU as a quasi-state.

[11] Directive 2000/31/EC of the European Parliament and of the Council of 8 June 2000 on certain legal aspects of information society services, in particular electronic commerce, in the Internal Market ('Directive on electronic commerce') [2000] OJ L178/1.

[12] There is not yet a paper which has pulled the bits and pieces together.

[13] In particular through the ex officio doctrine; Anthi Beka, *The Active Role of Courts in Consumer Litigation: Applying EU Law of the National Courts' Own Motion* (Intersentia 2018).

Perhaps the most important move forward in Casarosa and Grochowski's book is the focus on pointing to enforcement through private regulation, contracting, and online dispute resolution. One of the merits of EU law is the legacy of the common law, in which rights and remedies go hand in hand, quite differently from continental law, where substantive and procedural law are kept distinct from each other, particularly in private law.

Again, dispute settlement forms part of co-regulation. The EU digital policy legislation emphasizes in-house complaint handling and online dispute resolution, as is done prominently in the DSA. The binding legal requirements are at best understood as a framework. ISO, the International Standardisation Organisation, developed a set of standards dealing with customer satisfaction in ISO 10002[14] and dealing with complaint handling ISO 9000 and 9001.[15] These standards incorporate complaint handling into quality management. They were elaborated initially in 1987, but they gained pace through the globalization of the economy and the growing interest in transnational (private) law. The ISO standards entered the ESOs as European and national technical norms.[16] Technical norms are not binding; they provide guidance and leave space for developing an in-house business culture. Dispute settlement is firmly anchored in the European private (consumer) law acquis. The EU introduced harmonized requirements through the legislative procedure, defining a level playing field in dispute settlement outside courts despite the Member States' different legal cultures and traditions.[17] EU regulation is most developed in B2C relations, distinguishing between offline and online dispute settlement. The previous Commission had proposed to withdraw and replace the unsuccessful ODR regulation through mere recommendations.[18] The new Commission will likely bring this project to an end as it fits nicely with the rationality of the Draghi report. Emphasizing ADR, or even more strikingly, understanding contracting and ADR as pillars of private regulation opens vast space for reinvigorating the role and function of private law tools. It requires the combination of the two levels to fully understand the depth and reach of the privatization of the law through EU co-regulation, through the combination of broadly worded legal requirements in the EU

---

[14] ISO 10002 <https://www.iso.org/standard/71580.html>.

[15] ISO 9001 <https://www.iso.org/standard/62085.html>.

[16] CEN-CENELEC GUIDE 22 Guide on the organizational structure and processes for the assessment of the membership criteria of CEN and CENELEC Edition 5, 2021-12 (Supersedes CEN-CENELEC Guide 22:2018), <https://www.cencenelec.eu/media/Guides/CEN-CLC/cenclcguide22.pdf>.

[17] Directive 2013/11/EU of the European Parliament and of the Council of 21 May 2013 on alternative dispute resolution for consumer disputes and amending Regulation (EC) 2006/2004 and Directive 2009/22/EC (Directive on consumer ADR) [2013] OJ L165/63.

[18] <https://ec.europa.eu/consumers/odr/main/?event=main.home2.show>.

digital policy legislation, and through the massive relevance of private regulation in all its various forms to concretize these requirements.

Casarosa and Grochowski's book wonderfully combines three distinct sets of issues – the more theoretical and conceptual one ('the privatization of the law'), the highlighting and elaboration of the two forms of enforcement through contracting and alternative dispute resolution, and last but not least the key role national private law orders will have to play in order to subject private regulation to judicial review. The book sets a new agenda for research, maybe even a new field of 'law'. It should be understood not as closing the regulatory gap but as opening space for rethinking. In that sense, the book is just the beginning of a new era. Co-regulation – the combination of the public and the private, no longer in one business sector or as regards particular products like in the industrial age, but as a cross-cutting means tied to the use of the new technology alone – certainly deserves deeper thinking as to whether the public and the private is gradually vanishing and as to whether private administrative law[19] should be established as a third field of law between the public and the private, where the traditional distinction fails to do justice to the novelties and where well-established boundaries must be rethought. The same applies to the conceptualizing of private regulation. Natali Helberger, Michael Veale, and others[20] identified eight stacks or layers in the design of recommender systems, highlighting the immense complexity of the type of rules, the actors involved, and the interconnection between the eight layers. One wonders whether their findings could be transferred to the analysis of private regulation as such. If so, what does it mean for national private law orders, for our thinking in legal boxes, even beyond the three established levels of the governance discussion?

I belong to the growing group of scholars who are somewhat skeptical about the potential effectiveness of the EU pre-market control approach, which is to be realized through due diligence and technical standards and more broadly through private regulation. The reasons are manifold: the highly bureaucratic nature of the approach, which is manageable for the VLOPs and the VLSEs, but unbearable for SMEs; the overtly complex structure of public enforcement enshrined in the EU digital policy legislation; the lack of explicit coordination between EU and national authorities inbuilt through the Treaty of Rome; the many hundreds of public authorities competent in the 27 Mem-

[19] Rodrigo Vallejo Garretón, The Idea of Private Administrative Law, phd EUI 2021 <https://cadmus.eui.eu/handle/1814/71519>.

[20] Laurens Naudts and others, 'Toward Constructive Optimisation: A New Perspective on the Regulation of Recommender Systems and the Rights of Users and Society', in Natali Helberger and others, *Digital Fairness for Consumers* (BEUC Report 2024) <https://www.beuc.eu/sites/default/files/publications/BEUC-X-2024-032_Digital_fairness_for_consumers_Report.pdf>.

ber States.[21] The foreseeable difficulties will bring private law and national courts competent for adjudicating data privacy, commercial practices, and standard terms into a prominent position, similar to the rise of product liability cases in the 1960s. The CJEU has the last word if national courts interpret the private law acquis. Still, private regulation reaches beyond the acquis and leaves crucial questions open, thus calling for legal scholarship and calling upon courts to seek new avenues. Casarosa and Grochowski's book should be seen and read in that context, underpinning the key role of private law and national courts in filling the gap left by the EU digital policy legislation, a gap resulting from this legislation's disregard and neglect of its impact on private economic and social relations. As with the Treaty of Rome, the EU legislature, the EU organs, and the Member States seem to be convinced that national private law orders, complemented through the EU private law acquis, suffice to deal with all the loose ends, the uncertainties, and the potential risks to the health, safety, and economic interest of European citizens. The EU might be proven wrong unless national courts, with or without the participation of CJEU, take the leading role in this process.

[21] Hans-W Micklitz and Giovanni Sartor, 'Compliance and Enforcement of the AIA through the AI' [2025] YEL <https://doi.org/10.1093/yel/yeae014>.

Beyond the State or in Its Proximity?

Private Regulation in the Platform Economy and Its Enforcement

Federica Casarosa and Mateusz Grochowski

I. Private Regulation – The Backbone of the Platform Economy

Online platforms not only form the pillar of the present-day economy but also involve themselves intensively in regulating the communities of users participating in them. This pertains to the entire spectrum of platforms in the present-day economy, such as those that intermediate in the provision of goods (eg Amazon and eBay)[1] or other services (eg Airbnb, Uber),[2] peer-to-peer lending sites (eg Kickstarter, Indiegogo), and social media platforms (eg Facebook, Twitter). Besides other similarities in their business models,[3] the

---

[1] Christine Riefa, *Consumer Protection and Online Auction Platforms. Towards a Safer Legal Framework* (Ashgate 2015).

[2] Nestor M Davidson and others (eds.), *The Cambridge Handbook on the Law of the Sharing Economy* (CUP 2018); Vassilis Hatzopoulos, *The Collaborative Economy and EU Law* (Bloomsbury 2018).

[3] See eg (among a plethora of literature) Nick Srnicek, *Platform Capitalism* (Polity 2016); Philipp Staab, *Digitaler Kapitalismus. Markt und Herrschaft in der Ökonomie der Unknappheit* (Suhrkamp 2021).

platforms in question involve themselves intensively in private regulation.[4] This activity takes place primarily through two main regulatory toolbox elements: (a) the contractual clauses imposed on platform users through terms of service (ToS)[5] and (b) the internal dispute resolution schemes adopted.[6] Acting through these channels, platforms address internal interactions happening not only between the platform and its users but also between the users themselves. The content and scope of rules and standards set in this way depend on multiple factors, including the market sector,[7] the geographic location and its regulatory environment,[8] and even surprising causes such as habits and inertia in the legal services accompanying the platform economy.[9]

In all instances, platforms attempt to draft rules capable of providing a smooth and seamless operation of the services offered to users. This draws platforms' attention to a broad range of issues of a mostly technical nature, eg how user accounts can be created, altered, and deleted; to what extent the seller of a good on an intermediary platform bears liability for the product; how hate speech in the social media sector is defined; and the like. The regulatory schemes developed by platforms are relevant not only for vertical user-platform relations but also for horizontal links between individual users. In this way, platforms determine, for instance, the conclusion of supplier-customer contracts, the basic elements of customer protection, and the mechanisms of mutual evaluation (reviewing) and reputation building.[10] In many

[4] Tarleton Gillespie, 'Governance of and by Platforms' in Jean Burgess and others (eds), *The Sage Handbook of Social Media* (Sage 2017) 254.

[5] In practice, this document takes a variety of forms and names – 'user agreements', 'general terms and conditions', 'policies', etc; see eg Mateusz Grochowski, 'Default Rules Beyond a State. Special-Purpose Lawmakers in the Platform Economy' in Stefan Grundmann and Mateusz Grochowski (eds), *European Contract Law and the Creation of Norms* (Intersentia 2021) 235–236.

[6] Colin Rule, 'Designing a Global Online Dispute Resolution System: Lessons Learned from eBay' (Winter 2017) 13(2) UStThomas LJ 354; and even earlier, Ethan Katsh, Janet Rifkin and Alan Gaitenby, 'E-Commerce, E-Disputes, and E-Dispute Resolution: In the Shadow of "eBay Law"' (2000) 15(3) OSJDR 705.

[7] See, for instance, Molly Cohen and Arun Sundararajan, 'Self-Regulation and Innovation in the Peer-to-Peer Sharing Economy' (2015–2016) 82 UChi LRev Dialogue 116, 129-132.

[8] See Catalina Goanta, Giovanni De Gregorio and Mateusz Grochowski, 'One Rule of Law to Rule them All? Geography of the Terms of Service on Social Media Platforms' (manuscript on file with authors).

[9] On general deviations from the rationality paradigm in standard terms drafting, see Mitu Gulati and Robert E Scott, *The Three and a Half Minute Transaction Boilerplate and the Limits of Contract Design* (Chicago UP 2012); Stephen J Choi, Mitu Gulati and Robert E Scott. 'Variation in Boilerplate: Rational Design or Random Mutation?' (2018) 20(1) ALER 1.

[10] Robert Gorwa, 'The Platform Governance Triangle: Conceptualising the Informal Regulation of Online Content' (2019) 8 Internet Policy Review <https://doi.org/10.14763/2019.2.1407>.

instances, platforms also tackle sensitive issues related to fundamental rights (including non-discrimination, freedom of expression, and hate speech). Platforms also routinely create intricate, extrajudicial dispute resolution systems to enforce the rules adopted. They contribute not only to the settlement of private disputes but also – much more importantly – to establishing 'internal' standards for the communities gathered around platforms (eg determining the exact understanding of discrimination or drawing the boundary between permissible and objectionable forms of expressing one's opinion). One of the most prominent examples in this regard is the Facebook Oversight Board (the 'Supreme Court of Facebook'). However, the practice of other platforms provides multiple examples of such private adjudicatory frameworks, ranging from mediation to arbitration systems.[11]

For these reasons, private regulatory schemes in the platform economy are achieving a growing prominence in regulatory schemes and political debates in the EU and beyond.[12] Many of the relevant instruments center around the Directive on unfair terms in consumer contracts (UCTD),[13] which provides the most direct and most feasible instrument for reviewing particular ToS clauses. The CJEU has already addressed the UCTD-based approach,[14] but more robust case law is being developed at the domestic level. One of the most vivid examples is the case law of the German Federal Court (*Bundesgerichtshof*), which in a recent decision, intervened in the ToS of online platforms (such as Facebook), using the unfair contract terms framework to review the fairness of the rules created by platforms and to assess their compliance with fundamental rights. The recently adopted Digital Service Act (DSA)[15] added another layer to the inquiry; arts 14 and 44–48 provide an

[11] Maria Lorena Florez Rojas, 'Industry Self-Regulation Models in Dispute Resolution of E-Commerce B2C' (Law and Technology Master Program, Tilburg University 2015); Kate Klonick, 'The New Governors: The People, Rules, and Processes Governing Online Speech' (2018) 131 Harv LRev 1599.

[12] On the origins and nature of regulatory problems regarding intermediary platforms, see generally Chad Marzen, Darren A Prum and Robert J Aalberts, 'The New Sharing Economy: the Role of Property, Tort and Contract Law for Managing the Airbnb Model' (2017) 13 NYU JLB 295, with further references; Daniel E Rauch and David Schleicher, 'Like Uber, but for Local Government Law: The Future of Local Regulation of the Sharing Economy' (2015) 76 Ohio St LJ 901, 920–926; Vassilis Hatzopoulos and Sofia Roma, 'Caring for Sharing? The Collaborative Economy under EU Law' (2017) 54 CMLRev 81, 88. On similar debates about social media regulation, see IV.3, below.

[13] Council Directive 93/13/EEC of 5 April 1993 on unfair terms in consumer contracts [1993] OJ L95/29 (UCTD).

[14] CJEU 28 July 2016, C-191/15 *Verein für Konsumenteninformation v Amazon EU Sàrl*, ECLI:EU:C:2016:612.

[15] Regulation (EU) 2022/2065 of the European Parliament and of the Council of 19 October 2022 on a Single Market for Digital Services and amending Directive 2000/31/EC (Digital Services Act) [2022] OJ L277/1.

elaborated framework for dealing with various types of out-of-state regulatory schemes created in the platform economy.

This new substantive set of rules calls for a more precise understanding of the state-platform dynamic in rulemaking that has emerged in this way. In the same way, a plea for a (re)conceptualization of the private regulation of enforcement platforms has been posed by the new framework for alternative dispute resolution in DSA, arts 20–21. These phenomena represent a pressing challenge for state regulatory policy and call for a more comprehensive legal and socio-economic analysis. A significant concern is how rules created by platforms function in the market and in social practice, asking in particular how they are enforced by states and the EU as well as by platforms themselves.

II. The Concept of the Volume

The volume highlights the role of online platforms as creators of private regulation and explores the interrelation between these rules and the mechanisms of oversight and enforcement. In this regard, it builds on existing theoretical and practical accounts of the platform economy while also striving to provide a more systematic and comprehensive picture of private regulatory practices than has been offered in existing scholarship.

The private regulatory dimension of the platform economy is attracting growing attention in scholarship. The accounts of this issue tackle both the overarching patterns and conflicts of values.[16] The major portion of the relevant literature belongs to the 'digital constitutionalism' ambit and delves mainly into the issue of the role of platforms in addressing fundamental rights through their internal rules and enforcement schemes. The other publications take a sectoral approach and delve into private regulation in selected market spheres, such as freedom of speech,[17] employment,[18] and contracts and consumer protection.[19] The existing scholarship has drawn, however, a somewhat

---

[16] See Giovanni De Gregorio, *Digital Constitutionalism in Europe: Reframing Rights and Powers in the Algorithmic Society* (CUP 2022); Edoardo Celeste, *Digital Constitutionalism: The Role of Internet Bills of Rights* (Taylor and Francis 2022); Edoardo Celeste and others (eds), *Constitutionalising Social Media* (Hart 2022); Hans-W Micklitz and others (eds), *Constitutional Challenges in the Algorithmic Society* (OUP 2021).

[17] Emily Laidlaw, *Regulating Speech in Cyberspace – Gatekeepers, Human Rights and Corporate Responsibility* (CUP 2015); David Bromell, *Regulating Free Speech in a Digital Age – Hate, Harm and the Limits of Censorship* (Springer 2022).

[18] Jo Carby-Hall and Lourdes Mella Méndez (eds), *Labour Law and the Gig Economy – Challenges Posed by the Digitalisation of Labour Processes* (Routledge 2020).

[19] See eg Caterina Gardiner, *Unfair Contract Terms in the Digital Age. The Challenge of Protecting European Consumers in the Online Marketplace* (Edward Elgar 2022) and Vanessa Mak, *Legal Pluralism in European Contract Law* (OUP 2020).

incomplete picture and focuses mainly on describing selected phenomena rather than on building a coherent conceptual framework. Apart from the general perspective of the platform economy as a legal and socio-economic phenomenon, the existing scholarship provides a broad array of accounts that pertain to other types of private norm-setting on the market (eg spontaneous creation of contract rules in market communities, such as guilds and trade unions).[20] The applicability of these theories in the platform economy is, however, significantly limited. This is primarily due to the specific role of platforms (which create market and social domains in an arbitrary way, not by bottom-up association) and the massive harvesting and processing of personal data as the cornerstone of the platform economy. At the same time, so far only a few authors have directly addressed private regulation created by platforms. Moreover, this aspect of the scholarship is rather insular and in no way provides a comprehensive understanding of the involved questions and problems.

The volume results from transdisciplinary research and brings together specialists from various social sciences. Apart from lawyers, the volume encompasses participants with education and expertise in sociology, economics, and political science. This will allow us to foster an in-depth discussion about the social and economic relevance of the private regulatory schemes in the platform economy. Furthermore, such an approach will enable us to go beyond an analysis of legal issues (the usual focus of the existing studies) and approach the regulatory role of platforms more thoroughly.

The volume consists of three parts: the first contains contributions that address the foundational issues of private regulation in the entire platform economy or in its substantive segments. The second part focuses on the cross-sectoral questions of the private regulation of platforms, such as the enforcement of rules created by platforms under EU contract law and the relationship between the 'internal' and 'external' enforcement of such private regulatory frameworks. The third part looks at the question of how the enforcement of rules created by platforms is depicted in the judicial, academic, and policy discourse in selected EU Member States. This part provides a comparative background allowing a mapping of the responses to platforms' rulemaking activities, particularly in terms of the judicial interaction between domestic courts and the CJEU and the implementation of EU law and policy framework at the national level. The book merges a more general perspective on the platform economy and its legal background with more detailed insights on a broad range of EU jurisdictions. This approach is unique in the existing scholarship, which has thus far never endeavored to provide a wide-ranging

[20] See eg Lisa Bernstein, 'Private Commercial Law in the Cotton Industry: Creating Cooperation through Rules, Norms and Institutions' (2001) 99 Mich LRev 1724; Thomas Dietz, *Global Order Beyond Law. How Information and Communication Technologies Facilitate Relational Contracting in International Trade* (Hart 2014).

overview of the various responses towards platform rulemaking as adopted across multiple EU jurisdictions. In this way, the book takes a step forward from the general theoretical background – already addressed in the scholarship – and aims to better understand how this general framework works in the practical experience of several European legal orders.

In so doing, the book addresses four core questions:

1) To what extent may platforms serve as effective governors of socially or economically important concerns (such as freedom of expression and the protection of vulnerable social groups)?
2) What is the exact dynamic of the interrelations between rules created privately by platforms and the state governance system? In particular, to what degree may states enforce platform rules, and on what basis may they review and limit the platform's regulatory power?
3) Should the problem of enforcement of platform-created regulation be considered from the global and universal perspective, or does it also have substantial local idiosyncrasies? If so, how can such idiosyncrasies be defined, and to what extent do they result in a geographical fragmentation of platforms' private regulatory regimes?
4) What conclusions for regulatory policy (at the EU and domestic level) stem from the EU's experience with enforcing platform rules so far? Does the current interrelation between platforms and states suggest a need to reform existing approaches in legislation and/or case law?

In its outlook on the platform economy, the volume combines two perspectives: a theoretical account (with strong interdisciplinary insights) and a comparative analysis. Both approaches are present throughout all the contributions, incorporating more abstract and universal thinking about online platforms and the digital economy with examples from the experiences of specific national and supranational legal orders. In this way, the volume seeks to provide both a broad outline of overarching issues in the platforms' private regulation and a variety of responses – to this regulation – as adopted or contemplated in various jurisdictions. In other words, both parallel analytical paradigms reinforce and deepen each other. Reference to concrete national and supranational experience substantiates the theoretical framework. Conversely, comparative analysis is informed by a more structured conceptual agenda – and hence, contributions offer a comparison not merely of legal institutions but of legal discourses as facilitated by various actors involved in platform regulation.

In its comparative part, the volume accommodates insights into the experience of EU Member States in approaching the private regulation of global and domestic platforms. The sample of countries chosen for comparison was selected along two lines: (a) the intensity of regulation of the internal rules produced by platforms through legislation and case law and (b) the geopolitical and economic diversity of the jurisdictions under inspection. It encompasses jurisdictions (such as France) where the domestic responses towards platforms' private regulatory practices are especially well-developed or innovative.[21] Additionally, it encompasses jurisdictions with legal orders that have been oriented towards EU law and liberal market concepts (eg Italy and Netherlands).[22]

A particularly unique regulatory perspective is discussed in the chapter authored by Joana Campos Carvalho. She discusses the Portuguese legislation on the liability of online intermediary platforms in instances where the goods, digital content, or digital services do not conform with the consumer agreement.[23] Under these rules, platforms bear joint liability with the sellers or providers of services towards a consumer. As observed by the author, these rules were inspired not only by EU legislation but also by the 'soft' rule drafted at the European Law Institute as a part of model rules on online intermediary platforms.[24]

III. The State-Platform Dynamic in Rule Setting and Enforcement

1. *Why Enforcement Matters*

The volume does not focus on private regulation as such, instead considering enforcement as its primary perspective. The volume understands enforcement as a range of legal and extra-legal mechanisms (eg social consent) that allow the realization of the rights and obligations created by platforms. This encompasses enforcement through dispute settlement schemes as well as other means of filling platform-created rules with actual 'meaning' and 'gravity'.

The focus of this volume on enforcement is for an apparent reason, as it plays a pivotal role in the entire regulatory edifice created by platforms. The economic sense of private regulation rests not exactly on the question of who is apt to set rules but rather on who can enforce them. In essence, private regulation as a market and legal phenomenon boils down to the question of

[21] See Sara Migliorini and Constance Bonzé, 'Regulating the Digital Revolution. France's Blueprint for Platform Governance', in this volume, 255.

[22] Respectively, see Dianora Poletti and Federica Casarosa, 'Enforcing Platform Rights – The Italian Case Law', in this volume, 239, and Eric Tjong Tjin Tai, Paul Verbruggen and Ruşen Öncü, 'Private Law Regulation of Online Platforms in the Netherlands', in this volume, 273.

[23] Portuguese Decree-Law 84/2021 of 18 October 2021.

[24] European Law Institute, Model Rules on Online Platforms, 2019 <https://www.europeanlawinstitute.eu/fileadmin/user_upload/p_eli/Publications/ELI_Model_Rules_on_Online_Platforms.pdf> accessed 1 October 2024.

the economic or social power that allows non-state actors to impose rules on particular communities and execute them (which mainly includes determining sanctions when the rules are breached).[25] The platform economy became one of the most vivid areas of such an allocation of power. Due to the exponential growth of their social impact and their increasing market dominance, platforms have been enjoying a significant role as de facto governors of various social and economic domains. In this way, platforms compete in many ways with classical sovereigns (states and meta-state structures, such as the European Union). For these reasons, some scholars in the fields of law and political science tend to perceive platforms as 'special-purpose sovereigns'[26] who accompany and supplement the state's governance of society and the market.

2. *Platforms as Constitutional Actors*

By setting forth rules for the users' communities, online platforms do not grapple with issues of a merely technical nature. In many instances, they step directly into the domain of some of the most critical and sensitive values of a democratic society. At the same time, however, the sole logic of their operation can be profit maximization, as they are not subjected to the rule of law (in the same manner as are public authorities) nor to any duty to pursue the public interest.

One of the most conspicuous instances of actual platform power is content moderation, whereby social media platforms actively set boundaries on the users' freedom of speech. In this way, platforms take on a task traditionally reserved for public entities with democratic legitimation.[27] In the case of platforms, the political mandate in the classical sense is replaced with empowerment through market mechanics, where a platform's capacity to moderate speech is proportional to the number of clients (users) it attracts. At the same time, the emerging private speech regulation has led to a situation where platforms compete with public entities or even supplant their functions. As Giovanni De Gregorio and Pietro Dunn point out in their chapter, by leaving this issue unattended, public entities are empowering platforms as private enforcers of public policies. This shift can lead to the creation of functions that compete with or even supplant traditional public entities. The proper

[25] Fabrizio Cafaggi, 'New Foundations of Transnational Private Regulation' (2011) 38 JLS 20.

[26] The term was used for the first time by Jack M Balkin to label the de facto regulatory aptitude of social media platforms in terms of freedom of expression: Jack M Balkin, 'Free Speech in the Algorithmic Society: Big Data, Private Governance, and New School Speech Regulation' 51 (2018) UCDavis LRev 1149, 1153.

[27] Orla Lynskey, 'Regulating "Platform Power"' [2017] LSE Law, Society and Economy Working Papers 1/2017; Daniela Stockmann, 'Tech Companies and the Public Interest: The Role of the State in Governing Social Media Platforms' (2023) 26(1) Information, Communication & Society 1.

regulation of these matters necessitates addressing potential abuses of the private freedoms of platforms (represented mostly on the grounds of private law) as they are transformed into private powers. From the comparative vantage point, the question of limiting private speech regulatory power is intricately linked to how constitutional systems respond to the interplay between market dynamics and democracy. While in the US regulating social media is seen primarily through the prism of the First Amendment,[28] EU law tends to be understood as a collaborative mechanism for enforcing public policies. The recent digital market rules of the EU to a growing extent embrace this private/public interlink. For instance, while the DSA acknowledges platforms' capability to shape internal regulatory mechanisms,[29] at the same time – as many chapters in this volume clearly illustrate – it imposes several limits on the shape and enforcement of these rules. In general, these regulatory instruments aim to reconcile private power with public policy and values.

The evolution of big tech companies and their constant efforts to limit the government's influence on their operations meant that for a long time they were not perceived as a subject of public law regulation. At the same time, one can now observe their increasing influence on the sphere where individuals exercise their rights and freedoms. The business model of internet platforms is based on processing personal data, which affects the individual's privacy.[30] Privacy is often seen as the exercise of autonomy coupled with control over the sphere of seclusion. However, it is also widely recognized that the right to privacy is directly related to ensuring equal participation in the democratic process.[31] The importance of privacy has led to the adoption of personal data protection instruments in Europe. The most important one, the General Data Protection Regulation (Regulation (EU) 2016/679, GDPR), includes the use of private regulatory instruments such as codes of conduct and certification. The decision to include such solutions led to the responsibility for ensuring the proper framework for protecting personal data being shifted from public to private actors. Katarzyna Łakomiec's chapter analyses how the coexistence of public regulation and private rules under the GDPR affects the protection of privacy. Her inquiry attempts to answer the follow-

---

[28] Marco Bassini and Oreste Pollicino, 'The Reshaping of the Freedom of Expression in the Digital Environment in Light of the Role of Social Networks' in Andrej Savin and Jan Trzaskowski (eds), *Research Handbook on EU Internet Law* (Edward Elgar 2023).

[29] See especially DSA, art 14.

[30] Shoshana Zuboff, *The Age of Surveillance Capitalism: The Fight for a Human Future at the New Frontier of Power* (PublicAffairs 2019); Julie Cohen, *Between Truth and Power: The Legal Constructions of Informational Capitalism* (OUP 2019); Robert L Soane and Richard Warner, *The Privacy Fix: How to Preserve Privacy in the Onslaught of Surveillance* (CUP 2021).

[31] Paul M Schwartz, 'Privacy and Democracy in Cyberspace' (1999) 52(6) Vand LRev 1624.

ing questions: What is the relationship between privacy protection standards created by states and solutions adopted by private actors? How does the inclusion of co-regulation affect the enforcement mechanisms of privacy protection? How proportionality review and context analysis can enrich the public-private toolbox used to search for the best solutions for protecting privacy?

3. *Private Dispute Settlement*

In setting their governance schemes, platforms usually aim to create comprehensive and self-contained regulatory systems which incorporate the full spectrum of stages – from setting policy goals, to setting a rule and its application, to resolving disputes arising in the context of this rule. In other words, the dispute resolution system created by platforms should be seen as part and parcel of the private regulatory edifice in the online economy.[32] By examining the conflict management activities that online platforms engage in when monitoring and managing violations of their users' terms of service, the volume aims to contribute to the ongoing debate about the changing relationship between public authorities and private actors in the wake of platform capitalism. By looking at the space between 'platform regulation', in the sense of the state delegating regulatory tasks to these corporations, and 'regulation by the platform', which emphasizes corporations as agents of the social order, the text will further explore the theoretical explanations and implications of the digitization of dispute resolution in platform capitalism. When do platforms become agents of the state in taking over the administration of legal requirements, and when do they ultimately revolutionize the processes of norm creation and conflict management?

The general conceptual contours of dispute resolution schemes in the platform economy are discussed in this volume by Friederike Bahl, who looks at this issue from the socio-legal vantage point. One of the distinctive features of this sector is defining a new relationship between supply and consumption that extend beyond traditional consumer services. At the same time, being an intrinsic part of platforms' private regulation, dispute resolution mechanisms have a strong governance potential in society and on the market. As Bahl notes, many platforms mediate core legal and political concepts such as fairness and transparency.[33]

---

[32] Luca Belli and Jamila Venturini, 'Private Ordering and the Rise of Terms of Service as Cyber-Regulation' (2016) 5 IPR 1; Robert Gorwa, 'What Is Platform Governance?' (2019) 22 Information, Communication & Society 854; Marta Cantero Gamito, 'Regulation.Com. Self-Regulation and Contract Governance in the Platform Economy: A Research Agenda' (2017) 9 EJLS 53.

[33] This links the dispute resolution question with the involvement of platforms in constitutional matters, as discussed by Friederike Bahl, 'Theorizing Platform Regulation. A Sociological Account Between Private and Public Governance' in this volume, 53.

In this vein, out-of-state dispute resolution can be seen as part of a multilayer regulatory framework that comprises various frameworks of local or global scope created by platforms themselves or through various modes of platform-state cooperation. In her chapter, Barbara Warwas delves more deeply into the nature and mechanics of these dispute resolution schemes, looking at intermediary platforms such as eBay and Amazon and the social media sector. Her analysis is wrapped around the concept of multilevel regulation, understood as a framework comprising a network of rules and actors operating at various administrative levels.[34] This approach addresses complex regulatory activities with direct or indirect legal implications beyond the boundaries of a single state. Apart from the typical 'private' dispute resolution schemes (such as the Facebook Oversight Board), the multilevel regulation in the platform sector also incorporates – as Warwas observes – more specific internet governance mechanisms, such as the Uniform Domain Name Dispute Resolution Policy established by the Internet Corporation for Assigned Names and Numbers (ICANN). The complex nature of enforcement facilitated through the multilevel framework makes it hard to grasp at both the theoretical and practical levels. They create a specific hybrid enforcement mechanism that merges public and private elements and that, as Warwas suggests, should be considered a *sui generis* scheme.

At the same time, the emergence of out-of-state dispute resolution schemes poses several questions about the fairness of such mechanisms and respect for procedural guarantees and other basic values and rights. The pivotal concerns in this regard pertain to the consistency of decisions and the lack of arbitrariness (especially the platforms' impartiality in balancing their own market goals with users' interests). Following Bahl's observations, the dispute resolution mechanisms developed by platforms are often marked by a high degree of arbitrariness and opacity (for instance, in the case of the instant blocking of a social media account for publishing a controversial photo or the unilateral termination of an Amazon membership without explanation). This problem is further amplified by using algorithms commonly employed by platforms to track infractions and resolve conflicts. The application of such automated schemes puts in question – as Bahl further argues – the fundamental premises of the free market, namely a contractual meeting of the minds characterized by shared understanding and mutual commitment.

Specific problems in this regard pertain to content moderation on social media platforms. Under growing political and social pressure, these types of platforms have developed multifaceted instruments for ex-ante and ex-post content moderation, yet the mechanics in question are often plagued with shortcomings and injustices. For these reasons, as scholarship has pointed out,

---

[34] Fabrizio Cafaggi and Hans-W Micklitz (eds), *New Frontiers of Consumer Protection: The Interplay between Private and Public Enforcement* (Intersentia 2009).

there is a need to ensure the interplay between technological and human control.[35] One of the instruments intended to enhance the human dimension of content governance is 'trusted flaggers', as introduced by the DSA – ie persons and entities able to provide a final decision regarding the potentially illegal nature of online content. However, as argued by Federica Casarosa in this volume, the rules defined by the DSA still leave several questions open. This regards especially the criteria used to accredit flaggers, as well as the verification process that would evaluate the quality of the notifications provided by such trusted flaggers and the allocation of liability in the event of mistaken communication between the online intermediary and the trusted flagger.

IV. Regulating Private Regulation

1. Two Strategies

Apart from the general importance of the platform economy, private regulation and its enforcement also pose another foundational question: How do states (and other bearers of sovereign political power) and the platforms interact in regulating economic and social matters? The problem has two interconnected dimensions.

First, in the plainest scenario, states and other bearers of sovereign political power can focus on reviewing and invalidating regulation established by platforms (eg through review of standard contract terms under the UCTD and the private regulation scheme in the DSA) and limiting it through market regulation (eg by domestic or EU competition and consumer protection measures). In more elaborated settings, the state may serve as an indirect enforcer of rules created by platforms. In most instances, the state enforcement apparatus recognizes the platforms' rules as any other type of content created by contracting parties. From a negative perspective, states may occasionally refuse to enforce platform-created rules, especially when they violate users' rights or, in other ways, amount to an abuse of the platform's regulatory power. As Grochowski explains in his chapter, the logic behind the application of these instruments is, however, rather traditional. It focuses almost exclusively on the individual platform-client relationship and does not attempt to acknowledge the specific contracting structure in the platform economy.[36]

[35] Federica Casarosa, 'When the Algorithm Is Not Fully Reliable: The Collaboration between Technology and Humans in the Fight against Hate Speech' in Amnon Reichman and others (eds), *Constitutional Challenges in the Algorithmic Society* (CUP 2021); Valentina Golunova, 'In Tech we Trust? Fixing the Evolutionary Interpretation by the Court of Justice of the Prohibition of General Monitoring in the Era of Automated Content Moderation' in Evangelia Psychogiopoulou and Susana de la Sierra (eds), *Digital Media Governance and Supranational Courts* (Edward Elgar 2022).

The development of regulatory frameworks in the greater body of EU consumer law triggers responses on the side of platforms. Confronted with the growing degree of constraints, resulting from both the general contract law and the specific rules (especially of the DSA), platforms employ adaptive compliance strategies. As Marta Cantero Gamito discusses in her contribution, in the early stages of the digital market, platforms' business models were designed to disregard state-created rules; over time, the regulatory grip became increasingly effective. Such gradual alignment prompted by regulatory pressures can be seen in the history of GDPR compliance in the platform economy.

Second, the link between state and private enforcement can also be perceived from the flipside: platforms may serve as enforcers of state-created regulations. By creating well-structured communities of users – and by gathering immense amounts of data about them – platforms may in some instances be more efficient in applying and enforcing standards created by states (eg by detecting discriminatory patterns among users). In this way, they may play the role of 'enforcement intermediaries', being prompted or obliged by states to adopt standards and values in their private regulatory schemes.[37] The balancing in question occurs on two interconnected levels: the global and the regional. Although the attention on policymakers, media discourse, and academic analyses focuses mostly on the former, the key to understanding the exact role of platforms' governance freedom in many cases lies with the particular countries. The volume attempts to grasp the specificity of platforms' regulation at these two interconnected levels. First of all, it maps the key features of platform self-regulation as a universal phenomenon in the global online economy. Secondly, it also tries to better understand the role of individual state policy towards online platforms and its role in building the overall state/platform balance in the governance of the market and society. In this regard, we refer to examples from domestic legal systems, using them as substantiation for our general claim regarding the dynamic between state and platform rulemaking and enforcement.

2. *The Limited Potential of Private Law*

Given that the self-regulatory activities of platforms are rooted in contractual frameworks, contract law instruments are the most obvious and conceptually 'closest' options. This is particularly true for the applicability of general standards, such as good faith and the prohibition of exploitation or discrimination, which enable the correction of contract terms that undermine the interests of one party. In the context of platform economics, which predomi-

---

[36] See also IV.2, below.

[37] Christine Riefa and Mateusz Grochowski, 'The Enforcement of EU Consumer Law' in Miroslava Scholten (ed), *Research Handbook on the Enforcement of EU Law* (Edward Elgar 2023).

nantly involves business-to-consumer relationships, more specialized consumer law instruments – especially the UCTD – can provide an additional basis for regulating platforms.[38]

The national legal experience evidenced in this volume confirms the primary position of private law as the regulatory toolbox 'of first choice' for reviewing the private regulatory schemes of online platforms. The overarching private law and contract law tools, along with consumer law regulations, can significantly restrict and guide the regulatory authority of platforms in the Netherlands. However, as noted by Eric Tjong Tjin Tai, Paul Verbruggen, and Ruşen Öncü, the current framework is somewhat ineffective in addressing the platform economy. This ineffectiveness largely stems from the particular enforcement mechanisms that back traditional contract law, which, as previously mentioned, do not align well with the real power dynamics present in the digital marketplace. Similar general conclusions apply to Portugal. However, as Joana Campos Carvalho points out in her contribution, Portuguese lawmakers have been more audacious in implementing the UCTD and decided to extend its scope to all standard term contracts on the market and not merely to B2C agreements. This creates a substantially stronger potential to grasp various dimensions of platforms' regulatory activity also beyond the strict consumer context.

Likewise, an illustrative instance of such an active approach is platform regulation in Italy, discussed by Federica Casarosa and the late Dianora Poletti. Italian jurisprudence was some of the first to acknowledge the evolution of the information society structure, where the role of the platforms was moving from mere intermediaries to active parties in online contractual exchanges. Since 2008, judges have started to evaluate whether the hosting providers could be qualified as passive or active providers, identifying criteria that are in line with the ones provided by the Court of Justice of the EU. Since then, however, the rulings emerging in the most recent jurisprudence addressing the role of platforms are very limited. The latest cases refer mostly to the interplay between freedom of expression and contractual freedom – with specific attention on the extent to which contractual terms and conditions may limit the forms and content of the users' expression and whether the conduct of users on platforms may qualify not as a breach of contract but also as contractual fraud. It may seem that no claims have been presented against platforms. This is, however, not true, as the national Market and Consumer Authority (*Autorità Garante della Concorrenza e del Mercato*) has increasingly played a role. As a matter of fact, this regulatory authority is in charge of verifying compliance with consumer protection rules, including those relating to unfair commercial practices and unfair contract terms. Its decisions show

[38] Christoph Busch and others, 'The Rise of the Platform Economy: A New Challenge for EU Consumer Law?' (2016) 5 EuCML 3; Cantero Gamito (n 32).

how the consumer protection rules have been interpreted and, eventually, how their violation has been sanctioned by the relevant independent authority.

A more contoured approach in this regard has been adopted in the French case law. Generally, the Supreme Court (*Cour de Cassation*) has actively constrained platforms' private regulatory practices through the UCTD. The Court has also stepped in to safeguard vulnerable workers using these platforms, reclassifying them as employees who are entitled to the protections provided by French labor law. France's executive branch has been instrumental in overseeing the regulation of platforms. Their regulatory strategy often surpass the private regulations set by these platforms. As Sara Migliorini and Constance Bonzé explain in their chapter, the French Constitutional Court (*Conseil d'État*) at the same time understands platforms as vital enablers of essential freedoms and rights. It has affirmed that these platforms can enhance freedom of speech, especially during elections, by encouraging citizen engagement. Additionally, platforms play a key role in closing social gaps, including those related to geographical disparities. They contribute significantly to democratic processes by facilitating open dialogue. Overall, the importance of platforms in promoting participation and equality is widely acknowledged. Building on this premise, in certain cases the Constitutional Court has defended the regulatory autonomy of platforms. For example, it annulled the 2021 law that banned users from sharing the locations of police patrols through social traffic apps like Waze, deeming it an excessive violation of freedom of speech.

At the same time, despite their apparent attractiveness, private law instruments are far from optimal in the domain of online platforms. The primary disadvantage of this legal toolbox is its litigious nature. Most instruments within the classical private law framework simply establish an entitlement that must be exercised by a specific agent, typically the party harmed by a particular transaction. Consequently, when applied to online platforms, these instruments require activation by the platform user. In practice, however, the protection offered by this mechanism may often be superficial. Utilizing these tools requires resources – such as information, time, and money – that many platform users either lack or are unwilling to invest in disputes with a platform.[39] In this regard, the classical private law toolbox operates similarly in traditional business-to-consumer contexts. It was recognized early in the development of EU consumer protection that legal remedies dependent on self-initiated actions to assert one's rights are not the optimal solution for market realities, which are

[39] This is confirmed by the recent statistics of the 2022 Consumer Conditions Survey – standard survey <https://commission.europa.eu/document/download/0cdcc170-e877-4b3b-b4eb-404f47596896_en?filename=Consumer%20Conditions%20Survey%20-%20standard%20survey.xlsx> accessed 24 August 2024. Here, the results show that at least a quarter of the 71.2% of citizens who have purchased goods and services online have experienced problems regarding such purchases. However, only two-thirds have decided to take some manner of action.

characterized by the substantial structural advantages that business actors possess in terms of economic power.

In addition, contract law instruments are primarily effective in regulating classical contract law relationships, where both the parties involved and the contract's content can be clearly defined. However, the situation regarding online platforms has become much more complex. First, as mentioned earlier,[40] the private regulations created by platforms impact not only the platform-user relationship but also the horizontal relationships established among users. This means that a platform's internal regulatory framework can influence other contractual relationships, as Grochowski discusses more extensively in his chapter. Consequently, it is not always feasible to regulate this manner of internal governance using contract law instruments, especially in cases where such regulations affect the legal standing of specific users. Secondly, and to some extent as a result of the first point, contract law tools do not adequately account for the broader effects that a regulation created 'internally' by platforms has on the entire user community, beyond the isolated contractual relationship being considered. Thirdly, consumer regulations – including the UCTD – do not apply to platform-to-business relationships. This exclusion removes a significant group of legal relationships from the regulatory framework, specifically those in which regulations established by platforms affect their users who are entrepreneurs (eg, suppliers of goods and services offered on online marketplaces). In the platform marketplace, strong structural inequalities often persist between the parties in these relationships, resembling the imbalances found in traditional trader-consumer dynamics.

3. *Between Substance and Procedure*

An alternative to the weaknesses of private law instruments is to consider public law solutions, which are administered by regulatory authorities and do not require (or necessarily need) the involvement of the platform user. These solutions may include administrative oversight of the content of terms of service (ToS) and other elements of the regulatory framework. This applies particularly to systems that offer administrative control over the content of standard contract terms in the consumer market. By contrast, modern platform regulation in the EU has adopted a different approach, shifting the regulatory focus from ex-post control of rules created by platforms to a mixed strategy. This approach combines limited interference with the content of ToS by establishing a catalogue of mandatory elements that must be included in them, along with oversight of the rules' form and their implementation by the platform.

This approach is clearly articulated in the DSA, which presents a new regulatory framework for standard contract terms, to some extent diverging from

---

[40] See section I.

the model established by the UCTD. Central to this framework is DSA, art 14, which mandates that platform operators include specific information in their ToS, partially tailored to the nature of the services or users.[41] Additionally, the provision imposes a general obligation on platform operators to 'act in a diligent, objective, and proportionate manner' when applying any restrictions on services offered to users,

> 'with due regard to the rights and legitimate interests of all parties involved, including the fundamental rights of the recipients of the service, such as freedom of expression, media freedom and pluralism, and other fundamental rights and freedoms as enshrined in the Charter [of Fundamental Rights of the EU].'

This provision focuses less on the substance of the ToS and more on their enforcement by the platform. Finally, DSA, art 14 concludes by requiring Very Large Online Platforms (VLOPs) and Very Large Online Search Engines (VLOSEs) to observe certain formal (procedural) prerequisites – namely, to provide users with an easily accessible and transparent summary of their ToS and to make them available in an appropriate number of different languages.

A similar regulatory logic was also applied in an earlier piece of EU platform legislation, namely the 2019 Platform-to-Business (P2B) Regulation.[42] In art 8, the Regulation does not only oblige platforms to include certain contractual clauses in their ToS; it also prohibits retrospective changes to the existing ToS and introduces general standards of good faith and fair dealing as a benchmark for the assessment of the other, more specific rules.

The approaches adopted in the DSA and the P2B Regulation aim to find a 'middle ground' in relation to the private regulation established by platforms. Notably, these solutions largely respect the autonomy of platforms in developing their regulations, restricting it only through framework requirements concerning form and content. Another consequence of this approach is that it creates broader opportunities to view private entities as 'regulatory intermediaries'. This topic will be discussed in the subsequent section.

4. *Platforms as Regulatory and Enforcement Intermediaries*

Looking into the enforcement question is vital for understanding the extent to which the rules created by platforms can actually serve as efficient means of addressing social and economic concerns. This problem is crucially important

---

[41] Martin Senftleben, 'Human Rights Outsourcing and Reliance on User Activism in the DSA' (*Verfassungsblog*, 21 February 2024) <https://verfassungsblog.de/human-rights-outsourcing-and-reliance-on-user-activism-in-the-dsa> accessed 23 August 2024; João Pedro Quintais, Naomi Appelman and Ronan Fahy, 'Using Terms and Conditions to Apply Fundamental Rights to Content Moderation' (2023) 24 GLJ 881, DOI:10.1017/glj.2023.53.

[42] Regulation (EU) 2019/1150 of the European Parliament and of the Council of 20 June 2019 on promoting fairness and transparency for business users of online intermediation services [2019] OJ L186/57 (P2B Regulation).

for the entire volume, as the enforcement of private regulation remains much more heterogeneous and harder to conceptualize than the enforcement of state-created rules. What is particularly significant in this context is the dynamic relationship between the state and private enforcement mechanisms. This issue extends beyond a simple inquiry on enforcing state-created rules against platforms; it encompasses various complex interdependencies. Specifically, it relates to the different roles platforms play as intermediaries in the regulation and enforcement of rules. In this framework, platforms can act as creators of rules that are later enforced by the state, and they can also serve as 'enforcement intermediaries' for state-imposed rules and standards. These interdependencies arise within the highly unpredictable landscape of state-platform interactions, which hinges on a delicate balance between cooperation and conflict.

One of the instances of such balance is discussed by Cantero Gamito with regard to consumer law. In her contribution, she considers whether and to what extent online platforms may be deemed 'regulatory intermediaries'. In particular, she attempts to identify which regulatory practices in the platform economy may serve this purpose. The growing scope and intensity of platforms' private regulation has triggered, as she points out, a significant shift in the EU regulatory strategy for the digital market. Instead of more robust engagement with the substance of regulatory schemes developed by platforms, in recent legislation the EU has opted for a procedural approach. This regulatory strategy assumes that platforms should remain free in determining the exact content of their consumer protection policies as long as they observe the framework requirements regarding the incorporation of 'private' rules and the resolution of disputes. As mentioned in the previous section, this approach is particularly evident in the latest EU regulations, which, although they do not exclude the application of the UCPD, shift the focus to procedural issues related to ex-ante content regulation instead of emphasizing an ex-post approach.

At the same time, the effectiveness of platforms as regulators of public (collective) challenges is limited in several regards. In some areas – such as counteracting discrimination in contracting and consumer protection – platforms actively involve themselves in establishing internal provisions and standards, yet many other areas fall beyond their regulatory schemes. The specific reasons for this may vary; sometimes, it is due to the platform's lack of interest in regulating a particular situation or the greater cost-effectiveness of not doing so. Regardless of the exact reason, however, the pragmatic logic usually sets a constraint on the effectiveness of the governance of economic and social matters by online platforms without the involvement of public authorities.

In the dispute resolution phase, the role of platforms as enforcement intermediaries becomes more prominent. This is evident from the requirements imposed by the DSA. DSA, art 17 indicates the form and manner of statements of reasons for any decision taken by platforms. The leeway left to platforms is, however, limited, as the transparency requirements regarding the statement of reasons indirectly impose how the decisions are to be structured. As mentioned by Cantero Gamito, the technical specifications for the API (Application Programming Interface) used by platforms for reporting decisions can become an example of the 'code is law' approach being adopted by private regulators. The interaction with state standards is even more evident when looking at the subsequent enforcement steps, namely the internal complaint mechanisms and the out-of-court dispute resolution mechanisms that should be configured by platforms, according to DSA, arts 20 and 21. In particular, in the case of out-court dispute mechanisms, the provisions transplant 'judicial' fair trial standards into a non-judicial process.[43] This trend is also confirmed by the proposed modernization of the ADR/ODR package,[44] where the same standards will apply to alternative dispute resolution bodies that will address illegal commercial practices, such as consumer disputes in relation to refunds, restitution, or repair of a defective product, resolution of contracts based on unfair terms, etc.[45]

V. Platforms and Vulnerable Users

A specific dimension of platforms' regulatory policies – which intersects with fundamental rights and public policy goals – is the question of protecting users who, for various reasons, are in a disfavored position vis-à-vis the other participants in the platform economy. In essence, the issue of user protection rests on the question of the extent to which online platforms are responsible for considering the interests of vulnerable and deprived users and to what extent they should balance these interests against the aim of profit maximization.

The recent debates about social media regulation spotlight the protection of minors as the prime category of vulnerable users that are exposed to an especially high risk of harm.[46] Under regulatory and social pressure, platforms began implementing private regulatory policies to create a safer online

[43] Federica Casarosa, 'Out-of-court Dispute Settlement Mechanisms for Failures in Content Moderation' (2023) 14(3) JIPITEC 391.

[44] Proposal for a Directive of the European Parliament and of the Council amending Directive 2013/11/EU on alternative dispute resolution for consumer disputes, and Directives (EU) 2015/2302, (EU) 2019/2161 and (EU) 2020/1828 Brussels, 17 October 2023, COM/2023/649 final; Proposal for a Regulation of the European Parliament and of the Council repealing Regulation (EU) 524/2013 and amending Regulations (EU) 2017/2394 and (EU) 2018/1724 with regard to the discontinuation of the European ODR Platform, COM/2023/647 final.

[45] Vanessa Mak, 'Consumer ODR – Redefining pathways to dispute settlement in a post-consumer society' (*DSA Observatory*, 22 January 2024) <https://dsa-observatory.eu/2024/01/22/consumer-odr-redefining-pathways-to-dispute-settlement-in-a-post-consumer-society/> accessed 24 August 2024.

environment for young users. However, as Costanza Di Francesco Maesa warns in her paper, we are witnessing an increasing degree of violations in this regard despite these developments. They include exposure to harmful content online, grooming, cyberbullying, and sexual exploitation, as well as minors being lured into gaming or gambling schemes. Moreover, as Di Francesco Maesa points out, the new rules at the EU level – especially the DSA – remain largely unsatisfactory due to disproportionate intrusions into user privacy and a lack of sufficient enforcement tools. It is highly uncertain to what extent these deficits can be cured through private regulation introduced by the platforms themselves.

A similar logic may also apply to consumer protection instruments created by platforms in parallel with the state-made consumer protection schemes.[47] As Grochowski indicates in his chapter, in many instances, platforms may be willing to give up on short-term profit in expectation of longer-term gain. Platforms may be interested in counteracting discrimination in contracts concluded between their users in order to create a more secure contracting environment, so as to quash social and political unrest and preempt potential public regulation.

A specific vulnerability issue in the platform economy – one often overlooked in the legal and policy discourse on platform regulation – is employee rights. It is particularly vivid for the so-called 'labor platforms', such as Uber or Amazon Mechanical Turk, that intermediate in providing services (gigs) to clients.[48] In this context, however, the issue of employee protection becomes particularly problematic, as the nature of contracts concluded via such platforms is often quite questionable from the perspective of traditional labor law classifications. Moreover, as with other contracts intermediated by online platforms, also the agreements in question are heavily regulated by the platforms themselves. This issue is further explored by Claudia Schubert and Johannes Ipsen, who take a look at the ToS's of selected platforms from the labor law perspective. In particular, they are interested in the relationship between these terms and state-made labor law, which, both at the EU and at the domestic level, consists primarily of mandatory rules. The analysis by

[46] Marta Cantero Gamito and Hans-W Micklitz, 'Too much or too little? Assessing the Consumer Protection Cooperation (CPC) Network in the protection of consumers and children on TikTok' (*BEUC*, February 2023) <https://www.beuc.eu/sites/default/files/publications/BEUC-X-2023-018_Assessing_CPC_Network_in_the_protection_of_consumers_and_children_on_TikTok-Report.pdf> accessed 24 August 2024.

[47] On a similar phenomenon of consumer protection policies introduced by platforms, see Jane K Winn, 'The Secession of the Successful: The Rise of Amazon as Private Global Consumer Protection Regulator' (2016) 58 Ariz LRev 193.

[48] Brishen Rogers, 'The Social Costs of Uber' (2015–2016) 82 UChi LRev Dialogue 85; Ryan Calo and Alex Rosenblat, 'The Taking Economy: Uber, Information and the Power' (2017) 117 Colum LRev 1623, 1645–1670; Arun Sundararajan, *The Sharing Economy. The End of Employment and the Rise of Crowd-Based Capitalism* (MIT Press 2017).

Schubert and Ipsen tackles, for instance, the arbitration and mediation clauses imposed by platforms on their users, explaining the boundaries for such clauses in German labor law. Building on these observations, Schubert and Ipsen also examine the proposed EU directive on platform work.[49] They attempt to evaluate to what extent it may deliver the promise of bolstering the enforcement of labor law in the digital landscape and how it may interact with the platforms' private regulatory frameworks.

VI. Conclusions

If we were to pinpoint a single overarching question raised by all the chapters in this book, it would be the following: Should the rule-setting practices of online platforms, along with regulations established by their users, be subject to oversight or guidance from state or international regulations?[50] The expanding landscape of the platform economy has led to increased regulatory scrutiny at both national and transnational levels, as well as locally. At the same time, the existing regulations tend to be limited to sector-specific and narrow issues, thereby lacking a more comprehensive theoretical framework. The current policy debate leans towards some middle ground between a purely laissez-faire approach and a strongly regulatory approach. The most recent pieces of platform regulation in the EU, especially the DSA, attempt to achieve this middle ground by shifting attention from substantive to procedural matters.

The search for a balance between autonomy in the creation of private regulation and respect for public or community values is, however, rather far from a conclusion. As the contributions to this volume clearly show, this question is largely predicated on another issue: Should online platforms be recognized as a distinct category of market entities that carry unique responsibilities for their market activities? Considering the self-regulatory externalities present in the platform economy, responses to this question may vary based on the type of negative consequences involved. It can be hypothesized that platforms may, in the interest of the community of users, bear certain responsibilities where significant moral issues arise or where there are risks in respect of contract efficiency (such as exploitation of cognitive biases or discrimination[51]). However, this hypothesis requires further exploration.

---

[49] Proposal for a Directive of the European Parliament and of the Council on improving working conditions in platform work, COM/2021/762 final.

[50] See, among others, Vanessa Katz, 'Regulating the Sharing Economy' (2015) 30 Berkeley Tech LJ 1067, 1107–1126; Orly Lobel, 'The Law of the Platform' (2016) 101 Minn LRev87, 142–166; Calo and Rosenblat (n 48) 1670–1689; Sundararajan (n 48) 138–142.

There can be no doubt that the allocation of regulatory power between platforms and states requires much more than simple regulation based on mandatory prohibitions and generic standards, which represent the classical regulatory toolbox applied to private regulatory practices. The market power and epistemic capabilities of platforms – their ability to extract and process information about users and to adjust regulatory policy accordingly – clearly exceed the typical instances of private regulatory activities that legal systems have historically grappled with. Therefore, the legal framework for self-regulatory practices necessitates a more innovative approach that could embrace and possibly leverage the unique economic and regulatory aptitude of platforms. Recent EU regulation shifts the focus from ex-post approaches typical of contract law toward a more open regulatory environment, where platforms are invited – and, in many ways, incentivized – to take part in regulating certain social and economic matters. The underlying logic thus evolves from traditional regulation to co-regulatory schemes. This shift is further reinforced by the growing popularity of codes of conduct and standardization as means of 'outsourcing' regulatory tasks beyond the state apparatus. The EU regulation of the digital market and other spheres where the economic and epistemic powers of public authorities are substantially limited increasingly relies on these regulatory means.

In a parallel vein, the detection of misbehavior (ie the monitoring function) carried out through technical and organizational means by the platform[52] is followed by an enforcement mechanism that is no longer autonomously defined by the same platform. According to the most recent legislative initiatives, not only should other stakeholders be involved – as represented by trusted flaggers – dispute resolution mechanisms should also comply with standards and rules that mimic the judicial ones. As a result, platforms become increasingly involved in a multilevel enforcement system,[53] but additional coordination efforts should still be adopted.

---

[51] Online platforms' awareness of discrimination issues indeed seems to increase among platforms that attempt to introduce regulatory frameworks to cope with it (see, eg, Lobel (n 50) 164–165; Vauhini Vara, 'How Airbnb Makes It Hard to Sue for Discrimination' *The New Yorker* (3 November 2016) or that open themselves to state scrutiny (Nathan Heller, 'The Gig Is Up', *The New Yorker* (15 May 2017)).

[52] See James Grimmelmann, 'The Virtues of Moderation' (2015) 17 Yale JLT 42.

[53] Fabrizio Cafaggi, 'A Comparative Analysis of Transnational Private Regulation: Legitimacy, Quality, Effectiveness and Enforcement', EUI Working Paper, 2014 <https://cadmus.eui.eu/handle/1814/33591>.

Part 1

Out-of-State Regulation in the Platform Economy

Online Platforms as Private Regulators

Giovanni De Gregorio and Pietro Dunn

I. Introduction

Online platforms have assumed an increasingly prominent role as private regulators in the digital age. From the processing of data to content moderation, policy-makers across the globe are still discussing how to deal with the increasing power these actors can exercise in different areas.[1] This transformation is driven by their immense influence over the flow of information, communication, and commerce defining the characteristics of information capitalism.[2] As a result, the traditional regulatory power of public actors has been complemented by the power wielded by transnational private actors, thus leading to questions of transparency and accountability.[3]

The evolving landscape of online platforms as global regulators underscores the need for a coordinated and nuanced approach from governments, regulatory bodies, and civil society. Their agility and adaptability have led to the emergence of entirely new industries and business models.[4] Online platforms have,

---

[1] Martin Moore and Damian Tambini (eds), *Regulating Big Tech: Policy Responses to Digital Dominance* (OUP 2021).

[2] Julie E Cohen, *Between Truth and Power: The Legal Constructions of Informational Capitalism* (OUP 2019).

[3] Giovanni De Gregorio, *Digital Constitutionalism in Europe: Reframing Rights and Powers in the Algorithmic Society* (CUP 2022).

[4] José van Dijck, Thomas Poell and Martijn de Waal, *The Platform Society* (OUP 2018).

in this respect, been drivers of innovation, bringing about transformative changes in how users communicate, conduct business, and access information. Striking the right balance between fostering innovation and protecting the public interest is a complex and ongoing challenge in the digital age.

However, this innovation has, at times, outpaced the ability of traditional regulatory frameworks to keep up, leading to concerns about issues like privacy and fair competition. Emblematic of such challenges are well-known cases such as the Cambridge Analytica scandal, which has had a significant impact in terms of privacy and data protection and which carries consequences for democratic processes.[5] Similarly problematic is the use of online platforms in the spreading of disinformation, as seen in the context of the COVID-19 pandemic[6] and also as relates to recent instances of warfare.[7] The acquisition by Elon Musk of what was formerly known as Twitter has raised, in turn, questions about the legal (but also the ethical and philosophical) implications of allowing single individuals to buy and own services that have become central in the enjoyment of fundamental rights.[8] Considering the critical role of online spaces for democracy, these transformations raise constitutional questions.

This context is also promoting a different interplay between public and private actors in the digital age. The traditional demarcation between government and business is becoming increasingly blurred as online platforms wield significant influence over areas that were traditionally the domain of government, such as law enforcement, public discourse, and even diplomacy.[9] This changing landscape requires a re-evaluation of how these entities work together, share responsibility, and collaborate in addressing the challenges and opportunities presented by the digital era. Recent events have already underlined the inherent fragility of this relationship. Thus, for instance, in the aftermath of Hamas' attack on Israel of October 2023, EU institutions held Elon Musk's X not to be in compliance with the Digital Services Act as it had failed to counter the dissemination of disinformation concerning the conflict

---

[5] Brittany Kaiser, *Targeted: The Cambridge Analytica Whistleblower's Inside Story of How Big Data, Trump, and Facebook Broke Democracy and How It Can Happen Again* (Harper Collins 2019).

[6] Ruairi Harrison, 'Tackling Disinformation in Times of Crisis: The European Commission's Response to the Covid-19 Infodemic and the Feasibility of Consumer-Centric Solution Special Issue: Covid and EU Law' (2021) 17 Utrecht LRev 18.

[7] Sofia Ranchordas, Giovanni De Gregorio and Catalina Goanta, 'Big Tech War Activism' (*Verfassungsblog*, March 2022) <https://verfassungsblog.de/big-tech-war-activism/>.

[8] Giovanni De Gregorio, Pietro Dunn and Oreste Pollicino, 'Shareholder Power as a Constitutionalising Force: Elon Musk's Bid to Buy Twitter' (*Verfassungsblog*, 21 April 2022) <https://verfassungsblog.de/musks-bid-to-buy-twitter/>.

[9] Oreste Pollicino, 'The Quadrangular Shape of the Geometry of Digital Power(s) and the Move towards a Procedural Digital Constitutionalism' (2023) 29(1–2) ELJ 10.

between Israel and Palestinians,[10] while a study committed by the European Commission found that platforms' mitigation measures against risks connected to pro-Kremlin (dis)information warfare were 'largely ineffective' and 'insufficient to respond to the crisis'.[11]

Within this framework, this chapter underlines the role of online platforms as private regulators and provides examples of how the European regulatory strategy addresses their power. It argues that the liberal approach of public actors has not only led to the consolidation of new business models but has also increased the interdependency between public and private actors in the digital age. The present analysis does not argue that online platforms have been playing the role of state actors but, rather, that they are increasingly considered as critical centers of collaboration by public actors. The first part of this work focuses on platforms as private regulators, underlining in particular their role as governors. The second part focuses on three main areas of regulation in the EU which aim to mitigate the role of online platforms as private regulators. The third part examines how this new phase of regulation has not only limited the power of online platforms but has also opened the door towards a new collaborative relationship between public and private actors in the digital age.

II. The Role of Online Platforms as Private Regulators

The liberal approach adopted by constitutional democracies at the end of the last century triggered the rise and consolidation of online platforms. Precisely when the internet was promising to bring new opportunities of growth, the choice to leave the digital dimension free from public interferences boosted the role of private actors in developing new business models and performing their activities. The technological evolution together with such an approach has led platforms to rely on their private autonomy to set their own standards as underlined by the mix of publicized terms of services (ToS) and opaque internal rules.[12]

---

[10] Lisa O'Carroll, 'EU Warns Elon Musk over "Disinformation" on X about Hamas Attack' (*The Guardian*, 10 October 2023) <https://www.theguardian.com/technology/2023/oct/10/eu-warns-elon-musk-over-disinformation-about-hamas-attack-on-x>.

[11] Directorate-General for Communications Networks, Content and Technology, 'Digital Services Act: Application of the Risk Management Framework to Russian Disinformation Campaigns' (European Commission 2023) 64 <https://data.europa.eu/doi/10.2759/764631>.

[12] Giovanni De Gregorio, 'From Constitutional Freedoms to the Power of the Platforms: Protecting Fundamental Rights Online in the Algorithmic Society' (2019) 11 EJLS 65.

These rules can be considered as the (unaccountable) legal basis according to which platforms exercise their functions.[13] By defining the criteria according to which these decisions will be enforced as well as the procedural and technical tools underpinning their ToS and internal rules, platforms establish the rules of their respective community (ie quasi-legislative power). Although this autonomy is limited in some areas, such as in regards to data protection and consumer protection law, the global application of their platform services and the lack of any regulation of content moderation has given them broad margins of discretion when setting the rules governing their digital spaces.

Until the adoption of the regulatory framework addressed in the following sections, online platforms had been – essentially – free to unilaterally establish what users can do in their digital spaces. From a private law perspective, these agreements can be considered mere boilerplate contracts. Users cannot exercise any negotiation power; rather, as adhering parties, they can only decide whether to accept pre-established conditions. At first glance, the significance of this situation from a public (or rather constitutional) perspective may not be evident, since boilerplate contracts are very common even in the offline world, and online platforms' ToS do not seem to differ from the traditional contractual model.[14]

However, online platforms can directly enforce contractual clauses provided for in the ToS and internal rules, without the need to rely on a public mechanism such as a judicial order. For instance, the removal or the blocking of online content is performed directly by online platforms without the involvement of any public body ordering the infringing party to fulfil the related contractual obligations and without checking whether there is compliance with internal norms. Here, the code assumes the function of the law.[15] By relying on the network architecture as a modality of regulation, online platforms can directly enforce their rights, and they can exercise this role without the mediation of any public authority (ie a quasi-executive function). This private enforcement is the result of an asymmetrical technological position in respect of users.

Behind these normative and executive functions, the two above-mentioned examples have shown how platforms can perform a function which is similar to that of the judiciary, namely the balancing of fundamental rights (ie quasi-judicial power). When receiving a notice from users asking for content remov-

[13] Luca Belli and Jamila Venturini, 'Private Ordering and the Rise of Terms of Service as Cyber-Regulation' (2016) 5(4) Internet Policy Review <https://policyreview.info/articles/analysis/private-ordering-and-rise-terms-service-cyber-regulation>.

[14] Regarding the role of private law in governing the Internet, see Peter Zumbansen, 'The Law of Society: Governance Through Contract' (2007) 14(1) IJGLS 191; Lee A Bygrave, *Internet Governance by Contract* (OUP 2015).

[15] Lawrence Lessig, *Code and Other Laws of the Cyberspace* (2nd edn, Basic Books 2006).

al or the delisting of personal data, platforms assess which fundamental rights or interest should prevail in the case at issue so as to render a decision, as in the case of alleged defamatory content reported by a user which leads online platforms to assess the boundaries of the right to freedom of expression.

Nonetheless, with the lack of any regulation, online platforms are not obliged to respect of the rule of law. When exercising their activities, these platforms do not need to rely on legal bases to perform their functions, nor are they required to consistently enforce their ToS or to strike a balance between conflicting constitutional interests. As private actors, online platforms can discretionarily apply their standards.[16] In particular, the primary concern is the low level of decision-making transparency,[17] which strongly affects users' fundamental rights, considering the automated characterization of these functions. Indeed, online platforms also rely on artificial intelligence technologies to perform their functions. Automated decision systems, powered by data and based increasingly on machine-learning tools, are implemented as technical instruments supporting the functionalities of online platforms such as the organization of online content. At the same time, such technologies constitute technical self-executing rules, obviating even the need for a human executive or judicial function.

This technological asymmetry underlines how the setting, enforcement, and interpretation of the rules defined by online platforms are not strictly dependent on the role of the public authority. This discretion could be considered a clue to the exercise of quasi-public power by these platforms. While users, as citizens, are usually subject to the exercise of legitimate authority, online platforms govern their digital spaces through instruments of private law mixed with technology (ie the law of the platforms). Online platforms can be seen as rulers since they can define the norms governing their spaces.[18] Such power is of special concern from a constitutional perspective since it represents a form of disintermediation (or marginalization) of the rule of law and the role of public actors in enforcing fundamental rights in the digital age.

---

[16] Paul Schiff Berman, 'Cyberspace and the State Action Debate: The Cultural Value of Applying Constitutional Norms to Private Regulation' (2000) 71 UColo LRev 1263.

[17] Frank Pasquale, *The Black Box Society: The Secret Algorithms That Control Money and Information* (Harv UP 2015); Matteo Turilli and Luciano Floridi, 'The Ethics of Information Transparency' (2009) 11 Ethics and Information Technology 105; Tal Z Zarsky, 'Transparent Predictions' (2013) 4 UIll LRev 1503.

[18] Angelo Golia and Gunther Teubner, 'Societal Constitutionalism in the Digital World: An Introduction' (2023) 30(2) IJGLS 1; Gunther Teubner, 'Societal Constitutionalism: Alternative to State-Centred Constitutional Theory?' in Christian Joerges, Inger-Johanne Sand and Gunther Teubner (eds), *Transnational Governance and Constitutionalism* (Hart 2004).

III. Regulating the Power of Online Platforms

The rise of the role of online platforms as private regulators in the context of the digital market can indeed be observed from a variety of perspectives. A first, clear angle revealing their capability to act as creators of law, enforcers, and judges of rules is represented by the field of content moderation,[19] where these actors have the power to define which types of content or conduct may or may not be compliant with community standards and ToS. Through their content moderation practices, online platforms can thus structure and organize the flow of information online in configurations that are in line with their business interests and needs as well as with the company's own *Weltanschauung*.

Second, the power of online platforms as private 'governors' emerges also from their role in the framework of the digital market defined as gatekeeping.[20] Indeed, major online platforms have increasingly become dominant players whose services often represent essential tools in the context of the market (eg intermediation services, search engines, browsers, operating systems, cloud computing services). The way in which they offer and implement such services can thus significantly affect both business users and consumers' rights and interests, and it can contribute to an overall shaping of the exchange of goods and services online.[21] This raises, namely, important questions in terms of competition law and consumer law.

A third aspect consists of the possibility for online platforms to access and gather data about their end-users, information which can then be used for business purposes (including, for example, targeted political advertising[22]) and also in the development and deployment of AI systems (eg to detect emotions[23]). If data and computational power have become the 'new oil' of the digital market,[24] the ability of platforms to gather and exploit such resources clearly reflects an increasing relevance of these actors in the algorithmic age.

Aware of the risks, as well as of the potential for the pursuit of public interests – as represented by the emergence of the role of online platforms as private regulators – the EU has tried to react by regulating online platforms

---

[19] Kate Klonick, 'The New Governors: The People, Rules, and Processes Governing Online Speech' (2017) 131 Harv LRev 1598.

[20] Emily Laidlaw, 'A Framework for Identifying Internet Information Gatekeepers' (2010) 24(3) IRLCT 263.

[21] Nicolas Petit, *Big Tech and the Digital Economy. The Moligopoly Scenario* (OUP 2020).

[22] Max Zeno van Drunen, Natalie Helberger and Ronan Ó Fathaigh, 'The Beginning of EU Political Advertising Law: Unifying Democratic Visions through the Internal Market' (2022) 30(2) IJLIT 181.

[23] Damian Clifford, *Data Protection Law and Emotion* (OUP 2024).

[24] Massimo Durante, Computational Power: The Impact of ICT on Law, Society and Knowledge (Routledge 2021).

with a view, on the one hand, of setting the boundaries of such power, while attempting, on the other hand, to harness it to promote the goals of the Union itself. The following subsections will analyze, precisely, how the Union has reacted to platform power in the fields of content moderation, competition, data, and artificial intelligence.

1. *Procedural Safeguards in Content Moderation*

The regulation of content moderation in the context of the EU has undergone a rather significant development from the second half of the 2010s onwards, moving away from the original liberal approach that characterized the Union's strategies at the turn of the millennium, when the E-Commerce Directive (ECD)[25] established a safe harbor system rather favorable to providers of intermediary services. Increasingly, the Union has recognized wider margins of responsibility for intermediaries, namely online platforms, with a view to encouraging them to remove content and materials that are at odds with public values and goals.[26] Such a novel strategy entails, in practice, an increased reliance (and dependency) on the capabilities and practices of online platforms with respect to the pursuit and enforcement of the Union's public interests.

At first, the Union's new wave of content moderation policies was mostly characterized by a sectoral perspective. Thus, the 2018 Refit of the Audiovisual Media Services Directive (AVMSD)[27] focused on the audiovisual market, requiring providers of video-sharing platform services (VSPs) to take 'appropriate measures' to protect the public from a range of unwarranted materials, including content that is harmful to the full development of minors and hate speech.[28] Similarly, the so-called 'value-gap' provision of the DSM Copy-

---

[25] Directive 2000/31/EC of the European Parliament and of the Council of 8 June 2000 on certain legal aspects of information society services, in particular electronic commerce, in the Internal Market ('Directive on electronic commerce') [2000] OJ L178/1 (ECD).

[26] Claudia E Haupt, 'Regulating Speech Online: Free Speech Values in Constitutional Frames' (2021) 99 WashU LRev 751, 760; Giovanni De Gregorio, 'The Rise of Digital Constitutionalism in the European Union' (2021) 19 IJCL 41.

[27] Directive (EU) 2018/1808 of the European Parliament and of the Council of 14 November 2018 amending Directive 2010/13/EU on the coordination of certain provisions laid down by law, regulation or administrative action in Member States concerning the provision of audiovisual media services (Audiovisual Media Services Directive) in view of changing market realities [2018] OJ L303/69.

[28] Directive 2010/13/EU of the European Parliament and of the Council of 10 March 2010 on the coordination of certain provisions laid down by law, regulation or administrative action in Member States concerning the provision of audiovisual media services (Audiovisual Media Services Directive) [2010] OJ L95/1, art 28b (AVSMD). On the legal regime concerning VSPs following the AVMSD Refit Directive, see Ľuboš Kukliš, 'Video-Sharing Platforms in AVMSD: A New Kind of Content Regulation' in Pier Luigi Parcu and Elda Brogi (eds), *Research Handbook on EU Media Law and Policy* (Edward Elgar 2021).

right Directive[29] obliges providers of content-sharing services who have failed to obtain the relevant authorization from rightsholders to make 'best efforts' to expeditiously block access to or remove copyrighted materials and to ensure their unavailability.[30] Furthermore, Regulation (EU) 2021/784 on terrorist content online (TERREG)[31] recognizes the power of Member States to issue orders to remove or disable access to terrorist content against providers of hosting services[32] and establishes a specific regime for providers 'exposed to terrorist content', who have to put in place mitigation systems that address the risk of dissemination of terrorist content online.[33]

On top of these sectoral pieces of legislation, the Digital Services Act (DSA) serves as a general horizontal framework;[34] the instrument has the purpose of promoting and guaranteeing the protection of individuals' fundamental rights in the context of the digital landscape, including the right to freedom of expression and the right to non-discrimination as well as consumer rights, while countering the dissemination of illegal content and the perpetration of illegal conduct across the internet. Through the DSA, EU lawmakers have attempted to reform the previous, already mentioned framework set by the ECD. While the DSA has maintained the liability exemption regime designed by the ECD, at least with respect to the area of content moderation, it has nevertheless innovated the system by introducing a wide range of procedural obligations for a transparent and safe online environment, aimed at promoting wider responsibilities for providers of intermediary services.[35] The 'asymmetry' characterizing the new duties, which are scaled depending on the dimension and nature of the service offered, reflects 'a supervised risk management approach',[36] in conformity with the general trends in Union digital policies that tend to favor a risk-based approach.[37]

---

[29] Directive (EU) 2019/790 of the European Parliament and of the Council of 17 April 2019 on Copyright and Related Rights in the Digital Single Market and Amending Directives 96/9/EC and 2001/29/EC [2019] OJ L130/92 (DSM Copyright Directive).

[30] DSM Copyright Directive, art 17.

[31] Regulation (EU) 2021/784 of the European Parliament and of the Council of 29 April 2021 on Addressing the Dissemination of Terrorist Content Online [2021] OJ L172/79 (TERREG).

[32] TERREG, art 3.

[33] TERREG, art 5.

[34] Regulation (EU) 2022/2065 of the European Parliament and of the Council of 19 October 2022 on a Single Market For Digital Services and amending Directive 2000/31/EC (Digital Services Act) [2022] OJ L277/1 (DSA).

[35] Martin Husovec, *Principles of the Digital Services Act* (OUP 2024).

[36] European Commission, 'Communication of 21 April 2021, Proposal for a Regulation of the European Parliament and of the Council on a Single Market For Digital Services (Digital Services Act) and amending Directive 2000/31/EC' COM/2020/825 final 11.

[37] Zohar Efroni, 'The Digital Services Act: Risk-Based Regulation of Online Platforms' (*Internet Policy Review*, 16 November 2021) <https://policyreview.info/articles/

Furthermore, not only are online platforms required to enforce measures intended to foster a safer environment, they are, additionally, tasked with the often-countervailing goal of ensuring the protection of fundamental rights, notably freedom of expression.[38] Many obligations set by the DSA are specifically addressed at reducing actively the level of risk for fundamental rights, with a view to promoting a safer digital landscape in line with the Union's aspirations. In this respect, the most emblematic new obligation is represented by the need for very large online platforms (VLOPs) and search engines (VLOSEs)[39] to establish a mechanism for the assessment and mitigation of the 'systemic risks in the Union stemming from the designing or functioning of their service and its related systems, including algorithmic systems, or from the use made of their service'.[40] On top of being highly symbolic of the risk-based approach characterizing the DSA, by vesting providers of VLOPs and VLOSEs with the duty – but at the same time with the discretion – to adopt and implement the necessary mitigating measures, these obligations reflect a regulatory strategy that has been defined as 'enforced self-regulation' or 'meta-regulation', a description that is fitting in the sense that there is a macro-regulator (the EU) that oversees how other micro-regulators (VLOPs and VLOSEs) manage the governance of those 'systemic risks'.[41] In other words, VLOPs and VLOSEs, as private actors, become the primary enforcers of the policy objectives set by the Union.

In this respect, online platforms are directly vested with the role of striking a balance between interests having a significant constitutional status. This specific aspect emerges, for instance, from the DSA clause according to which the mitigation of systemic risks must be deployed with 'particular consideration to the impacts of measures on fundamental rights'.[42] Overall, the DSA thus externalizes to providers of intermediary services the implementation of goals that are, ultimately, of a public nature. That is, the DSA tries to push providers to counter, on the one hand, all online content and conduct that is considered harmful or illegal while, on the other hand, guaran-

news/digital-services-act-risk-based-regulation-online-platforms/1606>. See also Giovanni De Gregorio and Pietro Dunn, 'The European Risk-Based Approaches: Connecting Constitutional Dots in the Digital Age' (2022) 59 CMLRev 473.

[38] DSA, art 14(4). Joao Pedro Quintais, Naomi Appelman, Ronan Ó Fathaigh, 'Using Terms and Conditions to apply Fundamental Rights to Content Moderation' (2023) 24(5) GLJ 881.

[39] DSA, art 33.

[40] DSA, art 34.

[41] Nicolo Zingales, 'The DSA as a Paradigm Shift for Online Intermediaries' Due Diligence: Hail To Meta-Regulation' in Joris van Hoboken and others (eds), *Putting the DSA into Practice: Enforcement, Access to Justice, and Global Implications* (Verfassungsbooks 2023) 214.

[42] DSA, art 35(1).

teeing that all measures adopted are respectful of the principle of proportionality and, thus, of principles and values oriented towards democracy and pluralism. To achieve these public interests, moreover, the DSA envisages the possibility for providers to refer to co-regulatory codes of practice, which are to be drafted in a cooperative way by all relevant stakeholders, the Commission, and the newly created European Board for Digital Services (EBDS).[43]

Additionally, the trajectory towards an increased delegation of public policies towards online platforms does not seem to have reached its end with the DSA. Indeed, the proposal put forward by the Commission in May 2022 concerning the adoption of a Regulation on Child Sexual Abuse Material (CSAM) aims precisely at making providers of intermediary services responsible to reduce online child sexual abuse materials (CSAM) and solicitation of children (grooming).[44]

The developing framework in EU law on content moderation, as signaled not only by the DSA but also by the other sectoral interventions mentioned above, is thus moving towards increased forms of crossover between the regulation 'of' platforms and the regulation 'by' platforms, meaning that 'the EU legal framework (*regulation of*) leaves ample margins of discretion for private ordering by large-scale platforms (*regulation by*) to shape their relationship with users'.[45] As has been noted, such an approach marks a shift from a merely negligence-based 'liability' scheme towards a framework focused instead on the 'responsibility' to proactively implement and pursue publicly relevant policies,[46] thus making platforms, in practice, online watchdogs.[47]

2. *Regulating Gatekeepers*

The DSA was devised and developed as part of a packet together with the Digital Markets Act (DMA),[48] which is notably aimed at ensuring 'fairness and contestability' within the Single Market vis-à-vis the rise of platforms

---

[43] DSA, art 45.

[44] Proposal for a Regulation of the European Parliament and of the Council Laying down Rules to Prevent and Combat Child Sexual Abuse, COM/2022/209 final.

[45] João Pedro Quintais, Giovanni De Gregorio and João C Magalhães, 'How Platforms Govern Users' Copyright-Protected Content: Exploring the Power of Private Ordering and Its Implications' (2023) 48 CLS Rev 105792, 3.

[46] Giancarlo Frosio and Martin Husovec, 'Accountability and Responsibility of Online Intermediaries' in Giancarlo Frosio (ed), *Oxford Handbook of Online Intermediary Liability* (OUP 2020); Husovec (n 35).

[47] Giancarlo Frosio, 'Why Keep a Dog and Bark Yourself? From Intermediary Liability to Responsibility' (2018) 26 IJLIT 1.

[48] Regulation (EU) 2022/1925 of the European Parliament and of the Council of 14 September 2022 on Contestable and Fair Markets in the Digital Sector and Amending Directives (EU) 2019/1937 and (EU) 2020/1828 (Digital Markets Act) [2022] OJ L265/1 (DMA).

which have reached such dimensions and importance that they have in fact become 'gatekeepers' of digital markets.[49] In so doing, the DMA recalls to a certain extent the Platform to Business (P2B) Regulation,[50] effective since July 2020, which established new transparency rules for platforms, with a specific view to favoring smaller businesses and traders relying on search engines and online platforms for their activities. Like the DSA, in this respect the DMA takes a more horizontal approach to the concentration of powers in the hands of a few private companies and, adopting an antitrust perspective, has the goal of fostering the interests of the general public and of the European market in general.

Whereas the targets of the widest range of provisions under the DSA are VLOPs and VLOSEs, the DMA focuses its attention upon 'gatekeepers', ie upon undertakings that have a significant impact on the internal market, that provide a 'core platform service' representing an important gateway for business users to reach end users, and that enjoy an 'entrenched and durable position', also where such a position is foreseeable in the near future.[51] The new rules affecting gatekeepers focus on a variety of goals, including the promotion of increased transparency (especially with respect to advertising), the overcoming of the phenomenon of 'platform envelopment', the fostering of interoperability, and the countering of unfair market practices.[52] Further, the imposition of positive obligations upon gatekeepers represents a rather unusual approach towards the protection of competition in the European Single Market.

The DMA indeed limits online platforms' discretion and their role as private regulators. It limits the possibility for online platforms to lock their instant messaging services by requiring interoperability,[53] and at the same time it prohibits a more favorable treatment of their own services.[54] Likewise, users are also empowered by obligations to disclose how algorithms rank content and how ads are targeted.[55] Additionally, the DMA requires explicit consent for data use in targeted advertising and enables easy changes to de-

---

[49] From the start, the goal of the Digital Services Act Package has indeed been that of 'taming the giants'. See Martin Eifert and others, 'Taming the Giants: The DMA/DSA Package' (2021) 58 CMLRev 987.

[50] Regulation (EU) 2019/1150 of the European Parliament and of the Council of 20 June 2019 on Promoting Fairness and Transparency for Business Users of Online Intermediation Services, OJ L186/57 (P2B Regulation).

[51] DMA, art 3.

[52] DMA, arts 5–6. See Alexandre de Streel and others, 'The European Proposal for a Digital Markets Act. A First Assessment' (Centre on Regulation in Europe 2021) 19 <https://cerre.eu/wp-content/uploads/2021/01/CERRE_Digital-Markets-Act_a-first-assessment_January2021.pdf>.

[53] DMA, art 7.

[54] DMA, art 6(5).

[55] DMA, art 6(11).

fault settings, thereby empowering users and promoting a more competitive online platforms environment.[56] Particularly, this point has raised questions after the decision of the CJEU in *Meta Platforms*, which has led to the introduction of the pay or consent system.[57]

The DMA distances itself from the generally traditional body of EU (and state) competition law and takes a rather innovative turn; this is done by adopting a strategy towards the market that, rather than being merely proscriptive, is in great part prescriptive.[58] In other words, the DMA develops a framework which does not simply react to the failures of the market but which sets specific rules and obligations for market actors so as to avoid, ex ante, any malfunctioning. In other words, gatekeepers are entrusted with duties actively aimed at promoting a 'sustainable development of Europe' based on 'a highly competitive social market economy', in line with the principles set out in the Treaty on European Union.[59] Similar to the DSA and to the new wave of content moderation regulation, the DMA thus ends up delegating to the private targets of regulation the pursuit of objectives and goals that are fundamentally of a public interest in the context of the EU.

Therefore, vis-à-vis the alleged failure of traditional competition law against the background of the rise of online platforms, the DMA seeks to overcome the asymmetry of powers characterizing the digital single market by promoting – through the adoption of proactive due responsibility obligations imposed on those same platforms – the values of 'contestability' and 'fairness', the first encompassing the possibility for undertakings to overcome barriers to entry and expansion and to challenge gatekeepers with respect to the products and services they offer, and the second focusing precisely on reducing the imbalance of power between gatekeepers and business users.[60] The shift from an ex post and economy-driven approach to an ex ante regulation of competition and a largely value-driven system reflects the novel governance relationships between platforms and EU institutions,[61] whereby the former are made the prime actors vested with the responsibility of guaranteeing the values of 'fairness' and 'contestability' (rather than simple efficiency) in the digital context.

---

[56] DMA, art 5(2).

[57] CJEU 4 July 2023, C-252/21 *Meta Platforms and Others,* ECLI:EU:2022:704.

[58] Natalia Moreno Belloso and Nicolas Petit, 'The EU Digital Markets Act (DMA): A Competition Hand in a Regulatory Glove' (SSRN, 5 April 2023) <https://papers.ssrn.com/abstract=4411743>.

[59] Treaty on European Union, art 3(3).

[60] DMA, recitals 32–33. Alba Ribera Martínez, 'An Inverse Analysis of the Digital Markets Act: Applying the Ne Bis in Idem Principle to Enforcement' (2023) 19 ECJ 86, 89.

[61] Rupprecht Podszun, 'From Competition Law to Platform Regulation – Regulatory Choices for the Digital Markets Act' (2023) 17 Economics 20220037.

The peculiar nature of the DMA against the backdrop of traditional approaches to competition policies also emerges from the fact that the chosen legal basis is not, as might have been expected, art 103 of the Treaty on the Functioning of the EU but, rather, art 114.[62] Such a choice arguably suggests that the DMA aims to go beyond traditional competition tools and to foster, more generally, a market for digital services that is respectful of the central tenets and principles of the Union's constitutional framework. Put in this perspective, the full complementarity between the DSA and the DMA, that is, the two souls of the Digital Services Package, emerges with full clarity.

The Package, recognizing the inherent triangular structure of the power dynamics characterizing the algorithmic society,[63] strives to profit from the increasing role of online platforms in general and online platforms in particular, with a view to exploiting their resources and (algorithmic) powers in such a way that is advantageous for society and the Union as a whole. By promoting obligations based on particular business models and market positions, the DMA, like the DSA, renders online platforms co-protagonists in the promotion of Union values and interests.

3. *Data, Artificial Intelligence, and Risks*

The online platform economy is mostly data-based and data-driven, while AI systems have increasingly become paramount tools for the correct functioning of the services platforms offer. Online platforms resort on a daily basis to the analysis of data and to the profiling of recipients of their services for a plurality of goals, including optimization of their own services, content moderation and curation, and targeted advertising.[64] Strategies which delegate to the targets of regulation the responsibility of adopting measures adequate for respecting not only privacy and data protection rights but also, more generally, fundamental rights potentially affected by the use of AI tools contribute to online platforms being understood – here again –as subjects directly responsible for the promotion and attainment of public and constitutionally driven principles and goals.

---

[62] Eifert and others (n 49) 1001.

[63] Jack M Balkin, 'Free Speech in the Algorithmic Society: Big Data, Private Governance, and New School Speech Regulation' (2018) 51 UCDavis LRev 1149; Jack M Balkin, 'Free Speech Is a Triangle' (2018) 118 Colum LRev 2011.

[64] See, among others, Cass R Sunstein, *#Republic: Divided Democracy in the Age of Social Media* (PUP 2017); Federico Galli, 'Online Behavioural Advertising and Unfair Manipulation Between the GDPR and the UCPD' in Martin Ebers and Marta Cantero Gamito (eds), *Algorithmic Governance and Governance of Algorithms: Legal and Ethical Challenges* (Springer International 2021); Giovanni De Gregorio and Pietro Dunn, 'Artificial Intelligence and Freedom of Expression' in Alberto Quintavalla and Jeroen Temperman (eds), *Artificial Intelligence and Human Rights* (OUP 2023).

In the field of privacy and data protection, the General Data Protection Regulation (GDPR),[65] consistent with the principle of accountability embedded within it, also tends to exploit the capacities of data controllers themselves, by entrusting them with the role of defining, in practice, the means by which to ensure the protection of privacy and data protection rights. Online platforms as data controllers have been entrusted with the responsibility of ensuring that the processing of personal data is aligned with the protection of the general principles the GDPR sets. They are required to concretely ascertain the degree of risks to data subjects' rights when processing personal data, and, based on that assessment, to design the appropriate mitigation responses. As noted by Quelle, such a legal regime requires that data controllers and data processors engage in a manner of 'compliance 2.0', ie 'a form of compliance that does not merely 'tick boxes', but is tailored to respect the rights and freedoms of data subjects'.[66] The GDPR is, in other words, inherently grounded on making the data controller accountable. In this sense, the system of responsibilities established by the GDPR is focused on a risk-based approach,[67] one which vests data controllers with the direct task of actively protecting privacy and data protection rights, that is, those rights that have effectively been defined as 'Europe's First Amendment'.[68] As an example, this central role in the European framework has been clearly underlined in the questions raised by the pay-or-consent model. The questions related to the possibility of processing personal data for the purposes of targeted advertising based on alternative legal bases of consent have led European institutions and the CJEU to underline the central role of consent as a legal basis that aims to protect data subjects' fundamental rights.

Thus, consistent with the DMA scheme and the content moderation policies of the DSA, the GDPR's risk-based approach reflects a will to horizontally involve non-public actors, including online platforms, in the pursuit of desirable outcomes for society.[69] Through the GDPR, the EU lawmakers aimed namely at promoting values such as transparency, data minimization, and accountability in

---

[65] Regulation (EU) 2016/679 of the European Parliament and of the Council of 27 April 2016 on the Protection of Natural Persons with Regard to the Processing of Personal Data and on the Free Movement of Such data, and Repealing Directive 95/46/EC (General Data Protection Regulation) [2016] OJ L119/1 (GDPR).

[66] Claudia Quelle, 'Enhancing Compliance under the General Data Protection Regulation: The Risky Upshot of the Accountability and Risk-based Approach' (2018) 9(3) EJRR 502, 506.

[67] Milda Macenaite, 'The "Riskification" of European Data Protection Law through a Two-Fold Shift' (2017) 8 EJRR 506; Raphaël Gellert, *The Risk-Based Approach to Data Protection* (OUP 2020); De Gregorio and Dunn (n 37).

[68] Bilyana Petkova, 'Privacy as Europe's First Amendment' (2019) 25 ELJ 140.

[69] See, for instance, De Gregorio (n 12); Oreste Pollicino, *Judicial Protection of Fundamental Rights on the Internet: A Road Towards Digital Constitutionalism?* (Hart 2021).

the context of the collection and processing of data, also for the purposes of their use in the context of the development and deployment of automated systems.[70]

Building on such principles, the EU has, furthermore, come to address specifically the legal framework concerning the development, deployment, and use of AI systems. The AI Act seeks to ensure that AI systems respect fundamental rights;[71] this should be done by guaranteeing a proper governance framework of those systems (with a view to fostering legal certainty), by further encouraging the development of the Digital Single Market, and by preventing market fragmentation. With respect to the AI Act, particularly worthy of mention is the legal regime established for the wide category of 'high-risk' AI systems. Providers and deployers of those systems, in particular, will have to establish, implement, document, and maintain a risk management system, with a view to adopting suitable measures to face any known or foreseeable hazard.[72] Additionally, providers of high-risk AI systems will be required to put in place a quality management system to ensure compliance with the entire Regulation.[73] Once again, therefore, the regulatory dynamics of the AI Act are based on a strict inter-relation between the public institutions and the actors subjected to the new provisions of the Regulation.

Furthermore, in relation to online platforms, the AI Act establishes connections with the DSA, particularly for VLOPs. Indeed, the AI Act obligations do not affect the risk assessment obligations which VLOPs are required to comply with under the DSA.[74] As a result, while the AI Act augments the rules for online platforms as providers and deployers of AI systems, these obligations need to be coordinated with the requirements applying to online platforms as VLOPs under the DSA.

Both the GDPR and the AI Act thus vest online platforms with the fundamental role of monitoring, guaranteeing, and promoting the well-being of society at large and the rights of individuals. In the case of both the GDPR and the AI Act, platforms are in fact responsible for decisions concerning the practical implementation and enforcement of the Union's purposes and goals. These actors therefore play the role of the long arm of European public institutions. Such a strategy reflects a relationship between EU policies and private actors, namely online platforms, that is in many ways ambiguous: on the one hand, EU institutions aim to rein in and set some constraints on those plat-

---

[70] GDPR, art 22.

[71] Regulation (EU) 2024/1689 of the European Parliament and of the Council of 13 June 2024 Laying Down Harmonised Rules on Artificial Intelligence and Amending Regulations (EC) 300/2008, (EU) 167/2013, (EU) 168/2013, (EU) 2018/858, (EU) 2018/1139 and (EU) 2019/2144 and Directives 2014/90/EU, (EU) 2016/797 and (EU) 2020/1828 (Artificial Intelligence Act) [2024] OJ L2024/1689 (AI Act).

[72] AI Act, art 9.

[73] AI Act.

[74] AI Act, art 2(9).

forms' powers; on the other hand, such an aspiration is counterbalanced by an awareness of the possibilities those powers entail for the promotion of public interests as well as of the need to guarantee the advancement of a sector of the internal market which is becoming more and more strategic internationally.

IV. Platforms as Enforcers and Collaborators

The regulatory strategies developed by the EU in the context of the digital landscape reflect a remarkable evolution in the relationship between public institutions and private online platforms, whereby the former rely increasingly on the powers of the latter for the purposes of balancing and enforcing public interests. Even if the Union has expanded its regulatory intervention, often in the forms of regulatory horizontal instruments, it has not adopted a top-down approach but instead underlined the critical role of online platforms as private regulators.

This approach shifts attention to the responsibilities of online platforms. Particularly evident is, in this respect, the rise in the resort to legal provisions characterized by an inherently risk-based approach towards the governance of the internal market. This emerges, particularly, from European regulation on content moderation practices, where the choice of policies and technical tools is largely left to the discretion of the providers of intermediary services and their ToS, with these providers obliged to respect fundamental rights. Still, the decision about how to confront unwarranted materials is ultimately at the remit of private actors, even if VLOPs are subject to additional obligations based on risk mitigation measures. The risk-based approach, furthermore, also emerges clearly from law regulating data and AI. Despite the differences, both the GDPR and the AI Act, especially with respect to 'high risk' AI systems, delegate to the discretion of the regulated actors the identification of the strategies to be implemented to protect and foster fundamental rights and democratic values.

The choice to rely on risk-based regulatory instruments reflects, first of all, an awareness of EU public institutions as regards the quasi-public powers and capabilities developed by private actors in the digital landscape and thus of the inescapable need to rely on those powers to achieve public goals and interests. This emerges specifically also from the new and already mentioned ex ante approach of the DMA, which, in contrast to the traditional ex post strategies of previous legislation, manifests a dependence on digital 'gatekeepers' to avoid a malfunctioning of the Digital Single Market. Second, the resort to legislative strategies based on risk-based approaches reflects the concerns of the EU with respect to the need to guarantee the establishment of a framework that is as friendly as possible to the private digital actors themselves, especially in light of the importance acquired in the last years by the services those actors provide to society. In other words, EU digital legislation is marked by the recognition of online platforms' responsibilities to society and thus by the will to govern and steer their practices and activities, as well as by the aspiration to ensure that the advantages of digital technologies and services are not lost.

In this respect, the resort of the EU to these approaches is in large part oriented towards developing a proportionate framework in which private market actors may be made responsible of their actions and practices while avoiding their being drowned by legislative requirements.[75] From such a perspective, another element appears to be particularly significant with respect to the development of digital policy strategies, specifically the increasing role played by codes of conduct and codes of practice, which acquire, under the new laws, the status of 'co-regulatory' instruments.[76] This is particularly evident, first of all, from the text of the DSA. Indeed, the DSA complements the rules on providers' new due diligence obligations by recognizing the possibility of developing voluntary codes of conduct at Union level,[77] which acquire nevertheless a central harmonizing role once adopted. These codes apply, namely, to the obligation of VLOPs and VLOSEs to assess and mitigate systemic risks entailed by their services.

An important advantage of the codes of conduct is represented by the possibility to introduce more specific commitments tailored to address certain systemic risks. Further, to the advantage of providers of VLOPs and VLOSEs, these additional commitments are identified and defined not on a top-down basis, but rather as a result of negotiations that take into account the economic and financial interests of providers and of the Digital Single Market as such. At the same time, once they have been agreed upon, under the text of the Regulation the codes of conduct tend to acquire a rather compelling force which affects not only those actors that have participated in their drafting but, more generally, all VLOPs and VLOSEs. On the one hand, the choice to adhere to and comply with a code of conduct may strengthen the position of a VLOP or VLOSE in proving their compliance with the DSA's due diligence obligations (even though such a choice may not be per se sufficient to constitute an inescapable presumption); on the other hand, the refusal to apply a

---

75 De Gregorio and Dunn (n 37).

76 On the notion and role of co-regulation in the EU, see Interinstitutional Agreement of 31 December 2003 on Better Law-Making, OJ C321/1 paras 18, 22; Linda AJ Senden and others, 'Mapping Self- and Co-Regulation Approaches in the EU Context: Explorative Study for the European Commission, DG Connect' (Utrecht University Repository 2015) 5–6; Christopher T Marsden, *Internet Co-Regulation: European Law, Regulatory Governance and Legitimacy in Cyberspace* (CUP 2011).

77 DSA, art 45.

code of conduct represents a strong piece of evidence against providers.[78] As argued by Griffin and Vander Maelen, while the DSA repeatedly reiterates the 'voluntary' nature of codes, 'given their role in risk mitigation and auditing, VLOP/VLOSE participation is all but inescapable as part of DSA compliance'.[79] In this respect, Twitter's recent choice to withdraw from the 2022 Strengthened Code of Practice on Disinformation may well expose it to a serious risk of being held accountable.[80] In other words, compliance with a code of conduct ends up representing an important baseline in proving the provider's compliance with the Regulation.

Rather than resorting to top-down forms of regulation or self-regulation, the EU seeks to establish a collaborative framework where the practical implementation of governance measures is negotiated and agreed upon by the major market powers acting within the Digital Single Market. Nonetheless, this strategy, which emerges not only from the DSA but is present also within the AI Act when considering the role of codes of conduct, requires its being supported by a coherent regulatory regime which provides safeguards to mitigate the lack of transparency and accountability resulting from this collaboration. Nevertheless, increasing collaboration raises questions for the rule of law. Although they promote innovative forms of cooperation between the public and the private in terms of digital policy, these new relationships – taking the form of a risk-based approach or co-regulation – also raise challenges precisely because of the increasing reliance of public actors upon private actors, which could lead to opaque forms of governance.

Overall, the evolving EU framework on digital policies is moving towards a regulatory approach which, albeit through the use of legal tools that are traditionally connected to hard law, is characterized by the injection of co-regulatory (if not even of soft law) features. Such an approach reflects the EU's awareness of the inescapable need for the contribution of platforms and online platforms for the purposes of reaching institutional goals.

---

[78] In this respect, see DSA, recital 104. According to Vander Maelen, the DSA's new framework on codes of conduct has an important impact on both their functioning and their legal nature. See Carl Vander Maelen, 'Hardly Law or Hard Law? Investigating the Dimensions of Functionality and Legislation of Codes of Conduct in Recent EU Legislation and the Normative Repercussions Thereof' (2022) 47 E LRev 752, 764–768.

[79] Rachel Griffin and Carl Vander Maelen, 'Codes of Conduct in the Digital Services Act: Exploring the Opportunities and Challenges' (SSRN, 30 May 2023) 6 <https://papers.ssrn.com/abstract=4463874>.

[80] See Natasha Lomas, 'Elon Musk Takes Twitter out of the EU's Disinformation Code of Practice' (*TechCrunch*, 27 May 2023) <https://techcrunch.com/2023/05/27/elon-musk-twitter-eu-disinformation-code/>; Carl Vander Maelen and Rachel Griffin, 'Twitter's Retreat from the Code of Practice on Disinformation Raises a Crucial Question: Are DSA Codes of Conduct Really Voluntary?' (*DSA Observatory*, 12 June 2023) <https://dsa-observatory.eu/2023/06/12/twitters-retreat-from-the-code-of-practice-on-disinformation-raises-a-crucial-question-are-dsa-codes-of-conduct-really-voluntary/>.

V. Conclusions

Online platforms have increasingly emerged as private regulators in the context of the provision of their services. The ways in which they draft, enforce, and decide upon their own ToS represent forms of para-constitutional (quasi-legislative, quasi-executive, and quasi-judicial) powers. It is against such a backdrop that EU legislation concerning the digital landscape is evolving, taking into account precisely such developments in the power dynamics of the internet.

The new wave of EU legislation concerning the digital market has indeed attempted to harness these para-constitutional powers of digital platforms. Such an attempt is, furthermore, oriented first of all on a desire of the EU to put some limits on the absolute discretion enjoyed by platforms since the beginning of the millennium. Second, legislation has been triggered by an awareness that many public interests are, in today's world, unattainable without the direct cooperation of those private market actors. Third, the first two purposes have to be counterbalanced with the awareness that regulation should avoid suffocating the development of digital technologies, as this would be detrimental to the market as well as to the lives and rights of the recipients of digital services. To this extent, the described legislative tools reflect a situation of dependency between the EU and online platforms, whereby the former seemingly wishes to contain but is at the same time dependent on the powers of the latter.

Such an inter-relation between private and public powers emerges clearly from many of the choices made in most legal instruments enacted in recent years, including (but not limited to) the DSA, DMA, GDPR, and AI Act. All these instruments, indeed, share a heavy reliance upon private online platforms for the purposes of implementing and enforcing the rules set by the Union, with a view to ensuring an approach that is as balanced as possible. The increasing resort to strategies which include a risk-based approach or to the adoption of codes of conduct agreed upon by all major relevant stakeholders is clearly moved by the EU's aspiration to foster a cooperative governance system which is capable of exploiting, in a positive way, the new power dynamics of the internet.

At the same time, such an approach also reveals a deeply ambiguous relationship between the regulator and the regulated, between the public and the private. The potential impact of such ambiguities on the constitutional framework should not be ignored; rather, this impact should be carefully addressed by Union institutions in the future, especially with a view to ensuring that paramount principles, including notably transparency and the rule of law, are in fact guaranteed.

Theorizing Platform Regulation

A Sociological Account Between Private and Public Governance

*Friederike Bahl**

Platform-based regulation has reshaped the global economy and its legal foundations. But the conditions underlying this internal regulatory interest in platforms have not yet been explored in much sociological detail. Drawing on the example of privatizing judicial functions, this contribution is dedicated to giving a systematic account of the explanations offered for this emerging regulatory phenomenon. Analyses thus far tend to point to the far-reaching trend of international platforms such as Google and eBay to move in the direction of digital dispute resolution, with internal methods for addressing such issues as the administration of trademark infringements, the moderation of hate speech, or the removal of links to websites under data protection law. In retracing this evolution, the text will offer two overlooked potential avenues for further research. The first is a matter of combining explanatory perspectives: as between platform-internal interests in self-regulation and their practices for avoiding intermediary liability in cases of damage, there is no one-size-fits-all explanation. Rather, we need an approach that is sensitive to the systematic interdependency of private and public interests in platform adjudication. The second relates to a rethinking of the theoretical concepts we use to describe their relationship. Confining itself to the dualistic tension between privately regulating market actors and publicly regulating authorities, the research performed to date tends to leave an essential gap that no

* I thank Mateusz Grochowski, Federica Casarosa, Thomas Cannaday, Michael Friedman, and Janina Jentz for their thoughtful comments on earlier versions.

combined approach alone can fix, namely the regulatory relevance of actors who are neither public agents nor private platform.

I. Introduction

Platform corporations have reshaped the global economy and its legal foundations. With revenues sometimes exceeding 100 million euros, online retailers, social media channels, and search engines are not only among the largest companies in the world; they have also fundamentally altered the regulatory framework governing social activity and decision-making in cases of conflict. As the leading providers of comprehensive software solutions for reporting rule violations and also private adjudication mechanisms for resolving dispute, international companies such as Google, eBay, Alibaba or Meta (formerly Facebook) are part of a far-reaching trend toward digital dispute resolution and the platformization of judicial functions.[1]

As social relationships and everyday transactions on the internet have increasingly become transnational by relying on online auction houses and social media platforms, there is a growing interest in uncomplicated and often algorithmically controlled means of monitoring legal transgressions and in resolving conflict online.[2] Internet companies are not only among the first to pick up on this trend and develop such law tech expertise;[3] their often extensive on-platform systems for dispute resolution are also the most comprehensive of their kind worldwide.[4] Whether as a Meta-community or via Amazon Prime, companies tie down membership in the millions and channel, limit, and regulate their users' legal transgressions at an unprecedented level.[5] This includes both a safeguarding of transactions concluded between direct clients of their platform services and an examination of their users' behavior with regard to possible infringements of rights vis-à-vis third parties. From establishing whole sets of rules for digital communication and implementing their associated reputation systems, to editing content for publishing and monitoring copyright infringements as well as violations of personal data contained therein, the scope of regulatory action that platforms assume in some cases equals the decision-making power of state courts.

---

[1] Frank Pasquale, 'Digital Capitalism – How to Tame the Platform Juggernauts' (2018) 6 WISO direct 1, 2.

[2] Ethan Katsh, Janet Rifkin and Alan Gaitenby, 'E-Commerce, E-Disputes, and E-Dispute Resolution: In the Shadow of "eBay Law"' (1999) 15 OSJDR 705, 725.

[3] Richard Susskind, *Online Courts and the Future of Justice* (OUP 2019).

[4] Benjamin H Barton, 'Rebooting Justice: ODR is Disrupting the Judicial System' (2018) 44 Law Prac 32.

[5] Ulrich Dolata, 'Plattform-Regulierung. Koordination von Märkten und Kuratierung von Sozialität im Internet' (2020) 29 BJS 179.

Despite their steadily growing importance, however, the various forms and origins of these dispute resolution practices have thus far only been minimally researched. Against this backdrop, this article is dedicated to providing a systematic account of the reasons offered for this platformization of judicial functions with the aim of laying out the ground work for future research. Both exploring existing strengths to be fostered and identifying possible desiderata awaiting further analysis, the text will make two arguments. First, I will argue that a comparative review of the existing platform adjudication research discloses the multidimensional nature of its underlying mechanisms. Bearing in mind the inevitable tension between those regulatory activities that the platforms have installed on their own initiative and those that have been officially delegated to them despite the platforms' resistance,[6] a systematic account of existing literature can reveal the regulatory interdependency of private and public interests in furthering platform-based adjudication, an interdependency that our research designs must respond to. However, this interdependency also brings to light a theoretical challenge that goes beyond the possible benefits of combining analytical perspectives, and therein lies the second argument I would like to make: there is a need to rethink the conceptual tools we use to explore this interdependency. By inscribing any analysis of platform-based regulation in the contrasting landscape of private self-coordination and public delegation, the previous works imbue every attempt to theorize it with a conceptual duality that cannot do justice to the matter at hand. Focusing primarily on the relationship between private profitability and public organization, this body of literature emphasizes the tension between private regulation *by* platforms and the public regulation *of* platforms that obscures the significant influence of those actors that are neither platform nor public personnel.[7]

In order to outline both arguments in greater detail, the following sections initially concentrate on describing the main features of the trend towards expand-

---

[6] While regulatory tasks, such as trademark protection, can be delegated by the state, for instance, other regulatory activities of the platforms, such as the implementation of reputation systems, might be implemented on the platform's own initiative to absorb, for example, the uncertainties of anonymity that arise within digital markets and the issues of transactional trust that come with it.

[7] Tarleton Gillespie, 'Governance of and by Platforms' in Jean Burgess, Alice Marwick and Thomas Poell (eds), *The SAGE Handbook of Social Media* (SAGE 2017) 254. As we will develop in the text that follows – the platform-internal development of reputation systems that is done to generate trust can still be described as private self-coordination, just as a potential state requirement that search engines administer personal rights can be understood as an expression of public regulation. However, when platform-initiated regulatory services react, for example, to tech whistle-blowers and other actors who can be attributed neither to the platform itself nor to the state, regulatory dynamics begin to emerge that cannot be adequately captured in the conceptual duality of private self-coordination and public regulation.

ing platform-based adjudication (II) and then work out the form and content of the offered explanations for this trend (III–IV). By considering both platform-internal self-initiative and the efforts such platforms undertake to avoid liability, these explanations can suggest possible avenues for mutual gain through a combination of perspectives (V), but they also demonstrate the shortcomings of the dualistic vocabulary used to describe their interrelation (VI).

II. Platform Adjudication as Part of a Trend Towards Digital Regulation

Under the term platform economy,[8] a steadily growing number of conceptual analyses as well as empirical studies have been produced in recent years that describe a wide range of regulatory intervention undertaken by large internet corporations – such as Amazon, Google, eBay, and Meta.

Platform companies are not just manifestations of innovative business models that coordinate profitable markets having nation-sized dimensions. They also enable novel forms for organizing trade, labor, and other social relations.[9] Their platforms may serve a wide variety of purposes. These include trading (eg Amazon, eBay, Alibaba); networking, messaging, and search services (eg Meta, Instagram, WhatsApp, Google); and offering intermediary functions for a mixture of products or services (eg etsy, Airbnb, Deliveroo, myHammer). What they have in common is that they all provide their own socio-technical infrastructures, with which the leading providers among them have become core players in a trend toward the digital regulation of social action.[10] At the center of this regulatory shift are two essential areas

---

[8] Martin Kenney and John Zysman, 'The Rise of the Platform Economy' (2016) 32 Issues in Science & Technology 61; Kathleen Thelen, 'Regulating Uber: The Politics of the Platform Economy in Europe and the United States' (2018) 16 Perspectives on Politics 938; Tarleton Gillespie, *Custodians of the Internet: Platforms, Content Moderation, and the Hidden Decisions that Shape Social Media* (YUP 2018) 15, 21–22; Frank Pasquale, 'Two Narratives of Platform Capitalism' (2016) 35 YLP Rev 309. See also Kate Klonick, 'The Facebook Oversight Board: Creating an Independent Institution to Adjudicate Online Free Expression' (2020) 129 YLJ 2418, 2428.

[9] Ulrich Dolata, 'Privatization, Curation, Commodification. Commercial Platforms on the Internet' (2019) 44 ÖZS 181; Nick Srnicek, *Platform Capitalism* (Polity Press 2017); Paul Langley and Andrew Leyshon, 'Platform Capitalism: The Intermediation and Capitalisation of Digital Economic Circulation' (2017) 3 Finance and Society 11; Christian Fuchs, *Social Media. A Critical Introduction* (SAGE 2014).

[10] Steven Vallas and Juliet B Schor, 'What Do Platforms Do? Understanding the Gig Economy' (2020) 46 Annual Review of Sociology 273, 282; Dolata (n 5), Dolata (n 9) 187; Jean-Marie Chenou and Roxana Radu, 'The "Right to Be Forgotten": Negotiating Public and Private Ordering in the European Union' (2019) 58 Business & Society 74; Christoph Busch, 'Self-Regulation and Regulatory Intermediation in the Platform Econo-

of platform performance:[11] on the one hand, there is the re-organization of capitalist markets.[12] Commercial platforms fundamentally coordinate the exchange practices and trading processes taking place on them and determine their competitive conditions, production models, and respective labor relations. On the other hand, it is equally important to see that platforms also pursue adjudicatory tasks – serving legal protection – by structuring and curating all social relationships established on them and by resolving conflict.[13] This is the area of research that the present analysis is interested in. Through the contractual agreements that all users must sign before they can use the respective services, platforms not only control access to the goods and services they offer and shape the forms and modes of market transaction; rather, their infrastructures also represent virtual spaces for social activity,[14] within which platforms play a fundamental role in re-organizing tasks serving legal protection, such as safeguarding consumer welfare, monitoring compliance with the standards of democratic rights, and sanctioning possible violations. From the moderation of hate speech to the tracking of copyright infringements, they assume essential adjudicatory functions, which in some

---

my' in Marta Cantero Gamito and Hans-W Micklitz (eds), *The Role of the EU in Transnational Legal Ordering: Standards, Contracts and Codes* (Edward Elgar 2019); Susskind (n 3); Pasquale (n 1); Thelen (n 8); Gillespie (n 8); Jack M Balkin, 'Old School/New School Speech Regulation' (2014) 127 Harv LRev 2296.

[11] Dolata (n 5) 184.

[12] Daniel Beverungen, Dennis Kundisch and Nancy V Wünderlich, 'Transforming into a Platform Provider: Strategic Options for Industrial Smart Service Providers' (2021) 32 J Serv Manag 507; Alain Marciano, Antonio Nicita and Giovanni Battista Ramello 'Big Data and Big Techs: Understanding the Value of Information in Platform Capitalism' (2020) 50 Eur JL Econ 345; Philipp Staab, *Digitaler Kapitalismus. Markt und Herrschaft in der Ökonomie der Unknappheit* (Suhrkamp 2019); Srnicek (n 9); Stefan Kirchner and Wenzel Matiaske, 'Plattformökonomie und Arbeitsbeziehungen – Digitalisierung zwischen imaginierter Zukunft und empirischer Gegenwart' (2020) 27 IndBez 105; Justus Haucap and Ulrich Heimeshoff, 'Google, Facebook, Amazon, eBay: Is the Internet Driving Competition or Market Monopolization?' (2014) 11 Intl Econ & Econ Pol 49.

[13] Chenou and Radu (n 10); Jack M Balkin, 'Free Speech in the Algorithmic Society: Big Data, Private Governance, and New School Speech Regulation' (2018) 51 UCDavis LRev 1149; Laura DeNardis and Andrea Hackl, 'Internet Governance by Social Media Platforms' (2015) 39 Telecommunications Policy 761; Tarleton Gillespie, 'Platforms Intervene' (2015) 1 Social Media+Society 1; Sal Humphreys, 'Predicting, Securing and Shaping the Future: Mechanisms of Governance in Online Social Environments' (2013) 9 IJ Media Cult Pol 247; Rebecca MacKinnon and others, *Fostering Freedom Online: The Roles, Challenges and Obstacles of Internet Intermediaries* (UNESCO 2014); José van Dijck, *The Culture of Connectivity: A Critical History of Social Media* (OUP 2013); Ben Wagner, 'Governing Internet Expression: How Public and Private Regulation Shape Expression Governance' (2013) 10 JITP 389.

[14] Ulrich Dolata and Jan-Felix Schrape, 'Platform Architectures. The Structuration of Platform Companies on the Internet' (2022) 1 SOI Discussion Paper 1, 21.

cases endow them with the decision-making power of national-level courts.[15] This extensive reach of platform generated regulatory intervention in the area of dispute resolution begs the question of its origins.

Searching for explanations, existing literature provides us with two lines of analysis having a potential interconnectedness. While the first focuses on the platforms' own initiative in taking on these adjudicatory tasks against the backdrop of regulatory loopholes and state permissiveness (III), the second complements this perspective by exploring cases involving an official delegation of these tasks done over the platforms' resistance (IV).

III. Privately Initiated Platform Adjudication

A first important means of explaining the regulatory efforts of platforms can be found by exploring these activities from the perspective of their profitability for the platforms. Often adopting an economic perspective on market organization, the studies point to the fact that such regulatory services benefit the platform operators in their role as reliable market coordinators.[16]

Starting from the platform's interest in facilitating a transaction, the comprehensive regulatory efforts they undertake – so it is argued – are a corporative response to a challenge that is increasing with the digitization of markets: creating user trust in an environment of transactional uncertainty.[17]

If we consider trading markets, for example, there are at least three forms of uncertainty that their participants face:[18] uncertainty about the value of a traded product, uncertainty about successful competition for profit opportunities, and uncertainty about the cooperative behavior of all participating transaction partners.[19] While the uncertainty as regards value is linked to the difficulties in assessing the quality of products,[20] the uncertainty regarding competition arises from not knowing whether one's own market participation will result in profit.[21] The 'problem of cooperation' or trust,[22] on the other hand,

---

[15] Balkin (n 13); Dolata and Schrape (n 14) 15.

[16] Stefan Kirchner and Jürgen Beyer, 'Die Plattformlogik als digitale Marktordnung. Wie die Digitalisierung Kopplungen von Unternehmen löst und Märkte transformiert' (2016) 45 ZfS 324; see also, Dolata (n 5) 184; Gillespie (n 7).

[17] Katsh, Rifkin and Gaitenby (n 2) 729, 730.

[18] Jens Beckert, 'The Social Order of Markets' (2009) 38 Theo Soc 245; Andreas Diekmann and Wojtek Przepiorka, 'Reputation auf Märkten' in Andrea Maurer (ed), *Handbuch der Wirtschaftssoziologie* (Springer 2017) 241.

[19] Beckert (n 18); Kirchner and Beyer (n 16); Diekmann and Przepiorka (n 18).

[20] Beckert (n 18) 253–255.

[21] Beckert (n 18) 257–259; Ulrich Dolata, 'Volatile Monopole. Konzentration, Konkurrenz und Innovationsstrategien der Internetkonzerne' (2015) 24 BJS 505.

stems from the risk of fraud, cheating, and other refusals to cooperate as caused by a fear of betrayal.

In attempting to understand the interest of platforms in embarking on far-reaching regulatory engagement, the above-described line of argument can provide us with a first important explanation: successfully handling such uncertainties (eg through implementing community rules, offering reputation systems that measure their compliance, and punishing their possible violations) can help to facilitate further transactions in the realm of the platform operators.[23] Conversely, where trust is lacking – as in the case of many black market transactions – the interactions of market participants are sometimes limited to the controllable simultaneity of corresponding actions.[24] Moreover, the significance of absorbing such transactional uncertainty increases when specifically focusing on *digital* markets.[25] Although online transactions and conversations often do not conflict,[26] in a world where sensitive information can be distributed worldwide within a split second, where virtual communication extends the conditions of anonymity, and where trade relations reach across national jurisdiction and regional customs, providers and customers in digital markets are burdened with considerable uncertainties, whereas the analogue world's solutions for these problems can only to a limited extent be transferred to a digital setting.[27]

To illustrate this extended level of uncertainty, we don't need to venture into the transaction structures of the darknet, where issues of transactional trust become more evident and the judicial enforceability of damage claims faces challenges of traceability.[28] Rather, this dynamic is encountered already

[22] Diekmann and Przepiorka (n 18); Beckert (n 18) 259–261; Ulrich Brinkmann and Matthias Seifert, '"Face to Interface": Zum Problem der Vertrauenskonstitution im Internet am Beispiel von elektronischen Auktionen' (2001) 30 ZfS 23; Katsh, Rifkin and Gaitenby (n 2) 729; Heinrich Popitz, *Die normative Konstruktion der Wirklichkeit* (Mohr Siebeck 1980).

[23] Gillespie (n 7).

[24] Popitz (n 22).

[25] Kirchner and Beyer (n 16) 325.

[26] Katsh, Rifkin and Gaitenby (n 2) 724. For example, according to estimates, only about 1% of purchases on eBay cause a problem that is ultimately addressed by the platform's own dispute settlement system. See BBC NEWS, 'eBay-Style Online Courts Could Resolve Smaller Claims' (16 February 2015) <http://www.bbc.com/news/uk-31483099> accessed 31 January 2024.

[27] Kirchner and Beyer (n 16) 325.

[28] Despite being unofficial, the term 'darknet' or 'dark net' describes an overlay network within the internet that hides its user's identity and is accessible only with specific software or browser configurations (eg Tor), sometimes also requiring invitation. Of course darknets are being used for illegal and legitimate reasons alike. See Mihnea Mirea, Victoria Wang and Jeyong Jung, 'The Not So Dark Side of the Darknet: A Qualitative Study' (2019) 32 Secur J 102. Yet the anonymity they provide not only facilitates the sharing, purchasing, and

in online trading. In assessing the quality of a smartphone offered on Amazon or eBay, potential buyers cannot undertake a haptic test-run of its functions and quality as they would in a traditional showroom.[29] Instead, even material products exist merely as digital representations portrayed in videos and images. In the meantime, the uncertainty of reliable profits is increasing with the rising number of competitors in a global digital market, where competing offers are often just one click away.[30] Finally, trust in cooperative behavior, such as providing correct information and making prompt payment, might face new challenges in a setting where transnational transactions minimize face-to-face interactions and transcend local customs.[31]

By taking such regulatory services into their own hands – be it in the form of implementing reputation systems, installing access controls, or offering in-house-procedures for resolving potential conflicts – platform operators can ultimately increase their respective sales markets. As noted by Amy Schmitz and Colin Rule, major internet intermediaries like Amazon and PayPal realized early on 'that the consumer trust problem was creating friction on the internet and that solving it could provide a valuable market advantage'.[32]

These economic references to the profitability of market coordination for the platforms are often set in the context of a political economy of privatization.[33] According to this conception, these platform-based regulatory efforts become fully comprehensible only against the backdrop of what can be described as a regulatory permissiveness of the state and other public agencies towards private governance. While different reasons are attributed to this

---

selling of software, goods, and services but also impedes the traceability of legal transgressions. See Michael Chertof and Tobby Simon, 'The Impact of the Dark Web on Internet Governance and Cyber Security' (2015) 6 GCIG Paper Series I, 7.

29 Paul Eisewicht, *Die Kunst des Reklamierens. Beitrag zum Verständnis von Konsum als Handlungsproblem* (Springer 2015); Paul Eisewicht, 'Amazon, Zalando und Co.: Schrei vor (Un)Glück!?' in Tilo Grenz and Gerd Möll (eds), *Unter Mediatisierungsdruck* (Springer 2014) 77; Kirchner and Beyer (n 16) 325.

30 Dolata (n 21) 518.

31 Kirchner and Beyer (n 16) 331; Eisewicht (n 29); Tilo Grenz and Paul Eisewicht, 'Outlaws in App Stores: die Nebenfolgenanfälligkeit digitaler Dienste als blinder Fleck der Service Science' (2015) 8 AIS-Studien 76; Andreas Diekmann and David Wyder, 'Vertrauen und Reputationseffekte bei Internet-Auktionen' (2002) 54 KZfSS 674; Brinkmann and Seifert (n 22).

32 Amy J Schmitz and Colin Rule, 'The New Handshake: Where We Are Now' (2016) (3)2 IJODR 84, 97.

33 Jonas Pentzien, 'Conceptualizing the Role of the State in the Digital Platform Economy' in Indre Maurer, Achim Oberg and Dominika Wruk (eds), *Perspectives on the Sharing Economy* (Cambridge Scholar 2019); Staab (n 12). See also Neil Fligstein, *The Architecture of Markets. An Economic Sociology of Twenty-First-Century Capitalist Societies* (PUP 2001); Susan Strange, *The Retreat of the State: The Diffusion of Power in the World Economy* (CUP 1996).

permissiveness – to either a loss in state control or to inner-governmental conflicts of interest[34] – they both stress the shared need to contextualize the regulatory efforts of the platforms by including the political conditions that allowed it.[35] Building on the argument of the assumed advantageousness of internal regulation for the platform operators, all perspectives on state permissiveness reflect the institutional framework that has favored the privately initiated efforts of platform operators. Some argue that this trend towards governance by platform can only be seen as a comprehensive disruption of state power, insofar as platforms such as eBay, Amazon, Airbnb, or Uber cross the borders of national territories and thereby can evade mechanisms of public control and supervision.[36] For others, it is less the transnational market power of the platform companies itself than the intra-governmental conflict of interest between curbing and facilitating their activity that obstructs consistent public strategies and regulatory guidelines.[37] What these explanations have in common is the following: in understanding state regulation more in the sense of an intervening push back,[38] the studies repeatedly focus on failed public attempts at containing the private activities of platforms – starting from an inability to address tax evasion and moving on to the lack of democratic control for the dispute resolution procedures established by them.[39] Even if the market and political economy perspectives rarely explicitly address it, this complementary difference in their *foci* of analysis effectively binds them together. While the market perspective on transactional trust focuses on the inner profitability of private regulation for the platforms, the political economy approach complements this view by looking at the lack of its outside containment. Together they depict a tension between public and private interests in market coordination, whereby regulation *by* platforms prevails over regulation *of* platforms,[40] a dominance which is an important aspect for future study. With this line of

[34] As to the argument on lost state power, see Staab (n 12) 18; Oliver Nachtwey and Philipp Staab, 'Das Produktionsmodell des digitalen Kapitalismus' (2020) 23 Soziale Welt 285; Dolata (n 5) 202; Dolata (n 21) 21. For understanding possible conflicts of interest, see Pentzien (n 33).

[35] Gillespie (n 7).

[36] Dolata (n 5) 202; Rachel Botsman and Roo Rogers, *What's Mine is Yours: How Collaborative Consumption is Changing the Way We Live* (HarperCollins 2010).

[37] Pentzien (n 33).

[38] Based on an entrepreneurial understanding of the state, the expansion of platform regulation is depicted as a politically intended privatization of public goods, one which, however, has unintended side effects.

[39] Dolata (n 5) 201–202; Pentzien (n 33) 157; Staab (n 12) 18; Sandra Hannappel, Rebekka Rehm and Steffen J Roth, 'Welche Faktoren bestimmen, ob digitale Plattform-Märkte einer Regulierung bedürfen?' (2017) 3 Otto-Wolff-Discussion Paper 1; Robert W McChesney, *Digital Disconnect: How Capitalism is Turning the Internet Against Democracy* (NY New Press 2014).

[40] Dolata (n 5) 191, 202; Gillespie (n 7).

regulatory argument, we see what classic perspectives on economic market competition tend to miss: commercial platforms are not just 'two-sided markets' insofar as they connect a group of providers with a group of buyers and facilitate network effects between them.[41] In addition, they always represent hierarchical organizations that embed their own institutional arrangements into the exchange between all participants.[42]

IV. Publicly Delegated Platform Adjudication

However, having set out to give a systematic account of the various ways that platform-based dispute resolution has come into being, we have to take into consideration that the self-interest of platforms in market coordination is not the only explanation to be found in academic literature. There is also platforms' interest in avoiding intermediary liability.

To put it differently: to understand the origins of their adjudicatory efforts, we have to differentiate these activities according to the content of the various services they offer. While reputation systems and in-house complaint procedures for unsatisfactory transactions might fit into the theory of platform-initiated adjudication as regards the quest of platform companies to attract more customers, the same does not necessarily apply in respect of the dispute resolution services they offer in respect of trademark law, content management, and personal data protection.

In creating a systematic account of the platforms' interest in dispute resolution, these mechanisms of legal protection are indispensable for at least two reasons. On the one hand, they function at a high adjudicatory level. From complaint management systems for hate speech allegations on social media platforms to the execution of data protection protocols by search engines, the regulatory power of platforms is – as I will show in the following section – sometimes equivalent to the decision-making power of state courts. On the

[41] Ralf Dewenter, Jürgen Rösch and Anna Terschüren, 'Abgrenzung zweiseitiger Märkte am Beispiel von Internetsuchmaschinen' (2014) 151 Helmut Schmidt Working Paper 1; Mark Armstrong, 'Competition in Two-Sided Markets' (2006) 37 RJE 668; Jean-Charles Rochet and Jean Tirole, 'Platform Competition in Two-Sided Markets' (2003) 1 JEEA 990; David S Evans and Richard Schmalensee, *Matchmakers. The New Economics of Multisided Platforms* (Harvard Business Review Press 2016); David S Evans and Richard Schmalensee, 'The Industrial Organization of Markets with Two-Sided Platforms' (2007) 3 CPI 151, 154.

[42] Here, this strand of research also gives important indications that the quality and scope of these regulatory activities by private companies – if not being a distinguishing feature of digital markets – has reached a new level that awaits further examination. In this regard it would be interesting to compare the characteristics of dominant platforms with those of 19th century economic tycoons.

other hand, these legal protection mechanisms challenge the idea that the extensive regulatory efforts assumed by platforms are first and foremost a matter of their own initiative.

Let us return to eBay to illustrate this challenge. With its in-house eBay Resolution Center, the company not only operates one of the first and still largest online dispute resolution systems in the world;[43] rather, as emphasized in literature on the dispute resolution services of platforms, the company has also revolutionized the previous conflict management systems that saw disputes related to the international exchange of goods often subject to lengthy and costly court hearings. Now, approximately 60 million disputes of this nature are settled each year[44] – with only a fraction of these ever appearing before a judge.[45]

However, the comprehensive dispute resolution services that a platform provides to facilitate transactions are by no means exclusively an expression of the operator's own initiative in its quest for self-regulation. Rather, we also have to take into account that some of their features, such as the monitoring of copyright issues and brand protection, prove to be platforms' less deliberate response to the European readjustment of their legal liability for third-party content.[46] In order to gradually understand this complementary shift in perspective,[47] it is fitting to examine the trajectory of a ground-breaking legal decision on trademark liability issued by the Court of Justice of the European Union in the case *L'Oréal v eBay International* on July 12, 2011.[48] In their judgment, the European Court held that digital trading platforms, as intermediary bodies, have fundamental obligations to act in order to address and prevent cases of copyright piracy in user transactions. Convinced that the involved companies could not invoke the statutory exceptions to liability for trademark infringements if their platforms facilitated the selling of counterfeit products by professional traders, for example by means of advertisements, the

[43] Louis F Del Duca, Colin Rule and Kathryn Rimpfel, 'eBay's De Facto Low Value High Volume Resolution Process: Lessons and Best Practices for ODR Systems Designers' (2014) 6 Yearbook on Arbitration & Mediation 204, 204.

[44] Susskind (n 3); BBC NEWS (n 26).

[45] See Del Duca, Rule and Rimpfel (n 43) 205.

[46] Harald Frey, *Die Haftung von Host-Providern für Immaterialgüterrechtsverletzungen. Schriften zum geistigen Eigentum und zum Wettbewerbsrecht* (Nomos 2018) 86.

[47] This shift is complementary because it doesn't call for exchanging one explanation for the other, instead pointing out the necessity of further analyzing the interconnectedness of a regulation *by* and a regulation *of* platforms. See Gillespie (n 7).

[48] CJEU 12 July 2011, C-324/09, ECLI:EU:C:2011:474. In that case, the trademark proprietor L'Oréal complained that eBay had to take stronger action against trademark infringements. L'Oréal originally filed the lawsuit in England. However, since it concerned the interpretation of the Trade Marks Directive, the E-Commerce Directive, and the Directive on the enforcement of intellectual property rights, the English High Court referred the case to the CJEU.

CJEU ultimately held eBay responsible for the monitoring and punishment of such infringements of intellectual property rights.[49]

The CJEU court ruling has significantly impacted the dispute resolution efforts undertaken by platforms. Beyond observing that eBay has comprehensively expanded the scope of its private dispute resolution mechanisms in the wake of the CJEU decision,[50] it bears emphasis that this expansion can hardly be characterized as privately-initiated regulation given that the platform engaged in an ongoing law suit trying to prevent it. Moreover, eBay's resistance is not an isolated case. Since 2010, there has been a fundamental change in European jurisprudence on the intermediary liability of platforms, shifting regulatory responsibilities onto their operators.[51]

How far-reaching this trend is can be illustrated by a second example: the *right to be forgotten* as raised in a case involving Google.[52] In May 2014, the CJEU imposed comprehensive supervisory obligations on Google in the administration of personal data protection.[53] In extending the definition of a data controller to search engines,[54] the court ruled that it was Google's task to examine and, if necessary, enforce requests from individuals to remove website links resulting from a search for the person's name. Similar to the previous case, the court judgment initially arose from a single legal dispute, this time involving Google, the Spanish Data Protection Authority *Agencia Española de Protección de Datos* (AEPD), and the property owner Mario Costeja González. Originally, Mr Costeja had sued Google for not removing the website link

---

[49] A significant amount of counterfeit goods is offered on eBay. See Jörg Staniczek, *Tatort eBay: Der Handel mit Modeplagiaten im Zeitalter von Web 2.0* (Akademische Verlagsgemeinschaft München 2010). Thus, the corresponding ads generate a significant proportion of the platform's revenue.

[50] To deal with disputes over trademark rights, the platform operators have developed their own system that enables manufacturers to report offered products as counterfeits and effectively counteract further infringements. In such cases, the provider's eBay account will be suspended. Moreover, all EU Member States can now oblige the operators of trading platforms to end such violations as well as to prevent them.

[51] The question of whether the platforms, as intermediaries, are responsible for the content of the trade and exchange conducted on them, or whether they enjoy immunity from the criminal and civil law claims of their users regarding trademark and personal rights violations, has triggered an exceptionally lively debate between rights holders, service providers, and internet users in recent years. See Béatrice M Farano, 'Internet Intermediaries' Liability for Copyright and Trademark Infringement: Reconciling the EU and U.S. Approaches' (2012) 14 TTLF Working Paper 1.

[52] Rolf H Weber, 'The Right to be Forgotten: More than a Pandora's Box?' (2011) 2 JIPITEC 120.

[53] CJEU 13 May 2014, C-131/12 *Google Spain SL and Google Inc v Agencia Española de Protección de Datos (AEPD) and Mario Costeja González*, ECLI:EU:C:2014:317.

[54] Which initially were not assigned the data controller's duty of overseeing the procedures and purposes of data usage.

to an auction announcement that was published in 1998 in connection with unpaid social security debts. Although the auction had long since been completed, a Google search for his name still retrieved the announcement more than ten years later. In requiring Google to delete this single link, the CJEU imposed regulatory obligations on Google and other platforms reaching far beyond Mr Costeja's individual case. The court held that Google, as the operator of an internet search engine, was responsible for nothing less than the processing of personal data,[55] and it thus made the company subject to the European Data Protection Directive 95/46/EC.[56] In the European Union, the platform has subsequently been obliged to remove 'inadequate', 'excessive', and 'irrelevant or no longer relevant' website links from the list of results that its search engine generates for a person.[57] On the whole, the scope of Google's regulatory activities effectively reaches the level of a first instance court within a national jurisdiction.[58] Furthermore, in requiring that the platform operators take affirmative steps to build the necessary infrastructure, the European court case represents another example of the continuing trend that we have already seen with the eBay case. Namely, the ruling constitutes an official delegation of previously state-supervised regulatory duties to private companies,[59] a dynamic which hardly corresponds to the preceding combination of platform-initiated adjudication and a state permissiveness allowing as much. 'By creating a right to be forgotten, the European Union has, in effect, deputized a private organization to become its governing agent. The state (or in this case, the EU) coopts Google's growing system of private governance to turn it to the state's ends'.[60] Moreover, the fact that Google – and the same goes for eBay – legally contested any expansion of its regulatory commitment before extending its services suggests that this regulatory engagement cannot be sin-

[55] The activity of a search engine consists in finding information published by third parties or posted on the internet, automatically indexing it, buffering it, and finally making it available to internet users in a specific order. According to the court, this procedure should be classified as processing personal data.

[56] This Directive was replaced in 2018 by the General Data Protection Regulation (Regulation (EU) 2016/679 of the European Parliament and of the Council of 27 April 2016 on the protection of natural persons with regard to the processing of personal data and on the free movement of such data, and repealing Directive 95/46/EC (General Data Protection Regulation) [2016] OJ L119/1 (GDPR)) which, for EU Member States, incorporated the right to be forgotten in art 17 as a right to erasure ('right to be forgotten'). As to the impact of the GDPR on platform-based regulation see also n 78.

[57] CJEU 13 May 2014, C-131/12, ECLI:EU:C:2014:317, 92, 93, 94.

[58] We will return to the novelty of this decision-making power when contrasting it with traditional notice-and-takedown procedures.

[59] Busch (n 10); Chenou and Radu (n 10) 96.

[60] Balkin (n 13) 1207. Google will be granted legal immunity with regard to transactions carried out on its platform on the condition that the platform guarantees in return the administration of personal data protection. See Farano (n 51); Chenou and Radu (n 10).

glehandedly explained by its economic profitability for the platform. Rather, in this case the search engine assumed a cost-intensive administrative task that can only be understood in the context of (avoiding) intermediary liability; unlike algorithmic options for tracking and deleting ads for counterfeit products, the *right to be forgotten* at least partially demands human review, which for its part is accompanied by corresponding personnel costs, in all likelihood generating more costs than profits for the owner of a platform.[61]

V. Combining Perspectives – The 'End' of Monocausal Explanations and the Chances for Mutual Benefit

If we take the previous considerations into account, especially one thing becomes clear: upon placing the economic and socio-legal analyses side by side, we see them less as mutually exclusive alternatives and more as a call for rejecting monocausal explanations. Platform regulation is neither absorbed in a process of private self-regulation nor can it be reduced to an idea of public delegation. Even if the previous investigations focus on different aspects, the conclusion drawn for further sociological analysis cannot consist in the abandonment of one perspective in favor of the other.

Rather, in combining perspectives that analyze regulation *by* platforms with those that focus on the regulation *of* platforms, there is room for mutual benefit. Not only does it take both aspects to provide a viable argument for understanding markets as a social process of institutionalizing rules that goes beyond mere patterns of economic transaction,[62] an interconnected study of both approaches is also essential for making clear that an investigation into platform regulation needs to describe the existing tension between private and public governance mechanisms – regardless of whether we are interested in platform-initiated market coordination or are exploring delegated responsibilities.[63]

---

61 The same applies to Meta's complaint management of hate speech allegations.

62 See Marie-Laure Djelic and Sigrid Quack, *Globalization and Institutions. Redefining the Rules of the Economic Game* (Edward Elgar 2003); Sigrid Quack, '"Global" Markets in Theory and History: Towards a Comparative Analysis' in Jens Beckert and Christoph Deutschmann (eds), *Wirtschaftssoziologie* (KZfSS special issue 49, Springer 2010) 130; Gillespie (n 8); Beckert (n 18).

63 As regards concepts such as 'special purpose sovereigns' (Balkin (n 13) 1193) or 'regulatory intermediaries' (Busch (n 10)), the socio-legal contributions do not pointedly argue against the private market power of the platforms as identified from a market perspective. Rather, they point to the incompleteness of these arguments by differentiating external and internal measures for the dispute resolution arrangements of platforms. See Mateusz Grochowski, 'Default Rules Beyond the State: Special-Purpose Lawmakers in the Platform Economy' in Stefan Grundmann and Mateusz Grochowski (eds), *European Contract Law and the Creation of Norms* (Intersentia 2021); Gillespie (n 8), Gillespie (n 7).

Economic perspectives sensitize us to the diversity of the regulatory efforts engaged in by different platforms. Here, socio-legal research can benefit from keeping an eye on the inventiveness of the platforms when monitoring conflict and the individual design of rules and procedures they come up with to resolve them. Depending on their special purpose, the various internet platforms constitute not one but several markets on which they implement comprehensive guidelines, ranking systems, and dispute resolution procedures for all participants across jurisdictional boundaries, and it should be stressed that a comparative analysis of these markets is needed. In addition, even the platform-based conflict management services that have been delegated to platform operators will, once again, potentially allow for profitable options of market coordination. For example, leading platforms in the fields of legal-tech, such as Modria, have started to sell their patented software systems for alternative dispute resolution to private companies and public authorities alike.[64]

Conversely, the strength of socio-legal research lies in revealing the regulatory significance of particularly *legal* institutions – above all courts – in defining the scope of action available to platform companies. A perspective on *political* economy, which registers law primarily as legislative design, might, by contrast, miss out on such significance. To illustrate this line of thought, let us return to the two judgments of the CJEU that we explored earlier. When we take the trademark law case involving eBay and compare it with the respective cases in the US, a political economy approach would identify hardly any differences in the legislative requirements for intermediary liability. The respective legislation applicable to the legal problem at issue – especially the US Digital Millennium Copyright Act (DMCA)[65] – is almost congruent with the European legislation.[66] Moreover, the EU E-Commerce Directive for the liability of hosting providers was specifically modeled on the DMCA.[67] However, their judicial

---

See also Kate Klonick, 'The New Governors: The People, Rules, and Processes Governing Online Speech' (2018) 131 Harv LRev 1598, 1604.

[64] Modria is an online dispute resolution (ODR) platform. Founded as a PayPal-offshoot in 2011 by a team who had previously overseen the development of the dispute resolution systems at eBay and PayPal, Modria was bought by Tyler Technologies in 2017. As one of the world's leading providers of court software and technology, Tyler Tech intends to utilize Modria's software in courts and plans on adding an ODR step to every US litigation process. See Barton (n 4) 36.

[65] Digital Millennium Copyright Act (DMCA), 17 USC, s 512(1201–1205), (1301–1332) and 28 USC, s 4001.

[66] While the DMCA applies only to copyrights and is not applicable to trademark infringements, there are similar legal principles that have been applied in the US on the basis of co-fault and performance liability, so that the legislative framework governing the intermediary liability of e-commerce platforms for copyright and trademark infringements can widely be considered equivalent. See Farano (n 51) 65.

[67] Directive 2000/31/EC of the European Parliament and of the Council of 8 June 2000 on certain legal aspects of information society services, in particular electronic commerce,

interpretations diverge massively and expose the significance of a *court-initiated* re-localization of law to platforms in Europe, a significance that further analysis has to take into consideration. As compared to a 2010 ruling in which the US Supreme Court (in a similar case brought against eBay)[68] ruled in favor of relieving the platform of all responsibility,[69] the European decision is significantly more pro-active and explicitly promotes the expansion of the dispute resolution activities undertaken by platform operators.[70] If the eBay case thus reveals the value of a juridical dimension when analyzing the possible *varieties* of platform capitalism, in the Google case this socio-legal perspective proves its relevance in identifying transnational *spillover* effects. Although the original court decision refers exclusively to Google and the EU, the ruling has unsurprisingly already had far broader consequences. Not only did Google subsequently begin to build a comprehensive infrastructure for reviewing deletion requests inside as well as outside European jurisdictions, corporate competitors of Google that weren't immediately affected by the ruling nevertheless reacted similarly. For instance, Microsoft's Bing, as the second major search engine in Europe, has set up a comparable system for managing online requests to delete information.[71] A sole focus on the *political* economy of the platforms, which registers law primarily as legislative guidelines, cannot fully grasp this dynamic.[72] Rather, it requires a combination of

---

in the Internal Market ('Directive on electronic commerce') [2000] OJ L178/1 (E-Commerce Directive). For a detailed analysis of similarities and differences between the two pieces of legislation, see also Farano (n 51).

68 US Supreme Court 29 November 2010, 10-300 *Tiffany & Co v eBay Inc.* In this case, Tiffany argued that eBay was liable for false advertising because they advertised the availability of Tiffany jewellery in various ways, although most of the products offered were in fact fakes. This claim was rejected by the District Court – which explained that eBay's advertisement was not literally wrong, since real products were actually sold on the website; Tiffany's subsequent petition to the Supreme Court for a 'writ of certiorari' was similarly rejected on 29 November 2010.

69 Based on the court's decision, eBay does not have to check the authenticity of the goods offered on its platform. Rather, it falls upon trademark owners to report counterfeit products, at which point eBay is then obliged to take action. This means that the responsibility of the platform begins only after a complaint has been lodged and that no tasks of monitoring or preventing violations of this nature are imposed.

70 In addition to handling incoming complaints, the company is obliged to minimize possible violations – for example, through a comprehensive monitoring of private sellers as well as professional dealers or by providing complaint options for trademark owners.

71 Chenou and Radu (n 10) 83.

72 This shortcoming is even more pronounced in respect of European case law as a political revision of CJEU court rulings is hardly practical. Given that decisions can generally be revised only by coordinated action of the Member States, the EU Commission, and the EU Parliament, the binding effect of CJEU rulings is mostly presupposed and the Court is effectively an actor in its own right. See Martin Höpner, 'Wie der Europäische Gerichtshof und die Kommission Liberalisierung durchsetzen. Befunde aus der MPIfG-Forschungs-

economic and socio-legal approaches to reveal the fact that platform regulation entails a multiple number of public and private actors operating at the national, transnational, and supranational levels and that this combination of approaches is needed to properly trace how the regulatory actions of those different actors are mutually reinforced, overlap, and sometimes counteract one another.[73]

VI. Remaining Challenges – Beyond the Duality of Private Regulation *by* and Public Regulation *of* Platforms?

Taken together, the dispute resolution research presented so far can lay the groundwork for describing a polycentric system of intervention that has facilitated a platformization of judicial functions. However, in terms of further study, it also reveals a conceptual challenge. Regardless of whether we look at the entrepreneurial initiative of the platform operators, address the transformation of state regulation, or combine both of these approaches, the descriptions are recurrently embodied in dualistic pairings of 'private-public' or 'market-state' relationships that reflect a prejudicing of our conceptual perspective and consequently miss crucial aspects.

An illustrative example of this prejudicial effect is provided not least by analyses that use the conceptual tension between 'market and state' or 'private and public regulation' to actually emphasize their hybridization. From a 'blending of private and public rule making'[74] to a 'post-regulatory state',[75] their strength lies in specifically allowing the inclusion of various forms of private and public authority as well as in the different ways they can be com-

gruppe zur Politischen Ökonomie der europäischen Integration' (2014) 14 MPIfG Discussion Paper i; Walter Mattli and Anne-Marie Slaughter, 'Revisiting the European Court of Justice' (1998) 52 International Organization 177, 177; R Daniel Kelemen and Susanne K Schmidt, 'Introduction – the European Court of Justice and Legal Integration: Perpetual Momentum?' (2012) 19 J Eur Pub Pol 1; Marcus Höreth, 'Europäischer Gerichtshof' in Rüdiger Voigt (ed), *Handbuch Staat* (Springer 2018); Ran Hirschl, 'The Judicialization of Politics' in Keith E Whittington, Gregory A Caldeira and R Daniel Kelemen (eds), *The Oxford Handbook of Law and Politics* (OUP 2008) 119; C Neal Tate and Torbjörn Vallinder, *The Global Expansion of Judicial Power* (NYUP 1997).

[73] Gillespie (n 7). See also Fligstein (n 33); Richard Whitley, *Divergent Capitalisms* (OUP 1999); John Campbell and Leon Lindberg, 'Property Rights and the Organization of Economic Activity by the State' (1990) 55 ASR 634; Quack (n 62) 125; Marcus Höreth, *Die Selbstautorisierung des Agenten: Der Europäische Gerichtshof im Vergleich zum U.S. Supreme Court* (Nomos 2008); Michael Mann, *The Sources of Social Power, vol I: A History of Power from the Beginning to AD 1760* (CUP 1986).

[74] Quack (n 62).

[75] Colin Scott, 'Regulation in the Age of Governance: The Rise of the Post-Regulatory State' in Jacint Jordana and David Levi-Faur (eds), *The Politics of Regulation: Institutions and Regulatory Reforms for the Age of Governance* (Edward Elgar 2004).

bined. In depicting their intersection, however, this body of literature perpetuates a perspective that traces platform regulation along the lines of a duality that needs to be tested not only for its conceptual advantages but also for its analytical restrictions.

The advantage of such dualistic thinking is that it inherently offers opportunities for comparison by placing any social phenomenon we look at within a horizon of multiple perspectives. Often following the logic of functional differentiation,[76] it thus can expose various rationalities and modes of regulatory operation as regards, for example, the relationship of different social subsystems or social fields.

However, this strength is countered by a reductionist description. We can acquire a first sense of it by looking back at the judicial cases investigated earlier. Starting with the fact that eBay was assigned the task of monitoring offered products for cases of copyright piracy or trademark infringement and sanctioning respective offences, it is less persuasive to contend a privatization of dispute resolution than to conclude that eBay has been integrated into the justice system as a governing agent that is judged by its respective standards. However, describing this process as a way of public regulation is equally misleading. While it is true that the platform's regulatory system is turned to the state's ends, eBay is neither becoming a public organization in the process nor being bound to using official court procedures in order to fulfil the task assigned to it. This conceptual challenge to a private-public-duality becomes even more evident when we add the case of Google in administering a *right to be forgotten* under data protection law. While the platform operators are granted an even wider scope for the interpretation of the law than any traditional notice-and-take-down procedures would allow, describing this transfer using the concepts of public and private regulation is nevertheless similarly unfitting. Since the operators are officially equipped with European jurisdiction and, in case of doubt, are equally liable for its prosecution, the delegation of the task at hand challenges any depiction of operator schemes as 'private' regulation in the modern sense.[77] Analogously, the traditional concept of outsourcing public tasks to private actors is also not fitting. Without fixed rules for the implementation of the task, a transparent documentation of performance, and an option to retrieve the task, the CJEU ruling can neither be understood as a project-related delegation nor as a delegation in the actual sense of the word: instead of transferring far-reaching powers to a

---

[76] A logic of differentiation that, if not explicitly, then implicitly seems to be borrowed either from Niklas Luhmann's approach to system theory or Pierre Bourdieu's conception of social fields. See Niklas Luhmann, *Die Gesellschaft der Gesellschaft* (Suhrkamp 1997) 598; Pierre Bourdieu, 'Die Logik der Felder' in Pierre Bourdieu and Loïc JD Wacquant (eds), *Reflexive Anthropologie* (Suhrkamp1996).

[77] Cf Stephen E Sachs, 'From St. Ives to Cyberspace: The Modern Distortion of the Medieval 'Law Merchant'' (2006) 21 AmU Intl LRev 685, 708.

'private' provider, the court ruling effectively *integrates* Google into the European judicial system as a quasi-legal decision-making body.[78]

This conceptual reductionism becomes even more visible when we dive further into the respectively presumed rationalities that come with the duality of a public regulation *of* and a private regulation *by* platforms. To illustrate this fact, let us take the example of the platforms' assumed interest in regulatory action. In sorting all platform and state activity along the conceptual guidelines of private and public modes of regulation, we tend to identify commercial platforms first and foremost as single market players. Whether regarding their motivation to create trust in order to secure profits or their regulatory efforts to avoid financial liability, in both cases the companies are largely treated as rational, profit-oriented *units with homogeneous interests.* Meanwhile, differing inner-organizational logics and dynamics that do not conform with this homogeneity remain underexposed.[79]

The final passages of this text are, therefore, devoted to the fact that – and the manner in which – such inner-organizational rationalities further challenge the private-public dualism we set out to investigate. Using the example of tech whistle-blowers,[80] I will offer less a conceptual alternative to such dualism than a suitability test for examining the limits we face when entertaining it within dispute resolution research as well as within the context of platform-based regulation in general.

In March 2022, Meta's parent company, Instagram, began setting up parental security tools for its Instagram app. For children between the ages of 13 and 17, legal guardians can limit the period of the app's use and also see who their children follow and who follows them. While this is undoubtedly a regulatory act that is relevant to the debate we have set out to explore, we encounter difficulties as soon as we try to explain this platform-based activity

[78] Moreover, GDPR, art 17 reinforces this trend rather than changing its direction. In May 2018, the new GDPR incorporated the right to be forgotten for EU states as the 'right to erasure ("right to be forgotten")'. Since then, it is European law that data subjects 'have the right to obtain from the controller the erasure of personal data'; moreover, as the data controller, it is the search engine operator's responsibility to review these requests and remove links from search results on the satisfaction of certain conditions.

[79] The fact that this involves not necessarily discarding theories of functional differentiation, but rather considering various strands of organizational logic, is to be seen not least in Luhmann's system theory. Here, organizations – be they courts or platform companies – are explicitly not to be aligned with the operational modes and functions of subsystems. Rather, such organizations can be situated precisely at the intersection between different subsystems and their (partly conflicting) rationalities.

[80] James Clayton, 'Silenced No More: A New Era of Tech Whistleblowing?' *BBC* (11 October 2021) <https://www.bbc.com/news/technology-58850064> accessed 31 January 2024; Michael Mandelbaum, 'The Age of the Whistleblower' *The American Interest* (29 October 2019) <https://www.the-american-interest.com/2019/10/29/the-age-of-the-whistleblower/> accessed 31 January 2024.

along the duality of privately regulating market players and publicly regulating state authorities: neither were the new Instagram features initiated by the platform in a quest for self-regulation, nor were they a matter of official delegation by a public agency. Rather, the regulatory efforts were introduced by the platform mainly after whistle-blower Frances Haugen forced the company into action with her disclosure to the media of a number of internal company documents and her testimony to the US Senate Subcommittee on Consumer Protection the previous fall.[81] First of all, as a former platform employee, Haugen cannot be understood as belonging to the platform. Nor is she part of the state apparatus or other official initiatives – such as those launched by media, trade unions, or NGOs – such that her actions could be termed public regulation.[82] But even more important, in that she is a *former* employee, she poses a challenge to the way we usually conceptualize platform corporations. Instead of interpreting the regulatory efforts that platforms undertake against the backdrop of a homogeneous interest in platform profitability, her actions refer to the possible simultaneity of different – even conflicting – strands of organizational logic within one and the same platform, all of which must be taken into consideration.[83]

The conceptual challenge thus posed could also be reformulated in the following way: while the theoretical duality between public regulation of platforms and private regulation by platforms can make us aware of the conditions under which corporate organizations expand internal regulatory practices only on the basis of official – often state – requirements and under which they are willing to independently carry out such regulations even without state imposition, it risks overlooking the question of which actors *outside* private platforms and public agencies are relevant to the organizational decision-making processes of each of these entities, and it risks failing to differentiate between the regulatory impact of such actors.[84]

---

[81] She accused the platform of knowingly accepting the negative impact that the use of the app can have on the body image of, in particular, teenage girls. Shortly after Haugen's statement, Instagram CEO Adam Mosseri announced that the company would soon release its parental control tools, which it had been working on for a while.

[82] An observation that applies as well to state whistle-blowers such as Daniel Ellsberg, Chelsea Manning, and Edward Snowden.

[83] Tatiana Bazzichelli, 'Whistleblowing for Change. Disruption from Within' in Tatiana Bazzichelli (ed), *Whistleblowing for Change. Exposing Systems of Power and Injustice* (transcript 2021).

[84] A similar challenge to the one we see in the case of tech whistle-blowers is posed, for instance, by advertisers on platforms. As they are neither a part of the platform nor state actors, they equally resist categorization within the conceptual framework of private regulation by and public regulation of platforms. Nevertheless, they have an interest in placing their ads in a trusting environment and might not wish to pursue the official channels of a lawsuit to vindicate this interest.

From these considerations, there follows a call to examine the usefulness of the related private-public duality for the analysis of regulatory arrangements in contemporary markets[85] and to disclose the theoretical underpinnings of this duality. As long as we describe platform-based regulation as a combination of 'private regulation' and 'public governance', our attention is focused on capturing the tipping points between different rationalities and their dynamics.[86] How this predisposes our understanding of enforcing private regulation should be reflected on.[87] This challenge is most evident in the concept of a hybridization. Even if a 'hybridization of regulation'[88] takes the dissolution of contrasting market and state rationalities the furthest, the configuration of a hybrid,[89] borrowed from Greek mythology, is in the end a fused entity that is characterized by the duality from which it comes. While an analysis of hybridity need therefore be extremely sensitive to the combination of the individual components, it must remain bound to the inherent dualism out of which the hybrid arose – be it state and market[90] or private and public.[91]

Leaving the reader at this point with the conflict of an unresolved problem is perhaps unsatisfactory, but it is a necessary incentive in the collaborative quest to theorize digital economies.

---

[85] See David A Ciepley, 'Beyond Public and Private: Toward a Political Theory of the Corporation' (2013) 107 Am Pol Sci Rev 139.

[86] Quack (n 62) 138.

[87] In this context, the theorization of platform regulation could benefit from the debate on transnational law, and authors writing in this field have already begun challenging and replacing such dualities as they exist in the field of legal theory. See, for example, Peer Zumbansen, 'Neither 'Public' nor 'Private', 'National' nor 'International': Transnational Corporate Governance from a Legal Pluralist Perspective' (2011) 38 JLSoc 50.

[88] Chenou and Radu (n 10).

[89] Jean-Christophe Graz, 'Hybrids and Regulation in the Global Political Economy' (2006) 10 Competition & Change 230.

[90] Fligstein (n 33); Susan Strange, *States and Markets* (Continuum 1988).

[91] Jean-Christophe Graz and Andreas Nölke, *Transnational Private Governance and its Limits* (Routledge 2008); Rodney B Hall and Thomas J Biersteker, *The Emergence of Private Authority in Global Governance* (CUP 2002); Virginia Haufler, *A Public Role for the Private Sector: Industry Self-Regulation in a Global Economy* (Carnegie Endowment 2001).

Public Law and Co-regulation

The Influence of Fundamental Rights Discourse on the Standard of Privacy Protection Adopted by Online Platforms

*Katarzyna Łakomiec**

The slow evolution of big tech companies and their constant efforts to limit the government's influence on their operations meant they were, for a long time, not perceived as a subject of public law regulation. At the same time, we can now observe their increasing influence on the sphere in which individuals exercise their rights and freedoms. The business model of online platforms is based on processing personal data, which affects an individual's privacy. Privacy is often seen as the exercise of autonomy and control over the sphere of seclusion. However, it is also widely recognized that the right to privacy is directly related to ensuring equal participation in the democratic process. The importance of privacy has led to the adoption of personal data protection instruments in Europe. The most important one, the General Data Protection Regulation (Regulation (EU) 2016/679, GDPR), includes the broad use of self-regulatory and co-regulatory measures. The decision in favor of such solutions has led to a shifting of the responsibility for ensuring the proper framework for protecting personal data from the public to private actors. This chapter analyzes how the coexistence of public regulation and private rules under the GDPR affects privacy protection. It also describes how proportionality review and context analysis can enrich the public-private toolbox used to search for the best solutions for protecting privacy.

* Publication prepared as part of a research project financed by the National Science Center (grant no 2020/37/B/HS5/04212).

I. Introduction

Personal data is often declared to be a new oil[1] that fuels the digital economy. However, just as using oil products has a slow yet detrimental effect on public health and the environment, an unrestricted flow of personal data can have unforeseen consequences for democracies and fundamental rights.[2]

Traditionally, fundamental rights protection instruments were a part of public law. Governments, lawmakers, and courts were entrusted with the task of establishing and enforcing laws that safeguarded fundamental rights. Constitutions and international human rights treaties contain catalogues of rights and provide mechanisms for balancing them. Depending on the legal system, fundamental rights protection instruments were designed for individual-state relationships (such as in the US), or they also emphasized positive obligations of the state in shaping horizontal relationships, taking into account constitutionally protected values, such as dignity, equality, privacy, and freedom of speech (the model dominant in the EU).

Regulating new technologies introduced the need to change, or at least adapt, this model to present challenges. The first reason is the cross-border nature of operations enabled by technological advancements and the need to harmonize instruments based on different legal traditions. The second is the need to adjust the regulatory process to rapid changes in the realities of the network society. Thirdly, the effective enforcement of established standards is hindered by the length and rigidity of court procedures.

The other group of reasons is related to the appearance of online platforms on the market, creating alternative environments in which new rules regarding content, freedom of speech, intellectual property, and privacy are created.[3] Habermas points out that the functioning of social media has led to the creation of a myriad of semi-public spheres.[4] Creating similar conditions for human flourishing and meaningful public discourse in all of them is one of the most significant challenges for modern legal systems. One major obstacle to effectively regulating these digital spaces is the concentration of power in the hands of a few dominant online platforms, especially social media. Some authors have underscored the potential dangers associated with this concentration of power, as it can lead to 'mass digital dissemination of disinformation and hate speech' and 'political polarization through the selective dis-

[1] A quote attributed to Clive Humby, a British mathematician, and repeated many times in discussions about privacy in the digital economy.

[2] Paul M Schwartz, 'Privacy and Democracy in Cyberspace' (1999) 52(6) VandLRev 1609.

[3] Nicholas P Suzor, *Lawless: The Secret Rules That Govern our Digital Lives* (CUP 2019) 90.

[4] Jürgen Habermas, 'Reflections and Hypotheses on a Further Structural Transformation of the Political Public Sphere' (2022) 39(4) Theory, Culture & Society 145, 166.

tribution of content thanks to micro-targeting techniques.'[5] It can also cause the erosion of privacy due to the commodification of data flows.

Recent studies describe the regulatory regime's complexity and underline the need for interaction between general legislation and self- and co-regulation to meet the market's needs and ensure the protection of constitutional rights and freedoms.[6] Consequently, attempts have been made to adapt the regulatory process to the evolving realities of the information society.[7] Putting fundamental rights at the center of the debate on internet regulation was inevitable because of the extent to which big-tech companies influence how these rights are exercised. However, the process of finding optimal solutions in this regard is still in progress.

One area where these challenges are particularly evident is the regulation of information privacy, given the vast amounts of personal data processed by big-tech companies. The European Union has made enormous efforts to address these challenges. The legal instrument created out of the ambition to modernize and standardize personal data protection across Europe was the General Data Protection Regulation. While the GDPR represents a commendable endeavor, it has limitations. One of its main successes is that it proved wrong the assumption that every attempt at comprehensive regulation of new technologies would be futile. The regulatory logic of GDPR was developed by the Data Governance Act and the Data Act. The evolution of the regulatory process is also seen in the EU Digital Strategy, which consists of various acts regulating the internet, such as the Digital Services Act (Regulation (EU) 2022/2065, DSA), the Digital Markets Act (Regulation (EU) 2022/1925, DMA), and the AI Act (Regulation (EU) 2024/1689). All of these instruments experiment with measures pioneered by the GDPR, adjusting them to the respective subject of the regulation.[8]

The Chapter is structured as follows. In section II, I describe the current state of research on co-regulation, presenting it in the broader context of hard

[5] Julia Pohle and Daniel Voelsen, 'Centrality and power. The struggle over the techno-political configuration of the Internet and the global digital order' (2022) 14 Policy & Internet 13, 22.

[6] Christopher R Marsden, *Internet Co-Regulation: European Law, Regulatory Governance and Legitimacy in Cyberspace* (CUP 2011) 46; Irene Kamara, 'Co-regulation in EU personal data protection: the case of technical standards and the privacy by design standardisation "mandate"' (2017) 8(1) EJLT.

[7] Araz Taeihagh, M Ramesh and Michael Howlett, 'Assessing the regulatory challenges of emerging disruptive technologies' (2021) 15(4) Regulation & Governance 1009, 1012.

[8] For an extensive analysis of the relationship between these acts, see: Vagelis Papakonstantinou and Paul De Hert, 'The Regulation of Digital Technologies in the EU. Act-ification, GDPR Mimesis and EU Law Brutality at Play Act-ification, GDPR Mimesis and EU Law Brutality at Play' (Routledge 2024).

and soft regulation systems that nowadays coexist as a product of multilevel regulatory processes. In section III, I discuss different theoretical approaches to privacy and data protection and their relevance in the context of the regulation of new technologies. In section IV, I analyze the development of privacy protection in Europe and the EU approach to separating regulatory responsibilities between public and private actors. Section V addresses the relationship of the principle of proportionality and context. Section VI addresses codes of conduct and certification in the GDPR.

There are different methodologies for applying risk-based solutions in self-regulation and co-regulation.[9] The main goal of my Chapter is to contribute to the discussion about whether the use of tools specific to constitutional law, like proportionality review, can enrich this process from the perspective of private actors and provide for a more coherent approach or at least put the spotlight on protected constitutional values.

II. Hard Regulation, Co-regulation, and Self-regulation. Why Not All?

With large parts of the economy based on the flow of information and accumulation of power by online platforms, state and non-state regulators must deal with more complex problems requiring broad but in-depth expertise. The scale of risks generated by data processing is also growing so much that some propose to apply the precautionary principle, originally developed to counteract environmental and health hazards.[10] Changes are happening so fast that adjusting the legal framework may seem like shooting at a moving target. A new approach to regulation certainly requires more than just addressing new technological developments. Julie Cohen notes that the transformation in the political economy brought about by online platforms demands a corresponding transformation in regulatory logic.[11] Of course, this is difficult, given that legislative processes as a part of public law are subject to very slow changes that are more evolutionary than revolutionary. At the same time, changes in the balance of power between public authorities and online platforms may

[9] Felix Bieker, Michael Friedewald, Marit Hansen, Hannah Obersteller and Martin Rost, 'A Process for Data Protection Impact Assessment Under the European General Data Protection Regulation' in Stefan Schiffner, Jetzabel Serna, Demosthenes Ikonomou and Kai Rannenberg (eds), *Privacy Technologies and Policy* (Springer 2016).

[10] Joanna Mazur, 'Automated Decision-Making and the Precautionary Principle in EU Law' (2019) 9(4) TalTech Journal of European Studies 3.

[11] Julie Cohen, *Between Truth and Power. The Legal Constructions of Informational Capitalism* (OUP 2019) 200.

indicate the need for a more radical overhaul of how and where regulatory solutions are being prepared.

Changing the path of regulatory logic comes down to entrusting private actors (including platforms) with the responsibility of protecting fundamental rights and transferring to them some obligations previously associated with the state, such as transparency, involvement in policy-making, or impact or proportionality assessments. The European Union is currently experimenting with different scopes of assigning private actors with tasks previously entrusted to public authorities.

In this context, it is worth taking a look at currently prevalent forms of regulation. There are various studies on the history and evolution of self-regulation and co-regulation[12] that are impossible to summarize here.[13]

The difference between self-regulation and co-regulation, on the one hand and hard regulation, on the other, is that the former involve private actors in regulating their actions, with some or no government intervention. It is hard to pinpoint the origins of self-regulation. Historically it can be tied to the lex mercatoria, medieval merchant law,[14] Self-regulation originated in systems with little or limited state intervention and was developed in the United States, where codes of conduct were standard instruments prepared and implemented by industry associations.[15] It is now a global phenomenon that assumes independent regulation of commercial activities by private actors or their associations. Enforcement of self-regulation also remains in private hands. Therefore, it is indicated that self-regulation is not an optimal system for ensuring the protection of rights, as it offers limited safeguards and pro-

[12] Benoit Frydman, Ludovic Hennebel and Gregory Lewkowicz, 'Co-regulation and the rule of law' in Eric Brousseau, Meryem Marzouki and Cécile Méadel (eds), *Governance, Regulation and Powers on the Internet* (CUP 2012).

[13] One of the most comprehensive is the book Internet Co-Regulation European Law, Regulatory Governance and Legitimacy in Cyberspace, by Christopher T Marsden. See also Carmen Palzer, 'European Provisions for the Establishment of Co-Regulation Frameworks' (2003) 13 Media L&Poly 7; Paul Verbruggen, 'Does Co-Regulation Strengthen EU Legitimacy?' (2009) 15 Eur LJ 425; Johannes Brake, 'Co-Regulation or Capitulation? Addressing Conflicts Arising by AI and Standardization' (2020) 25 Lex Electronica 11; Christopher T Marsden, 'Internet Co-Regulation and Constitutionalism: Towards European Judicial Review' (2012) 26 Int'l RevL Computers & Tech 211; Dennis D Hirsch, 'The Law and Policy of Online Privacy: Regulation, Self-Regulation, or Co-Regulation' (2011) 34(2) Seattle ULRev 439.

[14] Clive M Schmitthoff, *The Unification of the Law of International Trade* (Gumpert 1964) 6; For a discussion on modern perspectives regarding lex mercatoria, see: Orsolya Toth, *The Lex Mercatoria in Theory and Practice* (OUP 2016).

[15] Hans J Kleinsteuber, *The Internet between Regulation and Governance* (2004) <https://www.osce.org/fom/13844?download=true>, 64.

cedures.[16] Initially, online platforms' various attempts at self-regulation were at least partly aimed at avoiding burdensome state regulation.[17] This approach was consistent with treating the internet as a space of freedom, where individuals can enjoy unlimited communication and the ability to obtain and disseminate information.

Co-regulation requires a certain degree of engagement from public authorities and private actors. This collaborative approach takes many forms, and the literature presents various typologies of co-regulation, depending on the origins of policy objectives, the division of regulatory responsibilities, and the form of public oversight and enforcement.[18] Finally, hard regulation means that public authorities create laws they enforce, particularly by the judicial system.

Much has been written about co-regulation; the common conclusions are that it allows policy goals to be achieved more flexibly and that it is often used in highly specialized and complex sectors such as technology or finance. It also creates problems concerning the need to implement constitutionally protected values by actors whose operating model significantly differs from the state. It creates challenges related to the oversight of co-regulatory activities, their transparency, and the inclusion of public participation, tasks in which states have achieved a specific benchmark through years of conforming to the rule of law and fundamental rights standards. Also, the mission to achieve optimal enforcement is still a challenge facing the public authorities.

Co-regulation could also be understood in a broader sense, one which is not limited to the private drafting, implementation, and enforcement of various instruments (eg codes of conduct and certification). In the case of the GDPR, it will also include entrusting data controllers with deciding on adequate data protection measures by applying a risk-based approach in a specific processing context.[19]

Despite the increasing transfer of responsibilities for regulating issues related to the impact of new technologies on fundamental rights to private actors (eg assessing the risk of data processing), there is not yet a clear model for the division of responsibilities between them and the public authorities. The most advanced regulations in this regard have been created by the Euro-

---

[16] Paul M Schwartz, 'Privacy and Democracy in Cyberspace' (1999) 52 VandLRev 1609, 1690; Hirsch (n 13) 464.

[17] One example of such action is the establishment of the Oversight Board by Meta, whose role is to resolve disputes regarding content moderation. Its credibility and independence have been criticized by various scholars and activists (Evelyn Douek, 'The Meta Oversight Board and the Empty Promise of Legitimacy' (2024) 37 HarvJoLT 373). See Elettra Bietti, 'Self-Regulating Platforms and Antitrust Justice' (2022) 101 Texas LRev 169.

[18] See Julia Black, 'Constitutionalising Self-Regulation' (1996) 59(1) Mod LRev 24; Marsden (n 6) 58.

[19] Maciej Pichlak and Klaudia Gaczoł, 'Simple and Advanced Reflexivity in GDPR Enforcement: Empirical Evidence from DPA Activity' (2023) 13 IDPL 267, 275.

pean Union, such as the GDPR, but even in this case the delegation of duties to private entities takes place in different scopes and through different approaches. Data controllers, who are private companies such as online platforms, exercise their freedom to conduct business, while public authorities implement constitutional norms to protect individual rights.

The new regulations introduced by the EU that apply to new technologies and digital markets include essential elements of self-regulation and, even more critically, co-regulation. My analysis will be devoted to the GDPR, which provides for a mix of solutions, combining hard regulation, co-regulation, and, to some extent, self-regulation to address the complexities of protecting privacy and adapting to an evolving technological landscape.

The first reason for using such hybrid regulatory solutions stems from the nature of privacy as a value and the need for a contextual analysis of data processing so as to achieve a proper protection of privacy. Public authorities alone may struggle to effectively perform appropriate context research in the case of data controllers who process data on a massive scale and whose purposes for processing are constantly evolving. Co-regulation is also helpful for addressing the technical aspects of data processing.[20] While hard law can determine the goals to be achieved, using appropriate technical and organizational measures, and selecting appropriate solutions, requires an analysis of the specific means of data processing.

The second reason is that some of the data controllers tend to change the logic of regulation, especially big-tech companies through their behemoth status. These companies invest considerable resources in lobbying[21] and litigation efforts, thereby influencing the creation and application of the law.[22] Their sophisticated and complicated operations, often based on proprietary technology, further complicate the regulatory landscape.

III. Privacy as a Value, Privacy and Context

In order to regulate effectively in the area of privacy and data protection, regardless of the entity that the task is entrusted to, it is necessary to carefully consider the nature of privacy as both an intrinsic and societal value. Privacy is safeguarded by the majority of modern constitutions and international human rights treaties. With the increasing reliance of contemporary society on

---

[20] Julie E Cohen, 'The Regulatory State in the Information Age' (2016) 17 Theo Inq L 369, 401.

[21] Corporate Europe Observatory, 'The Lobby Network: Big Tech's Web of Influence in the EU | Corporate Europe Observatory' (2024) <https://corporateeurope.org/en/2021/08/lobby-network-big-techs-web-influence-eu> accessed 1 April 2024.

[22] See Bietti (n 17) 168.

extensive data processing, many scholars have in recent years devoted their research to the content, significance, and optimal ways of preserving privacy.[23] In the ongoing debate surrounding the regulation of emerging technologies, including studies on the fourth industrial revolution, privacy has receded into the background, although it is still considered a value worthy of protection.[24] The reasons for this are primarily the focus on data protection as the most significant aspect of privacy and the technocratic nature of the solutions adopted. Those solutions are viewed as not addressing the holistic problems of online platforms infringing on individual autonomy or even altering the human experience. The need to protect fundamental rights other than privacy has also shifted the focus to other aspects of platform regulation. I believe that a broader discussion is needed. Still, at the same time, the narrow understanding of privacy concerning personal data protection mechanisms does not consider its nature as an instrumental value. In the classic book 'Privacy and Freedom,' Westin wrote that 'privacy is the shield for group and individual life.'[25] He then explained that privacy is essential for securing critical judgment and creativity in a liberal democratic society. Because of that, the societal systems provide privacy in various forms, ie securing freedom for associations and religious groups or creating conditions for conducting scholarly research away from public scrutiny.[26] Privacy is also 'vital to the development of individuality and consciousness of individual choice in life.'[27] For Westin, it is all about finding a balance between privacy and surveillance that is optimal for society.

Similar views were also represented in Europe, mainly based on Habermas's discourse theory and notion of the public sphere.[28] Ruiz emphasized close links between privacy and freedom:

'First, the protection of freedom to act in private guarantees the freedom to opt for participation in deliberation or to opt out of it. Second, it guarantees that, once it has been chosen, deliberation can be carried out freely, notably without the pressure of power relationships based on the possession of information about others. Third, it prevents free deliberation from being curtailed by the existence of power relationships other than those based on the possession of information […]'.[29]

---

[23] Helen Nissenbaum, *Privacy in Context Technology, Policy, and the Integrity of Social Life* (Stanford UP 2010); Daniel Solove, *Understanding privacy* (Harv UP 2008); Ignacio Cofone, *The Privacy Fallacy: Harm and Power in the Information Economy* (CUP 2023).

[24] Julie E Cohen, *Between Truth and Power: The Legal Constructions of Informational Capitalism* (OUP 2019); Shoshana Zuboff, *The Age of Surveillance Capitalism* (PublicAffairs 2019).

[25] Alan Westin, *Privacy and Freedom* (IG Publishing 2015 [1st edn 1967]) 26.

[26] Westin (n 25) 26–27.

[27] Westin (n 25) 37.

[28] Jürgen Habermas, *The Structural Transformation of the Public Sphere* (Polity Press 1992).

Reviewing the conditions that public debate should meet according to discourse theories, particularly the need to protect minorities from the pressure of the majority, privacy is an instrumental value that can guarantee free and equal participation in deliberation.[30] However, what is worth considering is the particular position that online platforms occupy in the discussed context of public debate. Like the state, platforms that base their activities on processing personal data will be in a unique position to influence public debate. Ruiz emphasizes the dependence of one's position in the public debate on knowledge about other individuals. In this context, the most important concern is that individuals about whom others know more will find themselves at risk of being 'too vulnerable to participate in deliberation without inhibitions.'[31] There are two conclusions to be drawn from this. Firstly, as private actors, online platforms have an unprecedented advantage in the public debate, obtained by overcoming the privacy barrier. Secondly, platform users are placed in a vulnerable situation as data subjects. One could even go so far as to say that protecting privacy from online platforms is a more significant challenge than protecting it from the state because data processing is secondary to the state's objectives, whereas in the case of platforms it may constitute the core of their activities.

The beginnings of modern privacy protection are most often associated with the article 'The Right to Privacy' by Warren and Brandeis.[32] Then, in the 20th century, various theories of the right to privacy were developed. The most important of them, to which contemporary scholars most often refer, are the theories of privacy as limited access and the theories of privacy as control.[33] In short, privacy as limited access assumes barriers to access to both the personal sphere and information about a person. In contrast, privacy as control assumes the possibility of deciding who can get to know an individual's private life or process personal information. Those theories no longer find direct application or are to some degree criticized, as they lack the com-

[29] Blanca R Ruiz, 'The Right to Privacy: A Discourse-Theoretical Approach' (1998) 11(2) Ratio Juris 155, 166.

[30] Ruiz (n 29) 159.

[31] Ruiz (n 29) 163.

[32] Samuel D Warren and Louis D Brandeis, 'The Right to Privacy' (1890) 4(5) Harv LRev 193. This article describes privacy as the 'right to be let alone.' Interestingly enough, the authors of this over 130-year-old text described threats to individual privacy caused by new technologies (in that case, connected with the printed press). It is a reminder that the problem of regulating 'new technologies' is not a dilemma that has arisen in our lifetime and that lawyers have always reflected on the conflicts of values associated with technological progress. It is evidenced by other concepts of privacy and justifications for its protection as adopted in legal and social theory.

[33] Björn Lundgren, 'A Dilemma for Privacy as Control' (2020) 24 The Journal of Ethics 165; Nissenbaum (n 23) 69.

plexity to tackle realities of contemporary privacy protection. They also focus on the individualistic dimension of privacy, and do not address the prevalence and societal impact of data processing. However, these theories play an essential role in shaping the modern understanding of privacy, and they allow us to understand the origins of modern privacy theories better. Nissenbaum writes that 'control over information about oneself is an important dimension of privacy, but so is the degree of access that others have to this information, irrespective of who is in control.'[34] It must also be mentioned that privacy as autonomy is still an essential component of data protection systems. It just has to be supplemented through robust 'by design' protection mechanisms and technical and organizational measures. In more detail, the social sciences discuss the difference between intrinsic and instrumental values.[35] Solove, among others, wrote about value of privacy.[36] He argues that the value of privacy is not possible to assess in the abstract, as 'privacy is a dimension of a wide variety of activities, each having a different value – and what privacy is differs in different contexts'. He adds that 'privacy does not possess a unitary value. Because privacy consists of a plurality of protection against different types of problems, its value is plural as well'.[37] The context mentioned by Solove is a very important concept in contemporary theories of privacy and will be developed further in the next section.

As mentioned above, contemporary theories of privacy emphasize the role of the context of data processing to determine the extent of the need for privacy protection and the optimal tools that can be used. Nissenbaum develops the theory of contextual integrity, which tackles the theory of privacy in the digital age, and points out that privacy is 'neither a right to secrecy nor a right to control but a right to appropriate flow of personal information'.[38] According to Nissenbaum: 'Contexts are structured social settings characterized by canonical activities, roles, relationships, power structures, norms (or rules), and internal values (goals, ends, purposes).'[39] She then goes on to identify the key variables that play a crucial role in determining privacy norms within different contexts. These variables include actors, information types, and transmission principles. Actors refer to the individuals or entities that are involved in data-sharing practices, such as senders of information, recipients of information, and information subjects.[40] Information types refer to the nature and what, in Europe, we would call the sensitivity of the processed

---

[34] Nissenbaum (n 23) 71.
[35] Max Weber, *Economy and Society* (University of California Press 1978).
[36] Solove (n 23) 84.
[37] Solove (n 23) 98.
[38] Nissenbaum (n 23) 127.
[39] Nissenbaum (n 23) 132.
[40] Nissenbaum (n 23)141.

data.[41] Transmission principles relate to constraints on the flow within a given context. Examples of transmission principles include confidentiality, reciprocity, desert, notice, and consent.[42]

The theory of contextual integrity attracted great interest at the beginning of the 21th century. This novel approach to a well-established subject matter, coupled with its ability to address the challenges posed by the advancement of new technologies, garnered considerable attention within the academic community. However, when utilized within the legal framework, this theory has its limitations, as it can be quite vague and not easy to implement.[43] Nonetheless, it undeniably offers a valuable framework for comprehending privacy in different contexts. It could be said that it provides a map for which a lawyer needs to find the right compass, a skipper, and, on top of that, a boat. In my opinion, the theory of contextual integrity has excellent potential for application in the European legal space if it is used to augment the proportionality test widely applied in Europe to assess the impact on fundamental rights. The advantage of integrating contextual integrity in the proportionality test is the possibility of adjusting the procedural and technical safeguards of rights and freedoms.

From a slightly different perspective, Solove points out that in order to examine privacy as a value in a broader social context and effectively balance it against other conflicting public values and interests, there is a need to examine some 'privacy problems'. The author indicates that problems presented in this way should be analyzed, taking into account activities compromised by each and potential harms.[44] The three harms he mentioned are essential from the perspective of the topic I am discussing. Solove draws a parallel between vulnerability harms and environmental pollution, highlighting the prevalence of such harms in the digital environment. Solove points out that 'there is often no single wrongdoer; instead, this digital pollution occurs through the combined activities of a multitude of institutions, each with different motives and objectives.'[45] The second relevant harm identified by Solove is the chilling effect.[46] This concept is applied to the relationship between the state and citizens, especially in the area of excessive use of power by the government. The privacy implications of the chilling effect are similar to Ruiz's view of the impact of a lack of privacy on public debate, presented above. This problem is currently being investigated in a promising analysis of the chilling effects of digital

[41] Nissenbaum (n 23) 143.

[42] Nissenbaum (n 23) 145.

[43] James B Rule, 'Contextual Integrity and Its Discontents: A Critique of Helen Nissenbaum's Normative Arguments' (2019) 11(3) Policy & Internet 260.

[44] Solove (n 23) 174.

[45] Solove (n 23) 177.

[46] Solove (n 23) 178.

dataveillance.[47] The third harm is the power imbalance, which is the result of the impact of privacy deficits on social structures.[48] It is currently one of the most widely commented aspects of a digital ecosystem that translates into the drift of legal regulation regarding the functioning of platforms from private to public law. As personal data is processed and analyzed by powerful tech companies, the balance of power tilts in favor of the private sector, potentially compromising the autonomy and agency of individuals.

IV. The Development of Privacy Protection in Europe

Privacy protection is an essential element of modern European constitutions. Its actual significance undoubtedly increased when the European Union adopted specialized instruments for personal data protection, implementing the guarantees provided for in the Charter of Fundamental Rights and the Treaty on the Functioning of the European Union. Currently, the Charter of Fundamental Rights provides that everyone has the right to respect for his or her private and family life, home, and communications (art 7), as well as the right to the protection of personal data (art 8(1)). It also contains basic rules for the processing of personal data (art 8(2)) and stipulates that an independent authority must be appointed to monitor compliance with them (art 8(3)). In accordance with the first sentence of art 52(1) of the Charter, any limitation on the exercise of the rights and freedoms recognized by the Charter must be provided for by law and respect the essence of those rights and freedoms. Under the second sentence of art 52(1) of the Charter, subject to the principle of proportionality, limitations may be imposed on those rights and freedoms only if they are necessary and genuinely meet objectives of general interest recognized by the Union or the need to protect the rights and freedoms of others. The Treaty on the Functioning of the European Union also ensures the protection of personal data (art 16(1)) and obliges the European Parliament and the Council to adopt relevant legislation (art 16(2)). The right to respect for private and family life is also protected by art 8 of the European Convention on Human Rights. The protection of personal data is 'of fundamental importance to a person's enjoyment of his or her right to respect for private and family life, as guaranteed by Article 8 of the Convention.'[49]

---

[47] Moritz Büchi, Noemi Festic and Michael Latzer, 'The Chilling Effects of Digital Dataveillance: A Theoretical Model and an Empirical Research Agenda' (2022) 9(1) Big Data & Society 1.

[48] Solove (n 23) 178.

[49] *Satakunnan Markkinapörssi and Satamedia v Finland App* no 931/13 (ECHR, 27 June 2017).

Art 1 GDPR sets protection of natural persons with regard to the processing of personal data as an important objective, but it also states that free movement of personal data is an important protected value. Recital 4 of the GDPR states that processing of personal data should be designed to serve mankind. This confirms not only that the processing of personal data is considered an important element of today's society but also that personal information flows are part of its reality. The abovementioned recital also states that 'the right to the protection of personal data is not an absolute right; it must be considered in relation to its function in society and be balanced against other fundamental rights, in accordance with the principle of proportionality' This is a direct reference to the provisions of the Charter of Fundamental Rights relating to limitations on fundamental rights.

The European data protection system draws on many of the privacy theories outlined above. First of all, it should be noted that, in addition to protecting the informational autonomy of individuals, it relies on strong procedural guarantees regarding processing. In other words, this system not only ensures the individual right to decide on the sharing of personal data but also recognizes the reality of modern society in which many activities of the public authorities and private entities are based on data processing.[50] The GDPR also repeatedly refers to the context of data processing. Extensive research would be required to try to find a legal definition of 'context' in the GDPR, if it is at all possible. However, its use allows us to point out a certain logic that is at the core of this system.

The Regulation introduces the need to take into account the context of data processing in various circumstances. The controller has to analyze the context in order to choose appropriate technical and organizational measures of data protection. Data protection by design and data protection impact assessment also require contextual analysis. The introduction of special data categories in the GDPR also proves that the context is an important factor in data protection, a point which I will come back to later.

The other principle that shapes the data protection system is the abovementioned principle of proportionality. Many solutions adopted in the GDPR are based on an examination of proportionality, starting from the main principles of the Regulation and continuing on to determinations regarding the permissible basis for data processing and transfers of personal data to a third country. The reason for adopting proportionality analysis is connected to the transfer of the responsibility to data controllers who will employ a risk-based approach; De Gregorio points out that proportionality can be 'considered the foundation of the risk-based approach based on the principle of accountabil-

[50] For a comparison of privacy protection models based on their individual and instrumental (societal) value, see: Daniel J Solove and Woodrow Hartzog, 'Kafka in the Age of AI and the Futility of Privacy as Control' (2024) 104(4) Boston ULRev 1021.

ity'[51] that is adopted in data protection system based on the GDPR. Pichlak and Gaczoł point out that the reform adopted in the GDPR introduces a data protection system based on three elements: self-regulation, a risk-based approach, and meta-regulation.[52]

The foundation on which the co-regulatory dimension of the GDPR is based is the principles relating to the processing of personal data (GDPR, art 5). While all the principles highlight parts of the data processing context relevant to privacy protection, the most important one for building public-private equilibrium is the principle of accountability. It is well established that the principle of accountability aims to ensure the compliance of data controllers to data protection norms,[53] but in my opinion it also constitutes the basis for imposing co-regulatory responsibilities on them.

The risk-based approach in the GDPR serves as the underlying logic and foundation for specific data protection solutions. These include, for example, data protection by design and by default (art 25), data protection impact assessment (GDPR, art 35), and security of processing (GDPR, art 32). These solutions require controllers to evaluate the risks to the rights and freedoms of natural persons and implement adequate measures to mitigate them, thereby ensuring data protection based on a broader understanding of the consequences of privacy loss. Supervisory authorities shape the risk-based approach through advisory activities as well as enforcement, which ensures a focus on fundamental rights and keeps broader principles of public law in the forefront of data protection discussions. An example of this involvement is the preparation of a (non-exhaustive) list of types of processing operations that are subject to the requirements for a data protection impact assessment (GDPR, art 35(4)).

V. The Principle of Proportionality and Context

In my opinion, it is worth briefly referring to the classic theories of proportionality to see what tasks are faced by online platforms and to identify the common ways with which these tasks are approached. There is no single model for examining proportionality; rather, its assessment varies depending, among other things, on the actor that applies this principle and the context in which fundamental rights are limited. Proportionality has been the subject of numerous studies, starting with Alexy,[54] moving on to Barak,[55] and ending

[51] Giovanni De Gregorio, *Digital Constitutionalism in Europe: Reframing Rights and Powers in the Algorithmic Society* (CUP 2022) 262.

[52] Pichlak and Gaczoł (n 19) 267, 268.

[53] De Gregorio (n 51) 74.

[54] Robert Alexy, *A Theory of Constitutional Rights* (OUP 2002).

with the growing body of literature on proportionality in private law.[56] It is obviously not possible to exhaustively quote or refer to these considerations here. However, I would like to present a few comments on the application of the proportionality test in the context of data protection and, more broadly, new technologies. The proportionality test is primarily used by the lawmakers to craft legal acts that effectively implement and balance constitutionally protected values. Constitutional courts and international courts play a vital role in overseeing the application of the proportionality principle by lawmakers. During proceedings, the constitutional courts evaluate the legislative process to ensure compliance with constitutional requirements. This control mechanism ensures that the lawmakers stay vigilant while imposing limitations on fundamental rights and freedoms. They can also take advantage of the jurisprudence of courts that set a certain standard, fill laconic provisions of the constitution and treaties with content, and adjust the interpretation of protected values if the development of societal standards or changes in technological advancements require it.

The formula of proportionality differs depending on the legal tradition, the core principles of the system (inter alia, constitutional identity), and the subject of regulation. The most common approach to proportionality testing includes three stages: suitability, necessity, and proportionality in the narrow sense (balancing). Prior to this assessment, the constitutionally valid aim must be identified. The suitability stage involves evaluating whether interference with protected rights will contribute to achieving a legitimate aim. As Möller notes: 'The point of the principle of suitability is to sort out those cases where, upon a closer look, there does not exist any conflict'.[57] The necessity condition is met if the chosen solution is the least restrictive but at the same time equally effective to the alternatives. For legal solutions regarding new technologies, the aspect of comparing different ways of achieving the goal will be particularly important. Perhaps some nuance is necessary here with respect to the classical stand on effectiveness and additional resources,[58] as data protection offers a wide range of alternative measures that affect the restrictiveness of the means. Proportionality, in a narrow sense, assumes a balancing of the limited value with the protected value or, from a different perspective, achieving the highest possible realization of both values.[59]

---

[55] Aharon Barak, *Proportionality: Constitutional Rights and Their Limitations* (CUP 2012).

[56] Franz Albert Bauer and Ben Gerrit Köhler (eds), Proportionality in Private Law (Mohr Siebeck 2023).

[57] Kai Möller, 'Proportionality: Challenging the critics' (2012) 10(3) IIJCL 709, 713.

[58] Möller (n 57) 713–714.

[59] Alexy (n 54); Kai Möller, 'Balancing and the structure of constitutional rights' (2007) 5(3) IJCL 453; Virgílio Afonso da Silva, 'Standing in the shadows of balancing: Proportionality and the necessity test' (2022) 20(5) IJCL 1738.

It must be noted that this three-stage proportionality test is applied by different groups of actors. The first of them is the lawmakers who apply the test most freely, choosing the appropriate solution based on systemic values as protected by constitutions and international treaties. The second are courts, especially constitutional and international courts, which are responsible for adjudicating matters related to the protection of individual rights and freedoms. Researchers point out that international courts have shown a certain reluctance to applying the first two stages of the proportionality test, and they refer mainly to proportionality in the narrow sense.[60] The reason for this is the need to limit interference with the autonomy of states, as the stages of suitability and necessity are deeply connected with policy choices. In my opinion, this limited approach cannot be maintained while at the same time transferring the protection of fundamental rights to such an integrated level as the European Union does in the GDPR.

Besides those traditional actors, the obligation to carry out the proportionality test has been transferred to a certain extent to private actors as a part of co-regulatory mechanisms. Proportionality also has to be assessed by the supervisory authorities established by Member States as they are responsible for advising, supervising, and enforcing compliance among private actors.

As the proportionality principle is removed from the monopoly of the public authorities, it is necessary to make it more detailed and adapt it to the realities of digital ecosystems involving complex technical realities, and there is a need for interdisciplinary research to assess specific risks.

As mentioned above, the concept of contextual integrity is deemed too vague, and the proportionality test has been deemed not particularly detailed. The response to these challenges is to include contextual analysis in the proportionality test. This will allow for a more specific risk assessment. In my book,[61] I have described this proposal at length: I based my inquiry in part on the analysis of legal protection of privacy and also on studies examining the jurisprudence of the Polish Constitutional Tribunal.[62]

The main claims of my proposal are: (1) New technologies have introduced a level of complexity in regulatory matters that requires additional analyses and research during the legislative process. (2) Contextual analysis is particularly useful at the stage of examining necessity and proportionality in the narrow sense; when examining necessity, it allows a determination of the least restric-

---

[60] Anna Śledzińska-Simon, *Analiza proporcjonalności ograniczeń konstytucyjnych praw i wolności Teoria i praktyka* (Wrocław 2019) 31.

[61] Katarzyna Łakomiec, *Konstytucyjna ochrona prywatności. Dane dotyczące zdrowia* (Wolters Kluwer 2020).

[62] For a different take on integrating contextual integrity into the framework of proportionality, see: Audrey Guinchard, 'Taking proportionality seriously: The use of contextual integrity for a more informed and transparent analysis in EU data protection law' (2018) 24(6) Eur LJ 434.

tive means by examining the context of data processing for each possible solution, taking into account measures that minimize the impact on privacy in a given context; when examining proportionality in the narrow sense, context analysis allows an examination of the depth of the impact of data processing on privacy and other values it protects, which allows the necessary balancing with other protected values. (3) The contextual analysis needs to be adjusted to European realities; accordingly, I have adjusted the elements of contextual analysis proposed by Nissenbaum so as to include the type of data, processing entities, the legal basis for data processing, data processing structures (specific features of data flow), and procedural and technical guarantees of processing.[63]

Now, I see that when examining the context we also need to take into account certain meta-tendencies prevalent in the digital public sphere. As I mentioned above, Solove identified vulnerability, chilling effects, and power imbalances as contextual harms to privacy. This is a good starting point for identifying problems that self- and co-regulation efforts must address. Including those meta-trends may be important when designing data protection tools, and they should be identified by lawmakers.

Conclusions from my research,[64] based on an analysis of the judgments of the Polish Constitutional Tribunal regarding the right to information privacy, covering all judgments from the adoption of the Constitution of 2 April 1997 to 2017 (in the subsequent years, the judicial activity of the Constitutional Tribunal was limited due to Poland's rule of law crisis). Elements of the theory of privacy as limited access dominated in cases in which the state was responsible for the processing of an individual's personal data, while in cases concerning the relationship between private entities and individuals, control theories dominated.

It should be noted, however, that even the Polish Tribunal – which was quite conservative in matters relating to new technologies – considered contextual elements in its judgments. Context is assessed as well by the lawmakers in the legislative process. Tools like public consultations and expert and comparative analysis aim to gather knowledge that will allow for proper impact assessment.

Moreover, the Polish Constitutional Tribunal has indirectly referred to contextual examination in its jurisprudence. This occurred in a case regarding the powers of Supreme Audit Office controllers to process sensitive personal data. The Tribunal stated:

> 'In the event of legislative interference with informational autonomy, meeting the requirement of proportionality in the narrow sense means, among others: a) the existence of statutorily determined procedural and technical guarantees for the safe processing of personal data; b) limiting the list of entities processing data to the minimum dictated by the type of

[63] Łakomiec (n 63).

[64] Łakomiec (n 63) 189.

data and the purpose of their processing; c) determining the time frame for data processing; d) introducing an effective anonymization mechanism; e) introducing provisions enabling stable financing and maintenance of databases to ensure their uninterrupted functioning in the era of dynamic development of modern technologies and various types of risks associated with it.'[65]

How does co-regulation fit into this? It should be noted that when a lawmaker or a court performs a proportionality assessment, taking into account the context of data processing, it is their sole responsibility to carry out this analysis. They can, of course, be supported by specialized analyses and scientific and technical research, but the main burden of the assessment of proportionality is assigned to one entity. Therefore, the question arises as to what exactly the proportionality assessment should look like in a situation when several entities shape the process of its examination and each of them has special knowledge available only to a limited extent to the other participants of this process. Moreover, those entities do not ultimately share the same goal. In my opinion, the role of the public authorities is to set the protected values but also to point out the context or the characteristics of the context that, from the perspective of protecting fundamental rights and the rule of law, require special measures from data controllers.

The GDPR introduces these kinds of elements of contextual analysis, eg the separation of special categories of personal data ('sensitive data') pursuant to art 9. In accordance with recital 51 of the GDPR, personal data, which is, by its nature, particularly sensitive in relation to fundamental rights and freedoms, merits specific protection as the context of its processing could create significant risks for fundamental rights and freedoms. This should be considered as part of the context firmly defined by law and online platforms, as data controllers have to take it into account while formulating their practices. In terms of data protection by online platforms, the other element of context firmly defined by law is the protection of minors. It consists of specific consent requirements (GDPR, art 8) and an obligation imposed on the providers of online platforms accessible to minors to put in place 'appropriate and proportionate measures to ensure a high level of privacy, safety, and security of minors, on their service' (DSA, art 28(1)).

The other example of defining the context is targeted marketing. This topic is regulated by the GDPR when it comes to consent to data processing, and it was the subject of a ruling by the CJEU in the case of *Meta Platforms Inc. and Others v Bundeskartellamt*. Currently, targeted advertising regulation is also introduced in the DMA.

---

[65] Polish CT 20 January 2015, K 39/12, OTK 1A 19.

The case of *Meta Platforms Inc. and Others v Bundeskartellamt*[66] revolved around the interpretation of the requirement of consent to data processing in relation to the operations of large online platforms and their dominant position on the market. One of the questions raised by the German court in the request for a preliminary ruling was whether the consent given by the user of an online social network to the operator of such a network could be considered as satisfying the conditions of validity laid down in art 4(11) GDPR, particularly the requirement that the consent must be freely given when the operator holds a dominant position on the market for online social networks.[67]

In response to the question, the CJEU emphasized that the dominant position of the operator of the social network may be an important factor in determining whether the consent was validly and freely given, and it is the responsibility of the operator to prove this. The CJEU also noted that the existence of such a dominant position may create a clear imbalance, as stated in recital 43 of the GDPR.

In my view, the ruling of the CJEU should be interpreted in a way that highlights the significance of the power imbalance between actors in the context of data processing by large social media platforms. This imbalance may be evident in the limited influence the user has on the contract's content or the difficulty in finding a comparable alternative service. The European Data Protection Board, in their opinion 'Valid Consent in the Context of Consent or Pay Models Implemented by Large Online Platforms', highlights the presence of lock-in and network effects that contribute to the power imbalance between online platforms and users.[68]

However, it should be noted that EU lawmakers have recognized that it is not possible to determine all contextual elements without the input of data controllers and that the elements of this context will both vary and require adjustments depending on the sector in which the data is processed. The assessment of the context should be based on cooperation – whereby the public authorities contributes knowledge of constitutional standards and requirements, including those relating to the rule of law and constitutionally protected values – and they should identify meta-tendencies; private actors, for their part, contribute to the knowledge of the sector, the processing, and technical aspects.

Finally, supervisory authorities engage in the process of assessing proportionality in co-regulation through their advisory and corrective powers (GDPR, art 58). It may lead to the development of a context loosely shaped

---

66 CJEU 4 July 2023, C-252/21 *Meta Platforms Inc. and Others v Bundeskartellamt*, ECLI:EU:C:2023:537.

67 Ibid.

68 European Data Protection Board, 17 April 2024 Opinion 08/2024 on Valid Consent in the Context of Consent or Pay Models Implemented by Large Online Platforms 23.

by law, as it does not have a universal application but instead focuses on investigating and commenting on specific examples of context assessment and specific activities of data controllers, as well as determining how to assess the context in a particular sector.

VI. Codes of Conduct and Certification in the GDPR

The co-regulatory tools such as codes of conduct and certification in the GDPR are voluntary and are to be created by data controllers and their organizations. Supervisory authorities, the European Data Protection Board, and the European Commission have an essential but advisory role in creating these measures.

One of the main co-regulatory instruments in the GDPR is codes of conduct (GDPR, art 40). Their introduction is justified by various specialized challenges confronting specific data processing sectors, on the one hand, and by the needs of smaller enterprises on the other. The European Data Protection Board noted that the preparation of codes of conduct facilitates discussions about standard data protection practices within the sector, which should result in well-tailored and specific data protection rules that meet the needs of the sector as well as the requirements of the GDPR.[69] The scope of codes of conduct tends to mirror the scope of the GDPR and aims to specify the application of the Regulation with regard to, inter alia, fair and transparent processing; the legitimate interests pursued by controllers in specific contexts; the collection and pseudonymization of personal data; exercise of the rights of data subjects; privacy-by-design measures and procedures; information obligations; and data breach proceedings (GDPR, art 40). An important aspect of codes of conduct is how they are adopted and enforced. Associations and other bodies representing categories of controllers or processors are responsible for preparing the codes of conduct. However, supervisory authorities also play an essential role in their adoption. They provide an opinion on whether the code complies with the GDPR, and if so, they approve that code (with transnational codes the procedure is more complex and involves European Data Protection Board). Codes of conduct may be monitored by specialized bodies established with the crucial role of supervisory authority.

The other co-regulatory instrument is certification. Origins of certification in the field of data protection date back to the early 2000s, and protection certification schemes were present in Europe even before the introduction of the GDPR.[70] From the perspective of fundamental rights protection, certifica-

[69] Guidelines 1/2019 on Codes of Conduct and Monitoring Bodies under Regulation 2016/679 5.

[70] Eric Lachaud, 'What GDPR tells about certification' (2020) 38 CLS Rev 4–5.

tion must be seen as a longstanding practice. It was a standard measure introduced in sectors where adherence to strict safety and quality standards was vital. For example, in the food industry, certification ensures that products are prepared under specific conditions and are safe for consumption. Currently, the basis for certification in data protection is included in arts 42 and 43 GDPR. In the area of data protection, certification is intended to demonstrate that data controllers meet specific standards of data processing and adhere to the other requirements specified in the GDPR. The use of certification by an online platform may present its users with a clear commitment to privacy protection.

Art 24(3) GDPR states that data controllers may use adherence to approved codes of conduct or approved certification mechanisms to demonstrate compliance with the obligations of the controller. GDPR co-regulatory tools may serve as guidelines for examining context and proportionality. There are many similarities in data flows in specific sectors, so essential components of context can be identified, risk can be assessed, and common remedies can be prepared. To date, co-regulatory measures in connection with the GDPR are not widely used. After more than five years of applying the GDPR, only limited codes of conduct have been adopted despite the conceptual work being carried out.

VII. Conclusions

At this stage, it is hard to determine whether co-regulatory approaches will fulfill the vast promises they make. There are big differences between the legal role of the public authorities and that of online platforms. It is obvious that the latter will not be able to meet the requirements that the rule of law imposes on public regulators, but at the same time – and to some extent – the law has to adjust to the realities of the digital society.

The solutions adopted in the GDPR assume various forms of cooperation in shaping the protection of privacy. EU lawmakers have created a legal framework for the protection of fundamental rights and entrust data controllers and processors operating in specific areas or sectors to develop detailed solutions appropriate to their model of operation. What distinguishes the new solutions in a new model of regulation, a model developed in the GDPR, is that private companies have a more active role in limiting the risks posed to fundamental rights and freedoms. This role consists not only of the passive implementation of obligations imposed by the lawmaker. It also provides for the creation of co-regulatory solutions based on the toolkit used in the past, mainly in public law. Part of this toolkit is employing the impact assessment process and basing the adopted solutions on its results. The mechanism relies heavily on the concepts of proportionality or contextual analysis, which have specific methodologies associated with them. Perhaps a deeper application of the theories described above can make risk assessment more value-oriented. It is important to note that the current legal framework is based on a combination of the principles of private and public law and a modern approach to fundamental rights.

Shadow Contract Law in the Platform Economy

Mateusz Grochowski[*]

I. The Platform Economy as a Self-regulatory Economy

There is no exaggeration in saying that the emergence of the platform economy became one of the most momentous and consequence-laden developments of early 21st century capitalism.[1] One of the clearest tenets of this development has been an immense concentration of various modalities of power –

[*] The chapter is based on the results of research project No. 2020/37/B/HS5/04212 of the National Science Centre.

[1] See eg Amy Kapczynski, 'The Law of Informational Capitalism' (2020) 129 Yale LJ 1460; Nick Srnicek, *Platform Capitalism* (Polity 2017). Julie E Cohen, *Between Truth and Power. The Legal Constructions of Informational Capitalism* (OUP 2019); Elke Schüßler and others, 'Between mutuality, autonomy and domination: rethinking digital platforms as contested relational structures' (2021) 19 Socio-Economic Rev 1217.

from economic to political[2] – in the hands of a relatively small cluster of market entities. It was accompanied by an enduring lack of meaningful control over the accumulation and exercise of this power. A specific fraction of this power, often pushed into the margins of the discourse over the platform economy, is the power to unilaterally establish and enforce rules[3] for horizontal contracts concluded between platform users.[4] These rules function in parallel to state-made contract regulation and, as such, they constitute a shadow law for platform-intermediated agreements. This phenomenon is particularly vivid against the backdrop of online marketplaces such as Amazon and eBay as well as other market intermediaries such as Uber and Airbnb. It can be traced, however, across the entire platform economy, including areas not traditionally associated with trading and contracts, such as social media.[5]

In all these instances platforms create an online venue, where private individuals may encounter each other and conclude agreements. In many instances online contracting, facilitated by platforms, allows the making of agreements between counterparties across different cultural or geographic venues,

---

[2] Julie E Cohen, 'The Regulatory State in the Information Age' (2016) 17 Theo Inq L 369, 375–382, 389–395; Oreste Pollicino, 'The Quadrangular Shape of the Geometry of Digital Power(s) and the Move Towards a Procedural Digital Constitutionalism' (2023) 29 ELJ 10.

[3] The private regulatory role of online platforms has long been observed in scholarship. It relates to both the general role of platforms as regulators of certain issues and more specific issues related to contracts as such. In the former regard, see eg Molly Cohen and Arun Sundararajan, 'Self-Regulation and Innovation in the Peer-to-Peer Sharing Economy' (2015–2016) 82 UChi LRev Dialogue 116; Hannah Bloch-Wehba, 'Global Platform Governance: Private Power in the Shadow of the State' (2019) 72 SMU LRev 27, 33–42; Kate Klonick, 'The New Governors: The People, Rules, and Processes Governing Online Speech' (2017–2018) 131 Harv LRev 1598.

[4] In greater detail on the out-of-state contract rules created by online platforms, Marta Cantero Gamito, 'Regulation.com. Self-regulation and Contract Governance in the Platform Economy: A Research Agenda' (2017) 9 EJLS 53–67; Niva Elkin-Koren and others, 'Social Media as Contractual Networks: A Bottom Up Check on Content Moderation' (2022) 107 Iowa LRev 987, 1019–1025; Mateusz Grochowski, 'Default Rules Beyond a State: Special-Purpose Lawmakers in the Platform Economy' in Stefan Grundmann and Mateusz Grochowski (eds.), *European Contract Law and the Creation of Norms* (Intersentia 2021); Lea K Kumkar, 'Plattform-Recht revisited. Umgang mit den Marktordnungen digitaler Plattformen de lege lata et ferenda' (2022) 30 ZEuP 530; Vanessa Mak, *Legal Pluralism in European Contract Law* (OUP 2020); Florian Möslein, 'Digitising Defaults: Methods and Mechanisms of Generating Default Rules in the Digital Age' in Birke Häcker, *Default Rules in Private Law* (OUP 2025, forthcoming); Florian Möslein, 'Digitized Terms: The Regulation of Standard Contract Terms in the Digital Age' (2023) 19 ERCL 300; Heike Schweitzer, 'Digitale Plattformen als private Gesetzgeber: Ein Perspektivwechsel für die europäische "Plattform-Regulierung"' (2019) 27 ZEuP 1.

[5] See eg Taylor Annabell and others, '(Un)disclosed brand partnerships: How platform policies and interfaces shape commercial content for influencers' (2024) 13 IPR 1.

parties who would have very low odds of trading for goods and services in the context of classic contracting. In so doing, platforms substantially reduce contracting costs by providing parties with developed infrastructure that encompasses both technical and logistical components (such as the IT-based tools that allow the listings of goods and services and that establish online communication between contractors) as well as the regulatory architecture (ie rules created to govern relations between a platform and its users). In this way, platforms act as regulators of the market, and they broadly supply rules of various nature and content to regulate conduct of parties who conclude contracts on a platform. The rules in question are established in various forms, usually through terms of service (ToS)[6] and elements of technical design (especially user interfaces).[7]

The rules established in these ways not only relate to the platform–user relationship (eg how an individual account on the platform should be maintained) but also tackle many horizontal agreement issues as between platform participants.[8] In this way, platforms create microsystems of rules that, in terms of design and function, closely resemble general contract law. In other words, regulation produced by online platforms has a strong community-oriented[9] nature. It is addressed to a particular group of users who gather under the canopy of a platform in order to engage in contractual dealings. The community in question creates an infra-market, governed by a platform. As a result, by entering a platform sellers and suppliers gain access not only to particular sector of the market but also to an elaborated regulatory framework for their future contract.[10]

---

[6] Further on modalities of these instruments, Michael Karanicolas, 'Too Long; Didn't Read: Finding Meaning in Platforms' Terms of Service Agreements' (2021) 52 UTol LRev 1.

[7] On online interfaces as a vehicle for conveying contractual obligations, see eg Woodrow Hartzog, 'Website Design as Contract' (2011) 60 AmU LRev 1635.

[8] See eg Vanessa Mak, 'Private Law Perspectives on Platform Services' (2016) 5 EuCML 19, 20–23; Molly K Land, 'The Problem of Platform Law: Pluralistic Legal Ordering on Social Media' in Paul S Berman (ed), *The Oxford Handbook of Global Legal Pluralism* (OUP 2020).

[9] The notion of community referred to in this chapter is understood in a particular sense – namely, as a group of platform users (individuals and legal entities) interacting with the platform and, through it, with each other. In this sense, this term (or its variations) is commonly used in various segments of platform-related discourse; see eg Julie E Cohen, 'Infrastructuring the Digital Public Sphere' (2023) 25 Yale JLT 1; Katarina Stanoevska-Slabeva, 'Toward a Community-Oriented Design of Internet Platforms' (2002) 6 IJEC 71.

[10] The evolution of platforms from facilitators of transactions to market regulators, is commonly observed in academic literature – see eg Anthony J Casey and Anthony Niblett, 'Self-Driving Contracts' (2017) 43 The JCorpL 1, 22: 'Uber and Airbnb might be viewed as third-party providers of self-driving contracts. In many ways, Uber is providing a contract platform between the drivers and the passengers. The prices are determined algorithmically and update based on various on the ground circumstances. The result is that the

Although the platform economy has been attracting immense attention in various areas of legal scholarship, the private regulatory issues have been mostly on the margins of inquiry. Despite this relatively limited attention, private regulation is in fact present in the background of most foundational problems associated with the platform economy – from the protection of individual users to cross-cutting competition issues.[11]

The following observations attempt to fill a part of this gap by offering a structured account of platforms as architects of alternative systems of contractual rules. The discussion will refer only to horizontal contracts concluded on platforms between their users. Contracts in which the user purchases goods or services directly from the platform[12] will remain outside the framework of the present analysis. Such transactions are much closer to typical business-to-consumer contracts and do not exhibit as many special features as the other contracts discussed below. In what follows, I take a closer look at these processes and attempts in order to map the common theoretical denominators for the contractual rules created by platforms (section II) and outline their overall structural features (section III). In a further step, the paper looks at the most specific concerns and risks generated by the parallel regulation of contracts (section IV). Section V outlines the potential regulatory responses. That being said, the aim of this paper is not to formulate normative proposals for the regulation of shadow contract law in the platform economy. While that task would clearly exceed the scope of this paper, a few structuring remarks in this regard are nevertheless appropriate so as to create a complete picture of shadow contract law in the online platform market sector.

II. The Mechanics of Shadow Contract Law

1. *Regulating Contracts in the Shadow of Law*

Apart from merely facilitating the conclusion of contracts by bringing individual contractors together and by reducing transaction costs, platforms typically[13]

vertical integration between driver, vehicle, dispatcher, pricing agent, is broken. The same can be said of Airbnb.'; discussing this phenomenon similarly, Jason Tanz, 'How Airbnb and Lyft got Americans to Trust Each Other' (*Wired*, 23 April 2014) <https://www.wired.com/2014/04/trust-in-the-share-economy/>: 'eBay evolved from a passive host to an active participant in every transaction'.

[11] See Elettra Bietti, 'Self-Regulating Platforms and Antitrust Justice' (2022) 101 Tex LRev 165, with further references.

[12] On this phenomenon, taking as an example the dual role played by Amazon (as a platform and as a seller in its own right), Lina M Khan, 'Amazon's Antitrust Paradox' (2017) 133 Yale LJ 710, 754–755.

[13] Various platforms display a divergent commitment to regulating user communities and the beta agreements. Some focus on creating and enforcing fairly detailed internal

act as co-regulators of these transactions, broadly supplying rules of various nature and content.[14] Since all the platforms in question operate their own self-contained marketplaces, horizontal contracts concluded between users are extensively subordinated to rules generated by the platforms themselves. Conventional (state-enacted) contract law plays only a secondary role in regulating transactions on platforms' infra-markets – although de jure it still applies to them. In this way platforms establish sets of privately created rules, which, from a practical perspective, operate almost exactly in the same fashion as contract law in the conventional sense.

This contract law for the platform economy emerges in parallel to the state systems of contract governance, and it imitates their structures and functionalities. In this sense, it can be perceived as a mirror image of classic contract law. Obviously, the image created by platforms does not exactly follow either the content or the scope of classic contract law. Platform-set rules are by nature much more selective in scope, and they are driven by a number of factors specific to the platform economy or to out-of-state lawmaking as such. For these reasons it would be more proper to describe those rules as 'shadow contract law'[15] rather than as systems of contract governance in a proper sense. As with every shadow, rules established by platforms outline only a silhouette of a fully-fledged contract, being precise only in selected and rather narrow details.

The shadow contract law of the platform economy emerges in the intersection of several economic dynamics and legal gaps. In the past few decades, markets and social life have been witnessing a gradual erosion of the regulatory functions of a state.[16] This involves, in particular, incremental empow-

---

regulations, while others opt for a more hands-off approach, leaving a much wider field for rule-making by the users themselves – see also Grochowski (n 4) 236–238.

[14] The typical model of a platform – which, acting as a contract intermediary, assumes hybrid interconnection of two opposing vectors – entails centralization in certain spheres of its activity and decentralization in the others; see Cohen and Sundararajan (n 3) 118. Building on this observation, authors conclude (with implicit reference to Ronald Coase's distinction) that platforms are 'market-firm hybrids'. Attempts at private regulation count undoubtedly as the first centralized and quasi-sovereign dimension of platform operation.

[15] This notion vaguely refers to the notion of the 'shadow of the law' developed in the seminal contributions by Robert H Mnookin and Lewis Kornhauser ('Bargaining in the Shadow of the Law: The Case of Divorce' (1979) 88 Yale LJ 950) and by Robert Cooter and others, 'Bargaining in the Shadow of the Law: A Testable Model of Strategic Behavior' (1982) 11 JLS 225. Further on the relevance of this conceptual framework for out-of-state contract regulation, see Stefan Grundmann and Mateusz Grochowski, 'The Creation of Norms: An Evolutionary View on European Contract Law' in Stefan Grundmann and Mateusz Grochowski (eds), *European Contract Law and the Creation of Norms* (Intersentia 2021) 31–32.

[16] Gunther Teubner, 'After Legal Instrumentalism: Strategic Models of Post-Regulatory Law' in Gunther. Teubner (ed), *Dilemmas of Law in the Welfare State* (De Gruyter 1986).

erment of private actors, who in various ways take over parts of the state's regulatory agenda. In the digital society this phenomenon assumes particularly specific forms: the role of the state is clearly reduced, and, as a consequence, private entities enter into a number of areas that thus far have been subjected to the state's regulatory monopoly.[17]

This pertains also to online platforms, which in various ways adopt a role of rule makers on the online market. Consequently, the regulatory agenda of the platform economy comprises rules created by the platform itself (and the classic legal rules, enacted by states or international entities).

At the same time, due to multiple premises, the latter fraction of regulation has limited impact on the platform economy. First of all, they are often limited to a particular state jurisdiction. Therefore, they do not apply to platforms, which usually function worldwide and thereby de facto exempt themselves from domestic rules through forum shopping[18] and by creating enforcement and dispute resolution systems. Secondly, the market profile of many online platforms excludes application of numerous classic pieces of regulation, which do not match the specificity of the platform economy. In this way, platforms blur conventional distinctions between employer and employee, between consumer and professional, and in respect of other categories that grounded the existing regulatory frameworks.[19] In this way, the emergence of the platform economy was taking place mostly in the fissures of the legal system where the existing rules were not precise enough or improperly enforced. While the law allowed platforms to set off and gradually establish their market prowess, by safeguarding data transfers and the enforcement of platform-user transactions, it was very poorly equipped to control the ways how this power was being exercised.[20]

---

[17] This transformation originated in the enforcement domain, where online platforms effectively took on the responsibilities of resolving disputes and enforcing rules, or received such responsibilities from states (see Barbara Warwas, 'Dispute Resolution within Online Platforms', in this volume, 213, along with further references). This key dynamic enabled the development of systems of substantive rules and governance schemes in the platform economy.

[18] See eg the practice tackled by CJEU in the judgment of 28 July 2016, *Amazon*, C-191/15, ECLI:EU:C:2016:612.

[19] See Caroline Meller-Hannich, 'Share Economy and Consumer Protection' in Reiner Schulze and Dirk Staudenmayer (eds), *Digital Revolution: Challenges for Contract Law in Practice* (Hart and Nomos 2016); Rolf H Weber, 'The Sharing Economy in the EU and the Law of Contracts' (2017) 85 Geo Wash LRev 1777, 1800; Cohen and Sundararajan (n 3) 121.

[20] See eg Joanna Mazur and Marcin Serafin, 'Stalling the State: How Digital Platforms Contribute to and Profit From Delays in the Enforcement and Adoption of Regulations' (2023) 56 Comp Pol Stud 101; Brishen Rogers, 'The Social Costs of Uber' (2015–2016) 82 UChi LRev Dialogue 85.

The existence of parallel systems of contractual rules that emerge beyond the state – or even in defiance of state-made contract law – is neither new on the market nor unknown in contract law theory.[21] The emergence of such parallel regulatory structures is in many regards inherent to the market as a domain of free dealing between individuals who, in pursuing their interests, choose forms of cooperation that to the highest extent possible align with their goals and resources.[22] Indeed, the existing legal and sociological scholarship provide abundant illustration of this phenomenon for various industry sectors and contracting communities.[23]

These theoretical and empirical accounts are, however, of limited applicability in the platform economy. Whereas in the classic paradigm of private (or self-) regulation the rules emerge as an outcome of the collective effort by all the participants of the contracting community, in the platform context the rulemaking activity is concentrated in the platforms' ToS.[24] In this way, platforms almost entirely[25] exclude participatory rulemaking, offering their regulatory design to users on a take-it-or-leave-it basis.[26] Such an immense concentration of regulatory power is one of the most specific features of shadow contract law – and it plays a decisive role in determining its structure, content, and shortcomings. The following sections will delve more deeply into various layers of the power structure that underpins shadow contract rules and their ramifications.

---

[21] See also Ralf Michaels, 'The True Lex Mercatoria: Law Beyond the State' (2007) 14 IJGLS 447.

[22] Especially important for a general account of these issues is the seminal work by Robert C Ellickson, *Order without Law. How Neighbors Settle Disputes* (Harv UP 1991); from the market economy perspective, see also Julian Arato, 'Corporations as Lawmakers' (2015) 56 Harv ILJ 230.

[23] See especially a series of studies on self-emerging structures of contract regulation by Lisa Bernstein: 'Private Commercial Law in the Cotton Industry: Creating Cooperation through Rules, Norms and Institutions' (2001) 99 Mich LRev 1724; 'Opting Out of the Legal System: Extralegal Contractual Relations in the Diamond Industry' (1991) 21 JLS 115; 'Social Norms and Default Rules Analysis' (1993–1994) 3 SCal Interdisc LJ 59; 'Beyond Relational Contracts: Social Capital and Network Governance in Procurement Contracts' (2015) 7 JLA 561. On similar issues, with a stronger focus on the impact of new technologies in contracting, see also Thomas Dietz, *Global Order Beyond Law. How Information and Communication Technologies Facilitate Relational Contracting in International Trade* (Hart 2014).

[24] See also Cohen and Sundararajan (n 3) 124.

[25] See, however, III.3, below.

[26] Cohen and Sundararajan (n 3) 121.

2. Two Layers of Platform-made Contract Law

The elementary framework of this phenomenon is based on a triangle, formed by three[27] relations.[28] Two of them link clients and suppliers with the platform itself and provide an organizational framework for participation in the community that is formed around a platform (eg rights and duties of the platform and participants and ways of exiting the community, sanctions for misconduct). For brevity, these two contracts will be referred to as 'alpha contracts'. The third contract is the 'ultimate' agreement between the client and supplier, concluded within the framework provided by the platform. It will be referred to below as the 'beta contract'.

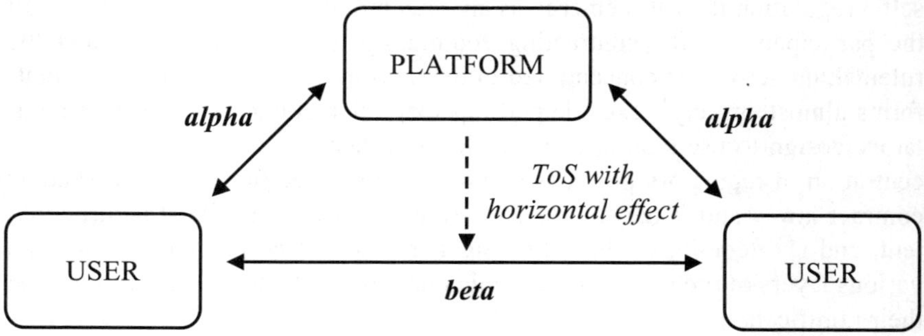

The dotted line in the middle of the diagram represents the essential dynamic of shadow contract law – ie the impact exerted by a platform over the beta agreement. Serving as vehicle for this impact are the alpha agreements, which not only bind each platform user with the platform as such, but which also oblige each of them to particular conduct vis-à-vis the other platform user who is a counterparty to the beta contract. In this way, although the alpha and beta contracts remain formally independent, the content of the platform-user relationship directly determines the formation, content, and enforcement of the user-user contract.

From this vantage point, alpha contracts play a two-pronged role. Besides being simple executory agreements, which produce rights and obligations between a platform and each of its particular users, they also perform an order-

[27] The structure of contractual relations in the platform economy, depicted below, is partially simplified. The relationships between alpha and beta contracts can be much more compound and inseparable – see eg, Khan (n 12).

[28] On the divergence between the 'triangle (ie platform) economy' vs the 'chain (ie classic) economy', see Aneta Wiewiórowska-Domagalska, *Online Platforms: How to Adapt Regulatory Framework to the Digital Age?* (European Parliament, Internal Market and Consumer Protection, PE 607.323, 2017) 1, 4; see also Christine Riefa, *Consumer Protection and Online Auction Platforms. Towards a Safer Legal Framework* (Ashgate 2015) 50.

ing function, setting the regulatory infrastructure for horizontal agreements between platform users. In conceptual terms, alpha agreements constitute contracts having a third-party effect. They create rights and obligations of platform users vis-à-vis the other platform users who concluded a – formally independent – alpha agreement with the platform. At the same time, however, the third-party effect in question is conditional on the entire structure of alpha agreements created within a platform. Alpha agreements may unlock their organizational potential only when they are accompanied by similar alpha contracts concluded by the other platform users. Otherwise, the imposition of certain rights and obligations related to beta contracts would have no purpose. The idea of regulatory contracts assumes, by definition, a certain community of beta contractors, all of whom adhere to the common regulatory framework set forth by a platform. Consequently, the alpha agreements are much closer to the conceptual grid of organizational contracts[29] or contractual networks[30] than to conventional agreements with third party effects.

3. *Shadow Contract Law and Palpable Power*

The shadow contract law of rulemaking vividly manifests one of the most distinctive traits of private regulatory processes within platforms: centralization of power and monopolization of its exercise.[31] For the reasons already discussed in the preceding section, the present-day economy situates platforms in a sphere that allows them to accumulate immense economic and epistemic power, which in turn creates the political power that has enabled platforms to develop regulatory schemes largely beyond state control. This overall governing power transpires at a more specific level and embodies the power to shape individual contracts (alpha agreements). Platforms typically enjoy almost exclusive bargaining power over particular alpha contractors.[32] For this reason, they are able to unilaterally impose rules on beta contractors, who can only accept them or reject them (a take-it-or-leave-it choice which in the latter case means not being able to enter the platform).[33]

These two types of power – the overall political capability to control the market and public sphere and the control over individual contractual design –

[29] Stefan Grundmann, Fabrizio Cafaggi and Giuseppe Vettori, 'The Contractual Basis of Long-Term Organization – The Overall Architecture' in Stefan Grundmann, Fabrizio Cafaggi and Giuseppe Vettori (eds), *The Organizational Contract: From Exchange to Long-Term Network Cooperation in European Contract Law* (Ashgate 2013).

[30] Elkin-Koreen and others (n 4).

[31] See also n 1, above.

[32] See also, Vanessa Katz, 'Regulating the Sharing Economy' (2015) 30 Berkeley Tech LJ 1067, 1100, 1101.

[33] On the take-it-or-leave-it issue in private economy self-governance schemes, see eg David A Hoffman, 'Relational Contracts of Adhesion' (2018) 85 UChi LRev 1395.

are indispensable in supporting shadow contract law. It would be too simplistic, however, to perceive the bargaining power as a simple manifestation of the overall governance power of platforms. While the economic and political power shield platforms from aspects of state supervision and regulatory intervention, the bargaining power vests platforms with the aptitude to set up internal regulatory schemes through (alpha) contracts. Without the political and economic status of platforms, the bargaining power in individual agreements would be impossible to wield. At the same time, the aptitude to unilaterally shape individual contracts is in many instances a necessary pathway to turn the general political power into a more concrete governance structure.

In this way, shadow contract law is both an emanation of the underlying allocation of power in the platform economy and a way to further entrench it. By virtue of a network of alpha contracts, platforms are able to create insulated spheres of market and social interactions that are governed predominantly by themselves. This dynamic extends, and partly modifies, the classical model – responding to a power-weakness relationship – that underlies contract law. In particular, it invalidates to some extent the conceptual structures conventionally employed to distinguish between various degrees of market and social power, structures such as consumer/business and employee/employer.[34] In the platform economy, all platform users (regardless of being suppliers of goods, services, or content) are generally in a deprivileged standing vis-à-vis the platform. Most illustrative for the advantage enjoyed by platforms are the instances in which platforms take over the same activity as their users (through self-preferencing[35] or introducing their own content or speech into the users' community). This turn in perceiving the power structures underlying contract law has been partly acknowledged in the EU law that puts forward new regulatory patterns for interactions between platforms and states. Such regulatory measures attempt to provide a feasible and sound solution to new power grids in the platform economy.[36] All of them are, however, in a rather experimental phase, and their actual effectiveness and future trajectories remain largely blurry.

III. The Architecture In Being

1. *Hybridization of Contract Types*

Due to the fragmentation of shadow contract law, it is difficult to analyze it in a similar way as one does with the architecture of conventional contract law.

---

[34] See also n 19, above.

[35] See eg Lina M Khan, 'The Separation of Platforms and Commerce' (2019) 119 Colum LRev 973.

[36] See V.3, below.

The structure of these regulations remains in a constant in-between state. It is in flux not only because of the differences between the models that each platform adopts – but also because the regulations themselves change within each platform (either on their own initiative or due to various regulatory pressures). Yet several common denominators can be identified that form the overall architecture of shadow contract law 'in being'.

The foundational feature of shadow contract law is its optionality. The regulatory systems created by platforms are inherently fragmented, reflecting the diversity of the segmented marketplaces and user communities governed by platforms. Platforms establish multiple parallel regulatory systems, allowing users to select one by creating an account and entering into a contract on a specific platform.[37] In this way, platform users are essentially choosing between different sub-types of their beta contracts, which can vary in terms of the specific rights and obligations established for the parties involved. These differences may sometimes be technical (eg the path a user must navigate through the platform's interface to finalize a contract) or may pertain to more fundamental issues, such as a client's right to withdraw from a beta agreement and the manner of performing the agreement. Each of these contracts is, of course, regulated in the first instance by the state-made law of the country in question, but in practice it is the rules created by the platforms that are crucial to the conclusion and execution of specific beta contracts.

Thus, in the platform market, a number of detailed sub-types of contracts emerge, based on two regulatory levels: the first is contract law in the proper sense, applied uniformly throughout the market; the second is the shadow rules created by the platforms, which vary depending on which of the platforms' infra-markets a client will choose. For instance, while purchasing a book on Amazon, clients enter a sale agreement subjected to the general sales law, supplemented by specific rule supplied by a platform.[38] The choice in question is usually a spillover of a client's decision to purchase a particular product or service via a certain platform. In several instances, however, this choice may be driven directly by differences in the architecture created by platforms to govern beta agreements. For instance, clients interested in an easier way out of a transaction may choose platforms with more liberal cancellation policies over those offering lower price or more convenient shipping modes.[39]

---

[37] See also Möslein (n 4) 62–63.

[38] See also Grochowski (n 4) 238.

[39] The exact motives behind choosing one platform over another rests on a much broader and more compound set of premises where the quality of a governance framework or the array of entitlements awarded to users can only be a part of a much more diverse constellation – see eg Claudio Panico and Carmelo Cennamo, 'User preferences and strategic interactions in platform ecosystems' (2020) 43 Strategic Management Journal 507; David S Evans, 'Attention Rivalry Among Online Platforms' (2013) 9 JCL&E 313.

2. *The Scope of Regulation*

The shadow contract law created by online platforms is to a great extent compartmentalized into various regulatory islands created by each online platform separately. Although it is possible to identify synergies between internal governance architectures adopted in particular sectors,[40] ultimately each of the platforms creates its own regulatory structure. At the same time, the regulatory islands created in this way heavily depend on public enforcement schemes, entrenching private power through the threat of public coercion (ie the general promise of the state to enforce all lawfully concluded agreements).

The array of shadow contract law is relatively similar to the range of issues covered in classical contractual rules. What is most obvious, platforms set multiple rules on the conclusion of beta contracts. While some of them are expressed verbally,[41] many others are established 'by design', ie through the technical architecture of user interfaces.[42] In many instances platforms also involve themselves directly in regulating the way contracts are performed.[43] Multiple platforms provide consumers with specific entitlements to exit the agreement[44] and for the return of product and payment.[45] Sometimes plat-

---

[40] See eg Catalina Goanta and others, 'One Rule of Law to Rule them All? Geography of the Terms of Service on Social Media Platforms' (manuscript on file with author).

[41] See eg Amazon's Conditions of Use & Sale (version of 9.8.2024 applicable in the EU), which sets forth rules on the meaning of a customer's order and the moment when the contract is concluded: 'Your order is an offer to Amazon to buy the product(s) in your order. When you place an order to purchase a product from Amazon, we will send you a message confirming receipt of your order and containing the details of your order (the "Order Confirmation"). […] The Order Confirmation is acknowledgement that we have received your order, and does not confirm acceptance of your offer to buy the product(s) or the services ordered. We only accept your offer, and conclude the contract of sale for a product ordered by you, when we dispatch the product to you and send e-mail or post a message on the Message Center of the website confirming to you that we've dispatched the product to you (the "Dispatch Confirmation"). […]' ('Conditions of Sale', section 2: 'Our contract').

[42] On online interfaces as a vehicle for conveying contractual obligations, see eg Hartzog (n 7).

[43] See eg the eBay User Agreement (section 12 'Additional items', subsection 'Simple delivery'): 'By using the label provided to you or not opting out, you and your buyer agree that you purchase the label from the delivery service provider, and you agree that no further delivery costs are owed to you by your buyer. Any delivery costs you owe to the delivery service provider to send your item are paid by the buyer to the delivery service provider on your behalf.'

[44] See for instance the eBay 'Order cancellation policy' (accessed 10 November 2024) with rules on the cancellation of orders (in many instances: contract termination) for sellers and buyers who transact on the platform.

[45] See eg an eBay default return policy (eBay User Agreement, section 13 'Additional terms', subsection 'Returns and cancellations'): 'Sellers can create rules to automate replacements, returns, and refunds under certain circumstances. For all new sellers, in list-

forms step even further towards bringing ToS closer to the conventional design of contractual rules. This may encompass, for instance, setting open-ended standards as a benchmark for users' conduct.[46]

Somewhat contrary to appearances, the relationship between conventional and shadow contract law is not always a one-way street. The state legal infrastructure does not merely regulate and channel private regulatory practices. At times, its bits and pieces are also appropriated by platforms as elements of their internal regulatory architectures. In this way, entitlements provided in platform-made contract law are in fact a more or less accurate mirror image of the universal legal framework. Such inclusion may occur in a multitude of forms. At times, it may be a mere restating of a rule binding anyway; at times it is an attempt to reshape a rule or to tinker with its scope. For instance, the Polish shopping platform Allegro introduced in its ToS a general 14-day cancellation period[47] that mirrors the withdrawal right for distance consumer contracts under EU law. At the same time, however, the right in question was extended to cover all buyers who use the platform irrespective of the transaction having a consumer or non-consumer character.

3. *User-created Rules*

The sub-types of contracts that emerge at the intersection of conventional and shadow contract law are convoluted even further by margins of flexibility left by platforms for users to co-regulate beta contracts with self-generated rules. User inclusion in the creation of the regulatory architecture may take place along two lines.

Firstly, platforms may resort to default (non-mandatory) rules in the conventional sense. In this scenario, selected rules for beta agreements in platforms' ToS are based on an opt-out or (less frequently) opt-in scheme.[48] The

---

ings where returns are accepted, eBay will set a default rule that automates the return process. Sellers may remove or customize their return preferences in their account settings within My eBay. Where settings have been set to automatically accept requests for returns or replacements, an eBay-generated return shipping label will be provided to Your buyer. You agree to comply with our returns policy.'

[46] See eg the General Terms (*Regulamin*) of the Polish trading platform Allegro: 'All actions taken by the User within Allegro should be in accordance with the Regulations, good morals and applicable laws, including those concerning the protection of consumer rights.'

[47] See Allegro General Terms, rule 2.13.

[48] For general discussion on the creation of default contract provisions by private actors, see also, Grochowski (n 4); Cohen and Sundararajan (n 3) 128, with further reference to Bernstein (n 23) 1726–1727; Stefan Grundmann and Philipp Hacker, 'Digital Technology as a Challenge to European Contract Law. From Existing to Future Architecture' (2017) 13 ERCL 255, 274; on the akin problems of privately-created default rules, see Fabrizio Cafaggi and Paola Iamiceli, 'Regulating Contracting in Global Value Chains. Institutional Alternatives and their Implications for Transnational Contract Law' (2020) 16 ERCL 44, 65–70.

majority of such rules are designed as gap-fillers, which aim to supplement lacunae in beta contracts[49] and are based on the opt-out pattern.[50] They aim to shape the relationship in a way that is optimal from the platform's perspective, leaving parties a margin of freedom to provide their own rules, with the margin varying significantly. The other basket of defaults are opt-in rules; introduced typically to enhance the efficiency of beta contracts, they provide parties with a broader array of choices[51] (sometimes chosen out of a broader menu of options).[52] Sometimes – as is especially typical for online platforms – the default rules are expressed in the form of particular applications or other solutions embedded in the technical architecture of a user's interface.[53] In some rare instances default rules supplied by platforms are designed to incentivize parties to introduce their own, tailor-made rules. Lastly, some of the default rules are introduced by platforms in order to nudge suppliers or clients, steering them to the ends intended by a platform.[54]

It must, however, be born in mind that, as explained earlier,[55] default rules of a different genre are inherent to platform regulation as such. Each of the internal regulatory structures (or, in other terms, the sub-types of contracts) is offered to platform users only as a non-binding option, which they can choose on an opt-in basis. Obviously, opting-out is only a spillover of market choice (ie the decision to join a particular platform and, subsequently, to make a beta contract). However, one of the factors driving this decision may be the regulatory design of a platform as such.[56] As a consequence, the privately-created

[49] See eg the eBay cancellation policy (quoted in n 45) that allows sellers to introduce individually tailored rules.

[50] See Grochowski (n 4) 239–244.

[51] See eg the 'InDemand' program (allowing users to continue a fundraising campaign – ie make additional beta agreements), available upon an opt-in basis on the Indiegogo platform <https://entrepreneur.indiegogo.com/how-it-works/indemand>.

[52] See eg the compound menu of shipping modes and shipping costs provided in the eBay Selling Practices Policy. The provisions in question list various options that can be chosen by parties on a take-it-or-leave-it or take-it-or-amend-it basis.

[53] For instance, if a passenger, who takes an Uber ride decides to tip the driver, she can use a dedicated facility within the Uber payment service (see also <https://help.uber.com/h/8459a496-5ed2-4f9d-b15c-d8afd9ccf34f>).

[54] One of the most elaborated schemes of this sort is applied by Uber, which – through different default rules – attempts to push drivers to drive in particular timeframes or certain geographic locations – *see* Alex Rosenblat and Luke Stark, 'Algorithmic Labor and Information Asymmetries: A Case Study of Uber's Drivers' (2016) 10 IJC 3758, 3775; Noam Scheiber, 'How Uber Uses Psychological Tricks to Push Its Drivers' Buttons' *New York Times* (2 April 2017). A more subtle 'nudging' default rule has been applied also by Airbnb, which – through its 'Price Tips' service – attempts to steer hosts into adopting particular pricing schemes in rental contracts – see Ellen Huet, 'How Airbnb Uses Big Data And Machine Learning To Guide Hosts To The Perfect Price' *Forbes* (5 June 2015).

[55] See III.1, above.

[56] See IV.2, below.

default rules in the platform economy have a two-tier structure: the choice of the entire regulatory regime (*opt-in*) and the choice of incidental defaults sewed into it (*opt-out*, rarely *opt-in*).[57]

To some (albeit highly limited) extent, the internal regulatory design of online platforms leaves space for bottom-up regulation by platform users themselves. Such rules emerge mainly on the margins of the main grid of a platform's regulatory architecture – either by unprompted use of lacunae in the design or by building on margins of freedom purposefully left by platforms. The most vivid manifestations of such a self-regulatory drive are the feedback schemes[58] employed by most platforms as a reputation- and trust-building device.[59] Providing ex post feedback on transactions allows the platform to generate, over time, standards and benchmarks (eg regarding acceptable delay in replying to client's messages, the technicalities of product shipping, or the handling of post-purchase claims) that spread across the community of users who read reviews left by others and who produce their own reviews. The relationship between such upstream-created rules and the rules established by platforms for beta contracts in many regards resembles the interdependence between conventional contract law and trade usages in the non-platform world.[60]

Usages established within the user community supplement the regulatory architecture created by a platform, provide it with a degree of flexibility, and constitute an additional source of regulatory knowledge. For several reasons, however, they are distinctive from more conventional types of usage. Firstly, while the typical usages assume a certain degree of proximity between contractors and a degree of permanence of market cooperation, bottom-up practices in the platform economy emerge mostly between strangers who meet only to conclude one particular contract. Secondly (and as a consequence), the usage in question heavily depends on infrastructures created by the plat-

[57] On the ramifications of these phenomena for the theory of default rules, see Mateusz Grochowski, 'The Majoritarian Concept of Default Rules: Towards a Shift in Paradigms?' (2020) 15 Studies in Private Law [Studia Prawa Prywatnego] 63, with further references.

[58] In a similar vein on feedback schemes in the platform economy, see also Cantero Gamito (n 4) 59–63, with further references.

[59] Feedback mechanisms in the platform economy have a strong regulatory potential. In particular, they create channels for community members to establish internal, detailed rules on the conclusion and performance of contracts. It is possible that reviews can also manifest embedded usages within the platform community (beta contractors may assess each other's conduct, based on pre-established, customary standards of behavior). Hence, feedback-giving schemes may allow a stronger integration of usages with the rest of self-regulatory content in the platform economy and, in turn, invigorate the regulatory significance of usages as such.

[60] Amongst the classic accounts, see eg, Robert C Ellickson, *Order without Law*, 188–206 and Lisa Bernstein, 'Merchant Law in a Merchant Court: Rethinking the Code's Search for Immanent Business Norms' (1996) 144 UPa LRev 1765.

forms themselves to develop and preserve rules (eg feedback records) created by users.[61] In this way, reputation in the platform economy is not only a vehicle of collective regulation (as in more conventional market settings); rather it is also an object of quite intensive regulatory activity by platforms. Thirdly, due to the naturally fractured character of platform communities, the usages may be much more limited in terms of scale and more detailed. At the same time, however, it may be assumed that within close-knit communities, linked by an efficient communication network, usages can gain faster and stronger recognition than in classic market settings.

IV. The Frailty of Shadow Contract Law

1. *The Internal Antinomy*

The vantage points on private regulation in the platform economy oscillate between two perspectives. The first looks at platforms as rule-makers in the strict sense, using various metaphors to capture their specific position in the regulatory landscape ('silicon states',[62] 'special-purpose sovereigns',[63] and multiple others). This view puts stronger emphasis on the role of platforms as alternative centers of governance, which compete with or supplement the conventional state-based schemes. It also often looks at platforms as de facto arbiters in fundamental disputes about rights and values such as freedom of speech[64] and equal treatment.[65] The second viewpoint interprets platforms' rulemaking activities as an emanation of economic power, sublimated into governance schemes that can be established and enforced beyond or against the state. This perspective underscores the role of private regulation within the overall business model in the platform economy.[66]

These two approaches are complementary as they pin down two sides of platform rulemaking existing in parallel. The dual focus is a direct consequence of the twofold role played by platforms, within the structure of alpha and beta contracts. Platforms act simultaneously as private enterprises and as

---

[61] See eg, Arun Sundararajan, *The Sharing Economy. The End of Employment and the Rise of Crowd-Based Capitalism* (MIT Press 2017) 60–65; Sergio Marti and Hector Garcia-Molina, 'Taxonomy of Trust: Categorizing P2P Reputation Systems' (2006) 50 Computer Networks 472.

[62] Lucie Greene, *Silicon States. The Power and Politics of Big Tech and What It Means for Our Future* (Counterpoint 2019).

[63] Jack M Balkin, 'Free Speech in the Algorithmic Society: Big Data, Private Governance, and New School Speech Regulation' (2017–2018) 51 UCDavis LRev 1149.

[64] Klonick (n 3).

[65] See eg Nancy Leong and Aaron Belzer, 'The New Public Accommodations: Race Discrimination in the Platform Economy' (2017) 105 Geo LJ 1271, 1319.

[66] See also n 3, above.

regulators,[67] pursuing their own economic goals while regulating the communities of contractors at the same time. Internally created regulatory architectures are, obviously, directly subordinated to a platform's market goals. Looking at shadow contract law from these two vantage points in parallel clearly elucidates both the potential and the perils of the gradual migration of contract law from conventional governance schemes into a realm of private regulation. The next three sections will take a glimpse at the most essential potentials and perils.

2. *Incentives and Opportunities*

The first of the potential advantages is epistemic. Since most of the platforms build their business models on a harvesting of user data, they obtain immense social and market knowledge, on various levels of granularity. In many instances, the degree of expertise far exceeds the information at the disposal of any state.[68] As a result, platforms are much more proficient than classic lawmakers (especially the state legislature and the judiciary) at learning about the regulatory needs and preferences of both individual clients and suppliers.[69] This allows them not only to supply regulation that is much more compliant with the actual regulatory necessities, but also – by analyzing big data (especially with the use of artificial intelligence algorithms) – to produce personalized rules, tailor-made for each particular platform user.[70]

Secondly, also the very market dynamics in the platform economy may – to some extent – push platforms towards nurturing the regulatory quality of beta contracts. Platforms are naturally incentivized to establish regulatory frameworks that attract users to establish and maintain accounts and to not

---

[67] Alex Rosenblat and Luke Stark identify the phenomenon of a, somewhat blurred, bipartite role for Uber, observing that 'attempts, through algorithmic management and communications, to mobilize its supply of drivers to meet demand ahead of time complicate its claim that it operates as a neutral intermediary.' – Rosenblat and Stark (n 54) 3768.

[68] A separate question in this regard is the actual efficiency of analytical schemes employed by platforms. The abundance of empirical evidence calls into question whether automated big data analysis can achieve full objectivity and a freedom from bias. Yet quite to the contrary, in many instances algorithms replicate biases already existing in the data pool; see eg Anupam Chander, 'The Racist Algorithm?' (2017) 115 Mich LRev 1023.

[69] The particular big data-based aptitude of online platforms to organize markets efficiently and cope with their dysfunctionalities has been identified by many authors, both in general terms as well as with regard to particular spheres or phenomena – see eg Rogers (n 20) 96–97; Sundararajan (n 61) 155; Tanz (n 10).

[70] On the personalization of rules by Uber, see Omri Ben-Shahar, 'Are Uber Drivers Employees? The Answer Will Shape The Sharing Economy', *Forbes* (15 November 2017); more generally on the personalization of rules based on automated analysis of big data, see Ariel Porat and Lior Jacob Strahilevitz, 'Personalizing Default Rules and Disclosure with Big Data' (2013) 112 Mich LRev 1417.

look for other opportunities outside of the platform. For these reasons, platforms usually develop multiple tools, which enhance the coherence and functionality of the community. One of the most characteristic types of these measures are tools for enhancing trust[71] – and, hence, for incentivizing users to increase the volume of transactions concluded on a platform. In market settings characterized by a certain degree of competitiveness, platforms may also effectively compete over elements of their regulatory design[72] (eg in terms of return policies, reviewing schemes, and other instruments that may boost users' confidence and willingness to stay active).

3. *Biased Rules*

Although the preceding section[73] portrayed platforms as competent rule-makers (who in many instances have a regulatory upper hand over states), this perspective should be taken with great reservation. Although platforms are positioned to produce rules well-suited for beta agreements, it will not necessarily be in their interest to take advantage of this aptitude. Obviously, in setting forth regulatory design for beta contracts, platforms follow their own particular economic interests, which will not necessarily conform to the needs and preferences of the regulated community. As a consequence, the above-described assumption of efficient regulation fails in many respects.

This may be reflected, first of all, in an allocation of preferences between the parties to beta contracts in a manner that is contrary to classical contract law paradigms, which heavily emphasize an equality of opportunities and equal protection of the interests of all parties involved in a transaction. Consequently, contract law remains generally averse to solutions having directly distributive effects. Shadow contract law does not always follow suit. In several instances platforms have designed their internal governance schemes in an unbalanced way, providing disproportionately higher rights and profits to one party.[74]

In many instances platforms do not seize upon the opportunity to craft efficient rules for beta agreements, keeping their regulatory architecture relatively impartial. This typically means that some beta contractors will be discouraged from making agreements or from entering a platform at all and that

---

[71] See eg Orly Lobel, 'The Law of the Platform' (2016) 101 Minn LRev 87, 146–156.

[72] On competition over contract law terms, see David Gilo and Ariel Porat, 'Viewing Unconscionability Through a Market Law' (2010) 52 Wm&Mary LRev 133, 162–170.

[73] See section IV.2, above.

[74] Distribution of profit or risks in the sense discussed here is distinctive from other types of distributive intervention in beta contracts. For instance, platforms quite often establish rules for beta agreements that have a protective flavor and which may resemble consumer protection frameworks – see further Jane K Winn, 'The Secession of the Successful: The Rise of Amazon as Private Global Consumer Protection Regulator' (2016) 58 Ariz LRev 193; Miriam R Albert, 'E-Buyer Beware: Why Online Auction Fraud Should Be Regulated' (2002) 39 Am Bus LJ 575.

they will thus not benefit from a magnification of the volume of contracts (and a consequential accrual of greater profits).[75] The existing regulatory frameworks developed by platforms provide many examples of terms that potentially create inefficient outcomes for beta contractors (eg by imposing oppressive terms of supply[76] or terms for the rendering of services[77]), especially terms that hinder an efficient allocation of risk (eg by obliging suppliers to indemnify clients for all losses, even those resulting from the platform's negligence)[78].

4. *Shortcomings of the Regulatory Model*

Besides the voluntary distortion of party parity, several concerns arise also in connection with the overall model of shadow contract law and its economic setting. The accumulation of regulatory power in the hands of platforms may create further negative outcomes when coupled with the monopolist or oligopolist structures that are typical for many sectors of the platform economy.[79] Even in settings where platforms are – formally – in a competitive milieu, the exact freedom of choice available to users may be low. Platforms develop a variety of schemes intended to confine users to a particular plat-

[75] Such an attitude of platforms is possible both in competitive markets as well as in situations of monopoly or oligopoly (as are relatively more common in the platform economy). In the second instance, platforms may still be interested in increasing the volume of contracts, by attracting new sellers and suppliers – and thereby accruing higher market rent, based on limited competition. Such practice was evidenced, for instance, by Uber (operating in an oligopolist setting), which – as a part of its policy of appeasing driver unrest – offered a number of additional advantages to drivers. As Greg Bensinger (Uber's Driver Dilemma: Fare Hikes and Cuts Don't Change Pay' *Wall Street Journal* (12 November 2017)) points out, these perks 'are generally funded by riders, easing the burden on Uber. The changes include extra payments for trips that require more than eight minutes to pick up a passenger, fees for some cancellations and fewer ride offers that require tolls.'

[76] Christoph Busch and others, 'The Rise of the Platform Economy: A New Challenge for EU Consumer Law?' (2016) 5 EuCML 3, 5, 7.

[77] This pertains, first and foremost, to platforms that operate on a quasi-employer basis (such as Uber); see eg Rogers (n 20) 98–101; Ryan Calo and Alex Rosenblat, 'The Taking Economy: Uber, Information and the Power' (2017) 117 Colum LRev 1623, 1626–1627.

[78] On illustrative instances of such schemes see eg Larry A DiMatteo, 'Regulation of Share Economy: A Consistently Changing Environment' in Reiner Schulze and Dirk Staudenmayer (eds), *Digital Revolution: Challenges for Contract Law in Practice* (Hart 2016) 99–101; Talia G Loucks, 'Travelers Beware: Tort Liability in the Sharing Economy' (2015) 10 Wash JL Tech & Arts 329, 335.

[79] See eg Lobel (n 71) 160–162; Teresa Rodriguez de las Heras Ballell, 'Refusal to Deal, Abuse of Right and Competition Law in Electronic Markets and Digital Communities' (2014) 22 ERPL 685, 688–689; Christopher Koopman and others, 'The Sharing Economy and Consumer Protection Regulation: The Case for Policy Change' (2015) 8 JEBL 529, 539; Vera Demary, *Competition in the sharing economy*, IW Policy Paper 19/2015 (Institut der deutschen Wirtschaft 2015) 14.

form, making it highly difficult for them to adopt the most efficient regulatory scheme for beta contracts.[80] This may even further diminish incentives to establish regulatory designs in the interest of users, thus encouraging platforms to engage in more opportunism.

Furthermore, apart from creating its own externalities, regulation created by platforms may also prove ineffective in coping with externalities already existing on the market. The most vivid instance of this problem is the issue of discrimination in contracting. Several empirical studies reveal that the platform economy is associated with a wide range of discrimination, especially gender- and race-based discrimination.[81] The regulatory schemes supplied by platforms may in some instances trigger or magnify these occurrences.[82] At the same time, the widespread problem of discrimination may strongly call for a self-regulatory response of platforms.

V. Taming Private Regulation

1. *Models of Regulated Regulation*

The emergence of shadow contract law in the platform economy poses several foundational questions about interactions between platform-made rules and various layers of the regulatory structure for digital markets as enforced by online platforms. First of all, the rulemaking aptitude of online platforms, as with any exercise of private power for public ends, raises a fundamental question regarding the checks and controls upon this practice. In the democratic, free market economy, the ultimate competence to create and legitimize any regulatory action on the market lies in the hands of a state. Although this

---

[80] One of the most illustrative instances in this regard can be seen in the manner which the regulatory design of reputational schemes is impacted by the competition between platforms. As trust constitutes one of the crucial assets in the platform economy, the extent to which it can be transferred (or shared between) platforms may in many instances be a crucial determinant of the user's willingness to migrate between platforms. Typically, platforms have developed various tools within their regulatory frameworks which limit feedback transferability and which hence have a competition-constraining effect; see also Zsófia Tóth and others, 'Social capital creation on professional sharing economy platforms: The problems of rating dependency and the non-transferability of social capital' (2022) 14 J BusRes 450.

[81] See eg Tamar Kricheli-Katz and Tali Regev, 'How Many Cents on the Dollar? Women and Men in Product Markets' (2016) 2 Science Advances 1; Sarah K Harkness, 'Discrimination in Lending Markets: Status and the Intersections of Gender and Race' (2016) 79 Social Psychology Quarterly 81; Benjamin Edelman, and others, 'Racial Discrimination in the Sharing Economy: Evidence from a Field Experiment' (2017) 9 American Economic Journal: Applied Economics 1; Nancy Leong and Aaron Belzer, 'The New Public Accommodations: Race Discrimination in the Platform Economy' (2017) 105 Geo LJ 1271, 1319.

[82] See, amongst others, Calo and Rosenblat (n 77) 1647.

paradigm acknowledges certain degrees of self-regulation, the state should have enough instruments at its disposal to supervise market practice and – whenever justified for policy reasons – intervene in shadow lawmaking.

This goal may be achieved, first of all, by creating mandatory elements that are to be incorporated into regulation elaborated by platforms[83] (eg certain duties that have to be included in every alpha user agreement).[84] Secondly, it is also possible to speculate about a less paternalistic approach premised on scrutiny of the rules emerging in the platform economy rather than on a direct regulation of them. The review in question may be applied ex ante (in a form of pre-approval) or ex post, by an administrative authority, courts, or private bodies vested with this competence by the state. This approach may also take the form of 'certification' of rules produced by platforms, which would officially confirm their quality and fairness towards the general public (by state agencies or self-regulatory bodies).[85]

2. *Fragmentated Regulation in EU Law*

Initially, both in the EU and beyond, the responses to the emerging private regulation of platforms were the result of the 'incidental' review of contract terms based on general (not platform-specific) instruments such as the unfairness test[86] in the UCTD[87] and unconscionability.[88] The scope of application of these oversight measures was limited only to selected areas and was largely

---

83 On examples of this approach in current EU law, see V.2, below.

84 The principal rationale for this sort of intervention is twofold. First of all, the state can intervene to protect public interest (eg to reduce negative externalities and to guarantee safety and the quality of products). Secondly, it can also act paternalistically toward participants on the platform (clients and suppliers) in order to guarantee certain economic values (such as efficiency and equality of contractors). In this way, the state can both protect alpha-contractors from one another as well as provide them paternalistic treatment vis-à-vis the platform. See Cohen and Sundararajan (n 3) 120, 131–132.

85 As one of the most recent embodiments of this idea, see arts 45–48 of Regulation (EU) 2022/2065 of the European Parliament and of the Council of 19 October 2022 on a Single Market For Digital Services and amending Directive 2000/31/EC (Digital Services Act) [2022] OJ L277/1 (DSA), describing codes of conduct and crisis protocols that can be created by online platforms and, ex post, monitored and approved by the relevant authorities.

86 On unfair terms regulation as a constraint upon platforms' private regulatory power, Jacobien Rutgers, Wolf Sauter, 'Promoting Fair Private Governance in the Platform Economy: EU Competition and Contract Law Applied to Standard Terms' (2021) 23 CYELS 343, 349–357.

87 Council Directive 93/13/EEC of 5 April 1993 on unfair terms in consumer contracts [1993] OJ L95/29 (UCTD).

88 See especially the decision of the Supreme Court of Canada 26 June 2020, *Uber Technologies Inc v Heller*, 2020 SCC 16 (it must be noted, however, that the ruling is related directly to the alpha and not the beta dimension).

incidental[89] (conditioned by the matter of individual disputes decided by the courts). At the same time, there was no clear enforcement strategy behind their use on the part of national authorities – even if they had the formal ability to review platforms' ToS on their own or to initiate such a review by the courts. However, all of these solutions are incidental and are limited to individual cases in which the courts have decided to review ToS provisions. At the same time, these rulings do not arrange themselves into any coherent pattern, and it would be difficult to define a common denominator within them that could serve as a starting point for the formulation of a more generalized principle.[90] At the more granular level, the classical unfairness test was also introduced in the Data Act[91] for clauses related to the transfer and (mis)handling of data.[92]

Over time, EU law has begun to address this issue through regulations crafted directly for the platform economy. The issue was addressed for the first time by the P2B Regulation, which introduced an extensive regulation of ToS[93] used by platforms in their relations with business users.[94] Unlike the classic UCTD solution, this instrument builds on the general transparency requirement coupled with the mandated content of ToS. A similar rule was also introduced – with a much broader scope of addressees – in the DSA.[95] Although both regulations do not explicitly for oversight of the ToS of platforms, they do in fact introduce this mechanism in disguise. The obligation to include rules on alpha contracts in the ToS is not monitored per se, what is monitored is how the platform provider uses ToS. Thus, while EU law does

---

[89] See eg Babette E Boliek, 'Upgrading Unconscionability: A Common Law Ally for a Digital World' (2021) 81 Md LRev 46, 86.

[90] On the general applicability of the unfairness test in the online context, see also Caterina Gardiner, *Unfair Contract Terms in the Digital Age. The Challenge of Protecting European Consumers in the Online Marketplace* (Edward Elgar 2022) 77–135 and Irina Domurath and Hans-Wolfgang Micklitz, 'EU Digital Private Law: Tattering or New Beginning?' (2024) 20 ERCL 263, 301–304.

[91] Art 13 of Regulation (EU) 2023/2854 of the European Parliament and of the Council of 13 December 2023 on harmonised rules on fair access to and use of data and amending Regulation (EU) 2017/2394 and Directive (EU) 2020/1828 [2023] OJ L2023/2854.

[92] Moritz Hennemann, 'A Fair Share? – Data Contracts and Unfair Terms Control' in Sebastian Lohsse, Reiner Schulze and Dirk Staudenmayer (eds), *Private Law and the Data Act* (Nomos 2024).

[93] Paola Iamiceli, 'Online Platforms and the Digital Turn in EU Contract Law: Unfair Practices, Transparency and the (pierced) Veil of Digital Immunity' (2019) 15 ERCL 392, 408; Mateja Durovic and Joseph Poon, 'Consumer Vulnerability, Digital Fairness, and the European Rules on Unfair Contract Terms: What Can Be Learnt from the Case Law Against TikTok and Meta?' (2023) 46 JCP 419, 421–427.

[94] Art 3 of Regulation (EU) 2019/1150 of the European Parliament and of the Council of 20 June 2019 on promoting fairness and transparency for business users of online intermediation services [2019] OJ L186/57 (P2B Regulation).

[95] DSA, art 14(3).

not allow for oversight of the actual ToS provisions, it does regulate how the platform uses them – and thus it influences their content. Consequently, the use of both ex ante mandatory content and ex post review produce somewhat similar effects as regards the ultimate content of the transaction.

3. *Towards a Meta-regulation*

The existing instruments of shadow contract law regulation in platform economies are based on a fairly conventional view in which the function of contract law is to provide a static instrument of control for the practice of private regulation. This approach, in other words, treats state-made instruments of control, such as the UCTD, as a means of one-directional state influence over the exercise by market actors of their regulatory private power. As such, it is firmly rooted in the classical vision of contract regulation, in which the state reserves to itself the ability to monitor the content of a contract from the perspective of its compliance with the law and underlying ethical standards.[96] Although for formal reasons this paradigm is in no way obstructed in terms of its application to ToS governing beta agreements, from a regulatory policy perspective it is plainly powerless as a meaningful regulatory tool.

It seems much more convincing to think of the novel foundations for the extrinsic regulatory structure of shadow contract law (as anchored in public sovereignty and democratically-legitimized power). Some groundwork in this regard has been already done in the EU digital market law that – as discussed in the previous section – has gradually shifted its accents from the classical unfairness test based on a general clause toward a procedural approach, one ensuring the transparency of clauses.

In parallel, however, another, much more significant process has taken place in EU law. The new digital market regulations (especially the DSA) are increasingly moving back to a governance model where platforms are not just treated as the object of regulatory action but also as an invited or mandated partner in creating rules for their users.[97] This applies not only to regulation in the strict sense, but also to circular activities, such as risk assessment.[98] In this model, the platform's task is to generate regulatory content, which is

[96] On the general conceptual basis for this approach, see Hugh Collins, *Regulating Contracts* (OUP 1999) 1–12 and Aditi Bagchi, 'The Political Economy of Regulating Contract' (2014) 62 Am J Comp L 687.

[97] On this tendency, see Rachel Griffin, 'Codes of Conduct in the Digital Services Act. Functions, Benefits & Concerns' (2024) Technology & Regulation 167; Hans-Wolfgang Micklitz, 'Contract Law under Regulatory Siege – Revival of Contract Law? Standardisation, Regulation and Consent' in Stefan Grundmann and Mateusz Grochowski (eds), *European Contract Law and the Creation of Norms* (Intersentia 2021) 217–223.

[98] See further Giovanni De Gregorio and Pietro Dunn, 'The European Risk-Based Approaches: Connecting Constitutional Dots in the Digital Age' (2022) 59 CMLRev 473.

subject only to ex post supervision and possible adjustments by the state. This approach applies to a broad spectrum of regulatory activities undertaken by platforms, including shadow rules created for beta agreements.

This approach – which partially recalls the former concept of platforms as regulatory intermediaries[99] – builds on two political pillars: the assumption that platforms are epistemically and technically capable of introducing and enforcing internal rules (which is hardly debatable) and the conviction that, if properly prompted by the state, they will potentially produce regulation that corresponds with the underlying constitutional values and collective interests of platform users. Against the backdrop of the earlier conclusions on the allocation of power and the actual structure of incentives that underpin platforms' private governance,[100] the latter assumption seems more than dubious. It rests on a high degree of optimism in the effectiveness of classical regulatory instruments and in the classical theories of economic incentives. The journey of the co-regulatory schemes provided for by the DSA is, however, still at the very beginning, and it is hard to predict its future progress and development with full certainty. At the same time, co-regulatory patterns seem nonetheless the most promising perspective for effectively, and not merely ostensibly, reining in the uncontrolled creation of shadow contract rules.[101] The political and epistemic parameters of such 'regulated regulation' demands, however, a separate and much more in-depth analysis.

VI. Conclusions: Shadow Contract Law and a Regulatory Contract

Shadow contract law can hardly be seen as a novel problem per se. The formation of parallel regulatory systems is a phenomenon as old as the market economy. Alternative contract regulation structures are an emanation of a centuries-old issue of economic power turned into political (regulatory) capacity. In the case of private regulation by platforms, however, the essence of the problem stems from the scale and specific forms of this phenomenon. With the previous observations in mind, it is possible to distinguish four key areas in which shadow contract law poses significant new challenges for legal theory and for digital market regulation.

---

[99] See Christoph Busch, 'Self-Regulation and Regulatory Intermediation in the Platform Economy' in Marta Cantero Gamito and Hans-Wolfgang Micklitz (eds), *The Role of the EU in Transnational Legal Ordering: Standards, Contracts and Codes* (Edward Elgar 2019) with further references.

[100] See especially sections IV.3–IV.4, above.

[101] In a similar vein, see also Möslein (n 4) 315–319, with further illustrations of this idea in current EU law.

First, the regulation of contracts by digital platforms is based on a much stronger concentration of economic and regulatory power on the side of the platforms themselves as compared to the parties to beta contracts. This allocation of power differs quite markedly from many conventional cases of private regulation, in which the ability to create rules is more cooperative in nature. The different distribution of power in the platform economy leads to an almost completely centralized regulation of beta relationships, through ToS. At the same time, the participation of users themselves in the creation of regulatory content is reduced to strictly limited spheres, largely subject to control by the platforms.

Second, as a consequence of this distribution of regulatory power, the platform's internal governance architecture lacks strong control instruments to ensure the objectivity of rules created for beta contracts. These rules are overwhelmingly created in the interest of the platforms, while at the same time possible corrective mechanisms (such as regulatory competition over regulatory design) prove largely ineffective. Admittedly, there are strong economic reasons incentivizing platforms to create effective and well-functioning rules for beta contracts. Internal regulatory design is part of the platforms' business model, and its effectiveness is an essential condition fostering customer trust and allowing them to build horizontal relationships within the platform. However, neither of these mechanisms guarantees that beta contracts pursue the central values of contract law, especially autonomy and equality. Shadow contract law is inherently regulatory – and its goals are directly subordinated to platforms' profit maximization.

This opens up – thirdly – the question of creating other mechanisms to limit and control how platforms create private regulation. So far, the piecemeal answers provided by private law have relied heavily on the classic paradigm of contract regulation, in which the state creates and enforces instruments that allow for ex post control of the content of contracts in terms of their compliance with the law and ethical standards. These instruments allow, however, only a selective monitoring of the terms, usually against the background of specific individual disputes between the platform and its users. In contrast, they do not allow for a systemic response to the general problems that may be raised by the regulatory beta design of contracts as applied by individual platforms. Rather, many of these issues relate to a collective dimension (eg the allocation of benefits and risks within the beta contractor community) and are thus very difficult to grasp from the perspective of classical contract control instruments.

This, in turn, raises the fourth central area of concern. Specifically, there exists a need to conceptualize a new regulatory approach capable of capturing the organizational (structural) dimension of the alpha contracts on which online platforms base their regulatory models.

Part 2

Enforcing Platforms Rules – Horizontal Perspective

Enforcement of Platform Private Regulation and EU Consumer Law

Marta Cantero Gamito[*]

I. Introduction

It is widely acknowledged that platforms hold significant regulatory authority, influencing not only digital governance but also reinterpreting the very foundations of contractual relations. Large online platforms operate in a context defined by two competing forces. On the one hand, they are private entities, in principle free to define their terms of engagement. On the other, their expansive reach has raised questions about their quasi-public role and the critical responsibilities that this role begets. The European Union (EU) has been at the forefront of responding to these digital behemoths. In doing so, the EU legislature initially sought to balance platforms' operational autonomy with the primary requirements of consumer protection, competition, and personal data protection laws.

Central to the EU's response has been the recognition that platforms, especially during the early days of the platform economy, have blurred the conventional lines of regulatory domains, ie the public-private distinction. Moreover platforms' influence expands across sectors, which requires a holistic

[*] Unless otherwise indicated, all internet links were last accessed on 11 September 2024.

approach to governance. Such an approach demands a reevaluation of the very nature of regulatory analysis in the digital domain. Not only should it encompass rulemaking, it also triggers novel considerations in compliance and enforcement mechanisms.[1] Accordingly, the role of digital platforms, arguably that of non-state regulators in the digital realm, underlines a recalibration of the boundaries between public and private regulatory spheres. A critical question arises: Do digital platforms serve as mere alternatives to state regulatory mechanisms or do they operate in tandem, complementing state-driven frameworks?

EU digital policy and regulation, with the complex system of the rules applicable to these phenomena, embodies this dialectic. Dedicated legislative instruments such as the Digital Services Act (Regulation (EU) 2022/2065, DSA) and the Digital Markets Act (Regulation (EU) 2022/1925, DMA) exemplify the EU's attempt to harmonize *platform self-regulation* with overarching public regulations, aiming for a synergetic rather than antagonistic relationship.[2] At the same time, consumer law, traditionally aimed at addressing asymmetries in bargaining power and information between traders and consumers, now deals with challenges posed by platforms' distinctive position.[3] The emphasis has been on enhancing transparency and ensuring fairness in platforms' terms of service.[4]

In this context, political scientists, constitutional theorists, and other scholars of governance have been studying the efforts of states to govern under technological complexity, with a focus mainly on the democratic compatibility of the political and regulatory role of technology.[5] Arguably, the hegemony of platform-created rules in the contemporary landscape mirrors the trajectory of transnational private regulation (TPR), shaped, to a significant extent,

---

[1] Robert Gorwa, 'The Platform Governance Triangle: Conceptualising the Informal Regulation of Online Content' (2019) 8(2) Internet Policy Review <DOI: 10.14763/2019.2.1407>.

[2] It is essential to acknowledge that many of the legal acts discussed in this chapter, such as the DSA, operate with broader categorizations of markets beyond consumers. These rules are not strictly consumer-specific but instead aim to create a more comprehensive framework that addresses the complexities of the platform economy, where the boundaries between consumers, traders, and platform are often blurred.

[3] Christoph Busch and others, 'The Rise of the Platform Economy: A New Challenge for EU Consumer Law?' (2016) 5 EuCML 3.

[4] Mateusz Grochowski, 'From Contract Law to Online Speech Governance' (*Verfassungsblog*, 18 May 2023) <https://verfassungsblog.de/contract-speech/> accessed 23 August 2024.

[5] Julie E Cohen, 'The Regulatory State in the Information Age' in Julie E Cohen (ed), *Between Truth and Power: The Legal Constructions of Informational Capitalism* (OUP 2019); Roger Brownsword, *Law, Technology and Society: Reimagining the Regulatory Environment* (Routledge 2020); Giovanni De Gregorio, *Digital Constitutionalism in Europe: Reframing Rights and Powers in the Algorithmic Society* (CUP 2022), to mention a few.

by the perceived inadequacies of traditional regulatory frameworks in a rapidly globalizing world.[6] The emergence of these platforms, particularly in the last three decades, highlights a shift from conventional state-centered regulatory paradigms to a more decentralized form of digital governance.[7] Not unlike the transition from the regulatory state to regulatory capitalism, the digital realm has experienced a metamorphosis in its regulatory *foci* – moving from primarily state-driven oversight to a complex blend of platform self-regulation and external directives.[8] However, the genesis and maturation of platform rule-making cannot be isolated from broader systemic underpinnings. This chapter is an attempt to identify the conditions giving rise to platform private regulation (PPR) to examine how it interacts with the enforcement of consumer law.

Similar to the factors contributing to the rise of TPR as identified by Cafaggi,[9] Section II describes how the evolution of platform governance to a quasi-regulator status is contingent on an array of institutional, economic, and socio-political drivers. Section III examines the interactions between PPR and the enforcement of consumer law, focusing on the enforceability of PPR, coordination, and mechanisms for sanctions. Section IV concludes. The chapter argues that the EU legal framework, in particular the DSA, incorporates PPR through a process of proceduralization or 'administrativization' of substantive law, which ultimately impacts the enforcement of consumer law at the domestic level and supports the need for further empirical research to define roles and responsibilities between public and private actors in the economy.

II. Drivers and Patterns of Platform Private Regulation

1. *Need for Regulation and Harmonization*

During the 1990s and early 2000s, online marketplaces such as Amazon or eBay were seen as digital utopias, producing a domain where users were able to engage in exchanges seemingly without interference by the platforms themselves. However, for those new businesses, it was also an open field for the redefinition of internet governance.[10] In a realm with limited jurisdictional

[6] Fabrizio Cafaggi, 'New Foundations of Transnational Private Regulation' (2011) 38 JLS 20.

[7] Siobhán O'Mahony and Fabrizio Ferraro, 'The Emergence of Governance in an Open Source Community' (2007) 50 Academy of Management Journal 1079.

[8] Natasha Tusikov, *Chokepoints. Global Private Regulation on the Internet* (UCalP 2016).

[9] Cafaggi (n 6).

[10] Lee A Bygrave, *Internet Governance by Contract* (OUP 2015); Matthias C Kettemann, *The Normative Order of the Internet: A Theory of Rule and Regulation Online* (OUP 2020).

and legal boundaries, they harnessed the power to reshape conventional regulatory dynamics.[11] This era, echoing Zuckerberg's mantra 'move fast and break things',[12] saw platforms transition from 'mere connectors' to the engineers of the rules in cyberspace. In these early stages, the lack of robust rules or the unsuccessful application of existing ones for online platforms led to these companies establishing their own legal frameworks, often contained in their Terms of Service (ToS).[13] This self-imposed regulatory framework spanned several layers – from technological structures, like codes and norms, to societal standards like reputation systems.[14] Yet the absence of concrete state rules for the online world was substantial. Even attempts at implementing regulatory structures were frustrated by factors like the complex nature of online relationships and the borderless operations of platforms. Acknowledging these challenges, the early 2000s witnessed the introduction of legislative frameworks such as the Digital Millennium Copyright Act (DMCA) and section 230 of the 1996 Communications Decency Act (CDA) in the US, or the 2000 E-Commerce Directive (Directive 2000/31/EC) in the EU. These rules were aimed at protecting creative works and safeguarding online freedom, but they, too, met with their share of contestation and challenges.

In the 2000s sharing economy platforms emerged and surged in popularity. Platforms like Airbnb or Uber were not just service providers; they embodied a departure from traditional norms.[15] Similar to other regimes of transnational private regulation, platform regulation was a reaction to international legislative fragmentation,[16] resulting even in the *standardization* of certain platform practices, such as content moderation.[17] Platform standardization refers here to the setting of standards by platforms themselves which, though not necessarily of a technical nature, prescribe the procedures for platforms' operations.[18] During this period, platforms evolved into regulatory agents, prompt-

---

[11] Orly Lobel, 'The Law of the Platform' (2016) 101 Minn LRev 87.

[12] Jonathan Taplin, *Move Fast and Break Things: How Facebook, Google, and Amazon Have Cornered Culture and What It Means For All Of Us* (Pan Macmillan 2017).

[13] Luca Belli and Jamila Venturini, 'Private Ordering and the Rise of Terms of Service as Cyber-Regulation' (2016) 5(4) Internet Policy Review <DOI: 10.14763/2016.4.441>.

[14] Robert Gorwa, 'What Is Platform Governance?' (2019) 22 Information, Communication & Society 854; Heloise Berkowitz and Antoine Souchaud, '(Self-)Regulation of Sharing Economy Platforms Through Partial Meta-Organizing' (2019) 159 J Bus Ethics 961; Rotem Medzini, 'Enhanced Self-Regulation: The Case of Facebook's Content Governance' (2022) 24 New Media & Society 2227.

[15] Marta Cantero Gamito, 'Regulation.Com. Self-Regulation and Contract Governance in the Platform Economy: A Research Agenda' (2017) 9 EJLS 53.

[16] Compare Cafaggi (n 6).

[17] Marta Cantero Gamito, 'Platform Content Standardization' (*TechReg Chronicle*, 15 June 2022).

[18] Cantero Gamito (n 17).

ing states to similarly expand their law enforcement capabilities in response to this transformation.[19]

Naturally, the (legislative and policy) trust in platforms as regulatory intermediaries was not without complications, and the self-regulatory power of platforms soon showed its limitations.[20] While platforms banned actions like harassment, consumer law enforcement in the platform-mediated economy remained a challenge. The operational secrecy of algorithm-driven rules, coupled with the monopolistic tendencies of big platforms, raised concerns about fundamental rights and the very nature of public values.[21] Consequently, legislation evolved, with the EU taking the lead to address emerging challenges by establishing rules that aspire to impact platforms' practices globally. Prominent examples are the General Data Protection Regulation (Regulation (EU) 2016/679, GDPR) and more recently the DSA, as both attempted to increase transparency and accountability for platforms' practices by establishing rules to ensure, for example, clear consent mechanisms and disclosures about data processing and content moderation, together with a substantial system of penalties to deter platforms from abusing their users' data. However, as these rules came about in the EU and beyond, the regulatory landscape became more complex, resulting in internal regulatory fragmentation and insufficient enforcement.

2. *Weaknesses in Enforcement*

Notwithstanding the above, it was not solely the lack of applicable legal frameworks that facilitated an increased role of online platforms as regulators. Consumer law has not only proven to be relevant within the platform economy but has, arguably, served as the primary regulatory framework governing the relationship between platforms and their users before the creation of dedicated legal frameworks for platforms.[22] The Court of Justice of the European Union (CJEU) reinforced this premise by acknowledging the application of the Unfair Contract Terms Directive (Directive 93/13/EEC, UCTD) to Amazon's Terms of Service (ToS).[23] This judgment highlighted that the contractual rela-

[19] Christoph Busch, 'Self-Regulation and Regulatory Intermediation in the Platform Economy' in Marta Cantero Gamito and Hans Wolfgang Micklitz (eds), *The Role of the EU in Transnational Legal Ordering* (Edward Elgar 2020).

[20] Orla Lynskey, 'Regulating "Platform Power"' [2017] LSE Law, Society and Economy Working Papers 1/2017; Kate Klonick, 'The New Governors: The People, Rules, and Processes Governing Online Speech' (2018) 131 Harv LRev 1599.

[21] José van Dijck, Thomas Poell and Martijn de Waal, *The Platform Society*, vol 1 (OUP 2018); José van Dijck, 'Governing Digital Societies: Private Platforms, Public Values' (2020) 36 CLS Rev 105377.

[22] Grochowski (n 4).

[23] CJEU 28 July 2016, C-191/15 *Verein für Konsumenteninformation,* ECLI:EU:C:2016:612.

tionship between a platform and its user is fundamentally a consumer contract, thereby falling within the scope of consumer law unless the user's activities become predominantly professional, as clarified in the judgment in *Schrems*.[24] Yet the institutional apparatus for cross-border consumer law enforcement has not always delivered, which resulted in an insufficient application of consumer protection rights and remedies in the platform economy.[25]

To keep pace with technology developments as well as to react to the rule-making activity of platforms, the European Commission announced that in the framework of the New Consumer Agenda, a fitness check would be undertaken to assess digital fairness in EU consumer law with the aim of ensuring consistent fairness across online and offline domains.[26] The rules emerging from such review are expected to clarify the suitability of horizontal consumer law to tackle the challenges of the digital era and to ensure alignment with existing and forthcoming rules, such as the DSA or the EU Artificial Intelligence Act (AI Act).[27]

Certainly, consumer law plays a critical role in safeguarding users of digital services. It can help to counterbalance the inherent power disparity between online platforms and their users.[28] However, in practice, the concurrence of different bodies – eg consumer and data protection authorities – introduces complexities. A detailed analysis of the reactions following BEUC's external alert on TikTok offers insights into the overlapping domains of EU law and the jurisdictional conflict of enforcement agencies.[29]

Both the EU consumer *acquis* and the GDPR offer different enforcement avenues and distinct interpretations of what an enforcement breach entails. The enforcement procedures that were triggered following infringements of EU regulations by TikTok serve as a major example of this divergence. Identical

---

24 Grochowski (n 4).

25 Alexandre Biard, 'The Age of Consumer Law Enforcement in the European Union: High Hopes or Wishful Thinking?' [2023] EJRR 1.

26 Communication from the Commission to the European Parliament and the Council, New Consumer Agenda Strengthening consumer resilience for sustainable recovery, COM/ 2020/696 final.

27 Regulation (EU) 2024/1689 of the European Parliament and of the Council of 13 June 2024 laying down harmonised rules on artificial intelligence and amending Regulations (EC) 300/2008, (EU) 167/2013, (EU) 168/2013, (EU) 2018/858, (EU) 2018/1139 and (EU) 2019/2144 and Directives 2014/90/EU, (EU) 2016/797 and (EU) 2020/1828 (Artificial Intelligence Act) [2024] OJ L2024/1689 (AI Act).

28 Christine Riefa, 'Consumer Protection on Social Media Platforms: Tackling the Challenges of Social Commerce' in Tatiana-Eleni Synodinou and others (eds), *EU Internet Law in the Digital Era: Regulation and Enforcement* (Springer International 2020).

29 Marta Cantero Gamito and Hans-W Micklitz, *Too much or too little? Assessing the Consumer Protection Cooperation (CPC) Network in the protection of consumers and children on TikTok* (16 February 2023) <https://www.beuc.eu/reports/assessing-consumer-protection-cooperation-cpc-network-protection-consumers-and-children>.

business operations (eg misleading practices to obtain consent from minors) can simultaneously be covered by consumer protection, data protection, e-commerce, and audiovisual rules. Naturally, an increase in applicable regulations intensifies potential conflicts. Yet even within consumer law, different national bodies might opt for either the Unfair Contract Terms Directive (UCTD, Directive 93/13/EEC) or the Unfair Commercial Practices Directive (UCPD, Directive 2005/29) to address similar business operations. Such decisions are often shaped by the agency's past experiences and understanding of the law in question.[30] For example, when it comes to the legal validity of contracts for processing personal data, especially as relates to minors, (some) data protection authorities argue that they lack the mandate to assess contractual validity.[31]

While consumer groups have the competence to initiate collective actions against practices infringing data subjects' rights by means of unfair commercial practices and unfair contract terms, consumer protection authorities do not have the competence to administratively oversee compliance with the GDPR or to impose penalties for its breaches.[32] The responsibilities vested in data protection authorities (DPAs) under the GDPR (GDPR, arts 51ff) undermine other national bodies' competence to enforce the GDPR. For instance, in Germany, proceedings initiated by the German Federal Cartel Office (FCO) against Meta culminated in the interruption of data processing as presented in Facebook's ToS. The FCO identified an abuse of dominance in obtaining consent for data processing. The authority of the FCO to scrutinize compliance with the GDPR can be assessed only in relation to an abuse of a dominant position requiring cooperation and consultation with the designated data supervisory authority.[33] As such, within the remit of competition law, a competition body may assess GDPR compliance as a secondary matter. Currently, the jurisdiction of entities other than DPAs in enforcing the GDPR is confined, and secondary supervisory bodies cannot reach beyond the primary DPA by approaching the judiciary unless specific conditions are met.[34]

To facilitate enforcement, new rules aim to increase cooperation mechanisms between different DPAs in the event of cross-border infringements of the GDPR.[35] As a result, the different sector-specific rules, coupled with

[30] Fabrizio Cafaggi and Hans-W Micklitz, *New Frontiers of Consumer Protection: The Interplay between Private and Public Enforcement* (Intersentia 2009).

[31] Irish Data Protection Commission, Decision on Meta (DPC Inquiry Reference: IN-18-5-5) 31 December 2022, see paras 4.13 and 4.16.

[32] CJEU 28 April 2022, C-319/20 *Meta Platforms Ireland*, ECLI:EU:C:2022:322.

[33] CJEU 4 July 2023, C-252/21 *Meta v Bundeskartellamt*, ECLI:EU:C:2023:537.

[34] CJEU 15 June 2021, C-645/19 *Facebook Ireland and others v Gegevensbeschermingsautoriteit*, ECLI:EU:C:2021:483.

[35] Proposal for a Regulation of the European Parliament and of the Council laying down additional procedural rules relating to the enforcement of Regulation (EU) 2016/679, COM/2023/348 final.

sector-specific enforcement agencies, pose challenges, especially in a context of diverse national enforcing bodies with different procedural rules, which significantly impairs the potential of applicable regulatory frameworks.

Furthermore, not only the overlapping scopes of application and enforcement jurisdictions led to an insufficient application of EU consumer law. An identified suboptimal operation of mechanisms within the EU CPC Regulation[36] questions the capacity of consumer protection rules and consumer law enforcement to protect consumers in digital environments.[37] The shortcomings in the application of the different regimes, not to mention the problem of regulatory capture in the enforcement of the GDPR,[38] arguably contributed to the increase of the regulatory power and authority of platforms.

3. *Technology Drivers – Code is Law?*

The interplay between law and technology has always been a delicate balance. Lessig's aphorism *Code is Law* underscores the idea that the architectural design of digital systems (the code) can regulate behavior similarly to traditional legal frameworks.[39] As such, the relationship between law and technology can arguably be seen as a binomial in which their interaction operates in a constant flux, where the assignation of different values to each element results in manifold possible outputs that depend on the need(s) for regulation and the agenda of legislators.

One of the most evident examples of this relationship is content moderation *in* and *by* digital platforms. Since online platforms struggle with the responsibility of moderating content, they face a complex web of jurisdictional standards, particularly reconciling differences between, for example, the EU and the

[36] Regulation (EU) 2017/2394 of the European Parliament and of the Council of 12 December 2017 on cooperation between national authorities responsible for the enforcement of consumer protection laws and repealing Regulation (EC) 2006/2004, OJ L345/1 (CPC Regulation).

[37] Marta Cantero Gamito, 'Do Too Many Cooks Spoil the Broth? How EU Law Underenforcement Allows TikTok's Violations of Minors' Rights' (2023) 46 JCP 281.

[38] For example, the Irish Data Protection Commission (DPC) handling of complaints against Facebook has drawn significant criticism. Despite numerous complaints and potential breaches of the GDPR by Facebook, the DPC's investigations have often been lengthy and resulted in relatively modest fines compared to the maximum penalties allowed under the GDPR. In some cases, it took years for the DPC to issue decisions, which has led to frustration among privacy advocates and other EU data protection authorities. See, for instance, Sebastian Golla, 'Is Data Protection Law Growing Teeth? The Current Lack of Sanctions in Data Protection Law and Administrative Fines under the GDPR' (2017) 8 JIPITEC 70; Siyao Li and Abraham L Newman, 'Over the Shoulder Enforcement in European Regulatory Networks: The Role of Arbitrage Mitigation Mechanisms in the General Data Protection Regulation.' (2022) 29 J Eur Pub Pol 10, 1698–1720.

[39] Lawrence Lessig, *Code and Other Laws of Cyberspace* (Basic Books 1999).

USA.[40] These standards are intertwined with politically charged issues, resulting in divergent perspectives on how platforms should exercise their moderation discretion.[41] Platforms find themselves in the position of moderating content that can often be politically or socially disruptive, leading to accusations of bias or censorship. The debate often revolves around the question of whether platforms should be viewed as holding moderating power, which comes with associated liabilities, or simply as neutral conduits. The erosion of trust in both the platforms and in the very institutions that seek to regulate them further complicates the matter. High-profile public disagreements, such as between Breton (EU Commission) and Musk (Twitter, now X),[42] or concerns as to whether TikTok is an instrument for Chinese Communist Party surveillance[43] highlight the challenges in finding common ground.

The DSA requires online platforms to disclose their moderation decisions and to provide a statement of reasons for content removal or restricted availability of user-generated content (art 17). These statements of reasons (SoR) are publicly available at the platform-funded *DSA Transparency Database*, in line with DSA, art 24(5). To date, more than 12 billion SoRs have been incorporated into the database since its launch in September 2023.[44] To comply with this obligation, the European Commission has set a series of technical specifications for the API (Application Programming Interface) used by platforms for reporting decisions.[45] These specifications outline how platforms should report these decisions, and as such they can be seen as an example of 'code is law', as effected by legislators. Accordingly, platforms are now in a position where they

---

[40] Philip L Verveer, 'Content Moderation in the United States and Europe: Similar Values, Different Approaches' (2023) M-RCBG Associate Working Paper No. 197; Daphne Keller and Paddy Leerssen, 'Facts and Where to Find Them: Empirical Research on Internet Platforms and Content Moderation' in Joshua A Tucker and Nathaniel Persily (eds), *Social Media and Democracy* (CUP 2020).

[41] Theresa Josephine Seipp and others, 'Dealing with Opinion Power in the Platform World: Why We Really Have to Rethink Media Concentration Law' (2023) 11 Digital Journalism 1542.

[42] Julia Tar, 'EU Commissioner Breton reminds X owner Musk of EU digital rulebook compliance ahead of Trump debate' (*EuroActiv*, 13 August 2024) <https://www.euractiv.com/section/platforms/news/eu-commissioner-breton-reminds-x-owner-musk-of-eu-digital-rulebook-compliance-ahead-of-trump-debate/>.

[43] Albert Fox Cahn, 'America Lost the Plot With TikTok' (*The Atlantic*, 29 April 2024) <https://www.theatlantic.com/technology/archive/2024/04/tiktok-ban-red-herring/678234/>.

[44] <https://transparency.dsa.ec.europa.eu/>.

[45] For a knowledgeable analysis of the practical implications of these technical specifications, see Daphne Keller, Rushing to Launch the EU's Platform Database Experiment (*The Center for Internet and Society Blog*, 16 July 2023) <https://cyberlaw.stanford.edu/blog/2023/07/rushing-launch-eus-platform-database-experiment>.

have to operationalize legal principles through code.[46] By defining the technical parameters, the Commission essentially dictates the technological processes that platforms must adopt in their moderation reporting operations. This does not only shape the submissions to the database; it also potentially reshapes how platforms approach content moderation, influencing the algorithms, the user interfaces, user experiences, and public access to information. As such, the API specifications (technical code) become a tool for law enforcement.

4. *Distributional Effects – From the Brussels Effect to the Big Tech Effect*

Over the years, the so-called 'Brussels Effect' has epitomized the EU's global regulatory clout.[47] Its influence was palpable when global corporations adapted their practices to comply with the EU's GDPR.[48] However, we are witnessing the rise of a new paradigm, the 'Big Tech Effect'. Large platforms have the resources and global reach to not only comply with stringent regulations but also to shape them to their advantage, effectively setting new industry standards that smaller competitors may struggle to meet. This regulatory burden can entrench the market power of Big Tech as it can create barriers to entry for new firms and perpetuate a concentration of power within a few dominant players. Moreover, platforms' operational decisions – shaped by the need to comply with regulations or preempt further regulatory scrutiny – can lead to distributional effects that extend beyond the marketplace. This was illustrated, for example, by Apple's move to prioritize user privacy in its iOS 14, by limiting third-party tracking. The decision had implications beyond the EU, influencing the dynamics of online advertising worldwide and prompting marketers to reconsider their strategies.[49] Likewise, Facebook's (now Meta's) internal content moderation policies have not only defined global online discourse but also prompted debates on freedom of speech and the role of platforms in guiding public discourse.[50]

In such scenarios, where Big Tech's decisions are often echoed globally, we are witnessing a shift from a world shaped predominantly by traditional

---

[46] Chris Marsden, 'Platform Law in Europe: Combatting Digital Harms through Co-Regulation' (2022) 15 JLE 34.

[47] Anu Bradford, 'The Brussels Effect' (2012) 107 NwU LRev 1; Anu Bradford, *The Brussels Effect: How the European Union Rules the World* (OUP 2022).

[48] Christopher Kuner, 'Extraterritoriality and regulation of international data transfers in EU data protection law' (2015) 5(4) IDPL 235. See also Christopher Kuner, 'The Internet and the Global Reach of EU Law' (2017) in Marise Cremona and Joanne Scott (eds), *EU Law Beyond EU Borders: The Extraterritorial Reach of EU Law* (OUP 2019).

[49] Casey Newton, 'Apple's Move to Make Advertising Harder on iOS 14 is Part of a Trend' (*The Verge*, 27 August 2020) <https://www.theverge.com/interface/2020/8/27/21402744/apple-idfa-facebook-fight-ads-advertising>.

[50] Tarleton Gillespie, *Custodians of the Internet* (YUP 2018); Klonick (n 20).

regulations to one dominated by corporate policies.[51] The result is greater market concentration and a redistribution of market power in favor of larger platforms. The size of the global userbases and economic power effectively enable large platforms to set de facto standards.[52] As such, the Big Tech effect suggests that the operational policies and compliance strategies of dominant tech firms reciprocally influence global norms and practices.[53]

Furthermore, this dynamic interplay carries significant distributional effects, impacting market entrants, consumer welfare, and the balance of power among states, corporations, and citizens. When EU rules like the GDPR, the DSA, or the DMA entered into force, they had the potential to recalibrate the market, affording protections that may favor smaller entities or enhancing consumer rights at the expense of corporate flexibility.[54] Also, the distributional effects are not limited to the market; they also permeate societal and political dimensions. Big Tech's compliance with EU regulations often translates into a global change in their operations, influencing the information and speech flow and potentially leading to 'splinternets', where online experiences are fragmented by jurisdictional compliance[55] and where access to services and information is increasingly dictated by regional legal frameworks and the platforms' interpretation of those laws.

Thus, while the new wave of rules was designed to further protect consumers and recalibrate the market, their distributional effects can have the unintended consequence of reinforcing the market power of dominant platforms, thus perpetuating a digital divide between larger firms having the resources to influence legislation and smaller entities struggling to survive given the existing barriers to entry and rules largely tailored to competitors.

III. Enforcement of Platform Private Regulation and EU Consumer Law

The transformation prompted by the private regulatory architecture of platform private regulation required a reevaluation of its foundational and analyt-

---

[51] Shoshana Zuboff, *The Age of Surveillance Capitalism: The Fight for a Human Future at the New Frontier of Power* (Public Affairs 2019).

[52] Natali Helberger, Jo Pierson and Thomas Poell, 'Governing Online Platforms: From Contested to Cooperative Responsibility' (2018) 34 The Information Society 1.

[53] Blayne Haggart, Kathryn Henne and Natasha Tusikov (eds), *Information, Technology and Control in a Changing World: Understanding Power Structures in the 21st Century* (Springer International 2019).

[54] Yane Svetiev, *Experimentalist Competition Law and the Regulation of Markets* (Hart 2020).

[55] David Kaye, *Speech Police: The Global Struggle to Govern the Internet* (Columbia Global Reports 2019) 113.

ical elements. The discourse shifted from the lens of the regulatory state to the broader picture of regulatory capitalism.[56] As seen above, such transformation transcended mere rulemaking, reaching also the layers of compliance and enforcement. The increasing influence of non-state actors in regulatory paradigms, including in both domestic and transnational arenas, does not overcome the distinction between the private and public spheres. Instead, it refuels a renewed examination into their respective roles and the ever-evolving demarcations between them. A predicament thus emerges: Should we perceive these online platforms – ultimately, transnational private corporations – as substitutes for traditional legal rules and institutions, or should we envision them as complementing, in a layered architecture, nation-states at their grassroots? The resolution of this quandary is contingent on the perceived interaction between the public and the private law domains.

In 'New Foundations of Transnational Private Regulation', Cafaggi documents the reallocation of rule-making power between public and private actors, the historical reasons and incentives that explained such a power shift, and the resulting competition between public and private regulatory bodies.[57] In the contemporary setting of digital regulation, the foundational framework of TPR proposed by Cafaggi offers valuable insights into the nuanced relationship between platform private regulation and the broader public regulatory structure and specifically addresses how that relationship operates at the level of enforcement.

Often, domestic judicial and administrative authorities enforce transnational regulation through a framework of vertical complementarity, where public legislation complements the transnational private regime.[58] However, as also seen above, one of the reasons explaining the emergence of TPR is the lack of effectiveness by state institutions in implementing transnational regimes.[59] Domestic enforcement, Cafaggi argues, tends to follow the interests of individual states or litigants in courts, which may not align with the goals of transnational bodies.[60] Yet despite the conflict between domestic and transnational objectives and despite the shortcomings of domestic enforcement, national courts and administrative bodies are still critical in the enforcement of TPR.[61] The issue to consider

---

[56] Petter Törnberg, 'How Platforms Govern: Social Regulation in Digital Capitalism' (2023) 10 Big Data & Society 20539517231153808.

[57] Cafaggi (n 6).

[58] Cafaggi (n 6).

[59] Cafaggi (n 6).

[60] Fabrizio Cafaggi, 'Chapter 2: Enforcing Transnational Private Regulation: Models and Patterns' in Fabrizio Cafaggi (ed), *Enforcement of Transnational Regulation* (Edward Elgar 2012).

[61] Cafaggi (n 6).

here is that, in the face of vertical institutional complementarity, TPR responds with innovative tools to overcome existing limitations.[62]

From an institutional perspective of complementarity, 'at the transnational level the effectiveness of private regulation strongly depends on the credibility and legitimacy of public institutions, including that of the judiciary both at domestic and international level'.[63] The delegation of regulatory power has traditionally been ring-fenced by constitutional limitations to ensure a balance of power and prevent overreach.[64] However, when it comes to digital platforms, the rationale for this delegation shifts. As seen above, platforms are believed to possess a larger capacity for enforcing their self-crafted rules, stemming from their granular understanding of their operational ecosystems. An example of this is the DSA's approach to regulating terms and conditions – transitioning from self-regulation to enforced platform private regulation. This move highlights the vertical and horizontal complementarity between private governance by platforms and public regulatory oversight. This complementarity seeks to ensure that rulemaking and enforcement are not solely at the discretion of platforms but operate within a framework that aligns with the public interest.

1. *Enforceability of Private Rules*

The enforcement of platform-created rules, or PPR, in a multilevel and multinational context such as the EU is particularly complicated. PPR must align with national private law and EU consumer law. For platform rules to be enforceable, they must comply with the legal framework of the jurisdiction in which the platform operates, leading to legal pluralism (and legal fragmentation). Since platforms typically use terms of service, user agreements, and policies to establish their regulatory regimes,[65] the enforceability of these rules depends on their compliance with statutory private law provisions. For instance, in the Netherlands, platforms must observe contract law and consumer law if they wish to enforce their rules under Dutch law.[66] In a case involving Airbnb's fee structure,[67] the Dutch Supreme Court examined the compliance of Airbnb's fees

[62] Cafaggi (n 6).

[63] Cafaggi (n 6) 41.

[64] Jacco Bomhoff and Anne Meuwese, 'The Meta-Regulation of Transnational Private Regulation' (2011) 38 JLS 138; Deirdre Curtin and Linda Senden, 'Public Accountability of Transnational Private Regulation: Chimera or Reality' (2011) 38 JLS 163.

[65] Edoardo Celeste, 'Terms of Service and Bills of Rights: New Mechanisms of Constitutionalisation in the Social Media Environment?' (2019) 33 Int'l RevL Computers & Tech 122.

[66] See Eric Tjong Tjin Tai, Paul Verbruggen and Ruşen Öncü, 'Private Law Regulation of Online Platforms in the Netherlands', in this volume, 273.

[67] Dutch Supreme Court 19 November 2021, 21/00168 *Airbnb*, ECLI:NL:HR:2021:1725, NJ 2021/396, annotated by TFE Tjong Tjin Tai.

with consumer protection legislation and, in particular, the UCTD.[68] Similarly, in Germany, civil law claims against platforms' practices and ToS were interpreted in the light of the UCTD.[69]

Moreover, domestic judicial review is crucial in ensuring the enforceability of platform rules. When platform participants contest decisions made under these rules, national courts review the validity and application of the PPR. In the *Booking.com* case, the Dutch Supreme Court assessed whether Booking.com's activities constituted intermediary services under Dutch law, thus impacting its obligation to participate in sectoral pension funds.[70] This ruling emphasized the importance of accurately defining the nature of platform services so as to determine their regulatory obligations. The Court concluded that Booking.com's business model – facilitating bookings and earning a commission – qualified it as an intermediary, therefore subjecting it to specific regulatory requirements.[71] Domestic judicial review has indeed been instrumental in interpreting the application of the E-Commerce Directive. In this way, the enforceability of platform rules or PPR is closely tied to the nuanced distinctions between active and passive hosting. Italian courts have provided significant guidance for domestic application and, taking into account rulings by the CJEU, the Italian Supreme Court unified the different interpretations under a list of 'interference indicators' to better facilitate a case-by-case assessment.[72]

2. *Coordination*

There are important differences in the enforcement of PPR by public (domestic and supranational) and private (transnational) actors and institutions. In terms of rationales, public enforcement is often general and territorially-based, whereas private regulation is largely functionally-based.[73] The result of this legal plurality is the existence of overlaps, which necessarily requires strong coordination.

There is not one single PPR regime; rather, there are as many regimes as there are private actors. The challenge lies not only in ensuring coordination between public institutions – such as courts and agencies – and private enforcement structures, but also among them. We highlighted above the coordination problems derived from the TikTok case under the CPC Regulation as a paradigmatic example of coordination failure between domestic and suprana-

---

[68] Tjong Tjin Tai, Verbruggen and Öncü (n 66).

[69] Grochowski (n 4).

[70] Dutch Supreme Court 9 April 2021, 19/04002 *Booking.com*, ECLI:NL:HR:2021:527, NJ 2021/206, annotated by TFE Tjong Tjin Tai.

[71] See Tjong Tjin Tai, Verbruggen and Öncü (n 66).

[72] See Dianora Poletti and Federica Casarosa, 'Enforcing Platform Rights – The Italian Case Law', in this volume, 239.

[73] Cafaggi (n 60).

tional enforcement structures. A possible solution to overlapping PPRs and a lack of coordination is the establishment of a transnational framework containing implementation and procedural principles.[74] The DSA indeed follows this path and establishes a meta-regulatory framework[75] that, while aimed at ensuring compliance with EU consumer and data protection law, is, arguably, more oriented to ensuring PPR enforcement.

This shift from content to substance constitutes an important burden for monitoring not only platforms' practices but also their internal procedures. Naturally, this will increase the role (and costs) of enforcement authorities.[76] At the same time, the proceduralization of PPR increases the administrative role of private actors. An example of this is dispute resolution under the DSA. Pursuant to art 20, platforms are mandated to establish accessible and user-friendly internal mechanisms, enabling users to lodge complaints regarding content moderation decisions. These mechanisms must function transparently and with due process guarantees, such as offering timely responses and clarifying the rationale behind decisions so that users are fully informed of the grounds for actions affecting their content or accounts. Furthermore, art 18 compels platforms to put in place appeals mechanisms that allow users dissatisfied with the initial adjudication an avenue for secondary review. The DSA also contains provisions on out-of-court dispute resolution mechanisms (art 21), which require the establishment of independent, impartial, and proficient bodies accredited by Member States to adjudicate disputes.[77]

The DSA's comprehensive procedural approach to dispute resolution by platforms legitimates their role as adjudicators,[78] effectively transforming platforms into administrative bodies that manage and resolve disputes. Consequently, the main claim of this chapter is that platform regulation, broadly understood, is more likely to be experiencing a process of *administrativization* than one of con-

---

[74] Cafaggi (n 60).

[75] Christoph Busch and Vanessa Mak, 'Putting the Digital Services Act into Context: Bridging the Gap between EU Consumer Law and Platform Regulation' (2021) 10(3) EuCML 109; Nicolo Zingales, 'The DSA as a Paradigm Shift for Online Intermediaries' Due Diligence' (*Verfassungsblog*, 2 November 2022) <https://verfassungsblog.de/dsa-meta-regulation/>.

[76] Zingales (n 75).

[77] Thomas Hughes, 'Practical Considerations for Out-of-Court Dispute Settlement (ODS) under Article 21 of the EU Digital Services Act (DSA)' (*DSA Observatory*, 8 February 2024) <https://dsa-observatory.eu/2024/02/08/practical-considerations-for-out-of-court-dispute-settlement-ods-under-article-21-of-the-eu-digital-services-act-dsa/>; Pietro Ortolani, 'If You Build It, They Will Come: The DSA's "Procedure Before Substance" Approach' (*Verfassungsblog*, 7 November 2022) <https://verfassungsblog.de/dsa-build-it/>.

[78] Moritz Schram, 'Emulated Guardians: On the Practice, Politics, and Performativity of the DSA and the Oversight Board' (2023), PhD thesis, on file with the author.

stitutionalization,[79] whereby administrative law principles are applied to private regulatory entities and contract law rules to international organizations.[80]

3. *Mechanisms for Sanctions*

Another important factor in the recognition of PPR is the possibility of imposing sanctions. Here, we shall discard the idea that compliance with a platform's terms and conditions (T&C) is voluntary and that, hence, there are weaknesses in the enforcement of PPR by platforms. Network effects, the ineligibility of platform contracts, and misleading practices in obtaining consent make platform contractual frameworks the statutory framework regulating the relationships between platforms and their users. As such, platorms' sanctioning mechanisms for violations of their T&C acquire regulatory significance. This quasi-regulatory authority is controversial as it often leads to platforms acting as both regulators and adjudicators, with limited external oversight. Under the DSA, platforms are authorized to impose sanctions, but they must do so in accordance with due process guarantees established by the regulation. SoRs mandated by DSA, art 17 arguably legitimize this mandatory nature of PPR. The DSA recognizes the power of platforms to administer sanctions, for example by removing, demoting, or disabling access to illegal content (sanctions on a statutory basis) or by any other restrictions imposed on the basis of incompatibility with the platform's T&C (sanctions on a contractual basis).[81]

In this sense, platforms continue to function as regulators and regulators in their own right, often leading to conflicts between their internal enforcement mechanisms and public regulatory objectives. As a reaction to this, the DSA's meta-regulatory approach attempts to mediate these tensions by providing for a procedural framework that harmonizes public oversight and private enforcement. Thus, the DSA marks a shift towards the administrativization of platform governance, which recognizes platforms' capacity to enforce their own rules while ensuring that such enforcement operates within a broader framework of consumer protection and public interest.

The limitations associated with the enforceability of PPR contained in a contractual framework are thus overcome by self-enforcement mechanisms. At the same time, the DSA can contribute to the enforceability of consumer law in the platform economy. By stripping certain platforms of their liability exemptions under the DSA when they fail to adequately inform consumers about the identity of traders or fail to present themselves as responsible for the transaction, the DSA will (try to) ensure that platforms do not escape

---

[79] Here I am in agreement with the view of Rodrigo Vallejo on platform/private administrative law.

[80] Cafaggi (n 6).

[81] See also DSA, art 4.

liability.[82] However, it remains to be seen whether this will effectively resolve the coordination challenge in the enforcement of consumer law.

IV. Conclusion

The consolidation of PPR, which complements EU and national regulation, is an important development in platform governance but also a new challenge from the perspective of fundamental rights, particularly consumer protection. PPR represents a transfer of power and responsibility from public to private actors and institutions, and it entails a distribution of regulatory power among market players. A critical aspect of the enforcement of PPR is legal pluralism; in this context, such legal pluralism refers to (1) the existence of overlapping legal regimes that simultaneously regulate the same space and (2) more specifically, the interactions between private regulation and public law.[83] At the same time, enforcement cannot be separated from compliance.[84] Arguably, the DSA represents the organic functional interdependence between rulemaking and enforcement power. This interdependence is eventually the result of the governance structure of private regulators,[85] which highlights the necessity for independent and impartial enforcers. However, as it was conceived, the DSA does not put forward a mechanism for achieving structural separation between rule-makers and enforcers. The DSA will arguably become the procedural framework upon which statutory consumer law will be interpreted and applied. Therefore, we will have to observe the role played by administrative bodies, Digital Services Coordinators, and national courts in coordinating the application of consumer protection rules and principles in the platform economy. As it currently stands, functional separation seems impracticable.

Ultimately, the enforcement of platform-created rules within the multilevel and multinational EU highlights the central role of both private and public entities in protecting consumers. Accordingly, this evolving regulatory landscape demands a delicate balance and not easily achieved coordination of the regulatory and supervising roles of both private (platforms) and public (administrative authorities and courts) bodies. This balance is critical for main-

[82] See DSA, recital 24.

[83] Vanessa Mak, 'Pluralism in European Private Law' (2018) 20 CYELS 202; Vanessa Mak, 'New Legal Pluralism and Transnational Private Law' in Vanessa Mak (ed), *Legal Pluralism in European Contract Law* (OUP 2020).

[84] Compare Fabrizio Cafaggi and others, 'A Comparative Analysis of Transnational Private Regulation: Legitimacy, Quality, Effectiveness and Enforcement' (2014) EUI Department of Law Research Paper no 2014/145.

[85] Compare Cafaggi and others (n 84).

taining impartiality and accountability. Continuous empirical research[86] will be central to address the dynamic interdependencies between platform private regulation and public ordering.

[86] Such research would need to be supported by tangible access to platform data (DSA, art 40), which would in turn require that this access was effectively operationalized. See Svea Windwehr and Joschka Selinger, 'Can We Fix Access to Platform Data? Europe's Digital Services Act and the Long Quest for Platform Accountability and Transparency' (*Internet Policy Review*, 27 March 2024) <https://policyreview.info/articles/news/can-we-fix-access-to-platform-data> accessed 2 September 2024.

Private Regulation by Digital Platforms: The Case of Minors

Costanza Di Francesco Maesa[*]

I. Introduction

Vulnerable users, and especially minors, suffer the most significant consequences of online platforms' poor regulation and poor enforcement of applicable laws. At the EU level, an increasing number of legal measures have been adopted in recent years to protect minors online.[1] Similarly, self-regulatory initiatives aiming to improve the online environment for minors have been autonomously undertaken by online platforms.[2] However, in practice, the fundamental rights of vulnerable users' are increasingly under attack, as minors are more frequently victims of cyberbullying, sexual exploitation, and grooming. In this regard, some research has found that the systematic exposure of children to inappropriate content and commercial practices, such as persuasive design, may over the long-term have negative neurologic consequences.[3] Furthermore,

[*] Except where otherwise noted, all links were last accessed September 2023.

[1] See section II.

[2] See section III.

[3] See Gadi Lissak, 'Adverse physiological and psychological effects of screen time on children and adolescents: Literature review and case study' (2018) 164 Environ Res 149;

children may risk a potentially lifelong adverse effect as resulting from the recent phenomenon of 'datafication'[4] of childhood, ie the collection and the extensive sharing of children's personal data by digital services.[5]

To interrupt such an unacceptable trend, both the EU and online platforms are adopting new rules to protect minors online. However, some of the proposed EU acts, such as the Proposal for a Regulation on Child Sexual Abuse,[6] may pose serious risk for internet users' privacy, which is a fundamental right that must be balanced alongside other fundamental rights. In addition, the enforcement mechanisms foreseen in the proposed legislation do not seem effective.

It is for this reason that we will first investigate whether some of the recently approved or proposed EU legislation on the topic, such as the Proposal for a Regulation on Child Sexual Abuse and the Digital Services Act (II), as well as the measures taken by online platforms (III), are adequate to effectively protect minors; secondly, we will examine whether effective enforcement mechanisms have been adopted (IV). In this context, we will then try to examine whether online platforms are the most appropriate actors in terms of protecting the fundamental rights of vulnerable users (V).

II. Recent EU Legislation Enacted to Protect Minors Online

Protecting the rights of children is one of the main objectives pursued by the EU,[7] and it is a fundamental right enshrined in art 24 of the Charter of Fundamental Rights of the European Union (the Charter). The latter, in particular, explicitly states that the 'child's best interests' must be considered foremost in all actions relating to children, 'whether taken by public authorities or private institutions'.[8] Every legislative act adopted at the EU level and any

---

see also the recent advisory from the US Surgeon General Vivek Murthy, available at: <https://www.hhs.gov/sites/default/files/sg-youth-mental-health-social-media-advisory.pdf>.

[4] With the term 'datafication', we refer to the recent trend of turning almost every aspect of our life into data, which is subsequently transferred as information, which is considered a new form of value.

[5] In the same sense, see the Commission Communication 'A Digital Decade for children and youth: the new European strategy for a better internet for kids (BIK+)' [2022] COM/2022/212, 7.

[6] European Commission, 'Proposal for a Regulation laying down rules to prevent and combat child sexual abuse' [2022] COM/2022/209 final.

[7] See art 3(3) TEU: the Union 'shall promote […] solidarity between generations and protection of the rights of the child'. See also art 3(5) TEU.

[8] Charter, art 24(2). According to the Explanations relating to the Charter of Fundamental Rights [2007] OJ C303/17, art 24 is based on the Convention on the Rights of the Child of 1989, where, like the Charter, the 'best interests of the child' is considered the

decision concerning children taken on the basis of EU law must, therefore, take into primary consideration the best interests of the child, and this principle is to be equally respected in online and offline contexts.[9]

Since 2012 the EU legal framework on the protection of children online has considerably evolved, even if there is not yet a European act specifically and exclusively dedicated to protecting children online.[10] The EU legal framework concerning the protection of minors online is the result of different provisions included in different European acts regulating different matters, such as the Audiovisual Media Services Directive, the General Data Protection Regulation, and the Digital Services Act. The existing legal framework is, therefore, fragmented and risks incoherence, especially as far as its enforcement in relation to minors is concerned. An effective enforcement of the rules concerning the online protection of minors should be based on a coherent legal framework tailored to meet minors' specific online needs and peculiarities. To this end, specific trainings for law enforcement officials and for online platform's content moderators, as well as detailed rules on the distribution of tasks between the different national and EU enforcement authorities, and between state and digital platforms' competent actors need to be adopted. To generally assess whether the EU legal framework is adequate for effectively protecting children online, it is nevertheless necessary to examine the other EU acts whose provisions are aimed at protecting children online. It is in this context that the Digital Services Act and the Proposal for a Regulation on Child Sexual Abuse have recently been adopted. Due to space constraints and given the specific problems that these acts pose for the fundamental rights of children and in terms of enforcement, this contribution will focus on the provisions concerning children's protection online that are included in those two acts, leaving aside the analysis of provisions contained in the other EU acts referring to the protection of children.

1. Digital Services Act

The Digital Services Act[11] is an EU act that includes rules for the protection of minors from online harmful content. It obliges all platforms to take into primary account the rights of child users and to take appropriate and effective

---

primary consideration in all actions concerning children. See art 3(1) of the Convention on the Rights of the Child [1989] General Assembly resolution 44/25.

[9] See Communication, 'A Digital Decade for children and youth', fn 3, which expressly refers to UN General Comment no 25 on the UN Convention on the Rights of the Child, to which all EU Member States are parties, which explicitly addresses children's rights in the digital environment.

[10] See the compendium of EU formal texts concerning children in the digital world at <https://digital-strategy.ec.europa.eu/en/library/european-strategy-better-internet-kids-bik-compendium-legislation>.

measures to ensure the privacy, safety, and security of children using their services. However, the amendments concerning child protection proposed by the European Parliament in 2022 were not adopted in the final text; recital 3 of the Regulation does not explicitly mention the necessity of taking into primary account the best interests of the child, as interpreted in the UNCRC General Comment no 25 on children's rights in relation to the digital environment.[12]

Similarly, the final text of the DSA does not entirely adopt the proposal for a children's clause in Chapter III requiring all digital service providers to assess whether their services are likely to be accessed by or have an impact on children. According to that proposal, in such instances 'providers should be required to undertake child impact assessments and mitigate systemic risks to children's rights, based on statutory standards'.[13]

In the final version of the text, rather than all digital service providers, only very large online platforms (VLOPs) and very large online search engines (VLOSEs) are required to consider systemic risks related to their services, such as the actual or foreseeable negative effects in relation to child protection.[14] Such risks may arise, for example, in the design of online interfaces which intentionally or unintentionally exploit the inexperience of children or which may lead to addictive behavior.[15]

VLOPs and VLOSEs are consequently required to put into place 'reasonable, proportionate and effective mitigation measures' to 'protect the rights of children, including age verification and parental control tools, [and] tools aimed at helping minors signal abuse or obtain support, as appropriate'.[16] Cyber-violence, including non-consensual sharing of intimate content, is an example of content that requires rapid processing if flagged by users, including children, and appropriate adaptation of the content moderation practices.

Providers of VLOPs and VLOSEs should also 'ensure that their services are organised in a way that allows minors to access easily mechanisms pro-

---

[11] Regulation (EU) 2022/2065 of the European Parliament and of the Council of 19 October 2022 on a Single Market For Digital Services and amending Directive 2000/31/EC (Digital Services Act) [2022] OJ L277/1 (DSA).

[12] See European Parliament, 'Amendments adopted on the proposal for a regulation of the European Parliament and of the Council on a Single Market For Digital Services (Digital Services Act) and amending Directive 2000/31/EC' (2022) P9 TA(2022)0014, particularly the amendments proposed under recital 3.

[13] 5Rights Foundation, 'Children's rights in the EU Digital Services Act' (2021) <https://5rightsfoundation.com/uploads/DigitalServiceAct-5RightsPositionPaper,June2021.pdf> 3.

[14] DSA, art 34(1)(d). Accordingly, a growing number of digital platforms, such as Tiktok and Facebook, are training their moderators to detect those types of content. See para 4.2 for a critical appraisal of the methods used to train moderators.

[15] DSA, art 34(1)(d).

[16] DSA, art 35(1)(j).

vided for in th[e] Regulation […] including notice and action and complaint mechanisms'; they should also provide tools to enable conditional access to information that may 'impair their physical, mental or moral development'.[17] Providers of intermediary services should also make publicly available in an easily accessible manner, at least once a year, clear reports 'on any content moderation that they engaged in during the relevant period'.[18] VLOPs and VLOSEs will be subject to fines of up to 6% of their total worldwide annual turnover in the preceding financial year if they intentionally or negligently infringe the relevant provisions of the DSA or fail to comply with decisions on interim measures and voluntary measures.[19]

In the DSA, it is also forbidden for providers of online platforms to present advertisements based on profiling if they are reasonably certain that the recipient of the service is a minor[20] – though in complying with the principle of data minimization,[21] the provider of the online platform cannot maintain, acquire, or process more personal data than it already has to assess the recipient's age.[22] Furthermore, just as with deceptive interface designs,[23] those restrictions only apply to online platforms as defined in the DSA, but not to websites, apps, or other intermediary services that, for example, embed Google ads. Worse, the DSA limits the prohibition to ads shown by platforms to their own users. Providers are therefore free to micro-target such ads to any other locations on the web, if they offer this kind of service. In practice, the prohibition in the DSA does not cover cookies and tracking banners that appear as advertisements on most webpages as resulting from Google ads services. In addition, art 26 does not address the use of proxy data for otherwise sensitive criteria. Consequently, while a platform is not allowed to target ads based on the sensitive category of 'race', they can simply replace prohibited references with a generic proxy such as 'interested in African-American culture' or 'K-pop'.

Therefore, while the DSA represents a relevant step in the direction of protecting children online, especially because it sets obligations for VLOPs and VLOSEs, it is many steps away from solving certain problematic issues regarding the protection of children online. The reasons for this will be explained further in sections III and IV.

---

[17] DSA, recital 89.

[18] The information that shall be included in those reports is listed in DSA, art 15. See para 1(a)–(e) for a list of the information that is to be included in the annual reports.

[19] DSA, art 74.

[20] See Costanza Di Francesco Maesa, 'La profilazione nel contesto del diritto internazionale' in Adelina Adinolfi and Andrea Simoncini (eds), *Protezione dei dati personali e nuove tecnologie* (Collana del Dipartimento di Scienze Giuridiche dell'Università degli Studi di Firenze 2022).

[21] The principle is enshrined in GDPR, art 5(1)(c).

[22] DSA, recital 71, art 28(2)–(3).

[23] See DSA, arts 25–26.

2. *Proposal for a Regulation on Child Sexual Abuse*

As far as the fight against online child sexual abuse is concerned, the European Commission has been very active in the last years, since 2020 when it became a priority in 2020 EU Strategy[24] and with the 2011 updating of the Child Sexual Abuse Directive.[25] At the time of writing, while the recently proposed Regulation 'laying down rules to prevent and combat child sexual abuse' (CSA Regulation)[26] is awaiting the Parliamentary Committee's opinion, an Interim Regulation[27] has been adopted to provide for temporary derogations from certain obligations under the E-Privacy Directive.[28] The aim of these temporary derogations is to enable internet service providers that were already doing it before, to continue their voluntary practices of detecting, reporting, and removing child sexual abuse material (CSAM) online. If other internet service providers would like to initiate the same activity they are, conversely, not allowed to do so.

The proposed CSA Regulation goes a step further. According to the impact assessment,[29] voluntary actions against child sexual abuse have proven insufficient for various reasons: they were adopted by only a small number of service providers, the private-public cooperation in this field was difficult to achieve, and Member States encountered considerable difficulties in preventing child sexual abuse online and guaranteeing appropriate assistance to the victims of those crimes. It is for these reasons that, according to the proposed CSA Regulation's Impact Assessment, the preferred option is to oblige ser-

---

[24] Communication from the Commission on a 'EU strategy for a more effective fight against child sexual abuse' [2020] COM/2020/607 final.

[25] Directive 2011/93/EU on combating the sexual abuse and sexual exploitation of children and child pornography, and replacing Council Framework Decision 2004/68/JHA [2011] OJ L335/1.

[26] European Commission 'Proposal for a Regulation laying down rules to prevent and combat child sexual abuse' [2022] COM/2022/209 final (CSA Regulation).

[27] Regulation (EU) 2021/1232 on a temporary derogation from certain provisions of Directive 2002/58/EC as regards the use of technologies by providers of number-independent interpersonal communications services for the processing of personal and other data for the purpose of combating online child sexual abuse [2021] OJ L274/41 (Interim Regulation). The derogations envisaged by the Interim Regulation will apply until 3 August 2024 or until an earlier date if the legislators adopt the proposal for a Regulation on child sexual abuse before that date.

[28] Directive 2002/58/EC concerning the processing of personal data and the protection of privacy in the electronic communications sector (Directive on privacy and electronic communications) [2002] OJ L201/37 (E-Privacy Directive). The European Electronic Communications Code (EECC) entered into force in December 2020.

[29] See Commission Staff Working Document Impact Assessment Report accompanying the document Proposal for a Regulation laying down rules to prevent and combat child sexual abuse [2022] SWD/2022/209 (Impact Assessment).

vice providers to detect grooming[30] and CSAM (also within interpersonal communication services), to prevent the imminent abuse, and to ensure full harmonization.[31] Providers of hosting or interpersonal communication services will thus be obliged, according to the proposed CSA Regulation,[32] to detect, report, and remove CSAM online.[33] The scope of the proposed CSA Regulation is wide, as it applies to practically every social media, messenger, and chat service operating in the EU, to web-based emails, image, and video hosting sites, and also to gaming platforms and dating apps offering chat functions: It will, therefore, constitute a derogation from the E-Privacy Directive (Directive 2002/58/EC) and *lex specialis* in respect of the DSA.[34]

The consequence of the obligations foreseen in the proposed CSA Regulation is the privatization of law enforcement tasks, as the obligation to detect, remove, report, or block content will be delegated to relevant information society services.

The measures under the CSA Regulation risk representing a disproportionate interference with arts 7, 8, 11, and 12 of the Charter,[35] as far as they incentivize service providers to remove end-to-end encryption and to scan everyone's private communications, thus circumventing the prohibition against an indiscriminate scanning of private conversations by law enforcement authorities.[36] Although the proposal allows the scanning of encrypted messages only if it is the result of detection orders, the whole framework is configured to incentivize providers to 'pre-empt legal detection orders by taking the strongest (and therefore most intrusive) measures possible'.[37] Providers of hosting services and of interpersonal communication services are, in fact, required to carry out a risk assessment for the purpose of online child sexual abuse for each service they offer, and they are consequently to take 'reasona-

---

[30] Grooming means the manipulation of children for the purposes of future exploitation or abuse.

[31] See Proposal for a CSA Regulation, p. 11.

[32] Proposal for a CSA Regulation.

[33] Proposal for a CSA Regulation, art 1(1)(b)–(d).

[34] In this sense, European Digital Rights (EDRi) 'Private and secure communications attacked by European Commission's latest proposal' (2022) <https://edri.org/our-work/private-and-secure-communications-put-at-risk-by-european-commissions-latest-proposal/>.

[35] For in-depth commentary on the Proposal for a CSA Regulation, see Teresa Quintel, 'The Commission Proposal on Combating Child Sexual Abuse – Confidentiality of Communications at Risk?' [2022] 2/2022, 262. On the risks posed for users' fundamental rights, see the Opinion of the Legal Service of the Council of the European Union on the Proposal for a Regulation laying down rules to prevent and combat child sexual abuse, Document no 8787/23, 26 April 2023, and Teresa Quintel, 'Renewed Concerns About Compliance of the Proposed 'Regulation to Prevent and Combat Child Sexual Abuse' with Essence of Right to Data Protection: The Council Legal Service Opinion' (2023) 9(2) EDPL 173.

[36] For a more in-depth analysis, see III.1 and III.2, below.

[37] EDRi (n 34).

ble mitigation measures, tailored to the risk identified' so as to minimize that risk.[38] If they fail to demonstrate in their risk assessment that there is no risk of child sexual abuse, they are liable to be issued with a detection order forcing them to introduce additional measures. However, as it has been remarked, 'this is an impossible standard to achieve, meaning that the law will likely have a coercive effect on providers to introduce [on] their own initiative as many 'mitigation measures' as possible'.[39]

Considering that the Impact Assessment considers encrypted communications without scanning to be inherently risky and sees end-to-end encryption is as one of the factors making services like WhatsApp or Signal potentially risky,[40] the provider may choose to remove end-to-end encryption so as to comply with the CSA Regulation. If such a solution is adopted, the confidentiality of internet users' communications would no longer be ensured and the right to privacy and data protection would be seriously at risk, as we will see below (III.1).

In conclusion, the right to privacy and data protection will be seriously at risk if the CSA Regulation is not amended, thus jeopardizing all users' – including minors' – right to privacy and data protection. Properly balancing the conflicting interests of, on the one hand, children protection online and, on the other every users' – including children's – right to data protection is therefore essential.

III. Role of Digital Platforms in Protecting Minors

Any digital services, from social media to interactive games, can expose minors to risks – such as bullying, grooming and harmful content – that can promote self-harm, violence, suicide, hate speech, sexual harassment, eating disorders or risky online challenges. Digital platforms therefore have an important role in protecting minors from online harmful content, as they can prevent, identify, and remove emerging threats potentially faced by children.[41] It is for this reason that in this section we will examine the role of digital platforms in protecting minors online. To this end, in the first instance, we will analyze the role of digital platforms in detecting and reporting online CSAM, especially where end-to-end encryption systems are used, and, in the second instance, we will analyze the case law of the CJEU on this issue to

[38] Proposal for a CSA Regulation, arts 3–6.

[39] EDRi 'European Commission's online CSAM proposal fails to find right solutions to tackle child sexual abuse' (2022) <https://edri.org/our-work/european-commissions-online-csam-proposal-fails-to-find-right-solutions-to-tackle-child-sexual-abuse/>.

[40] See Impact Assessment (n 29) 38 and 73.

[41] See 'Online Platforms' Moderation of Illegal Content Online Law, Practices and Options for Reform' (2020) Study for the IMCO Committee.

assess whether the proposed CSA Regulation and the practice of digital platforms in this respect are consistent with the CJEU's case law.

1. *End-to-end Encryption*

Some online platforms already voluntarily contribute to the effort to detect and report online CSAM. In 2022, for instance, the CyberTipline received more than 32 million child sexual abuse reports.[42] That system for reporting instances of apparent online child exploitation, including CSAM, is important for the protection of minors. However, while a great number of notifications have been sent by some digital platforms, such as Facebook, some others reported very few cases per year, ie reporting less than 10 cases of online sexual abuse per year.[43] According to some studies,[44] the use of end-to-end encryption systems represents one of the possible reasons for low detection rates; encryption of data for privacy and security purposes is in fact deemed to hamper the identification of perpetrators of children abuse and exploitation, since the investigative tools currently used by enforcement authorities are not usually effective when faced with end-to-end encrypted communications.[45] The decision of some social platforms, such as Facebook, to implement end-to-end encryption on its private messaging service by default[46] would thus make the detection of child sexual abuse online more difficult, 'when not impossible'.[47] Similarly, Europol determined that sex offenders targeting children use techniques such as the anonymization and encryption of their illegal activities to hinder law enforcement authorities investigations:[48] offenders mainly use dark net forums, social networking, and end-to-end encrypted communication applications, such as WhatsApp,[49] to distribute and share CSAM.

[42] For a list of the companies from which the NCMEC received notifications in 2019 and for the number of notifications each of them made, see <https://www.missingkids.org/ourwork/ncmecdata>.

[43] In 2022, Facebook identified and notified around 21 million instances of online child abuse cases, while other digital platforms identified and notified less than 100 cases, some of them even less than 10. See the NCMEC 'Reports by Electronic Service Providers' (2022).

[44] In this sense, see Impact Assessment (n 29) 27.

[45] See Communication from the Commission on a 'EU strategy' (n 24) 2.

[46] Mark Zuckerberg, 'A Privacy-Focused Vision for Social Networking' (2019) <https://about.fb.com/news/2019/03/vision-for-social-networking/>.

[47] Impact Assessment (n 29) 27.

[48] Proposal for a CSA Regulation. See also European Parliament 'Combating child sexual abuse online' Briefing, EU Legislation in Progress (2023) <https://www.europarl.europa.eu/RegData/etudes/BRIE/2022/738224/EPRS_BRI(2022)738224_EN.pdf>.

[49] Although WhatsApp has banned more than 300,000 accounts solely on the basis of unencrypted elements to which it has access, it's use by offenders is nevertheless popular. See in this respect, Salla Huikuri, *The Darkest Side of the Darknet: How Do Online Communities of Pedophiles Contribute to the Justification of Sexual Violence Against Children* (Reviews of the Police University College 25, 2022).

However, especially as regards online community forums, chat rooms, and messaging apps, end-to-end encryption is a crucial tool for protecting confidentiality and ensuring the protection of users' fundamental rights, such as the right to privacy, the right to data protection, and the right to freedom of expression. It is thus necessary to find a balanced solution to protect children online and, at the same time, to ensure the protection of the fundamental rights enshrined in the Charter. However, thus far such a solution is missing. In fact, in this regard some authors, including the National Center for Missing & Exploited Children ('NCMEC'), argued that is necessary to remove end-to-end encryption in private communications; Meta, for example, was asked in 2023 by an international group of law enforcement authorities – including Interpol, the FBI, the Australian Federal Police and others – not to introduce end-to-end encryption on Facebook Messenger and Instagram. On the other hand, others argue for the opposite, ie contending that end-to-end encryption is necessary to ensure the privacy and security of internet users' communications and that the solution recently proposed in the CSA Regulation is contrary to EU law, resulting in indiscriminate and unlawful mass surveillance. Tutanota, an end-to-end encrypted mail service, for instance, believes that the general surveillance, as foreseen in the recently proposed CSA Regulation, is 'completely disproportionate', arguing that there are better alternatives for protecting minors online.[50] According to former MEP Felix Reda, the planned level of surveillance also risks overloading enforcement authorities as the number of false positive is significantly high, and thus innocuous messages, chats, and photos of innocent people could end up in investigators' files.[51] Furthermore, the risk of false reports and the lack of adequate details on the methodology used by tech companies to detect CSAM would amplify the risks of infringing the fundamental rights of online users and particularly the right to data protection. The proposed CSA Regulation thus risks being inconsistent with the CJEU's case law, as we will see in the next sub-section.

2. CJEU's Case Law on the Indiscriminate Retention of Data

The CJEU has decided several cases addressing the legitimacy of general surveillance tools used by law enforcement authorities to detect serious crime, and it has always stated that blanket or indiscriminate data retention is

[50] Tutanota, 'CSAM Scanning: EU Commission's lies uncovered' (2022) <https://tutanota.com/blog/posts/eu-csam-scanning/>. See also Ian Levy and Crispin Robinson, 'Thoughts on Child Safety on Commodity Platforms' (2022) <https://arxiv.org/pdf/2207.09506.pdf>.

[51] See <https://www.asktheeu.org/en/request/technologies_for_the_detection_o#incoming-39916> and Laura Kabelka, 'MEPs sceptical on EU proposal to fight online child sexual abuse' (2022) <https://www.euractiv.com/section/digital/news/meps-sceptical-on-eu-proposal-to-fight-online-child-sexual-abuse/>.

not proportionate[52] and that indiscriminate data retention to fight serious crime is incompatible with EU law.[53] This interpretation, based on arts 7 and 8 of the Charter, was confirmed also in cases concerning international data sharing.[54] Recently, the CJEU reiterated its position at the end of 2020 in two judgments, *Privacy International*[55] and *Quadrature du Net*.[56] In both judgments, the Court ruled that the E-Privacy Directive,[57] read in the light of arts 7 and 8 of the Charter, must be interpreted as precluding national law 'enabling a State authority to require providers of electronic communications services to carry out general and indiscriminate transmission of traffic and location data to the security and intelligence agencies', even where such transmission of data is for the purpose of safeguarding national security.[58] In the *Privacy International* case, the CJEU reached the same conclusion as in *Tele2Sverige*,[59] but it went a step further, extending the prohibition of indiscriminate and general transmission of data not only to enforcement authorities for the purposes of combating crime, but also to intelligence agencies for the purpose of safeguarding national security.[60]

By contrast, in the *Quadrature du Net* case, the Court held that EU law does not preclude indiscriminate data retention measures if a Member State, for the purposes of safeguarding national security, makes recourse to an instruction requiring such retention and can prove that it is confronted with

> 'a serious threat to national security that is shown to be genuine and present or foreseeable, where the decision imposing such an instruction is subject to effective review, either by a court or by an independent administrative body whose decision is binding, […], and where that instruction may be given only for a period that is limited in time to what is strictly necessary, but which may be extended if that threat persists'.[61]

---

[52] CJEU 8 April 2014, C-293/12 and C-594/12 *Digital Rights Ireland and Others*, ECLI:EU:C:2014:238.

[53] CJEU 21 December 2016, C-203/15 and C-698/15 *Tele2Sverige*, ECLI:EU:C:2016:970.

[54] CJEU 6 October 2015, C-362/14 *Maximilian Schrems v Data Protection Commissioner*, ECLI:EU:C:2015:650; CJEU 8 April 2014 (n 52); CJEU Opinion 1/15 26 July 2017 on the EU-Canada agreement, ECLI:EU:C:2017:592; CJEU16 July 2020, C-311/18 *Data Protection Commissioner v Facebook Ireland Limited and Maximillian Schrems ('Schrems II')*, ECLI:EU:C:2020:559.

[55] CJEU 6 October 2020, C-623/17 *Privacy International*, ECLI:EU:C:2020:790.

[56] CJEU 6 October 2020, C-511/18, C-512/18 and C-520/18 *La Quadrature du Net and Others v Premier ministre and Others*, ECLI:EU:C:2020:791.

[57] Directive 2002/58/EC concerning the processing of personal data and the protection of privacy in the electronic communications sector (Directive on privacy and electronic communications) [2002] OJ L201/37 (E-Privacy Directive).

[58] CJEU 6 October 2020 (n 55) para 83(2).

[59] CJEU 21 December 2016 (n 53).

[60] CJEU 6 October 2020 (n 55) para 80. See also the jurisprudence cited by the Court, ie CJEU 8 April 2014 (n 52) paras 57–58, CJEU 21 December 2016 (n 53) para 105.

In this case, an exception to the general prohibition of indiscriminate data retention by law enforcement authorities and intelligent agencies was made by the Court, under the specific conditions enumerated, and only for the purposes of safeguarding national security.

Conversely, the CJEU stated that to combat serious crime only the targeted retention of traffic and location data under certain conditions is allowed.[62] However, as regards the retention of IP addresses, the Court ruled that where the criminal offence was committed online, the IP address 'might be the only means of investigation enabling the person to whom that address was assigned at the time of the commission of the offence to be identified',[63] explicitly mentioning cases of 'particularly serious child pornography offences, such as the acquisition, dissemination, transmission or making available online of child pornography', whose detection may prove impossible without recourse to the retention of IP addresses by providers of electronic communications services. The Court stated, therefore, that, even if a legislative measure providing for the retention of the IP addresses of all natural persons who own terminal equipment permitting access to the internet 'would catch persons who at first sight have no connection', and that internet users are entitled to expect, under arts 7 and 8 of the Charter, 'that their identity will not, in principle, be disclosed',[64] a legislative measure providing for the general and indiscriminate retention of exclusively IP addresses assigned to the source of a connection is not considered to be contrary to EU law, 'provided that that possibility is subject to strict compliance with the substantive and procedural conditions which should regulate the use of that data'.[65]

Finally, with regard to data relating to the civil identity of users, the Court stated that legislative measures concerning the processing of that data, 'including the retention of and access to that data solely for the purpose of identifying the user concerned, and without it being possible for that data to be associated with information on the communications made, are capable of being justified by the objective of preventing, investigating, detecting and prosecuting criminal offences in general'.[66] The retention of and access to that data is thus allowed in general to prevent, investigate, detect, and prosecute criminal offences, which need not even be 'serious'. The reason is that such data does not, in itself, 'make it possible to ascertain the date, time, duration and recipients of the communications made, or the locations where those communications took place or their frequency with specific people

[61] CJEU 6 October 2020 (n 56) para 229(1).
[62] CJEU 6 October 2020 (n 56) para 229(1).
[63] CJEU 6 October 2020 (n 56) para 154.
[64] CJEU 6 October 2020 (n 56) para 155.
[65] CJEU 6 October 2020 (n 56) para 155.
[66] CJEU 6 October 2020 (n 56) para 158.

during a given period, with the result that it does not provide, apart from the contact details of those users, such as their addresses, any information on the communications sent and, consequently, on the users' private lives. Thus, the interference entailed by the retention of that data cannot, in principle, be classified as serious'.[67]

In conclusion, we argue that, according to Court's case law, the proposed CSA Regulation may be considered legitimate only insofar as the general and indiscriminate retention concerns IP addresses assigned to the source of a connection if the conditions enumerated in *Quadrature du Net* are respected, and as far as it concerns data relating to the users' civil identities. By contrast, an indiscriminate scanning of everyone's private conversations by digital platforms, and especially by providers of hosting or interpersonal communication services, would not adequately protect internet users from arbitrary investigations according to the CJEU's ruling. This holds even more true if we consider that the use of AI tools is not always accurate, as is demonstrated by some studies on the topic; it is enough to mention that Meta, in a period of just 53 days, found that 207 people were wrongly flagged by their systems and that 4,500 other people are lodging complaints.[68]

Furthermore, the assertion is further reinforced if we consider that, in the case of the CSA Regulation, this form of 'mass surveillance' is not even carried out by law enforcement authorities but by private entities, such as digital platforms. In this regard, it therefore seems that no adequate solutions for detecting child sexual abuse within encrypted services have been found so far, nor have effective measures been taken by digital platforms to solve this serious issue.

IV. Ineffectiveness of Enforcement Mechanisms

Children are inadequately protected online also because of the ineffectiveness of the enforcement mechanisms. In this section, we will thus explore this issue while examining the rules and the role of digital platforms in moderating content, detecting illegal content, and reporting it to the competent authorities.

---

[67] CJEU 6 October 2020 (n 56) para 157.

[68] EDRi, 'Internal documents revealed the worst for private communications in the EU; how will the Commissioners respond?' (2022) <https://edri.org/our-work/internal-documents-revealed-the-worst-for-private-communications-in-the-eu-how-will-the-commissioners-respond/>. See also the data concerning LinkedIn, which found that only 31 of the 75 files identified by PhotoDNA as CSAM actually involved CSAM.

1. Illegal Content and the Limited Liability of Internet Service Providers

Internet service providers currently have few incentives to tackle illegal content proactively, as becoming aware of illegal content increases their risk of liability. Illegal content is thus not effectively detected and subsequently removed. The main reason is that according to the EU legal framework, online service providers fulfilling the role of 'intermediaries', including digital platforms, have neither an ex ante obligation to monitor the information transmitted through their services nor a preventive obligation to research the activities indicating the presence of illegal contents. The DSA instead affords certain categories of internet service providers with a limited exemption from secondary liability, ie the liability resulting from users' illegal behavior.[69] The DSA establishes that three categories of information service providers playing a neutral, passive, or merely technical role towards the specific information hosted[70] are exempted from secondary liability for 'information provided by a recipient of the service'.[71] Internet intermediaries are, however, exempted from liability for hosting third-party illegal content only if they do not have 'actual knowledge' of the illegal activity or information and if they expeditiously block or remove the content upon gaining such 'knowledge or awareness'. In this regard, the CJEU has provided some guidance on how 'actual knowledge' and 'awareness' is obtained in respect of intellectual property infringements. The jurisprudence on other aspects varies among Member States.[72]

Furthermore, the DSA lays down the key principle that Member States are not to impose a general obligation on intermediaries to monitor the information they transmit or store, or an obligation to actively 'seek facts or circumstances indicating illegal activity'.[73] However, internet intermediaries may be ordered by a court to prevent or terminate instances of infringement.[74] In such a case, they are to obey to the order of the competent authority and prevent or terminate the illegal activity.

---

[69] See in this respect, Giovanni Sartor, *Providers Liability: From the eCommerce Directive to the Future. In-Depth Analysis for the IMCO Committee* (2017). A distinction is made between liability for content created by the provider and liability for third party content, such as other users' content. See Grabitz/Hilf, *Recht der Europäischen Union* (CH Beck 2009) 40 Sekundärrecht A4 art 12 Vorbem para 2.

[70] A further condition for internet intermediaries is that they not have knowledge of or control over the information stored. See CJEU 12 July 2011, C-324/09 *L'Oréal/eBay*, ECLI:EU:C:2011:474.

[71] DSA, arts 4–6.

[72] European Commission, 'Overview of the legal framework of notice-and-action procedures in Member States' (2018) SMART 2016/0039, 2.

[73] DSA, art 8.

[74] DSA, arts 4(3), 5(2), 6(4).

In this regard, the CJEU's case-law on the E-Commerce Directive (ECD)[75] has shown a trend towards imposing stricter obligations on internet intermediaries to tackle illegal content. The main strategy has consisted in affirming that certain internet intermediaries do not fall within the ECD's scope of application, as they are not 'passive' intermediaries.[76] It has been asserted that automated processing, ie processing without human intervention, can also be considered non-passive. Consequently, social networks, such as Facebook, or content-sharing platforms, such as YouTube, and search engines, such as Google, could be deemed as not falling under the ECD's secondary liability exemption. In this regard, some scholars have argued that it is necessary to abandon the view that only 'passive' intermediaries should be protected, since the rationale for establishing an exemption from secondary liability for internet intermediaries is that they fulfil a function as communication enablers. And to perform this function effectively, it could be necessary for intermediaries to play an active role and create an environment in which users' communications are delivered and made accessible.[77] Making the protection from secondary liability conditional on passivity would induce intermediaries not to take initiatives against illegal, inappropriate, or irrelevant content or activity, with the result that the quantity of online illegality would increase and users who prefer not to be exposed to objectionable material will be unsatisfied.[78] It is also important to highlight that there is a difference between removing or blocking classes of items in domains such as child pornography or copyright infringements, where 'cost-effective automated means to identify illegal material exist',[79] as compared with other domains, such as hate speech or defamation, where such means are not available.[80] In general, as it has been argued, to protect fundamental rights, and particularly the right to freedom of expression and information,[81] the provider should be considered liable only when it has contributed to the unlawful behavior of its user 'by failing to exercise due care, namely, to adopt reasonable measures that could have prevented that behaviour or mitigated its effects'.[82]

---

[75] Directive 2000/31/EC on certain legal aspects of information society services, in particular electronic commerce, in the Internal Market ('Directive on electronic commerce') [2000] OJ L178/1 (ECD).

[76] See Sartor (n 69) 24.

[77] In this sense, see Sartor (n 69) 26.

[78] See Sartor (n 69) 27, who also recalls that these motivations lie behind the US good Samaritan clause (Communication Decency Act (CDA) [1996] section 230(c)(2)).

[79] See Sartor (n 69) 26.

[80] See Georgios N Yannopoulos, 'The immunity of internet intermediaries reconsidered?' in Mariarosaria Taddeo and Luciano Floridi (eds) *The Responsibilities of Online Service Providers* (Springer 2017) 43.

[81] See Charter art 11.

Another trend has consisted, by contrast, in ordering hosting providers to remove future unlawful information of identical or equivalent content under certain conditions specified by the CJEU; the removal of unlawful content thus fell within the area of responsibility of private parties, especially large service providers, which are increasingly gaining control over the content available on their platforms.[83] As a result, it has become more difficult for internet service providers to fulfil the conditions for the liability exemptions and to be considered non-liable for third-party content. The consequence is that they tend to over-block critical, but lawful, content, without taking other appropriate measures to protect lawful content (so-called 'collateral censorship'); secondary liability may in fact induce intermediaries to constrain the behavior of their users to avoid the risk of being sanctioned for not having prevented, terminated, or mitigated illegal activities.[84]

The consequences of imposing specific stricter obligations on internet intermediaries to tackle illegal content are therefore twofold and in tension: on the one hand, internet intermediaries are induced not to take initiatives against illegal, inappropriate, or irrelevant content or activity, while, on the other hand, they tend to over-block critical but lawful content ('collateral censorship'). This state of simultaneous under- and over-regulation creates legal uncertainty and does not promote the rights and interests of users, particularly those of minors. Consequently, there is a clear need to revise the EU legal framework so as to more effectively protect internet users and especially minors.

2. *Content Moderation*

The DSA aims to regulate another important function of digital platforms, one which is particularly important to protect children online: content moderation. To this end, a conditional liability regime similar to the one under the ECD and consistent with the jurisprudence of the CJEU has been established.

---

[82] See Sartor (n 69) 29. See also, on the duties of care of intermediaries, Peggy Valcke, Aleksandra Kuczerawy and Pieter-Jan Ombelet, 'Did the romans get it right? What Delfi, Google, eBay, and UPC Telekabel Wien have in common' in Mariarosaria Taddeo and Luciano Floridi (eds), *The Responsibilities of Online Service Providers* (Springer 2016) 101.

[83] See Anja Hoffmann and Alessandro Gasparotti, 'Liability for illegal content online. Weaknesses of the EU legal framework and possible plans of the EU Commission to address them in a "Digital Services Act"' (cepStudy 2020) 29.

[84] See Sartor (n 69) 11. This tendency is called 'collateral censorship', which is described as follow: 'Collateral censorship occurs when the state holds one private party A liable for the speech of another private party B, and A has the power to block, censor, or otherwise control access to B's speech'. See Jack M Balkin 'Old school/new school speech regulation' (2014) 127(8) Harv LRev 2309; Michael Meyerson 'Authors, editors and uncommon carriers: Identifying the "speaker" within the new media' (1995) 71 Notre Dame LRev 79.

The general rule prohibiting digital platforms from monitoring users' content that is set out in the ECD is reiterated in the DSA; digital platforms may therefore be held responsible only if they have 'actual knowledge' of the illegality of the content. Actual knowledge can be asserted only if the flagged content is manifestly illegal, ie 'where it is evident to a layperson, without any substantive analysis, that the content is illegal'.[85] According to the DSA, intermediary service providers can impose their own community standards and moderation policies on users in their terms and conditions, subject to the prerequisites that the transparency requirements set out in the DSA are respected and that procedures be put in place for the enforcement of terms and conditions. Among the transparency reporting obligations of intermediary services, there is the duty for service providers to make publicly available – 'in a machine-readable format and in an easily accessible manner' – reports on any content moderation practice that they engaged in during the relevant period, including information on the reasons for imposing specific moderation decisions on content and the way these decisions are imposed; information about the use of automated tools for content moderation purposes is also to be included.[86] If the intermediary service is primarily directed at minors, providers are to explain the conditions for and the restrictions on the use of their service in a clear and understandable way for minors. These rules aim at protecting the freedom of expression, at not incentivizing platforms to conduct surveillance of users' communications, and at encouraging companies to be more proactive when moderating content online.

This regime is coupled with a 'notice-and-action' system,[87] by which precise and 'adequately substantiated' notices may be submitted by users to the provider of hosting services, which for its part will take an 'informed and diligent' decision.[88] In addition, a further mechanism has been established to allow a quick removal of illegal content; namely, 'trusted flaggers' have been created.[89] If trusted flaggers acting within their designated area of expertise submit notices about illegal content or activities to providers of online platforms, the latter are to take all the necessary technical and organizational measures to ensure that those notices 'are given priority and are processed and decided upon without undue delay'.[90] Trusted flaggers also have reporting obligations, as they are required, once a year, to publish detailed reports on the notices submitted during the relevant period.[91]

---

85 DSA, recital 63.

86 DSA, art 15(1).

87 DSA, recital 53, art 16.

88 DSA, art 20, recital 89; as far as minors are concerned, art 14(1), art 15(1)(d), art 53.

89 DSA, art 22. See Federica Casarosa, 'Internal Mechanisms of Enforcement – What Role do Trusted Flaggers Play?', in this volume, 195.

90 DSA, art 22(1).

91 DSA, art 22(3).

In the DSA, a compliance system has been established too. In this regard, the Commission's proposal has been substantially revised to ensure a better protection of minors, as was requested in an open letter of December 2021.[92] In the open letter, it was particularly highlighted that under the Commission's proposal,[93] users did not have consistent ways to appeal platform decisions, especially in cases of inaction by platforms. According to art 17 of the Commission's initial proposal, the internal complaint handling system could in fact have been used by users whose content was removed, disabled, or otherwise restricted. However, users would not have had the possibility to complain against inaction on the part of a platform in cases of notification or where illegal content or content violating the platform's terms and conditions was not removed by the digital platform. This situation would have been particularly serious where the users involved in the illegal content published online were minors. In such a case, they would not have had any instrument of redress. However, in the final text of the DSA, the points raised in the open letter have been attentively considered; the proposal has been therefore added a possibility to complain against the inaction of digital platforms.[94]

A problematic issue is the question of how to train moderators. The cases of TikTok or Facebook are exemplary in this regard. Content moderators who work for Teleperformance, a third-party company which moderates content for big social media companies, including TikTok, are shown sexually explicit, uncensored, and exploitative images of children as a part of their training;[95] by contrast, Facebook moderators are instructed to assume that the subject in a suspected child abuse video or photo is an adult if they are unable to determine whether the individual is a minor or an adult.[96] Both practices raise doubts about the legitimacy of the methods used to train content moderators and about the effectiveness of digital platforms' content moderation.

To conclude, the DSA's rules on internet intermediaries' exemption from secondary liability and content moderation seem adequate in theory, but they

---

[92] Open letter to Members of the European Parliament, 'Shape the DSA so it can empower all users to act against wrongful platform decisions' (2021) <https://www.eurochild.org/uploads/2021/12/03122021-Open-Letter-platform-accountability-Art-17.pdf>.

[93] European Commission, 'Proposal for a Regulation of the European Parliament and of the Council on a Single Market For Digital Services (Digital Services Act) and amending Directive 2000/31/EC' (2020) COM/2020/825 final.

[94] DSA, art 20(1)(a)–(d). This is also established in art 20(4).

[95] See Alexandra S Levine, 'TikTok Moderators are being trained using graphic images of child sexual abuse', *Forbes* (4 August 2022) <https://www.forbes.com/sites/alexandralevine/2022/08/04/tiktok-is-storing-uncensored-images-of-child-sexual-abuse-and-using-them-to-train-moderators/>.

[96] See Jay Peters, 'Facebook moderators 'err on the side of an adult' when uncertain of age in possible abuse photos', *The Verge* (1 April 2022) <https://www.theverge.com/2022/3/31/23005576/facebook-content-moderators-child-sexual-abuse-material-csam-policy> accessed June 2023.

are neither sufficient nor appropriate to effectively protect children online in practice. There is no uniform and standard set of rules for digital platforms on content moderation, and every digital platform implements EU provisions on content moderation differently, often inadequately, with the result that children are not effectively protected in terms of harmful online content.

3. *DSA Enforcement Mechanisms*

A study published before the entry into force of the DSA,[97] where different models of enforcement for a future DSA are analyzed, highlights (i) the evident failure of self-regulation by online platforms; (ii) the importance of focusing on the internal operations of platforms and establishing an appropriate regulatory framing; and (iii) that the DSA may have a limited scope but it should nevertheless include consistent transparency and enforcement measures. Furthermore, data from the last 20 years shows that without liability for digital platforms, there is no incentive to comply.

The DSA plays a pivotal role in proposing solutions to solve the power imbalance between user and platform, platform and regulator, and platform and Member States. The solution proposed in the study consists in regulation by 'national enforcement bodies' that operate in a network across Member States, with an overall coordination by a central EU regulator. A peculiarity of this model is represented by the fact that the 'national enforcement bodies' should have sanctioning powers with specific penalties that should be proportionate to the platform's size. EU legislation should also establish internal rules for platforms, which should be structured by public values defined by EU legislators and not by the internal unsupervised moderation of platforms. Another aspect that should be increased is platform transparency as regards data sharing.[98] Furthermore, in the study mentioned above, it is argued that it is better to regulate digital platforms according to public and not private law values considering the pivotal role that platforms have in the public sphere and in shaping important values, such as non-discrimination and free speech.

The suggestions proposed in the study have been only partially adopted in the final text of the DSA, where enforcement and supervision is a duty shared by the European Commission and the Member States. According to this system, the EU Commission will be responsible for overseeing and enforcing the most stringent obligations for VLOPs and VLOSEs, even if VLOPs and VLOSEs are also required to establish independent compliance officers to monitor the compliance with the DSA internally. Member States, in turn,

---

[97] Melanie Smith, 'Enforcement and cooperation between Member States. E-Commerce and the future Digital Services Act', Study requested by the IMCO Committee, European Parliament (2020) <https://www.europarl.europa.eu/RegData/etudes/STUD/2020/648780/IPOL_STU(2020)648780_EN.pdf>.

[98] See Smith (n 97) 8, 30–33.

have the duty to oversee all the other intermediary service providers that are established or that have appointed a legal representative in their territory.[99]

In this context, a pivotal role is played by the digital services coordinator (DSC) – namely, an authority appointed in each Member State that is given the task of supervising the application and enforcement of the Regulation.[100] The most important features of DSCs, at least on paper, are their impartiality, transparency, and rapidity in performing their tasks.[101] DSCs have both specific powers of investigation and specific enforcement powers to carry out their tasks.[102] A DSC may also launch and lead joint investigations with the participation of one or more other DSC.[103] The Regulation also states that a European Board for Digital Services is to be established.[104] The Board will be an 'independent advisory group of DSC on the supervision of providers of intermediary services',[105] whose task is to give advice to DSCs and to the Commission so as to contribute to the application of the Regulation, to the effective cooperation of DSCs and the Commission, and to assist DSCs and the Commission in supervising VLOPs. It should contribute to the coordination and drawing up of guidelines on emerging issues related to the matters covered by the Regulation.[106] As far as the enforcement of the obligations laid down in the Regulation are concerned, the Commission is nevertheless the main actor responsible for investigating the compliance of VLOPs and VLOSEs. In fact, the European Commission may exercise investigatory powers and decide to initiate proceedings. At the end of a proceeding, the Commission will adopt a non-compliance decision in the event it finds that the VLOP or VLOSE concerned is not in compliance with the Regulation. Finally, the Commission may impose on the VLOP or VLOSE concerned fines not exceeding 6% of its total worldwide annual turnover in the preceding financial year, upon the satisfaction of certain specific conditions listed in the Regulation.[107]

To ensure compliance, the Commission and DSCs should set out detailed ground rules for services to comply with and specify how they will judge digital platforms' performance. To this end, regarding the protection of children

---

[99] DSA, art 49.

[100] DSA, recitals 110–115, 118–122; art 3(1)(n), (o), art 49(2)–(4), arts 50–53, art 55 concerning the duty of digital services coordinators to draw up annual reports on their activities under the Regulation.

[101] DSA, art 50(1).

[102] DSA, art 51(1), (2).

[103] DSA, art 60.

[104] DSA, art 61.

[105] DSA, arts 61(1) and 62 describe the composition and structure of the board, while art 63 describes the tasks of the board.

[106] DSA, art 61(1).

[107] DSA, arts 73–74.

online, the IEEE 'Standards for an Age Appropriate Digital Services Framework based on the 5Rights Principles for Children'[108] could be a basis for an EU standard used to implement the DSA's provisions related to children's rights. Developed by the international industry body 'Institute of Electrical and Electronics Engineers Standards Association' in collaboration with 5Rights, the IEEE Standards set out practical steps for companies regarding the design of age-appropriate digital products and services. Additional tools, such as guidelines dedicated especially to the protection of children online, would complete the specific rules regarding children's protection online and ensure that companies abide by the technical standards, accompanied by conformity assessments against which they can be judged. However, so far uniform standards for an age-appropriate Digital Service Framework do not exist.

Furthermore, there is a problem concerning the DSA's implementation process in terms of its enforcement in some EU countries. As we read in an open letter of 2023,[109] there will be problems in implementing the Regulation in jurisdictions where the protection afforded to children in cyberspace is higher than it is under the DSA. This is the case, for instance, in Germany, where the German Youth Protection Act, which was amended in 2021, prescribes a mandatory duty of care as regards the rights of the children for platforms having more than one million users, which is a threshold lower than the 45 million established in the DSA for the very large platforms who are subject to a similar obligation. According to the letter, however, 'small does not mean safe, as is evidenced by a significant part of extremist content migrating to the smaller platforms in 2021'.[110] In the open letter, it was thus suggested to add an exemption for the protection of children by stating that the Regulation does not affect measures taken at the national level in accordance with EU law for the protection of minors.[111] Through such an addition, the problem of coordination with, for example, German law would be solved.

Another problem mentioned in the open letter concerns the complaint mechanism and out-of-court dispute settlement. The problem arises because the costs incurred for out-of-court dispute settlement bodies fall onto the platform providers and decisions of certified out-of-court dispute settlement bodies are not binding.[112] The authors of the open letter assume, therefore, that

---

[108] Standards Committee of the IEEE Consumer Technology Society, 'Standards for an Age Appropriate Digital Services Framework based on the 5Rights Principles for Children' (2021) <https://5rightsfoundation.com/static/ieee-2089-2021.pdf>.

[109] National Coalition Germany – Network for the Implementation of the UN Convention on the Rights of the Child and others, 'Children's Rights and the Digital Services Act' (2022) <https://childrens-rights.digital/hintergrund/index.cfm/key.1747/topic.280> accessed June 2023.

[110] National Coalition Germany (n 109).

[111] National Coalition Germany (n 109) 2.

[112] DSA, art 21(2).

there will be a large number of complaints for which the platform providers will have to make compensation, with the consequence that they will act less strictly with regard to material that is not illegal in all the EU countries.

In this context, the Commission committed itself to facilitating the creation of a comprehensive EU code of conduct on age-appropriate design (the so-called 'BIK+ Code'). According to the Commission, the BIK+ Code will build on the new rules in the DSA. This process, aimed at ensuring the privacy and safety of children online, will involve industry, policymakers, civil society, and children themselves; it will thus be a co-regulatory instrument, to which digital platforms may adhere (the participation in codes of conduct is voluntary) and thereby commit themselves to taking specific risk mitigation measures and addressing specific risks or harms. Yet here as well, one can observe that the proposal is to create a soft law, non-binding instrument that cannot be adequately enforced in cases of non-compliance by digital platforms.

In conclusion, online platforms have become de facto regulators with increasing powers, notwithstanding the absence of adequate and effective oversight. Public oversight on digital platforms is divided among different sectoral regulators operating both at the EU and the national level – ie data protection authorities, regulators of audiovisual media services, competition authorities, regulators of electronic communication services, and digital services coordinators – with the scope of oversight depending on the size of the online platforms as well as other criteria.[113] Rules concerning public oversight and enforcement, in particular for cross-border situations, should thus be further improved, despite the important steps taken in this direction with the DSA.

V. Conclusions and Possible Solutions

From the foregoing analysis, we can draw some important conclusions.

In the first place, from the analysis of the EU legal framework regulating this important matter, we can affirm that, despite the protection of the rights of the child being one of the main objectives pursued by the EU and despite its being a fundamental right enshrined in the Charter, at the EU level there is no European act specifically and exclusively dedicated to children's protection online. Comprising a variety of provisions found in different European acts regulating different matters, the EU legal framework on the protection of children online is fragmented, especially as far as concerns its enforcement in relation to minors.

Second, our brief analysis of the provisions in the DSA makes clear that though these provisions may theoretically aim to ensure an adequate protection of minors online, protection is not ensured in practice because of the

[113] In this sense, see Hoffmann and Gasparotti (n 83) 28.

absence of a uniform set of rules adopted at the EU level regulating fundamental aspects for the protection of minors online (eg a standard set of rules for digital platforms on content moderation).

Third, from the analysis of the provisions of the recently proposed CSA Regulation and from an analysis of the CJEU's case law on 'mass surveillance', we can deduce that the proposed CSA Regulation may be considered legitimate only insofar as the general and indiscriminate retention of data concerns IP addresses assigned to the source of a connection where the conditions enumerated in *Quadrature du Net* are respected, and as far as such retention concerns data relating to the users' civil identity. By contrast, an indiscriminate scanning of everyone's private conversations by digital platforms, and especially by providers of hosting or interpersonal communication services, would not, according to the CJEU's ruling, adequately protect internet users from arbitrary investigations and would therefore violate their right to privacy and data protection. We therefor argue that no adequate solutions to detect child sexual abuse within encrypted services have been found so far, nor have effective measures been taken by digital platforms to solve this serious issue.

In the fourth place, we argue that the system of self-regulation by digital platforms connected with the limited secondary liability of digital platforms as set out in the DSA is not appropriate to effectively protect children online in concrete cases. The removal of unlawful content falls within the area of responsibility of large service providers, ie private parties, that are gaining increasing control over the content available on their platforms. However, at the same time it is becoming more difficult for internet service providers to fulfil the conditions which would exclude liability for third-party content. As a result, on the one hand, they are induced to not take initiatives against illegal, inappropriate, or irrelevant content or activity; on the other hand, they tend to over-block critical but lawful content ('collateral censorship'). In both cases, internet users and especially minors are not adequately protected from harmful online content.

Finally, from an analysis of the enforcement mechanisms set out to protect children online, we conclude that even if online platforms have become de facto regulators enjoying increasing powers, there remains a public oversight of digital platforms that is distributed among different sectoral regulators, both at the EU and the national level, with oversight depending on the size of online platforms and other criteria; responsible authorities include data protection authorities, regulators of audiovisual media services, competition authorities, regulators of electronic communication services, and digital services coordinators. Furthermore, uniform and detailed ground rules on age-appropriate digital products – and on services with which companies must comply – have not been incorporated into a EU binding act, nor does there exist a coherent legal framework tailored to meet minors' specific online needs and peculiarities. As far as enforcement mechanisms are concerned, for example, there are no plans for a specific training of either law enforcement officials or the content moderators of online platforms.

The question that arises spontaneously from the foregoing analysis is thus the following: in the absence of an appropriate regulatory framework and effective enforcement mechanisms, is it proper to delegate important unsupervised tasks – such as content moderation, age verification, and adoption or removal of end-to-end encryption – to digital platforms? Are online platforms the most appropriate actors when it comes to protecting the fundamental rights of vulnerable users and, in particular, minors?

Enforcement by Digital Labor Platforms – with Specific Regard to German Labor Law

*Claudia Schubert and Johannes Ipsen**

I. Introduction

Digital labor platforms are a phenomenon that labor law researchers worldwide have been dealing with since 2016.[1] The legal and legal policy discussion

* All links were last accessed on 19 April 2024.

[1] Eg Isabelle Daugareilh, Christophe Degryse and Philippe Pochet, 'Platform Economy and Social Law', ETUI, Working paper 2019.10; Chris Forde and others, *The Social Protection of Workers in the Platform Economy* (European Parliament, DG Internal Policies 2017); Willem Pieter de Groen, Zachary Kilhoffer, Karolien Lenaerts and Irene Mandl, *Digital Age. Employment and Working Conditions of Selected Types of Platform Work* (Eurofound 2019) 9ff; Harald Hauben, Karolien Lenaerts and Willem Waeyaerts, *The*

focuses primarily on four areas: (1) the classification of persons performing platform work as employees, or at least as economically-dependent persons with specific protection, (2) the collective bargaining autonomy for solo self-employed persons working through digital labor platforms,[2] (3) the unreasonable discriminatory treatment of persons performing platform work through the general terms and conditions of the employment relationship,[3] and (4) the further development of the legal situation *de lege ferenda*.

In practical terms, platform work is still a limited phenomenon, even though the number of persons performing platform work has grown significantly. In its 2021 draft directive on improving working conditions in platform work, the European Commission pointed out that 28 million workers are employed on digital labor platforms.[4] The total number of workers in the European Union was approximately 193 million in 2021.[5] Irrespective of the different business

---

Platform Economy and Precarious Work (European Parliament, Employment Committee 2020); Annarosa Pesole and others, 'New Evidence on Platform Work in Europe' (European Commission 2018); Agnieszka Piasna, Wouter Zwysen and Jan Drahokoupil, 'The Platform Economy in Europe', ETUI, Working paper 2022.5; Sara Riso, *Digital Age Mapping the Contours of the Platform Economy* (Eurofound 2019) 5ff; Maria Cesira, Urzì Brancati, Annarosa Pesole and Enrique Férnandéz-Macías, *New Evidence on Platform Work in Europe* (European Commission 2020); see also Christina Hießl, 'Case Law on the Classification of Platform Workers: Cross-European Comparative Analysis and Tentative Conclusions' (2021) (<https://papers.ssrn.com/sol3/papers.cfm?abstract_id=3839603>; see also German Federal Ministry of Labour and Social Security, Research Report no 462 (2016); Research Report no 490 (2016); Research Report no 499 (2017); Research Report no 508 (2018); Bertelsmann Foundation, *Deutschland/Plattformarbeit* (2019); Eva Kocher, 'Digitale Plattformarbeit – die Verantwortung von Marktorganisatoren' [2021] ZEuP 601; Daniela Mayr, *Arbeitsrechtlicher Schutz Soloselbständiger am Beispiel der Plattformarbeit* (Duncker & Humblot 2021) 74ff; Martin Risak and Doris Lutz (eds), *Arbeit in der Gig Economy* (ÖGB Verlag 2017).

[2] Eg Frank Bayreuther, *Sicherung der Leistungsbedingungen von (Solo-)Selbständigen, Crowdworkern und anderen Plattformbeschäftigten* (Bund 2018); Michael Doherty and Valentina Franca, 'Solving the "Gig-saw"? Collective Rights and Platform Work' (2020) 49 ILJ 352; Ioannis Lianos, Nicola Countouris and Valerio De Stefano, 'Re-thinking the Competition Law/Labour Law Interaction: Promoting a Fairer Labour Market' (2019) 10 ELLJ 291; José María Miranda Boto, Elisabeth Brameshuber and Daniel Pérez del Prado, *Collective Bargaining and the Gig Economy* (Bloomsbury 2022); see also Claudia Schubert, 'Guidelines on the application of Article 101 of the TFEU to Collective Agreements Regarding the Working Conditions of Solo Self-Employed Persons – An Analysis' [2023] ZVglRWiss 363.

[3] Eg Eva Kocher, 'Spinnen im Netz der Verträge – Geschäftsmodelle und Kardinalpflichten von Crowdsourcing-Plattformen' (2018) 18 JZ 862.

[4] Compare European Commission, Proposal for a Directive of the European Parliament and of the Council on improving working conditions in platform work, 9 December 2021, COM/2021/762 final, 1, 12.

[5] Eurostat. (2022). Europäische Union & Euro-Zone: Anzahl der Erwerbstätigen von 2011 bis 2021 (in Millionen). Statista <https://de.statista.com/statistik/daten/studie/249

models of the digital labor platforms,[6] it is relevant for the assessment of their general terms and conditions (GTC) that many of these platforms do not operate on the global labor or service market. Instead, they offer or mediate nationwide or regional services that are not provided virtually, but locally (eg cleaning services, craft services, courier services). Such enterprises are thus also related to the actual and legal conditions on site. The activity of these workers is not always a full-time occupation serving as their main source of income; rather, it is in many cases only secondary employment or part-time activity. Digital labor platforms offer access to the labor and service market for people who do not want or cannot take up permanent employment.

II. Private Regulation as a Means for the Enforcement of Interests by Digital Labor Platforms

1. *Typical Contractual Arrangements for Platform Work*

From a labor law perspective, it is also important to note that two forms of platform work exist: platforms either act as the contractual partner of the worker (the so-called service chain model) or they merely mediate a contract between the client and the worker (the so-called agency model).[7] In European academic literature, the former is also referred to as indirect crowdworking and the latter as direct crowdworking. In all cases, the digital labor platform concludes a framework agreement with the person performing platform work as the basis of their contractual relationship.[8] In this contract, the person performing platform work does not directly commit to the work; rather, the agreement contains the arrangement of the work assignments and the app used for the work.[9] In principle, the work assignments are only arranged via

097/umfrage/erwerbstaetige-in-der-europaeischen-union-eu/#statisticContainer>; in 2023, the number of persons employed was 195 million, see Eurostat. (2023). Europäische Union: Anzahl der Erwerbstätigen in den Mitgliedstaaten im 1. Quartal 2023 <https://de.statista.com/statistik/daten/studie/249104/umfrage/erwerbstaetige-in-den-eu-laendern/>.

[6] Riso (n 1) 5ff.

[7] Eg Valerio De Stefano, 'Introduction: Crowdsourcing, the Gig-Economy and the Law' (2016) 37 CLLPJ 471, 474f; Kocher (n 3) 863; Rüdiger Krause, 'Auf dem Weg zur unionsrechtlichen Regelung von Plattformtätigkeiten – Die Kommissionsinitiative zur Plattformarbeit' [2022] NZA 521, 524; Stefan Kreß, *Crowdwork* (Duncker & Humblot 2021) 27ff, 48ff; Mayr (n 1) 36ff, 46ff; Susanne Walzer, *Der arbeitsrechtliche Schutz der Crowdworker* (Nomos 2019) 61ff; see also Jan Marco Leimeister, Shkodran Zogaj, David Durward and Ivo Blohm, *Systematisierung und Analyse von Crowd-Sourcing-Anbietern und Crowd-Work-Projekten* (HSI 2016) 28ff.

[8] In detail on the design of the contractual relationship, Walzer (n 7) 57ff.

[9] Abbo Junker, 'Der Arbeitsvertrag zwischen Freiheit und Bindung' [2021] ZfA 502, 505f; Walzer (n 7) 59f.

the app. The content of the working tasks (orders) is described very specifically and regularly contains information on the time of performance. In the case of courier drivers, a shift system was, in some instances, agreed upon in the past, though this is no longer practiced today in order to avoid classifying courier drivers as employees.[10] The framework agreement also regulates the establishment of the account with the platform along with its conditions, payment, and termination of the contractual relationship.

2. Legal Classification of Contracts with Persons Performing Platform Work

Contracts with persons performing platform work can be classified as service contracts or employment contracts. This classification is of crucial importance for the legal status of the person performing platform work in all EU Member States. Social protection under labor law is generally limited to employees. Protection under social security law is also not uniform for employees and self-employed persons. In Germany, there is compulsory social insurance only for employees in order to cover the typical employment risks for dependent employees (illness, unemployment, old age), ie statutory health insurance, accident insurance, unemployment insurance, pension insurance. In contrast, social insurance is voluntary for self-employed persons, and they pay their contributions alone. These differences in social security mean that employing a self-employed person is significantly cheaper than employing an employee. As a result, in areas where both the employment of an employee or the employment of a self-employed person are conceivable, the competition between forms of employment will be decided in favor of self-employed persons. There is an incentive for companies to design their business model in such a way that self-employed persons are employed.

Some Member States within the European Union have specific regulations for solo self-employed persons who are economically dependent,[11] such as Austria, Germany, Italy, Portugal, and Spain.[12] They cover a group of self-employed persons who work without their own employees and who are in the need of social protection. The definition of these persons is not standardized in these Member States.[13] In Germany, such employee-like persons have to be economically dependent on a main client, with whom the main source of

---

[10] See Hießl (n 1) 46; Claudia Schubert, 'Beschäftigung durch Online-Plattformen im Rechtsvergleich – Zur Rechtsstellung von Fahrern bei Fahr- und Kurierdiensten in Europa, (2019) 118 ZVglRWiss 341, 369f.

[11] On economically dependent persons within the Member States of the European Union, see the country reports and the comparative analysis in Claudia Schubert (ed), *Economically-Dependent Workers as Part of a Decent Platform Economy* (Beck Nomos Hart 2023).

[12] See Schubert (n 2).

[13] Claudia Schubert, Comparative Analysis, in Schubert (n 2) paras 14ff.

income is earned or the majority of working time is spent.[14] The need for social protection does not apply to persons who have a particularly high income and are therefore able to provide for themselves.

In Germany, the legal status of so-called employee-like persons does not correspond to that of an employee. Although they are included in health and pension insurance schemes, they alone pay all contributions, whereas half of the contributions for employees are paid by the employer. Labor law applies to them only in certain areas where the legislature has extended to them the personal scope of application of labor law (eg holiday law, care leave, occupational health and safety, anti-discrimination law, data protection law). The Minimum Wage Act does not apply to them. However, they can form trade unions that conclude collective agreements on their working conditions and thereby regulate their remuneration in particular. In practice, however, the level of organization among these employee-like persons is very low, meaning that collective agreements exist primarily for media workers in radio and television.[15] More intensive social protection exists only for home workers, who are regarded as an 'extension of the employer's premises'. Their protection is therefore very similar to that of employees.

The classification of persons performing platform work as employees or as self-employed persons or as economically dependent persons often raises uncertainty. At the same time, the classification determines to a considerable extent the social protection enjoyed by the person. In this respect, the attempt to influence the classification as a self-employed person is of particular importance for digital labor platforms and thus also illustrates an attempt to prevent the application and the enforcement of mandatory employee protection laws (see III).

Digital labor platforms in particular have often tried to avoid or at least disguise the classification of contracts as employment contracts. The draft directive on improving working conditions in platform work therefore contains provisions to improve the enforcement of national labor law.[16] To this end, the draft stipulates not only a procedure for reviewing the classification

---

[14] Claudia Schubert, *Der Schutz der arbeitnehmerähnlichen Personen* (Beck 2004) 29, 32ff; Wolfgang Däubler, 'Arbeitnehmerähnliche Personen im Arbeits- und Sozialrecht und im EG-Recht' [2000] ZIAS 326, 327; Günther Wiese, *Buchautoren als arbeitnehmerähnliche Personen* (Manz 1980) 23, 60; Heinz Josef Willemsen and Michael Müntefering, 'Begriff und Rechtsstellung arbeitnehmerähnlicher Personen: Versuch einer Präzisierung' [2008] NZA 193, 195ff; see also Claudia Schubert, 'Germany' in Schubert (n 2) paras 10f.

[15] Claudia Schubert, 'Collective Agreements Regarding the Working Conditions of Solo Self-Employed Persons in Germany' [2023] ZVglRWiss 420, 421f; on the number of collective agreements, see also Manfred Löwisch and Volker Rieble, *Tarifvertragsgesetz* (4th edn, Vahlen 2017) s 12a para 9; Harald Schliemann, 'Zum Schutz wirtschaftlich schwacher Solo-Dienst- und Werkvertragsunternehmer – Ein Zwischenruf' in: Moderne Arbeitswelt. Festschrift für Rolf Wank (CH Beck 2014) 531, 542f.

of the contract as an employment relationship but also a rebuttable presumption of an employment contract. If a certain number of criteria listed in the provision are met, the existence of an employment contract is presumed.[17] However, the platform can rebut this presumption. As a result, labor law is not extended to all persons performing platform work. The concept of an employee under national labor law remains unaffected. It is only the enforcement of labor law that is to be simplified.

The opinions on this part of the proposed directive vary widely. While some are in favor of a much more far-reaching regulation,[18] others are generally opposed to such a regulation[19]. This has thus far hampered agreement on the proposed directive. Experience with such presumption-based regulations in other Member States (eg Croatia, Estonia, Greece, Malta, the Netherlands, Portugal, Slovenia, Spain) shows that they are not a game changer for the enforcement of labor law.[20] Only by changing the definition of an employee,

---

[16] Proposal for a Directive of the European Parliament and of the Council on improving working conditions in platform work, 9 December 2021, COM/2021/762 final.

[17] See arts 4 and 5 of the Proposal for a Directive of the European Parliament and of the Council on improving working conditions in platform work, 9 December 2021, COM/2021/762 final.

[18] Opinion of the European Committee of the Regions – Improving working conditions in platform work, 30 September 2022, OJ C375/45, 53f; compare also the Opinion of the European Economic and Social Committee on the Communication from the Commission to the European Parliament, the Council, the European Economic and Social Committee and the Committee of the Regions – Better working conditions for a stronger social Europe: harnessing the full benefits of digitalisation for the future of work (COM/2021/761 final) and the Proposal for a Directive of the European Parliament and of the Council on improving working conditions in platform work (COM/2021/762 final) 29 July 2022, OJ C290/95, 96, 101; Valerio De Stefano, 'The EU Commission's Proposal For A Directive On Platform Work: An Overview' [2022] ILLeJ 1, 3f.

[19] Compare eg Offener Brief mehrerer Arbeitgeberverbände, 2 November 2022, 'EMPL-Bericht Plattformarbeitsrichtlinie: Ende der Solo-Selbstständigkeit in Europa', <https://www.vgsd.de/wp-content/uploads/2022/11/Brief-Ende-der-Solo-Selbststaendigkeit-2.11.2022.pdf>; in academic literature, Stephan Gräf, 'Der Richtlinienentwurf zur Plattformarbeit – Analyse, Umsetzungsperspektiven und Alternativen' [2023] ZfA 209, 256ff; Claudia Schubert, 'Richtlinienvorschlag Plattformarbeit: Anwendungsbereich und Beschäftigungsstatus' in Richard Giesen, Abbo Junker and Volker Rieble (eds), *Arbeitsrechtsfragen bei Crowdworking und Plattformarbeit* (ZAAR 2023) 69, 83ff.

[20] On the national laws, see the contributions on 'The Concept of "Employee"' in Bernd Waas and Guus Heerma van Voss (eds), *Restatement of Labour Law in Europe* (Bloomsbury 2017) from Ivana Grgurev, 'The Position in Croatia', 59, 79f; Gaabriel Tavits, 'The Position in Estonia', 149, 166f; Costas Papadimitriou, 'The Position in Greece', 275, 287; Lorna Mifsud Cachia, 'The Position in Malta', 435, 454ff; Guus Heerma van Voss, 'The Position in the Netherlands', 477, 499f; José João Abrantes and Rita Canas da Silva, 'The Position in Portugal', 543, 553f; Polonca Končar, 'The Position in Slovenia', 641, 654f; Joaquín García Murcia and Iván Antonio Rodríguez Cardo, 'The Position in Spain', 657, 671f; see further Christina Hießl, 'The Legal Status of Platform

in particular by simplifying the definition of an employment contract (as has been done, for instance, in Californian labor law[21]), would we see the application of labor law significantly affected. Under this premise, there might also be a practical impact on persons performing platform work.

3. *Typical Enforcement Mechanisms by Digital Labor Platforms*

Additionally, the framework agreements contain continuing obligations. In practice, the enforcement of contractual obligations is limited by the fact that they must be performed personally and that there are limits for legal enforcement with regard to the execution procedure under civil procedure law. For an effective enforcement of rights and interests, the platforms therefore do not concentrate on regulating judicial and extrajudicial enforcement and will instead often require an agreement on contractual penalties or on a right to alter the legal relationship unilaterally in the case of a breach of obligations (eg reduction of remuneration, restriction or closure of the online account). The exercise of such rights may also be based on customer complaints or the monitoring and evaluation of work results by customers in rankings. As a result, contractual penalties and unilateral rights enjoyed by the platforms have a preventive effect and spare the digital labor platform from having to enforce the law because they can act unilaterally. At most, the contractual penalty must be sued for. It is thus up to the persons performing platform work to defend themselves against the platform's exercise of unilateral rights. Whether such an action is brought depends primarily on whether the person performing the platform work has an interest in continuing the contractual relationship with the digital labor platform. Legal disputes arise mainly in connection with the termination of employment by the platform.[22]

Platforms use GTC to regulate the contractual relationship as far as possible with regard to national statutory law. The platforms do not limit themselves to merely influencing the enforcement of their rights under the contract through alternative dispute resolution or online dispute resolution clauses. In the case of digital labor platforms in particular, there is only limited scope for this when it comes to employment relationships (see II.). In order to enforce the interests of the platform and control the behavior of the persons perform-

---

Workers: Regulatory Approaches and Prospects of a European Solution' [2022] ILLeJ 13, 19f; Miriam Kullmann, 'Platformisation of Work: An EU Perspective on Introducing a Legal Presumption' [2022] ELLJ 66, 68f.

[21] See the so-called ABC-Test, section 2750 (b)(1) State of California Labour Code; on its legal development, see William B Gould IV and Marco Biasi, 'The Rebuttable Presumption of Employment Subordination in the US ABC-Test and in the EU Platform Work Directive Proposal: A Comparative Overview' [2022] ILLeJ 85, 87ff.

[22] Eg BAG 1 December 2020, 9 AZR 102/20, 173 BAGE 111.

ing platform work, it is in some cases much more effective to provide for the aforementioned contractual rights and penalties in GTC.

The aim of this chapter is to illustrate the different mechanisms of enforcement, even if they occur prior to a judicial or extrajudicial dispute resolution proceeding (eg clauses on penalties, wage deductions, termination clauses or comparable measures). In practice, these measures have at least the same importance as the rules on judicial and extrajudicial dispute resolution, such that an evaluation of GTC that was limited to the latter would not give a realistic picture of the enforcement of digital labor platforms.

As the design of GTC can be determined to a considerable extent by the national legal system, the following is a brief overview of the legal framework that digital labor platforms have to deal with when designing their GTC and tailoring their enforcement strategy. This is followed by an evaluation of the clauses that are used in practice in the GTC of digital labor platforms. The focus is initially on clauses that digital labor platforms use to influence the classification of the contractual relationship. We then turn to clauses on remuneration, its payment, and its reduction, as well as contractual penalty clauses. These all serve to enforce the interests of the digital labor platforms during the ongoing contractual relationship. Finally, the clauses on the termination of the contractual relationship, which are also important in terms of their preventive effect, must be taken into account. Only in a last step do we turn to the clauses that deal specifically with legal disputes and dispute resolution.

III. Existing Legal Framework for Enforcement Design in German Law

1. Legal Assessment of Contractual Arrangements of Persons Performing Platform Work

The legal assessment and effectiveness of the contractual arrangement depends on which mandatory or dispositive regulations the legal system provides for such contracts. In the case of digital labor platforms, this legal framework is particularly dependent on whether the persons performing platform work have concluded employment contracts or service contracts with the platform. The demarcation between the contract types is not at the disposition of the contracting parties because employment contracts are structured by a multitude of (unilaterally) mandatory employee protection laws which cannot be deviated from to the detriment of the employees. The choice of the type of contract is not determined by the agreement of the contracting parties or the designation used in the contract, but by the actual performance of the contractual relationship.[23] This applies not only in German law (German Civil

Code, s 611a(1)(6)) but in all continental European legal systems. Even English courts no longer focus solely on the designation of the contract, since the Supreme Court decision of *UBER v. Aslam*.[24] This approach ultimately prevents the circumvention of compulsory labor standards. The classification of a contractual relationship is fraught with legal uncertainty particularly in the grey zones of labor law, which also include the contracts of digital labor platforms. This influences the drafting of the law and usually makes it more difficult for employees to enforce their rights.

Under German law, persons performing platform work are currently classified to a considerable extent as self-employed persons and to some extent as employees, even if the latest decision of the Federal Labour Court means that in the future it will be more common to assume that an employment contract has been concluded.[25] The persons performing platform work may also be employee-like persons, ie workers who are self-employed but economically dependent on a main client.[26] The classification of a contract as an employment contract depends on whether it is a matter of work that is bound by instructions and determined by others in a relationship of personal dependency (German Civil Code, s 611a(1)(1)). In practical terms, it is of crucial importance whether not only the individual work order offered by the platform but also the framework contract with the digital labor platform is an employment contract.[27]

---

[23] For German labor law in general, see eg BGH 14 July 1956, V ZR 223/54, 21 BGHZ 319, 333, 363; BGH 25 September 1985, IVa ZR 22/84, 95 BGHZ 393, 397, 399; BGH 9 May 2000, VI ZR 172/99, [2000] MDR 956, 957; Jan Busche, in Franz Jürgen Säcker and others (eds), Münchener Kommentar zum Bürgerlichen Gesetzbuch (9th edn, CH Beck 2021) § 133 para 64; on employment contracts, see BAG 15 March 1978, 5 AZR 819/76, 30 BAGE 30, 163; BAG 22 August 2001, 5 AZR 502/99, [2003] NZA 662, 663; BAG 17 April 2013, 10 AZR 272/12, 145 BAGE 26 para 15; see also Günter Spinner, in Franz Jürgen Säcker and others (eds), Münchener Kommentar zum Bürgerlichen Gesetzbuch (9th edn, CH Beck 2023) § 611a para 89; Roland Schwarze, 'Noch einmal: § 611 a Abs. 1 S. 6 BGB und der arbeitsrechtliche Formenzwang' [2020] RdA 231; offering a different approach, Karl Riesenhuber, '„Arbeitsgleiche Durchführung" als „arbeitsrechtlicher Formenzwang"?' [2020] RdA 226.

[24] Supreme Court 19 February 2021 – *Uber BV et al. (Appellants)/Aslam et al. (Respondents)*, UKSC 2019/0029.

[25] BAG 1 December 2020, 9 AZR 102/20, 173 BAGE 111 para 46.

[26] Compare Wolfgang Däubler, 'Digitalisierung und Arbeitsrecht' [2016] SR 32; Olaf Deinert, *Solo-Selbstständige zwischen Arbeits- u. Wirtschaftsrecht* (Nomos 2015); Michael Fuhlrott and Sönke Oltmanns, 'Der Crowdworker – (K)ein Arbeitnehmer?' [2020] NJW 958; Hans Hanau, 'Schöne digitale Arbeitswelt?' [2016] NJW 2613, 2616; Eva Kocher and Isabell Hensel, 'Herausforderungen des Arbeitsrechts durch digitale Plattformen – ein neuer Koordinationsmodus von Erwerbsarbeit' [2016] NZA 984, 989; Rüdiger Krause, *Gutachten für den 71. DJT* (CH Beck 2016) B 103ff; Claudia Schubert, 'Neue Beschäftigungsformen in der digitalen Wirtschaft – Rückzug des Arbeitsrechts?' [2018] RdA 200, 203f.

[27] Compare for German law BAG 1 December 2020, 9 AZR 102/20, 173 BAGE 111 para 46.

If the framework contract of the person performing platform work qualifies as an employment contract, a significant number of working conditions are subject to mandatory legal provisions which the contracting parties cannot disregard by deviating from them to the detriment of the employee or by choosing some other law.[28] In addition, as in the case of self-employed persons, courts will review the fairness of contractual terms, which is intended to prevent unreasonable disadvantages. Even though the European Unfair Contract Terms Directive (Directive 93/13/EEC, UCTD) does not include employment contracts in its material scope of application, the German legislator has extended the implementation of the Directive to employment contracts. This extension of the material scope of application of the review of GTC was accompanied by a regulation that requires the courts to consider the special features of labor law (German Civil Code, s 310(4)(2)). Furthermore, the classification of the contractual relationship also has an impact on the fairness test, because the deviation from the statutory provisions is part of the standard for an unreasonable disadvantage.

2. *Labor Law as Legal Framework for Standard Employment Contracts*

The contractual design of digital labor platforms and their legal assessment must be carried out against the background of the respective national labor law. There is only a partial European harmonization of labor law. Social security is not harmonized but merely coordinated within the EU. This makes uniform GTC for contracts with digital labor platforms in different Member States more difficult or even impossible.

In Germany, labor law is conceived as employee protection law and is predominantly a part of private law[29] because it is linked to the employment contract. The laws stipulate minimum standards for working conditions from which the parties may not deviate to the detriment of the employees (unilaterally binding statutes). Only very few standards are dispositive or bilaterally mandatory. Behavior-controlling regulations in the sense of nudging are not

---

[28] See Rome I Regulation, art 8(1)(2), Dieter Martiny, in Franz Jürgen Säcker and others (eds), Münchener Kommentar zum Bürgerlichen Gesetzbuch (9th edn, CH Beck 2021) Rom I-VO art 8 paras 22, 36ff.

[29] In many EU Member States, labor law is categorized as part of private law. However, in countries with a strong historical influence of communism (such as Russia, Serbia, Hungary, and Poland), labor law does not belong to civil law, but is a distinct legal branch. This approach is grounded in the premise that labor is not a commodity and that it should be treated in a different manner. The further remarks in this chapter focus on labor law as a private law domain, taking German labor law as the focal point. For Hungarian labor law, see György Kiss, 'Opportunities and Limits of Application Principles and Civil Code Rules in Hungarian Labour Law – Crisis Management with Means of Civil Law', ELLN Working Paper 4/2015, III; for Polish law, see Zygmunt Hajn and Leszek Mitrus, *Labour Law in Poland* (Wolters Kluwer 2019) 34f.

common in labor law due to its purpose. Parts of labor statutes are of a public law nature, which allows the labor authorities to enforce the law and to impose fines. In contrast to other countries (such as France), the labor administration (labor inspection) is not responsible for monitoring the implementation of all labor law, but its competence and authorization require a public law regulation. This applies in particular to occupational health and safety, but the Minimum Wage Act also contains sections of public law.

In addition, minimum working conditions in Germany are traditionally determined by the social partners, who regulate working conditions in collective agreements. Binding collective agreements are a key element of labor law. Collective labor law has considerable national peculiarities in the Member States, which are based on the respective socio-historical developments. Trade unions autonomously agree on working conditions with the employer or the employers' association. In doing so, they are bound by mandatory laws. In some cases, however, the legislature also permits deviations from employee protection laws to the detriment of employees (eg permissible fixed-term contracts without objective reasons). In such cases, the collective agreements of the social partners are nevertheless subject to a specific legal review, because the state – and therefore also the courts – are bound by positive obligations of fundamental rights.[30]

The number of employee protection laws has risen tremendously in the course of the development of labor law during the last 100 years. Legislators have partly codified the standards developed by the social partners and made them applicable to all employees. In some cases, legislators fill gaps where the social partnership and collective agreements become unproductive due to the insufficient number of employees who are organized in trade unions. This is particularly evident for the Minimum Wage Act in Germany.

If the contract with the digital labor platform is an employment contract, the law and collective agreements impose limits for the contract terms. Nevertheless, GTC play a significant role in employment contracts. Labor contracts not only stipulate core working conditions, such as wages, holidays, and working hours, but also contain a large number of other provisions. These relate to remuneration (eg bonuses, special allowances, cancellation clauses, voluntary clauses) and obligations of the parties to the employment contract (eg confidentiality obligations, non-competition clauses), but also to provisions on legal enforcement. Typical for employment contracts are time limits that lead to the expiry of the employee's and employer's claims if these are not asserted within a specific period (typically three, six, or nine months) – and thus long before the expiration of the statute of limitations. Such time limits are accepted by case law because they serve the effective execution of

---

[30] In detail, Daniel Ulber, *Tarifdispositives Gesetzesrecht im Spannungsfeld von Tarifautonomie und grundrechtlichen Schutzpflichten* (Duncker & Humblot 2010).

continuing obligations and legal certainty.[31] The GTC are limited not only by mandatory laws but also by court oversight of the contractual content, as is the case in consumer protection law.

Unlike consumer protection law, labor law is only partially harmonized by EU law. There is no generally applicable definition of an employment contract, an employment relationship, or an employee.[32] Furthermore, there are only minimum standards (TFEU, art 153(4)). Above all, the free movement of workers is intensively regulated in order to facilitate the internal market. There is also harmonization in labor protection law (occupational health and safety, maternal leave, child labor, youth work) and protection against precarious employment relationships (part-time, fixed-term, temporary work). The termination of employment relationships is not generally harmonized, but there is specific protection for employment relationships in the case of collective redundancies and transfers of undertakings. The information and consultation of employees as a collective are regulated only in their basic structures and in particular for Union-scale undertakings and Union-scale groups of undertakings. Collective bargaining and industrial action, in contrast, is not generally harmonized. In addition, EU anti-discrimination law and EU data protection law are of particular importance for labor law, although they are not exclusively a matter of labor law.

In comparison, the law for self-employed persons does not provide social protection. Only persons who are similar to employees enjoy minor protection under German law. Self-employed persons are primarily subject to the applicable professional law, commercial law, and competition law. Competition law in particular generally precludes self-employed persons from joining together in associations to determine prices and other contractual conditions (German Competition Act, s 1). Under German law, employee-like persons have had the right to enter into collective agreements through their associations since 1974 (Collective Agreement Act, s 12a).[33] However, if EU law is relevant to their agreements due to their cross-border nature, the ban on cartels in TFEU,

---

[31] BAG 30 March 1962, 2 AZR 101/61, [1962] NJW 1460, 1461; BAG 7 July 2010, 4 AZR 549/08, [2010] NZA 1068 para 94; BAG 16 March 2016, 4 AZR 421/15, [2016] NZA 1154 para 37; Hansjörg Weber, *Die Ausschlussfrist im Arbeitsrecht* (Duncker & Humblot 1983); critical on such time limits, Stephan Seiwerth, 'Schluss mit Ausschlussfristen?' [2020] ZfA 100, 111ff.

[32] See Robert Rebhahn, 'Die Arbeitnehmerbegriffe des Unionsrechts in der neueren Judikatur des EuGH' [2012] EuZA 3, 22ff; Felipe Temming, 'Systemverschiebungen durch den unionsrechtlichen Arbeitnehmerbegriff – Entwicklungen, Herausforderungen und Perspektiven' [2016] SR 158, 165; Katharina Ziegler, *Arbeitnehmerbegriffe im Europäischen Arbeitsrecht* (CH Beck 2011) 124ff.

[33] Draft Law of the Federal Government, BT-Drucksache 7/975, p 20f; on its development, Stephanie Rachor in Wolfgang Däubler (ed), Tarifvertragsgesetz (5th edn, Nomos 2022) § 12a para 7.

art 101(1) continues to apply, which national legislators cannot restrict to protect solo self-employed persons or employee-like persons. The extent to which such collective agreements of self-employed persons are not covered by the ban on cartels is disputed. On 21 September 2022, the European Commission published Guidelines on the application of EU competition law to collective agreements regarding the working conditions of solo self-employed persons. These assume that both collective agreements of economically dependent solo self-employed persons and collective agreements with digital labor platforms do not fall within the scope of TFEU, art 101(1).[34] However, such collective agreements are up to now rare. Furthermore, there are considerable doubts as to whether the CJEU will fully approve the Guidelines.[35]

In addition, there are only a few approaches for the co-operative design of contracts. In Germany, the Frankfurt Declaration on platform-based work by the trade union IG Metall in cooperation with international organizations and the voluntary declarations of commitment to these standards by digital labor platforms should be highlighted.[36] Some digital labor platforms, their association, and trade unions agreed on a Crowdsourcing Code of Conduct.[37]

3. *Legal Enforcement in Labor Law as Employee Protection Law – Legal Enforcement for Self-employed Persons*

For an assessment of the GTC of digital labor platforms, not only the minimum standard for working conditions but also their enforcement is essential. Enforcement is more strongly promoted for employment relationships than for self-employed persons.

The private enforcement as initiated by employees is supported by the obligation that the employer must provide employees with written proof of the essential aspects of the employment relationship at the beginning of the em-

---

[34] European Commission, Guidelines on the application of Union competition law to collective agreements regarding the working conditions of solo self-employed persons, 30 September 2022, OJ C374/2 under 3.1 and 3.3.

[35] Marco Bretzigheimer and Simon Maturana, 'Arbeitsmärkte und Kartellrecht – Der Leitlinienentwurf der Kommission zu Tarifverträgen von Solo-Selbstständigen' [2022] NZKart 246, 249; Clemens Höpfner, 'Die personelle Reichweite der Tarifautonomie', (2023) 41 VSSAR 105, 130; Jochen Mohr and Paul Mey, 'Kollektivverträge über die Tätigkeitsbedingungen von Solo-Selbständigen nach den neuen Leitlinien der Kommission' [2022] NZKart 665, 669; Schubert (n 2); see also Christina Hießl, '"Enforcement Priorities" as an Escape Route from European Competition Law? An Appraisal of the Commission's Guidelines on Collective Bargaining for the Solo Self-Employed' in Yves Jorens (ed), *The Lighthouse Function of Social Law* (Springer 2023) 123ff.

[36] The Frankfurt Declaration on Platform-Based Work <http://faircrowd.work/de/unions-for-crowdworkers/frankfurt-declaration/>.

[37] See <https://crowdsourcing-code.com/>.

ployment relationship.[38] This should ensure that employees are aware of their rights and thus facilitates the enforcement of their rights; finally, it should improve working conditions by promoting more transparent and predictable employment while ensuring labor market adaptability.[39]

In Germany, private enforcement does not take place before civil courts but before labor courts, which form a separate specialist jurisdiction and are not part of the civil jurisdiction. There are no court costs at first instance and each party bears its own costs. There is no obligation to be represented by a lawyer. Employees can also have their complaint recorded directly in the court by a court official. Each chamber of the court is staffed not only by a professional judge, but also by two lay judges; one represents the employee's side and one represents the employer's side. The court works towards a mutual settlement of the dispute at every stage of the proceedings. Arbitration and mediation are possible in and out of court. However, arbitral tribunals and arbitration proceedings are generally not available (see IV.5.b); the state courts therefore dominate the enforcement of labor law.

There is a private (out of court) arbitration mechanism specifically for digital labor platforms, known as the Ombuds Office. This is a privately established arbitration/mediation body that is accessible to all persons performing platform work whose digital labor platforms have signed the Crowdworking Code of Conduct. The persons performing platform work can submit a complaint to the Ombuds Office, which acts as a mediator and seeks to find fair solutions and reach a consensus between the digital labor platform and the complainant.[40] The Ombuds Office consists of five persons: a member of the German Confederation of Trade Unions, a representative of the German Crowdsourcing Association, a representative of the digital labor platforms which have signed the Code of Conduct, a worker who is registered on one of the platforms that has signed the Code of Conduct, and a neutral chair, regularly a judge. The Ombuds Office makes a recommendation but does not issue an arbitration award. It is only a supplement to the enforcement of rights before the state courts.

In addition, it should be noted that the social insurance schemes determine the status of the person performing platform work independently, because social insurance law has its own definition of a worker ('Beschäftigter') and this status is the basis for compulsory insurance. The status is determined in an administrative procedure conducted by the German Pension Insurance Association. The administrative procedure can be initiated by the digital labor platform, the per-

---

[38] Directive (EU) 2019/1152 of the European Parliament and of the Council of 20 June 2019 on transparent and predictable working conditions in the European Union [2019] OJ L186/105, art 4.

[39] Compare Directive (EU) 2019/1152, art 1.

[40] See the rules of the Ombuds Office <https://ombudsstelle.crowdwork-igmetall.de/en/seite/rules/>.

son performing platform work, or the German Pension Insurance. Its outcome can be challenged before specified administrative courts ('Sozialgericht').

Germany recognizes only individual legal enforcement actions for employees. In general,[41] there are no collective actions as in consumer protection law. However, trade unions have been calling for them for a long time, and there has been debate in academic literature.[42] At present, there is disagreement in legal practice on collective actions for mass procedures (eg in cases of unfair terms and conditions or as regards the application of tariffs).[43] Additionally, there is also no collective redress. Only in the case of collective agreements is it possible for the trade union concluding the agreement to claim that the employers' association should work towards the application of the collective agreements by its members.

In addition to private enforcement, there is legal enforcement by the labor administration and the customs officers in those areas of labor law that contain public law regulations. In addition to supervision measures, fines can be imposed for violations. Criminal sanctions are practically relevant in only a few areas, particularly in the case of a failure to pay social security contributions or taxes. Beyond the labor administration as an authority, there are almost no agencies for enforcing labor law – unlike in consumer law. The Federal Anti-Discrimination Agency is an exception. European Union law does not contain any specific requirements either, instead usually only stipulating that the Member States must provide for effective, proportionate, and dissuasive sanctions.

In comparison, self-employed persons generally only have access to civil courts. The only exception is for employee-like persons, who have access to labor courts. Only professional judges make decisions in the civil courts. Although there is no obligation to have a lawyer in small claims actions, the losing party must bear not only the court costs but also the costs of the other party, meaning that the losing party will also have to reimburse the other

---

[41] The implementation of Directive (EU) 2020/1828 of the European Parliament and of the Council of 25 November 2020 on representative actions for the protection of the collective interests of consumers and repealing Directive 2009/22/EC [2020] OJ L409/1, may also cover claims by employees who are consumers under German law – unlike under European law. See Martin Diller, 'Arbeitsrechtliche Verbandsklagen vor dem OLG?' [2023] NZA 673; Güray Bayat, 'Doch keine Verbandsklagen in Arbeitssachen' [2023] NZA 1165.

[42] See Ulrich Fischer, 'Betriebsratliche Rechtsdurchsetzung von gleichgelagerten betrieblichen Arbeitnehmeransprüchen – Alternative zur Massenklage?' [2003] RdA 269; Daniel M Klocke, *Rechtsschutz in kollektiven Strukturen* (Mohr Siebeck 2016); Wolfgang Däubler, 'Kollektive Durchsetzung individueller Rechte?' [1995] AuR 305.

[43] Compare DGB Diskussionspapier zur Verbandsklage im Arbeitsrecht, 14 March 2022 <https://www.dgb.de/themen/++co++4152699a-aa8e-11ec-ad1b-001a4a160123>; Bund-Länder-Arbeitsgemeinschaft; critical of such collective action, Bundesvereinigung der Arbeitgeber, 'Stellungnahme zu einer Erstreckung der Klagemöglichkeiten aus dem U-KlaG auf Arbeitsverträge sowie zur wettbewerbsrechtlichen Sanktionierung bestimmter Verstöße gegen arbeitnehmerschützende Vorschriften', 15 January 2024.

party for any attorney fees if one was employed. An advance on court costs must be paid when the action is brought. However, the plaintiff can apply for court cost assistance. Elements of conciliation and mediation are also anchored in civil courts, and there is access to arbitration. Due to the lack of specific social protection for self-employed persons, there are no special forms of legal enforcement with regard to the need of social protection.

IV. Evaluation of Selected General Terms and Conditions

1. Selected General Terms and Conditions

For the purpose of this part, the general terms and conditions (GTC) of 12 digital labor platforms[44] were analyzed in June 2023. The analyzed GTC come partly from reviewed platforms of Fair Crowd Work[45] and have partly been provided by persons performing platform work. Given the enormous number of online platforms, this evaluation cannot claim to be of an exhaustive nature, but it provides first indications for further research. It must be noted that 9 out of the 12 platforms have their (main) seat in Germany and were designed against the background of German law. Some companies that employ persons performing platform work in different states have several GTC with regard to the place of employment.

2. Classification of Contractual Relationship

Although the classification of the contract as an employment contract does not depend on the parties' designation of the contract, the majority of the GTC contains a provision on the legal classification of the contract (7 out of 12). As a rule, it is stated that the person performing platform work is an independent contractor.[46] In part, it is formulated in the negative, stating that no partnership, no joint venture, and no employment relationship is established (eg section 5 para 3 GTC AppJobber). In some cases, the employment relationship is indirectly excluded by stating that the person is not a consumer

---

[44] Amazon Mechanical Turk, Inc., clickworker GmbH, WorkGenius GmbH, content.de AG, Prolific Academic Ltd, IT2media GmbH & Co. KG (Crowdgurus), Dipl.-Kfm. Arnulf Mende (STUDENTENRING), wer denkt was GmbH (AppJobber), Testbirds GmbH, jovoto GmbH, Streetspotr GmbH, Lernigo GmbH.

[45] Fair Crowd Work is a joint project of IG Metall, the Austrian Chamber of Labour, the Austrian Trade Union Confederation, and the Swedish white-collar union Unionen, in association with research and development partners Encountering Tech and M & L Communication Marketing. See, therefore <http://faircrowd.work/platform-reviews/>.

[46] See GTC Amazon Mechanical Turk; section 1 no 1 Testbirds; para 2.2 and 4 GTC Content.de; GTC Clickworker; GTC Upwork.

(eg GTC WorkGenius)[47] or by stipulating that the person performing platform work pays tax on the income himself (eg GTC Crowdguru/IT2media) instead of the employer collecting the income tax from the employee's remuneration. If the platform wants to implement an agency model, it stipulates that all conditions in the framework agreement are only conditions under which the workers are placed (eg GTC Lernigo; GTC Streetspotr).

Such GTC are not, as a result, decisive for the application of unilaterally mandatory laws for the protection of employees or economically dependent persons. In all cases, it must be determined objectively on the basis of the facts whether an employment contract exists or not. Alternatively, the application of several labor law provisions may result from the classification of the worker as a solo self-employed but economically dependent person who is similar to an employee. This is also independent of the designation of the contract in the GTC.

3. *Enforcement During the Current Contractual Relationship*

a) *Remuneration clauses*

Remuneration is one of the core contract conditions and is addressed by all GTC. Regarding these regulations, the following can be observed: (1) only a minority of the analyzed GTC contain the exact remuneration for the person performing platform work[48] because the orders have specific prices, (2) in contrast, the majority of the analyzed GTC (10 out of 12) contain the right to reductions in the remuneration for a breach of contract, be it the primary requirements (eg quality of work, timely delivery) or be it the secondary requirement, and (3) almost all analyzed GTC regulate the disbursement of the remuneration, the manner of disbursement, and the time frame.

Reasons for a reduction in the remuneration are, primarily, non-performance and defective performance of the primary requirements.[49] This includes the client's rejection of the fulfillment.[50] Additionally, reductions in remuneration also enforce a number of obligations for the person performing platform work, which do not refer to the performance but facilitate the operation of the digital labor platform (eg entering or verifying information for

---

[47] On employees being consumers under German law, BAG 25 May 2005, 5 AZR 572/04, [2005] NZA 1111; 31 August 2005, 8 AZR 303/05, [2006] NZA 1273; 18 March 2008, 9 AZR 186/07, [2008] NZA 1004.

[48] While the GTC of one platform expressly stipulate the exact amount per hour (GTC Lernigo), the GTC of another refer for some cases to the categories shown on the webpage which provide estimates of the remuneration (ie no 7 of the GTC of content.de).

[49] Eg section 4 para 1 GTC AppJobber; section 7 GTC Lernigo; no 4.2, 6.1 GTC Crowdguru/IT2media; no 5.5 GTC content.de.

[50] See GTC Prolific; III.3.c GTC Streetspotr; section 3 para 2, section 5 para 1 GTC Testbird; section 4.4, 6.1 GTC AppJobber; no 7.1 WorkGenius.

disbursement, identification of the user)[51] and limits administrative burdens within continuing obligations (eg exclusion clauses).[52] Finally, digital labor platforms protect their economic interests through additional obligations, such as by prohibiting registration of more than one account or registration of a third party[53] or prohibiting unauthorized transfers,[54] but clarification is needed as to whether the scope of such prohibitions is appropriate.

Finally, the disbursement of remuneration is not uniformly stipulated. In some instances, the disbursement is exclusively or preferably carried out via PayPal;[55] in other instances the person performing platform work can choose between selected manners of disbursement.[56] Sometimes, a third party will be responsible for these monetary transactions.[57] In addition, the time frame for disbursement varies.[58] Further, the digital labor platforms reduce administrative burden by stipulating a minimum amount for disbursement.[59]

With regard to the enforcement of the digital labor platform's interests in cases of conflict, the clauses on the unilateral reduction of remuneration are of central importance. They allow the platform to unilaterally enforce its interests and subsequently change the relationship between performance and consideration, which is central to the exchange agreements. In German law, clauses that serve to unilaterally adjust remuneration are subject to strict substantive scrutiny. This applies to both employment contracts and service contracts, as the transformation of the Unfair Contract Terms Directive (Directive 93/13/EEC) was extended to employment relationships (see II). Even if performance descriptions and remuneration provisions[60] are not included in the review of the

---

[51] See no 6.3 GTC Jovoto regarding information for PayPal or bank account disbursement; see also no III.3.h GTC Streetspotr; section 2.2 GTC clickworker; Prolific; see also regulation 9.2 GTC content.de, which reserves the right to demand proof of identity and to withhold payment until identification can be verified. If such proof cannot be provided within 6 months (starting in the case of the request), content.de considers this a waiver of the right to payment.

[52] See GTC Prolific: 18 months for a claim of the minimum amount, 6 months or longer for specific rewards; no 7.4 GTC Crowdguru/IT2media: one year; no III.3.h GTC Streetspotr: three years.

[53] See section 2.4 GTC clickworker.

[54] Prolific.

[55] See no 6.1 GTC Jovoto; see no III.3.g GTC Streetspotr.

[56] See GTC Clickworker; GTC AppJobber; GTC Prolific; GTC content.de.

[57] See eg: 7.4 Work Genius GTC, Point 6 GTC Upwork.

[58] The GTC include, for example, how often money transactions will be carried out by the platform as well as the manners of payment by the platform; eg AppJobber, Jovoto.

[59] See Clickworker; content.de; Crowdguru/IT2media; Polific.

[60] Such remuneration provisions are agreements on remuneration as direct consideration for the work performed. This includes special allowances paid for the work performed (eg local bonuses, family bonuses, Christmas bonuses). See eg BAG 20 February 2008, 10 AZR 125/07, [2008] NZA 1124 para 14.

substance of contractual clauses (German Civil Code, s 307(3)),[61] all supplementary provisions that do not relate to pricing itself but that define the circumstances of the main performance promise made by the user (eg waiver clauses, time limits on working conditions, reduction clauses, contractual penalty provisions) are subject to judicial review.[62] The German Federal Labour Court has long-standing rulings holding that clauses which allow the employer to unilaterally reduce the remuneration are an unreasonable disadvantage if the employer can reduce the remuneration by more than 25%.[63] Moreover, the reduction of remuneration must not be arbitrary, ie the disbursement cannot be reduced for no reason. The clause must specify the reasons for which such a reduction of remuneration can be made.[64]

In the case of contracts between the platform and a solo self-employed person, the effectiveness of the clause in the context of the review of the GTC also depends on the weighing of the interests of the platform in amending an initial promise with the interest of the person performing platform work.[65] Due to the conflicting interests of both contracting parties, it usually depends on whether the adaptation of the contract is necessary for the platform.[66] Therefore, it is not permissible to reserve a right of change when not linked to a specific reason for such change.[67] The adjustment is necessary above all if the platform is entitled to a reduction under the applicable contract law due to deficiencies in the provision of services. The same applies if the platform has a claim for damages against the person performing platform work, which is enforced by the reduction of the remuneration.

---

[61] BAG 17 December 2012, 5 AZR 792/11, [2013] NZA 266 para 15; BAG 25 April 2023 9 AZR 187/22, [2023] NJW 2899 para 14.

[62] BAG 27 July 2005, 7 AZR 486/04, NZA 2006, 40, 45; BAG 20 February 2008, 10 AZR 125/07, [2008] NZA 1124 para 14; BAG 11 December 2018, 9 AZR 383/18, [2019] NZA 781 para 17; BAG 25 April 2023, 9 AZR 187/22, [2023] NJW 2899 para 15.

[63] BAG 27 July 2005, 7 AZR 486/04, [2006] NZA 2006, 40, 45; BAG 12 January 2006, 5 AZR 364/04, [2005] NZA 465f; BAG 19 December 2006, 9 AZR 294/06, [2007] NZA 809; BAG 24 January 2017, 1 AZR 774/14, [2017] NZA 777 para 25.

[64] Ibid.

[65] Compare Wolfgang Wurmnest, in Franz Jürgen Säcker and others (eds), Münchener Kommentar zum Bürgerlichen Gesetzbuch (9th edn, CH Beck 2021) § 308 Nr. 4 para 16.

[66] In general (without regard to platforms) BGH 21 December 1983, VIII ZR 195/82, 89 BGHZ 206, 211; BGH 30 June 2009, XI ZR 364/08, [2009] NJW-RR 1641; Wurmnest, ibid.; with regard to platform work, Walzer (n 7) 105ff.

[67] Eg BGH 21 December 1983, VIII ZR 195/82, 89 BGHZ 206, 211; BGH 12 January 1994, VIII ZR 165/92, [1994] NJW 1060, 1063; with regard to platform work, Walzer (n 7) 105f.

b) Penalty clauses

Penalty clauses for a breach of contract are an instrument which can be found in employment contracts as well as in service contracts. However, they are not a typical component in the GTC of digital labor platforms. Only three GTC contain terms which address penalization for a breach of contract (ie GTC Work Genius, GTC content.de, and GTC Lernigo). Subject to the penalty are shortcomings in the performance of the primary requirements, eg the failure of the person performing platform work to comply with an obligation to contact the client regarding the impossibility of fulfilling the project in the agreed time[68] or the production of content that violates the applicable law, the rights of a third party, or that contains defamatory or inciting statements.[69] However, penalties are also stipulated for a breach of secondary requirements, such as for poaching clients from the platform,[70] for (private) advertisement, and for self-promotion[71]. In such cases, the account of the person performing the platform work can be concurrently suspended. Further claims of damages remain unaffected.

4. Enforcement Through Termination of the Contractual Relationship or Comparable Measures

The GTC always regulate the termination of the contractual relationship between the digital labor platform and the persons performing platform work. In addition, there are provisions that give the digital labor platform the right to block or delete the account for the persons performing platform work, without these rules necessarily being linked to the termination of the contract. This is a severe restriction for the platform user, and it can factually result in a situation which is comparable to the termination of the contract itself. In the end, however, such account deletions are to be equated with a termination because the activity for or by means of the platform is possible only if such an account exists. From a legal point of view, its deletion is a termination of the framework contract with the platform. If the platform operates (or purports to operate) as a mediator, the right to terminate the contract does not affect the contract between the platform user and the client, as they share different and individual contractual relationships.[72] However, if the contract

---

[68] See no 4.5 GTC Work Genius (5% deduction of the agreed net remuneration per day, but not more than 20%).

[69] See 8.3, 8.9 GTC content.de.

[70] See 5.6 GTC content.de (lump sum of up to 1,000 Euros and immediate suspension of the account).

[71] See no 8.3, 8.9 GTC content.de, which forbids referrals to third parties or in his/her own company name (including the URL, e-mail addresses, telephone numbers as well as names).

[72] Expressly stated in point 13.1 of Upwork's GTC.

with the client is only for a specific order, the termination of the platform has – with regard to the economic consequences – the same effect as if the platform gives the orders itself.

The termination of the framework agreement is regulated uniformly in some of the GTC. The same rules apply to both the digital labor platforms and the persons performing platform work (eg Prolific, Streetspotr).[73] There is also no distinction between ordinary termination, ie termination with notice, and extraordinary termination. This is not expressly regulated, but some GTC include a right to immediate termination for compelling reason.

The other GTC distinguish between termination with notice, which does not require a reason for termination, and immediate termination for compelling reason, which takes effect upon receipt without a notice period. The notice period for both parties can be from 14 days (eg content.de) up to 4 weeks (eg AppJobber, Jovoto, Lernigo) or from 1 month to the end of the month (eg GTC WorkGenius).[74] Sometimes, the right to terminate the contract is restricted for the digital labor platform to cases in which the person performing platform work violates the GTC or other obligations arising from the contract (eg Testbirds, Crowdguru/IT2media, clickworker[75]). Sometimes, the platform is even obliged to give a warning before the termination, which allows the platform worker to remedy the abuse.[76] However, in the case of Lernigo, teachers must not terminate the contract without a four weeks' notice period.[77]

Unaffected by this remains the extraordinary termination without notice for both parties;[78] however, this does not affect already assigned orders and projects, unless there is a right to terminate the order or the project as well. The GTC regulate that both parties have the right to terminate the contract immediately and without further notice, especially in all cases of severe and persistent breach of the terms of the contract.[79] The digital labor platforms sometimes also reserve the right to stop operations and all associated services at any time.[80]

Generally speaking, the barriers for terminating the contractual relationship are not higher for persons performing platform work than for the digital labor platforms. Sometimes, the GTC introduce further rights to terminate the

---

[73] See no IV para 1 GTC Streetspotr; no 7 of the GTC of Prolific.

[74] See nos 9.1, 9.3 GTC WorkGenius; no 13.2 of the GTC Jovoto.

[75] In contrast, the person performing platform work can terminate or deactivate the account at any time, section 3.2 GTC clickworker.

[76] The GTC also list events in which a warning does not need be given, section 10 para 2 GTC AppJobber.

[77] See section 10 para 2 of the GTC Lernigo.

[78] See eg no 9.2 GTC WorkGenius; also section 10 para 2 GTC AppJobber.

[79] See no 10.4 GTC WorkGenius; see also no 13.3 GTC Jovoto, which gives examples of when an infringement of the contract is to be deemed serious.

[80] See no 10.7 GTC WorkGenius; compare GTC Jovoto.

contract for persons performing platform work.[81] Only one GTC does not include any regulation on the termination of the account by the person performing platform work (Crowdguru/IT2media). The person performing platform work can leave the account at least inactive; however, this is not the same legal situation as being not legally bound.

Supplementary provisions on the form or receipt of the termination are often included in the GTC. Regularly, the termination has to be in written form (eg WorkGenius) or in textual form (eg content.de; Streetspotr; Upwork).[82] Sometimes, it is additionally stipulated that the termination is effective only if the sender's address is identical to the e-mail address used by the user.[83]

The closure and deletion of the user account by the platform is partly carried out for administrative reasons of the platform (eg in a case of long-term inactive customer accounts or where there are uncertainties about the identity or availability of the user),[84] but also for the enforcement of contractual rights and obligations. In particular, violations of contractual obligations allow for the closure of the user account. Also, violations of the digital labor platform's GTC can be sanctioned by closure of the account.[85]

The assessment of these provisions depends to a particular extent on whether the person performing platform work is an employee or a self-employed person. While the provisions in the GTC fall far short of the requirements of German labor law for such employees who have been employed for more than six months (see German Dismissal Protection Act, s 1(1)), the protection of self-employed persons is much weaker. Even in the case of employee-like persons who are economically dependent on a main client and in need of social protection in the same way as an employee, there are no specific statutory notice periods (except for homeworkers). Despite the need for social protection, the Federal Labour Court has refused to further develop the law to protect these individuals and has not applied the notice periods under labor law by analogy to employee-like persons.[86]

5. Clauses on Legal Disputes

Concerning terms that address legal conflicts as well as procedural issues, the following regulations can be identified as typical: (1) regulations regarding

---

[81] See eg Testbirds, which allows the person performing platform work to delete the account at any time, section 2 no 5 GTC Testbirds.

[82] See no 9.3 GTC WorkGenius; no 10.2 GTC content.de; no IV para 1 GTC Streetspotr. With reference to textual form, section 10 para 5 GTC AppJobber.

[83] See no IV para 1 GTC Streetspotr.

[84] See no 10.3, 10.6 GTC content.de.

[85] See no 10.6 GTC content.de; compare section 2 no 5 GTC Testbirds; section 3.1 GTC clickworker.

[86] BAG 8 May 2007, 9 AZR 777/06, AP BGB § 611 Arbeitnehmerähnlichkeit no 15.

the applicable law, (2) regulations regarding the manner of dispute resolution, and (3) regulations regarding the place of jurisdiction.

a) *Choice of law*

Usually, the companies have used their freedom of choice to subject the contract to the law of the country where the platform has its head office. Of the 12 considered companies, the 9 which have their main seat in Germany have subjected the contract to German law. By contrast, companies having a main seat in other countries prefer their respective legal system (eg GTC Prolific, GTC Upwork), in part restricted to persons located in the respective state.[87] Also, through its choice of law, one platform has expressly excluded the application of private international law.[88] Another has excluded the application of the United Nations Convention on Contracts for the International Sale of Goods (CISG).[89] Others still have excluded both.[90]

A choice of law in GTC is generally permissible under the Rome I Regulation. For this purpose, it is irrelevant whether the contract is an employment contract or a service contract. The classification of the contractual relationship as an employment contract merely has the consequence that the employee protection laws continue to apply as mandatory rules within the meaning of art 8(1), (2) and art 9(1) Rome I Regulation, insofar as the contractual relationship falls within their scope of application. The choice of law must not deprive the employee of the protection afforded to him under national law. This protection cannot be derogated from by agreement.

b) *Dispute resolution*

Regulations regarding the settlement of disputes by arbitral proceedings can rarely be found. Only Amazon Mechanical Turk and Upwork address dispute settlement by arbitration in their GTC. Whereas Amazon Mechanical Turk's GTC stipulate that the Federal Arbitration Act and federal arbitration law and the laws of the state of Washington will apply, Upwork's GTC stipulate that 'the parties are expressly giving up any and all rights to a jury trial or court trial before a judge' and instead elect dispute resolution by arbitration. The

---

[87] '[…] [W]ithout regard to its conflict of law provisions; provided, however, that any Claims made by any Freelancer located within the United States will be governed by the law of the state in which such Freelancer resided at the time the dispute arose.' See regulation 14.2 GTC Upwork.

[88] See no 16.2 GTC Jovoto '[…] Die Anwendung des deutschen Internationalen Privatrechts ist ausgeschlossen.'

[89] Eg no 14.1 GTC Content.de.

[90] Section 11 para 2 GTC Appjobber; no 9.1 GTC Crowdguru/IT2media; no 12.2 GTC Work Genius.

arbitration award shall be final and binding on the parties and subject to review on the grounds set forth in the Federal Arbitration Act.

Alternative dispute resolution and online dispute resolution are covered only partly by the analyzed GTC. Only 5 of 12 GTC contain terms on alternative dispute resolution at all, and they differ with regard to the matters which are dealt with by alternative dispute resolution. The majority of platforms provide for alternative dispute resolution for disputes arising from the contractual relationship with the users in different ways. While Prolific stipulates an attempt to resolve the dispute through internal discussion before transferring the dispute to a court, Amazon Mechanical Turk provides for dispute resolution through arbitration.[91] AppJobber offers the possibility of a mediation procedure through the Ombuds Office of the trade union *IG Metall* following an internal dispute settlement procedure, but without binding itself to the outcome of this mediation or to an exclusion of court proceedings. Some terms limit the scope of alternative (dispute) resolution (by internal review and by mediation) to the deleting (and blocking) of accounts of the users (ie Clickworker).

Furthermore, Amazon Mechanical Turk's and Upwork's GTC contain several additional regulations on procedure, but they claim an exceptional position within the investigated GTC. Namely, they exclude class actions and consolidated actions and therefore restrict enforcement to claims on an individual basis. In addition to this, under these two companies' GTC, both parties waive the right to a jury.

The cautious regulation of legal enforcement by the platforms proves to be advantageous in view of the fact that some of the persons performing platform work are employees. German law has a special labor jurisdiction that allows mediation and conciliation but excludes arbitration for individual claims by employees. According to the German Labor Procedure Act, s 101(1), arbitration proceedings are only available to parties to a collective agreement if they are in dispute about the existence of a collective agreement or if the dispute concerns claims arising from a collective agreement. The social partners, as collective actors, do not need any special protection, so arbitration is open to them. This applies to individual disputes only in exceptional cases where the disputes concern claims arising from collective agreements, the collective agreements themselves provide for the possibility of arbitration, and the employees come from certain occupational groups exhaustively enumerated in the German Labor Procedure Act (eg film-makers, stage artists, performers). In the case of these occupational groups, it was

[91] The provision on the primacy of arbitration contains an exception for claims in small claims court if the claim qualifies; also, Amazon Mechanical Turk allows for dispute resolution proceedings to be conducted only on an individual basis and not in a class, consolidated, or representative action. However, if a claim for any reason proceeds in court rather than in arbitration, both sides waive any right to a jury trial.

considered advantageous, due to the peculiarities of their activities, to allow arbitration in which the arbitral tribunal is composed of persons who belong to or are close to these occupational groups and can therefore take into account the peculiarities of their activities.

In contrast to arbitration, conciliation and mediation form integral parts of labor court proceedings and out-of-court dispute resolution. The labor court procedure for individual disputes between employee and employer always starts with a so-called conciliation hearing before the judge. In addition, the German Labor Procedure Act, s 54(4), provides for the referral of the disputing parties to a conciliator. This is a judge who is specifically trained for such negotiations and mediations and who is also different from the judge who would later decide the dispute in court. In addition to this in-court mediation, the judge can also propose an out-of-court conciliation body to resolve the conflict, German Labor Procedure Act, s 54a. This possibility of mediation and out-of-court dispute resolution was introduced into procedural law in 2012. This applies not only to proceedings before labor courts; parallel provisions are also contained in the Civil Procedure Code. In this respect, the applicable procedural law gives the parties a range of options for dispute resolution, even if no contractual agreement on arbitration or mediation is included in the GTC.

c) *Place of jurisdiction*

As opposed to clauses addressing dispute resolution, we also find clauses on the place of jurisdiction in GTC. The digital labor platforms with their head office in Germany have prorogations for certain German cities, as is permissible under the law.[92] In the case of Prolific, the courts of England and Wales have exclusive jurisdiction, except for non-England or Wales residents, in which situation Prolific may begin proceedings in any court of the state of residence. Prorogation is, in part, explicitly limited to contractual relationships with merchants in the legal sense (see AppJobber, Jovoto, Streetspotr; less precise Clickworker: 'business relationship'). This avoids a violation of the German Civil Procedure Code, s 38(1). For the same reason, and with regard to art 25 Brussels Ia Regulation, one platform (Lernigo) limits prorogation to Germany, and the court of jurisdiction will be determined according to national law.

In German civil procedure law, an agreement on the place of jurisdiction is possible without further ado if it is concluded after the dispute has arisen and the parties reach an agreement with regard to the specific dispute. However, an agreement on the place of jurisdiction is only to a limited extent possible if it is

[92] See section 11 para 3 GTC AppJobber; section 10.3 GTC clickworker; no 14.2 GTC content.de; no 9.3 GTC Crowdguru/IT2media; no 16.1 GTC Jovoto; no VIII para 2 GTC Streetspotr; section 7 no 2 GTC Testbirds; no 12.3 GTC WorkGenius.

made before the dispute arises. The German Civil Procedure Code allows such an agreement on the place of jurisdiction only where merchants or legal persons under public law are involved on both sides of the dispute or where the case involves special funds under public law (German Civil Procedure Code, s 38).

The reference to merchants in the code – instead of companies – is based on the traditional demarcation in Germany of commercial law from the law governing the liberal professions. Unlike other states, Germany does not have a uniform regulation for merchants and freelancers. However, freelancers are covered by the provisions of commercial law if they are a legal entity in the form of a corporation entered in the commercial register (termed a formal merchant). This possibility has been opened up to freelancers only in recent times, with the result that the traditional separation between commercial law and the law governing freelancers has been partially softened.

In this respect, platforms will always be merchants. However, this does not apply in the same way to persons performing platform work. They are usually solo self-employed persons or employees. For employees, who are also consumers according to German law,[93] a jurisdiction agreement (choice of forum clause) before the legal dispute arises is ruled out from the outset. For solo self-employed persons, however, such a clause is permissible only if they exercise a commercial activity and not a liberal profession. An extension of the German Civil Procedure Code, s 38, to self-employed persons has so far been uniformly rejected by courts[94] and has only occasionally been discussed in academic literature.[95]

V. Conclusions

For digital labor platforms and the persons performing platform work, how the contractual relationship is classified is of central importance. Persons who are employees benefit from the mandatory employee protection law and the compulsory social security. In contrast, solo self-employed persons will at most enjoy a limited social protection if they are similar to employees.

---

[93] See German Civil Code, s 13 – Consumer: 'A consumer means every natural person who enters into a legal transaction for purposes that predominantly are outside the consumer's *trade, business or profession.*' (Emphasis supplied.) Thus, only self-employed persons are traders. Compare German Civil Code, s 14(1) – Trader: 'A trader means a natural or legal person or a partnership with legal personality who or which, when concluding a legal transaction, acts in exercise of their trade, business or profession.'

[94] OLG Zweibrücken 16 November 2018, 2 U 68/17, [2019] NZI 54; OLG Köln 29 June 2015, 8 AR 39/15, [2015] NJW-RR 1533; OLG Hamburg 18 January 2008, 13 AR 37/07, OLGR 2008, 340.

[95] Mathias M Siems, 'Fünf Jahre neuer Kaufmannsbegriff – Eine Bestandsaufnahme der Rechtsprechung' [2003] NJW 1297.

The determination of the employment relationship is primarily guided by the facts relating to the actual performance of work. The GTC and in particular the regulations on claims are not relevant. The status determination can be clarified by an action before the labor courts. Therefore, the directive on improving working conditions in platform work[96] focuses on the determination of the employee status by the courts. In this respect, effective access to the courts must be guaranteed.

The legal enforcement of labor law is through individual proceedings in state courts. Arbitration proceedings are excluded in this respect in Germany and other Member States of the European Union. In contrast, mediation and dispute settlements are typically provided both in- and outside courts. Such settlement can also be done through an Ombuds Office; however, individual claims before state courts are predominant in Germany. In addition, there is a public enforcement by the labor administration for occupational safety and health regulations.

In any case, the substantive scrutiny to which a contractual clause is subject protects persons performing platform work against a unilateral enforcement of interests by a platform in its GTC. Especially unilateral platform rights that serve to enforce interests without recourse to the courts must be checked for their fairness. Additional regulations on arbitration and mediation are not necessary if the courts utilize and embrace these possible mechanisms in any event and initially strive for a consensual resolution of disputes, also in the interest of an effective conduct of proceedings. Unless there is a particularly competent body that is preferable to the generally existing possibilities, the use of particular dispute resolution forums is not worth regulating in the GTC. In this respect, labor platforms do not require special regulation, regardless of whether an employment contract or a service contract is at issue.

---

[96] See n 4.

Internal Mechanisms of Enforcement – What Role do Trusted Flaggers Play?

Federica Casarosa

I. Introduction

The digital platform phenomenon is characterized by a number of revolutionary aspects that distinguish digital platforms from traditional media. Two of these are elements that mark a boundary with the other communication means: first, the role of the user, who plays a dual role as both the receiver of the digital platform's service and also as the author of the content published through the platform. In this sense, users are no longer defined as mere consumers but as producers-consumers or 'prosumers'. Second, digital platforms have changed their role from neutral intermediaries and service providers into powerful gatekeepers that intervene in the content published through moderation, screening, selection, cataloguing and, where necessary, the 'labelling' of such content.

These elements have challenged the lenses through which digital platforms were initially regulated by legislation.[1] The E-Commerce Directive[2] of 2000 acknowledged the importance of digital platforms – which were defined as

[1] For a historical perspective, see also Dianora Poletti and Federica Casarosa, Enforcing Platform Rights – The Italian Case Law, in this volume, 239.

[2] Directive 2000/31/EC of the European Parliament and of the Council of 8 June 2000 on certain legal aspects of information society services, in particular electronic commerce, in the Internal Market ('Directive on electronic commerce') [2000] OJ L178/1 (ECD).

internet service providers – in the internal market[3] and, in order to boost economic growth and investments in this sector by European companies, it established a system where digital platforms were exempted from liability for unlawful content published by users.[4] This approach relied on the fact that digital platforms did not interfere with the content and were mere passive intermediaries.

Soon, digital platforms changed their business model in order to provide more (tailored) services to users and to move from being passive providers to actors that can interfere with, if not manipulate, the choices and activities of users.[5] In this context, digital platforms not only define acceptable behavior but also envisage consequences for cases of misconduct. This control over content was justified by the existing legislative framework: upon the logic of the liability exemption, digital platforms were able to become censors of online content.[6]

This type of framework can be characterized as *transnational private regulation*, where the private regulator defines rules and sanctions, in the event of violation, that will apply to the regulatees.[7] As clarified by Cafaggi,[8] transnational private regulations are sector-specific private regulatory regimes that are set up by private bodies but which establish a complementarity with public rules as the latter provide a basic framework upon which the private standards (usually stricter) can apply. One feature of transnational private regulations is the fact that they are generally voluntary, leaving the parties free to choose whether they wish to join the regime; however, once the parties choose to participate, they are legally bound to internal rule and, in the event of violation, they are subject to sanctions.

When looking at the governance structure of digital platforms, the features of transnational private regulation can easily be identified: content moderation

---

[3] Note that at that time, the 'digital single market' was not yet envisaged. The concept was defined only fifteen years later. See European Commission, 'A Digital Single Market Strategy for Europe' (Communication) COM/2015/192 final.

[4] See ECD, arts 12–15.

[5] For the dark side of this process, see Shoshana Zuboff, *The Age of Surveillance Capitalism: The Fight for a Human Future at the New Frontier of Power* (PublicAffairs 2019).

[6] Damian Tambini, *Codifying Cyberspace: Communications Self-Regulation in the Age of Internet Convergence* (Routledge 2008); Christopher T Marsden, *Internet Co-Regulation: European Law, Regulatory Governance and Legitimacy in Cyberspace* (CUP 2011), chapter 'Private ISP Censorship', <https://www.cambridge.org/core/books/internet-coregulation/private-isp-censorship/B105B59C432D99D77E592171F2BFAA7E> accessed 3 July 2024.

[7] Fabrizio Cafaggi, 'New Foundations of Transnational Private Regulation' (2011) 38 JLS 20, 26–28; Fabrizio Cafaggi, 'A Comparative Analysis of Transnational Private Regulation: Legitimacy, Quality, Effectiveness and Enforcement' (2014) Working Paper <https://cadmus.eui.eu/handle/1814/33591> accessed 23 April 2024.

[8] Cafaggi (n 7) 22.

is at the core of the regulatory framework.[9] The terms and conditions, or community standards, are the ways in which digital platforms define the rules applicable to their users, distinguishing between acceptable content and prohibited content. Some of the rules are based on laws and regulations, such as laws relating to copyright material or child pornography, while others are based on the preferences of the digital platforms, relating, for instance, to manipulated content leading to misinformation or the scope of hate speech policy.[10]

Participation in the digital platform is voluntary; however, as soon as users register on the platform or even start using the services provided by the platform, the standards become mandatory. For instance, participation in the social media platform Instagram requires a registration that entails the acceptance of the platform's terms.[11] With Google, by contrast, the mere use of the service results in the user's acceptance of the terms of service.[12]

Within the terms and conditions, some clauses are devoted to conflicts between the platform and the users, allowing the platform to impose sanctions when misbehavior is detected. In this case, the sanctions include the possibility of removing content or the possibility of disabling or terminating the user's account.[13] This type of internal enforcement mechanism goes along with external enforcement that is provided by out-of-court dispute settlement or judicial proceedings.

The detection of misbehavior is based on the monitoring function, which is carried out through technical and organizational means, both ex-ante and ex-post. Digital platforms employ preventive mechanisms that are able to screen and eventually hamper uploads of content before they are published, thus simultaneously linking the monitoring function with enforcement of the

---

[9] Catalina Goanta and Pietro Ortolani, 'Unpacking Content Moderation: The Rise of Social Media Platforms as Online Civil Courts'.in Xandra Kramer, Jos Hoevenaars, Betül Kas and Erlis Themeli (eds), Frontiers in Civil Justice (Edward Elgar 2022).

[10] For a comparison between the different scopes of hate speech definition in several platforms, see Federica Casarosa, 'When the Algorithm Is Not Fully Reliable: The Collaboration between Technology and Humans in the Fight against Hate Speech' in Amnon Reichman and others (eds), *Constitutional Challenges in the Algorithmic Society* (CUP 2021).

[11] See the registration page at <https://www.instagram.com/accounts/emailsignup/>. The webpage clearly states: 'By signing up, you agree to our Terms. Learn how we collect, use and share your data in our Privacy Policy and how we use cookies and similar technology in our Cookies Policy'. The terms adopted by Instagram are available here: <https://help.instagram.com/581066165581870/?locale=en_US> accessed 2 July 2024.

[12] See the Terms of Service available at <https://policies.google.com/terms?hl=en-IT&fg=1> accessed 2 July 2024.

[13] See the section on 'Content Removal and Disabling or Terminating Your Account' in Instagram's Terms of Use (n 11).

rules.[14] However, content detection is definitely not free of flaws. In particular, in the case of technological tools, such as algorithms and artificial intelligence, their ability to recognize the substance of the content analyzed (eg whether or not it qualifies as hate speech or aggressive expression) and also the context in which the content is expressed (eg a quotation from another person, a joke, or a verbal attack) is not foolproof. If these factors are not correctly evaluated, then mistakes may occur, thereby having a subsequent effect on the decision of the online platform to remove or disable access to the content.

In order to improve the level of accuracy and demonstrate a concern for the need to consider the local context and cultures, digital platforms have started to create special routes for what are termed *trusted flaggers*.[15] Notices that come from individuals or institutions falling into this category will have more weight in the content moderation process, thus triggering either a swifter reply or a more thorough analysis of the notice, as their expertise is deemed higher than that of a general user in detecting both illegal materials and content contrary to platforms' standards.[16]

The current academic debate has devoted wide attention to the interplay between public and private actors, acknowledging the limits of state regulation in the digital environment and the redistribution of power emerging from the development of technologies,[17] as well as the shift towards manners of delegating

[14] See James Grimmelmann, 'The Virtues of Moderation' (2015) 17 Yale JLT 42. Note that automated content filtering has been used since the first years of internet development, as many tools have been deployed to analyze and filter content; among them, the most common and well known are those for spam detection or hash matching. For instance, spam detection tools identify content received at one's email address, distinguishing between clean emails and unwanted content on the basis of certain sharply defined criteria derived from previously observed keywords, patterns, and metadata. See Thamarai Subramaniam, Hamid A Jalab and Alaa Y Taqa 'Overview of Textual Anti-spam Filtering Techniques' (2010) 5 International Journal of Physical Science 1869.

[15] As will be clarified in the following analysis, the scope of this trusted flagging activity can be broad, covering any kind of content contrary to the platforms' terms and conditions, or it can be very topic-specific. For instance, in 2016, the Facebook platform established a partnership with fact-checking organizations in order to verify the truthfulness of news. See Mathew Ingram, 'The Weekly Standard and the Flaws in Facebook's Fact-Checking Program' *Columbia Journalism Review* (18 September 2018) <https://www.cjr.org/the_new_gatekeepers/the-weekly-standard-facebook.php> accessed 3 July 2024.

[16] This is the main justification provided by digital platforms, see Naomi Appelman and Paddy Leerssen, 'On "Trusted" Flaggers' (2022) 24 Yale JLT 452.

[17] Elettra Bietti, 'A Genealogy of Digital Platform Regulation' (3 June 2021) <https://papers.ssrn.com/abstract=3859487> accessed 8 February 2024; Giovanni De Gregorio, 'From Constitutional Freedoms to the Power of the Platforms: Protecting Fundamental Rights Online in the Algorithmic Society' (2019) 11 EJLS 65; Nicolas P Suzor, *Lawless the Secret Rules That Govern Our Digital Lives* (CUP 2019); Tarleton Gillespie, *Custodians of the Internet: Platforms, Content Moderation, and the Hidden Decisions That Shape Social Media* (YUP 2018).

enforcement power to private actors, leading to collaborative governance mechanisms.[18] However, within this literature, limited attention[19] has been devoted to the involvement of other stakeholders in the different phases of transnational private regulation and, in particular, to the role of trusted flaggers.

The present contribution will focus on the role of trusted flaggers in the monitoring function and on the impact of such mechanisms in the enforcement undertaken by digital platforms. It should be observed that the trusted flaggers system was initially a voluntary tool that could support the content moderation choices of digital platforms; now, thanks to the Digital Services Act,[20] it has become an institutionalized tool positioned at the boundary between monitoring and enforcement. The contribution will provide a short overview of the role of trusted flaggers in the last years, highlighting the interplay between the interventions of the digital platforms and the reiterated pushes coming from the European bodies so as to strengthen the role and importance of trusted flaggers. Thereafter, a detailed analysis of the current framework will be presented, emphasizing the challenges and the risks that may emerge from the institutionalization of such a mechanism. Conclusions will follow.

II. Trusted Flaggers: The Beginning

The use of (trustworthy) third parties in content moderation dates back to the allocation of intermediary liability on hosting platforms.[21] In order to meet the need for speed as well as accuracy in the evaluation of content, a flagging mechanism was provided by platforms to allow users to express concerns about potentially offensive content.[22] This mechanism allows for a reduction

---

[18] Natali Helberger, Jo Pierson and Thomas Poell, 'Governing Online Platforms: From Contested to Cooperative Responsibility' (2018) 34 The Information Society 1; José van Dijck and Thomas Poell, 'Understanding Social Media Logic' (2013) 1 Media and Communication 2; Jens-Peter Schneider, Kester Siegrist and Simon Oles, 'Collaborative Governance of the EU Digital Single Market Established by the Digital Services Act' (4 September 2023) <https://papers.ssrn.com/abstract=4561010> accessed 28 March 2024.

[19] Appelman and Leerssen (n 17); Sebastian Felix Schwemer, 'Trusted Notifiers and the Privatization of Online Enforcement' (2019) 35 Computer Law & Security Review 105339; Eleonora Rosati, 'The DSA's Trusted Flaggers: Revolution, Evolution, or Mere Gattopardismo?' (*Verfassungsblog*, 22 February 2024) <https://verfassungsblog.de/the-dsas-trusted-flaggers/> accessed 22 March 2024.

[20] Regulation (EU) 2022/2065 of the European Parliament and of the Council of 19 October 2022 on a Single Market For Digital Services and amending Directive 2000/31/EC (Digital Services Act) [2022] OJ L277/1 (DSA).

[21] Appelman and Leerssen (n 17) 11; Schneider, Siegrist and Oles (n 19) 11–12.

[22] Kate Klonick, 'The New Governors: The People, Rules, and Processes Governing Online Speech' (20 March 2017) <https://papers.ssrn.com/abstract=2937985> accessed 18 June 2024.

in the volume of content that is to be reviewed automatically and also identifies content that the automated system does not signal as offensive.

Such a voluntary mechanism then evolved into a more structured system which, however, was based on the needs and decisions of the digital platforms. The latter started to identify individuals or entities as experts or as knowledgeable institutions that may be more trustworthy in the flagging of content, thus becoming 'trusted flaggers'. For instance, YouTube defined trusted flaggers as individual users, government agencies, and NGOs that have specific expertise and, additionally, that have (already) flagged content frequently with a high rate of accuracy and are able to establish a direct connection with the platform.[23] Although it is important to highlight that, in the described case, the monitoring activity was only partially delegated to trusted notifiers,[24] such collaboration was deemed crucial in order to improve the results of content detection and removal.[25]

However, from the perspective of the general public, the use of trusted flaggers remained a less than transparent process: the selection process to identify and recruit trusted flaggers, their role and involvement in content moderation, and the rate of acceptance of their notifications was not disclosed.[26] The intervention of the European Commission in 2018 with the Recommendation on the measures to effectively tackle illegal content online[27] tried to provide some guidelines. According to the Recommendation text,

---

[23] Casarosa (n 10); Appelman and Leerssen (n 16) 3.

[24] See YouTube Trusted Flagger program, where it was stated that 'Content flagged by Trusted Flaggers is not automatically removed or subject to any differential policy treatment – the same standards apply for flags received from other users. However, because of their high degree of accuracy, flags from Trusted Flaggers are prioritized for review by our teams'. Available at <https://support.google.com/youtube/answer/7554338?hl=en>.

[25] It is interesting to note that a similar model was adopted earlier by online marketplaces in order to combat the sale of counterfeited goods online. The VeRO programme was adopted by eBay in 2010 in order to allow owners of intellectual propriety rights to report to the platform listings that may infringe their rights, see at <https://www.ebay.com/sellercenter/ebay-for-business/verified-rights-owner-program>. Such a programme was the reaction of the platform to the decision of the CJEU in case C-324/09, *L'Oréal v eBay*, [2009] ECD I-6073, where the Court affirmed that the operator of an online marketplace can be required to take measures which contribute not only to bringing to an end infringements of intellectual property rights by users of that marketplace, but also to preventing further infringements of that kind (see para 144). See Ansgar Ohly, 'The Liability of Intermediaries for Trade Mark Infringement', *Research Handbook on Trademark Law Reform* (Edward Elgar 2021) <https://www.elgaronline.com/edcollchap/edcoll/9781785366208/9781785366208.00023.xml> accessed 19 June 2024; Patrick van Eecke and Maarten Truyens, 'L'Oréal v. eBay: Is the Tide Finally Turning for Hosting Providers?' (2011) 12 Computer Law Review International 1.

[26] Schwemer (n 19) 8.

[27] Commission (2018) Recommendation 2018/334 of 1 March 2018 on measures to effectively tackle illegal content online, C/2018/1177, OJ L63/50.

platforms should 'publish clear and objective conditions' for determining which individuals or entities they consider as trusted flaggers. These conditions include expertise and trustworthiness and also 'respect for the values on which the Union is founded as set out in Article 2 of the Treaty on European Union'.[28] The Recommendation tried to strengthen the role of trusted flaggers in the notification of unlawful content on the basis of the positive results that emerged from the implementation of the EU Code of Conduct on countering illegal hate speech online.[29] Still, none of the companies involved in such a program changed their approach, leaving the procedure by which one becomes a trusted flagger undisclosed.[30]

This limited transparency was one of the factors that led to the inclusion of a specific provision dedicated to trusted flaggers in the much-awaited Digital Services Act.[31] This legislation aimed to provide a dedicated horizontal regulatory framework for online platforms with rules on digital services in order to prevent unfair practices by online intermediaries and to reduce the power of gatekeepers.[32] The European Commission presented the proposal for the DSA as an act reshaping the European rules on platform governance, yet the provisions addressing the liability of internet service providers followed the ones defined in the already mentioned E-Commerce Directive. The novelty of the DSA lies in the set of rules dedicated to the monitoring and enforcement process, which includes a clear procedure for removing content or disabling users, an obligation to provide a statement of reasons that led to the decision, and information on the redress possibilities available to the recipient of the service in respect of the decision, particularly through internal complaint-handling mechanisms, out-of-court dispute settlement, and judicial redress.[33] This set of rules also includes not only a provision dedicated to trusted flaggers, identifying their role in the monitoring and enforcement phases, but also measures that specify how their activities are to be supervised and measures adopted to avoid potential abuses.

---

[28] Ibid point 27.

[29] European Commission Press Release IP/16/1937 'European Commission and IT Companies Announce Code of Conduct on Illegal Online Hate Speech' (30 May 2016).

[30] Casarosa (n 10) 310.

[31] Supra (n 20).

[32] Miriam Buiten, 'The Digital Services Act: From Intermediary Liability to Platform Regulation' (21 June 2021) <https://papers.ssrn.com/abstract=3876328> accessed 19 June 2024.

[33] See DSA, arts 16, 17, 20, and 22.

III. The Institutionalization of the TF system

As mentioned above, the DSA has institutionalized the position of trusted flaggers (TF) with a specific provision dedicated to their role and the relationship they have with, respectively, digital platforms and the Digital Service Coordinators. Although some of the measures adopted are in line with the previous soft law instruments, others lay out more detailed obligations that run the risk of overburdening TF and, eventually, reducing the advantages of such a system for the providers of such flagging activity.

As emerges from the DSA's recitals, it is evident that the EU legislature regulated TF with a dual objective, on the one hand strengthening the position of TF in the content moderation process led so far by digital platforms and, on the other, limiting the occasions that may lead to abusive behavior. However, the system set up in the DSA is extremely elaborate and imposes several tasks and reporting obligations that may become a barrier to the participation of smaller organizations that have limited internal resources.

In order to clarify the challenges emerging in the application of DSA, art 22, the following analysis will distinguish the role of TF vis-à-vis the digital services coordinator and the digital platform, respectively.

1. The Relationship Between TF and Digital Services Coordinators

a) The selection of TF

The selection of TF is no longer an internal process defined by the digital platform. As mentioned above, the procedures previously adopted by a few platforms were not consistent and not always transparent, reducing the trustworthiness of such mechanisms in the eyes of users. This problem is tackled by DSA, art 22(2), which allocates to a digital services coordinator (DSC) the task of awarding the status of TF. The selection process is then harmonized across Europe, as all the DSCs decide on the basis of the same criteria listed in the DSA: the expertise and competence of the organization, its independence from any digital platform, and the ability to carry out the flagging task.

Before delving into the interpretation of the criteria indicated in the DSA, it is important to note that the objective of harmonization of standards across Europe may be hampered if no coordination among the DSCs is envisaged in advance in the selection procedure. The wording of art 22 implies that each DSC will follow a procedure that is defined at the national level, leaving timing, evidence requested, controls, and reporting choices to each DSC. Therefore, it will be a task of the Commission, after consulting the newly established European Board for Digital Services (EBDS),[34] to ensure a consistent applica-

---

[34] See DSA, art 61.

tion among the DSC and avoid misalignments.[35] Yet it seems that some DSCs have already started working on this issue together in informal groups in order to achieve a consistent approach. For instance, the Italian DSC (Autorità per le Garazie nelle Comunicazioni – AGCOM) published in February 2024 a public consultation on the interpretation of DSA, art 22, in particular on the type of entities that can be selected, the length of the TF award (proposed at three years), the documents and information that may provide proof of the three criteria specified by the DSA, and the areas in which the TF system will be adopted.[36] The final document is expected to be published in autumn 2024. Similarly, the Irish DSC (Coimisiún na Meán – CNAM) adopted in the same period guidelines to inform the interested entities about the assessment and decision-making process regarding TF selection.[37] Similar guidelines have been published since March 2024 by the Austrian, Danish, and Romanian DSCs.[38] The French DSC (ARCOM) chose to merely publish information on its website that replicated the articles of the DSA.[39]

With some small differences, the guidelines adopted by the mentioned national authorities are similar, with useful clarifications on the application of the DSA provision.

Upon looking at the criteria, the most difficult to interpret is the third one, where the applicant is asked to demonstrate how it will ensure diligence, accuracy, and objectivity in notice submissions. Since the DSA-based system is newly established, previous practices are non-existent; however, the applicants may submit their experience with the platform-specific system or within other programs.[40] It is interesting to note that the Irish DSC guidelines clarify,

---

[35] See DSA, art 22(8).

[36] See AGCOM Resolution 40/24/CONS on the public consultation on the 'draft regulation of procedure for the recognition of the status of Trusted Flaggers pursuant to art 22 of the Digital Services Regulation (DSA)'. The deadline for sending any comments on the consultation draft was 18 March 2024. The text of the consultation is available at <https://www.agcom.it/documents/10179/33213833/Allegato+15-2-2024+1708010469236/cba801de-88fa-4f0c-95c8-7bcd81455dbf?version=1.0>.

[37] <https://www.cnam.ie/wp-content/uploads/2024/02/20240216_Article22_GuidanceForm_Branded_vF_KW.pdf>.

[38] For the Austrian KommAustria, see <https://www.rtr.at/medien/was_wir_tun/DigitaleDienste/Regelungen/Trusted_Flagger.de.html>; for the Danish KFST, see <https://www.kfst.dk/forbrugerforhold/digitale-formidlingstjenester-dsa/paalidelig-indberetter-forsker-eller-tvistbilaegger/paalidelig-indberetter-af-ulovligt-indhold/>, for the Romanian ANCON, see <https://www.ancom.ro/uploads/forms_files/Proiect_decizie_aNCOM_notificatori_de_incredere_DSa1709646936.pdf>.

[39] See <https://www.arcom.fr/espace-professionnel/signaleurs-de-confiance-conditions-et-candidatures>.

[40] See, for instance, the EU Code of Conduct on Countering Illegal Hate Speech Online, adopted in 2016, available at <https://commission.europa.eu/strategy-and-policy/

in the explanatory part, that also newly established organizations may apply to the TF system, even if they do not have any prior experience in identifying, detecting, and notifying illegal content. The guidelines stress that, in this case, the evaluation will not be on the experience but rather will consider the expertise and capabilities of the staff carrying out the flagging.[41] The Italian text currently under consultation is even more detailed and stresses that in order to ensure the fulfilment of the due diligence criterion, the requesting entity should demonstrate three elements: a sufficient availability of human resources (ie adequate staffing), technical resources (ie technical/professional capacity with reference to detection, identification, and reporting), and financial resources (ie the economic/financial capacity of adequate funding sources) to perform the envisaged tasks.[42] Moreover, for the accuracy and objectivity requirements, the applicant entity should demonstrate that it uses a significant and relevant number of sources, that it has adequate tools and procedures to detect, identify, and report illegal content, and that it possesses internal policies for reviewing evaluation processes in cases of error.

The existence of such a level of organization is in line with the fact that the status of TF can no longer be awarded to individuals but only to entities,[43] which may be both public and private organizations.[44] The examples provided by DSA, recital 61 include, for instance, public organizations, such as the internet referral units of national law enforcement authorities or the European Union Agency for Law Enforcement Cooperation, and also private organizations, such as the INHOPE network of hotlines for reporting child sexual abuse material. This does not exclude, as suggested by Rosati,[45] creative

---

policies/justice-and-fundamental-rights/combatting-discrimination/racism-and-xenophobia/eu-code-conduct-countering-illegal-hate-speech-online_en>.

[41] CNAM Guidelines, p 10.

[42] AGCOM Consultation, p 17.

[43] DSA, recital 61.

[44] Note that the initial proposal only included entities representing collective interests, while now corporate entities representing private interests may apply.

[45] See Rosati (n 19). However, note the negative evaluation of the AIM – European Brands Association, which instead supported the possibility of individual IP holders receiving the status of trusted flaggers. According to their Position Paper, 'mandating the use of a third party such [as] an association through which notices must be filtered may be appropriate for certain user-generated content which may be subject to interpretation or nuance, such as disinformation or alleged harassment, but it is not for content that can be addressed automatically. Verification of an IP right holder is straightforward: it can prove its identity and provide evidence of its rights (for example by uploading a trade mark certificate) via a standardized form, with little, if any, human review needed of its notices thereafter.' See AIM, Position Paper – Recognising individual IP right holders as trusted flaggers under the DSA, available at <https://www.aim.be/wp-content/themes/aim/pdfs/23-12-12%20AIM%20position%20paper%20-%20trusted%20flaggers%20under%20the%20DSA.pdf>.

industries trade bodies or industry associations as long as they can satisfy the criteria set out in DSA, art 22(2).[46] This wide range of potential applicants is not, however, unlimited, as recital 61 provides that 'the overall number of trusted flaggers awarded in accordance with this Regulation should be limited'. Although so far only one Finnish copyright anti-piracy center is listed on the webpage of the EU Commission as TF, the expectation is to have several more that may address the more than sixty topics of expertise identified by the DSA. Again, the limits to be imposed on the number of TF will be a matter to be discussed and agreed upon at the European level through the coordination of the EBDS, as no criteria are indicated in the DSA, neither quantitative nor qualitative.

On a side note, it must be noted that the strength of the certification system has already been diluted indirectly by the European Commission. In a recent statement, the European Commissioner for Internal Market, Thierry Breton, affirmed that the TF system set up on the basis of the DSA will not affect the already existing ones created under other initiatives, such as the implementation of the Code of Conduct on Countering Illegal Hate Speech Online.[47] If this is the case, a set of questions emerge: Should the organizations already involved in such programs also be certified by the DSC? If the response is in the negative, then a problem may emerge as a parallel path is set up: the one for certification as a TF that will have transparency and reporting obligations to be verified by the DSCs, and the path leading to designation as a hate speech and disinformation TF.[48] In the latter case, the lack of certification will also result in an exemption from the obligations related to the designation as a TF. As a result, it is highly improbable that a TF already carrying out reporting activity for hate speech and disinformation will have any incentive to apply for certification, thus reducing the number of potential actors.

b) *Monitoring of TF activity*

The TF selected must then submit an (at least) annual report to the national DSC on their activities, pursuant to DSA, art 22(3). The report must include a quantitative analysis of the notices on the basis of the digital platform in-

---

[46] This is also confirmed by the approach adopted by the national DSCs so far, as industry federations and trade associations, such as intellectual property owners organizations, are included. See, respectively, CNAM Guidelines, p 19, and the Italian AGCOM Consultation document, p 2.

[47] See the answer given by Mr Breton on behalf of the European Commission, 9 January 2024, EN P-003315/2023, available at <https://www.europarl.europa.eu/doceo/document/P-9-2023-003315-ASW_EN.pdf>.

[48] The list of TF included in this programme has been added in the 7th Evaluation of the Code of Conduct, November 2022, available at <https://commission.europa.eu/system/files/2022-12/Factsheet%20-%207th%20monitoring%20round%20of%20the%20Code%20of%20Conduct.pdf>.

volved and the type of allegedly illegal content notified; additionally, it must also detail the action taken by the platform.

Although the annual report of the TF can be limited to a quantitative analysis of the reporting activity, it may be a useful tool from different perspectives. From the DSC side, it can be useful, first, as a means to verify that the TF has devoted time to the task of detecting and reporting illegal content, and secondly, to verify whether the activity has been carried out objectively, diligently, and accurately. As a matter of fact, if the actions taken by the digital platform are always contrary to the notices provided by the TF, this may trigger an investigation of the TF, eventually resulting in a revocation of the TF status.[49] However, this evaluation will have to be compared also with the transparency reports submitted by digital platforms, pursuant to art 15(c) DSA, where the latter are asked to provide information about the number of notices received – distinguishing the ones by trusted flaggers and the actions taken; and distinguishing the ones based on the terms and conditions and the ones based on legal provisions – the notices processed by using automated means, and also the time to process the notice.

Although the annual reporting enhances the transparency of the TF system, it does not come without costs: the reporting obligations add to the detailed procedure to become a TF and may become a barrier for smaller organizations and entities that have limited staff and limited resources to invest.[50]

2. *The Relationship Between TF and the Digital Platform*

a) *System set up and fast-track procedure*

DSA, art 22(1) obliges digital platforms to act expeditiously when they receive notices from a TF; however, in order for the platform to recognize the source of the flagging, technical and organizational measures should be put in place. As a result, as soon as the organization receives the status of TF, it will have to contact the digital platforms and acquire the necessary information about the privileged access and the procedure for notice. It is important to note that such access and notice procedures may be different for each digital platform, resulting in an additional burden for the TF to invest time and effort to become familiar with each system.[51] In this context, more than welcome is

---

[49] See DSA, art 22(6).

[50] See the Statement from Trusted Flaggers on the Digital Services Act negotiations, 21 March 2021, available at <https://hateaid.org/wp-content/uploads/2022/05/hateaid-trusted-flaggers-statement.pdf>.

[51] Note that the CNAM Guidelines indicate that the TF will have to commit to an 'onboarding' process and training programs provided by digital platforms, at p. 9. These training activities are hinted at also in DSA, recital 87, acknowledging the need for increased cooperation with TF, through training sessions and exchanges in order to reduce the processing time for specific types of illegal content.

the inclusion in DSA, art 44– a provision dedicated to standardization – of the reference to the 'electronic submission of notices by trusted flaggers under art 22, including through application programming interfaces'.[52] In this case, the Commission will support and promote the development and implementation of voluntary standards set by European and international standardization bodies. Although, at the moment, no standard is available on the market, it is probable that the obligations emerging from the DSA application will trigger the adoption of new standards.[53]

From a different perspective, it should be noted that the DSA-based TF system is not going to be the only one, as digital platforms will be able to maintain the parallel TF system that they already have. This is also acknowledged by recital 61, which affirms that private entities and individuals may enter into bilateral agreements with digital platforms. It is probable that digital platforms will maintain (or set up) their priority flagging systems,[54] distinguishing them from the DSA-based system on the basis of the point of reference used: the DSA-based TF system addresses the illegal content, whereas the platform-based system addresses the violation of terms and conditions.[55] Given that some of the clauses included in the terms and conditions replicate the relevant legal provisions, relating, for instance, to child pornography or terrorism content,[56] it is possible that the entities addressing these topics may have greater incentive to apply to the platform-based system rather than the DSA-based one, as the former entails less burdensome procedures and no subsequent reporting obligations.

---

[52] See DSA, art 44(1)(c).

[53] It should be noted that DSA, art 44(1) also includes, under letters (a) and (b), two other connected issues, namely standardization of the electronic submission of notices under art 16; and the templates, design, and process standards for communicating with the recipients of the service in a user-friendly manner on restrictions resulting from terms and conditions and changes thereto.

[54] See also DSA, recital 62, which explicitly refers to the application of alternative priority flagging systems so as to 'take quick and reliable action against content that is incompatible with their terms and conditions, in particular against content that is harmful for vulnerable recipients of the service, such as minors'.

[55] See, for instance, the Google Priority Flaggers Programme which runs parallel to the DSA trusted flagger system. The Programme establishes special channels for notification by the participating organizations, with a focus on violations of Google's policies and Community Guidelines. It must be highlighted that, according to the explanation provided, the issues reported by priority flaggers are not subject to any different policy treatment; 'however, because of [the] high degree of trust and expertise, our teams prioritize flags from priority flaggers for review'. As a result, similar to the DSA-based TF system, the notices from the organizations will be prioritized vis-à-vis common users. See <https://transparency.google/tools-programs/partner-programs/>.

[56] See Casarosa (n 10).

b) Participation in the enforcement process

A question that is left open by the DSA is the role of TF in the subsequent enforcement phase by the digital platform. As mentioned above, digital platforms are required to give priority and process the notices by TF without undue delay. However, no guidance is given regarding the further role of TF in the procedure, neither as is envisaged inside nor outside the digital platform's internal complaint system.

Looking at the content moderation system set up in the DSA, although the notice of the TF primarily serves to trigger an evaluation of the content by the digital platform, it is still relevant in the subsequent steps of the procedure. As presented in the figure below, after the notice is submitted, the digital platform will have to process it, following the fast-track procedure. However, it is not specified that this process be different than the one for notice and takedown as provided in DSA, art 16. Accordingly, the decision of the digital platform in respect of the notice can also be based on automated decision-making rather than through the analysis of an individual moderator.[57]

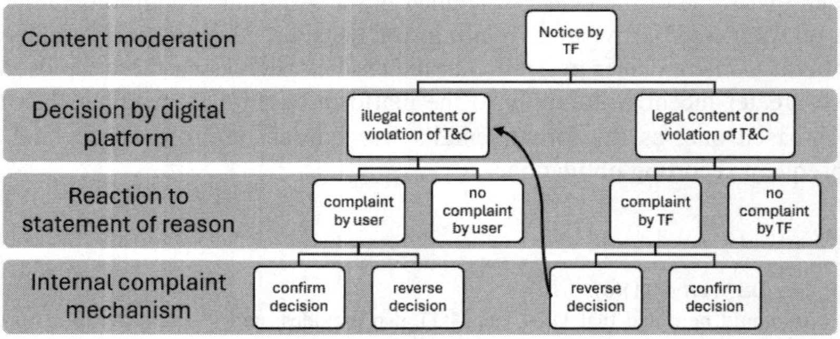

Internal complaint procedure triggered by TF notice

If the decision by the digital platform confirms the notice, acknowledging the content as illegal, then the digital platform will have to inform the user about the removal of the content and/or the user's profile having been disabled. The detailed statement of reasons required by DSA, art 17 also includes the factual circumstances considered and 'where relevant, information on whether the decision was taken pursuant to a notice submitted in accordance with art 16 or based on and voluntary own-initiative investigations, and, where strictly neces-

[57] As stated in DSA, art 16(6): 'Providers of hosting services shall process any notices that they receive under the mechanisms referred to in paragraph 1 and take their decisions in respect of the information to which the notices relate, in a timely, diligent, non-arbitrary and objective manner. *Where they use automated means for that processing or decision-making*, they shall include information on such use in the notification referred to in paragraph 5' [emphasis added].

sary, the identity of the notifier'.[58] In this case, this disclosure may apply both to the notices submitted on the basis of DSA, art 16 and also in the case of notices submitted by TF, as no differentiation is provided in the legislation.[59]

What is the added value for the user in learning that the decision was based on the notice of a TF? The internal complaint mechanism envisaged in DSA, art 20 does not include any kind of adversarial procedure: the complainant has the responsibility of submitting 'sufficiently precise and adequately substantiated complaints'[60] that can lead the platform to change its decision. It seems that there is no involvement of TF in the procedure. However, DSA, art 22(6) may lead to a different conclusion; the provision acknowledges that a TF could also be evaluated as regards the 'information gathered in connection to the processing of complaints through the internal complaint-handling systems referred to in Article 20(4)'. Thus, it seems possible to infer that the digital platform may decide (at their own discretion) to request additional information from the TF in order to evaluate the claim and subsequently use it to support its final decision.

Let us look instead to the other leg of the process. If the digital platform processes the notice of the TF but evaluates the content as legitimate, then it will be the TF which will receive the statement of reasons. Before the adoption of the DSA, an erroneous notice would not have had any consequence for a TF (or for an individual user). Now, this has changed, and in case of a significant number of erroneous notices, the digital platform may inform the DSC and trigger an investigation by the latter, leading in the worst-case scenario to revocation of the status as TF.[61] As a consequence, it is possible that a TF which has its notice rejected by the digital platform will decide to appeal against this decision through the internal complaint handling mechanism. Here, one important element in the choice to file an appeal is the TF's interest in safeguarding its status as a diligent, accurate, and objective notifier. Although revocation as a TF may not be an economic sanction, it may have an impact on the reputation of the TF.

The presenting of a complaint proceeds along the same path as the one followed by an individual user mentioned above, thus requiring the submission of a precise and substantiated claim. But in this case the legislation does not

[58] See DSA, art 17(3)(b).

[59] This is also confirmed by the information that the digital platform is obliged to enter in the DSA Transparency Database. According to the search form, the options available regarding the information source are: a notice submitted in accordance with DSA, art 16; a notice submitted by a trusted flagger; other types of notification; and voluntary own-initiative investigations. See the full form at <https://transparency.dsa.ec.europa.eu/statement-search>.

[60] See DSA, art 20(3).

[61] See DSA, art 22(6) and (7). Note that where individuals frequently submit notices or complaints that are manifestly unfounded, DSA, art 23(2) allows the digital platform to suspend the user for a reasonable period of time.

clarify whether a fast-track procedure is envisaged, as it specified a general obligation for digital platforms to adopt timely, non-discriminatory, diligent and non-arbitrary procedures.[62] Only if the digital platform reverses its decision will the process result in interaction with the user who initially posted the content.

3. *The Relationship with Users*

Although not mentioned in the DSA, it is interesting to add another dimension to this analysis, one evaluating the potential relationship between TF and users. The previous sections described a direct and regulated interaction between TF and DSC and between TF and digital platforms; however, the legislation makes no mention of the interplay between TF and individual users. As a matter of fact, it is possible that individual users may decide to report illegal content not through notices to the digital platform but rather through the intermediation of TF. This would have the added value that TF notices follow a fast-track procedure.

Interestingly, such a case is envisaged in the guidelines adopted by national DSCs. Among the criteria for the evaluation of the flagging process, the CNAM guidelines as well as the AGCOM Consultation Document include, for instance, the existence of an online mechanism for the public to report illegal content to the TF itself.[63] Although this feature may be helpful for TF certification, as it shows the different sources that a TF uses in order to carry out its tasks, it may become an additional burden for TF, which will have to screen and filter information before submitting notices.

IV. Concluding Remarks

Content moderation is at the core of the transnational regulatory framework adopted by digital platforms. It encompasses all the phases that are envisaged in a private regulatory regime, from rule setting to monitoring to enforcement. In the last years, the interactions between public and private actors in the different phases have changed and reflected the power struggle between the states and market actors.

In this context, other stakeholders have begun to assume increasing importance, delivering or contributing part of the tasks and activities envisaged in each phase of the regulatory regime.[64] One of the less analyzed roles is that

[62] See DSA, art 20(4).

[63] See, respectively, CNAM Guidelines, p 14, and AGCOM Consultation document, p 5.

[64] Matthias C Kettemann and Wolfgang Schulz, 'Platform://Democracy: Perspectives on Platform Power, Public Values and the Potential of Social Media Councils' <https://www.ssoar.info/ssoar/handle/document/86524> accessed 28 March 2024; Schneider,

of TF in the monitoring and enforcement phases. The TF system has developed as a tool designed to gather expertise and knowledge while legitimizing the content selection process.[65] The initial heterogeneity found across digital platforms will fade away as the DSA has institutionalized the position of TF in the enforcement phase. DSA, art 22 has clarified the role and the relationship TF have both with the digital platforms and Digital Service Coordinators.

This choice was a reaction to the lack of transparency in the system adopted by digital platforms; however, the set of detailed obligations included in the DSA-based system runs the risk of reducing the incentives of organizations to participate. The preceding analysis shows that the DSA-based system imposes several tasks and reporting obligations that may become a barrier to the participation of smaller organizations possessing limited internal resources.

Moreover, the level of complexity in the overall internal complaint process envisaged by the DSA has undoubtedly increased. This complexity affects both digital platforms and TF. The former are required to set up a notice and complaint handling mechanism that not only addresses the claims by users but also considers the potential appeals of TF. The latter are required to provide accurate and objective notices; additionally, they must monitor the reaction of the digital platform in order to avoid unwanted consequences. Again, looking only at the side of TF, the incentives for smaller organizations to participate in the DSA-based TF system may be minimal as they may not be able to follow such elaborate procedures.

Although the objectives of the EU legislature in regulating the TF system were laudable – namely, to strengthen the position of TF in a process previously guided by the discretionary power of digital platforms and to simultaneously limit potentially abusive behavior – what has resulted is an overburdening structure that may have the counterproductive effect of reducing the participation of organizations which protect the voices of marginalized communities and which have limited financial and human resources.

Siegrist and Oles (n 18); Robyn Caplan, 'Networked Platform Governance: The Construction of the Democratic Platform' (2023) 17 IJC 22.

[65] Appelman and Leerssen (n 16).

Dispute Resolution within Online Platforms

In Search of the Regulatory Paradigm and Systematic Function of Dispute Resolution in the Digital Platform Economy

*Barbara Warwas**

This chapter describes new provisions on dispute resolution within the EU digital market, namely art 11 (internal complaint-handling system) and art 12 (mediation) of Regulation (EU) 2019/1150 of the European Parliament and of the Council of 20 June 2019 on promoting fairness and transparency for business users of online intermediation services (the P2B Regulation); and art 20 (internal complaint-handling system) and art 21 (out-of-court dispute settlement) of Regulation (EU) 2022/2065 of the European Parliament and of the Council of 19 October 2022 on a Single Market For Digital Services and amending Directive 2000/31/EC (Digital Services Act, DSA). The chapter is exploratory in nature. The main hypothesis is that dispute resolution has played a fundamental role in the digital platform economy at the enforcement level, yet its function and the regulatory paradigm it follows (if any) have largely not been studied systematically. Against this background, I pose a research question of a fundamental nature for the digital platform economy, one that is two-fold: (1) What are the systematic regulatory goals of the EU regulations on dispute resolution within online platforms? (2) What regulatory paradigm do these regulations imply with a view to the enforcement of different types of rules and regulations produced by online platforms? Preliminary answers to these questions should offer us indications concerning the

* All links were last accessed on 21 June 2024.

(new) regulatory paradigm and systematic function of dispute resolution in the digital platform economy.

The chapter is organized as follows: First, I present a brief literature review on the role of dispute resolution in digital platforms. Second, I describe and emphasize the increasing practical role of dispute resolution within the platform economy. Third, I analyze the specific provisions on internal complaint-handling systems, mediation, and out-of-court dispute settlement as found in the P2B Regulation and DSA, thereby searching out the new regulatory paradigm behind them. Finally, I formulate general conclusions concerning the (new) regulatory paradigm and systematic function of dispute resolution within the digital platform economy and propose future lines of research on the topic at hand.

I. Literature on Dispute Resolution in the Platform Economy

First, it is appropriate to briefly review the academic literature on dispute resolution within online platforms. The goal is to better understand the role that dispute resolution plays within online platforms and how academics and, to some extent, also practitioners have viewed the (evolving) function of dispute resolution in the context of the digital platform economy and beyond, relating, for example, to the functioning of democratic systems and the society.

The literature review below largely follows the findings of the literature review by Rory Van Loo in his article 'Federal Rules of Platform Procedure,' complemented by the research conducted by the author of this chapter.[1] Van Loo distinguishes three main categories of literature on dispute resolution and online platforms, namely: (1) the literature on platform governance, (2) scholarship on alternative dispute resolution (ADR) in cross-border marketplaces, and (3) the writings on procedural privatization of justice and access to justice.[2] Based on the most recent global trends in the research and practice on justice needs around the world, I add another strand of literature here, namely the literature on people-centered justice that focuses on reducing barriers to justice for end-users (here, mainly platform users) through the use of technology.

As Van Loo notes with regard to the first three strands of literature, each of them is quite distinct, in comparison to the others. The first strand of scholarship on *platform governance* is mainly preoccupied with the resemblance of platforms to sovereign states regarding their governance. Here, large online platforms like Facebook, X (formerly Twitter), and Google are

[1] Rory Van Loo, 'Federal Rules of Platform Procedure' (2021) 88(4) UChi LRev 829–895, especially 831–835.

[2] Van Loo (n 1) 831–835.

compared to states that exercise 'quasi-sovereign influence over commerce, speech, elections, and myriad other spheres of activity.'[3] What is more, platforms tend to accumulate the powers of all three branches of government within their reigns, ie the legislative, the executive, and the judicial, with the last one having received little attention in practice or from academics.[4] The authors in this strand of literature point to the threats stemming from such accumulation of powers by online platforms for the functioning of democratic systems and society, especially given the lack of accountability on the side of platforms for their operations.[5] At the same time, scholars pose normative arguments supporting more procedural regulation of the judicial power of online platforms based on the very same analogy with sovereign states, where such power is subject to various democratic safeguards.[6]

The second category of literature concerns the writings on *ADR in online marketplaces.* According to Van Loo, this literature mainly describes the practicalities of adopting various forms of dispute resolution, like mediation, in online marketplaces such as eBay or Amazon.[7] Van Loo also points to the overlapping discussions from this strand of literature with the literature on private administration.[8] At the same time, this strand of literature, according to Van Loo, does not contain more daring proposals regarding how dispute resolution systems within online platforms could be reformed with a view to concrete regulatory or legal requirements toward the platforms.[9]

---

[3] Van Loo (n 1) 832.

[4] Van Loo (n 1) 832 with further references; Kate Klonick, 'The New Governors: The People, Rules, And Processes Governing Online Speech' (April 2018) 131(6) Harv LRev 1598–1670.

[5] For example, Jonathan L Zittrain, 'Engineering an Election' (June 2014) 127(8) Harv LRev Forum 335, 336, concerning the ability of platforms to influence the elections; K Sabeel Rahman, 'The New Utilities: Private Power, Social Infrastructure, and the Revival of the Public Utility' (2018) 39(5) Cardozo LRev 1621, 1632, 1641, pointing to the power of platforms over societies and the economy; as referred to by Van Loo in Van Loo (n 1) 832, with further references.

[6] This is the argument advanced by Van Loo himself after referring to a few scholarly writings proposing a similar argument, without directly referring to dispute resolution concerning online platforms (in fn 15), Van Loo (n 1) 832–833.

[7] Van Loo (n 1) 833, with further references; in addition to the review by Van Loo, worth noticing is the work by Colin Rule on global dispute resolution based on the eBay dispute resolution system, in Colin Rule, 'Designing a Global Online Dispute Resolution System: Lessons Learned from eBay' (Winter 2017) 13(2) UStThomas LJ 354–369; or an in-depth analysis of eBay's dispute resolution, in Ethan Katsh, Janet Rifkin and Alan Gaitenby, 'E-Commerce, E-Disputes, and E-Dispute Resolution: In the Shadow of "eBay Law"' (2000) 15(3) OSJDR 705–734.

[8] Van Loo (n 1) fn 17.

[9] Van Loo (n 1) 833.

Those proposals appear more frequently in the third strand of literature, namely that on *procedural privatization of justice and access to justice in the context of ADR*.[10] This is mostly so because – according to Van Loo – many authors within this group tend to view ADR, particularly mandatory arbitration, as methods that often endanger parties' access to the court.[11] Van Loo points to a noteworthy phenomenon here; namely, what often appears as an advantage of 'private justice' for ADR (for example, the principle of confidentiality) tends to be seen as the opposite by scholars working on the procedural privatization of justice, hence as a threat to judicial systems (eg, lack of transparency of private proceedings).[12] The relative nature of those perspectives and approaches can be explained by the regulatory models (or paradigms) regarding ADR assumed by the authors of those contributions, which I explain more below.

For now, I find it relevant to complement the literature review by Van Loo presently under analysis with an additional strand of literature, namely the one on *people-centered justice*. This literature goes hand-in-hand with the new policy proposals concerning a surveying of and reflection upon the people's (citizens') justice needs in the judicial reforms in different jurisdictions.[13] The starting point of these discussions is that formal judicial systems

---

[10] This is implied by Van Loo's analysis of this strand of scholarship, including an approach more critical of ADR, as opposed to the approach of ADR scholars in the first group. See Van Loo (n 1) 833–834; the author of this chapter also contributed to this strand of literature, although not concerning online platforms. See Barbara Warwas, 'Access to Privatized Consumer Justice: Arbitration, ADR, and the Future of Value-Oriented Justice' in Loïc Cadiet, Burkhard Hess and Marta Requejo Isidro (eds), *Privatizing Dispute Resolution: Trends and Limits* (Nomos 2019) 325–351. The approach taken in that article is mixed: on the one hand, it points to the discussion that is critical of the privatization of justice through ADR as encountered in academic literature, while on the other hand, it points to the opportunities that ADR may bring to the disputants.

[11] Van Loo (n 1) 833–834.

[12] Van Loo (n 1) 833–834.

[13] The movement on people-centered justice concerns both national and international developments. The former include the discussions on justice systems in Canada, Sweden, the US, and the Netherlands. See The Hague Institute for Innovation of Law (HiiL), Prof Dr M Barendrecht (contact person for the proposal), 'Consortium Versterkt Conflictoplossend Vermogen' (2023) 11 <https://www.hiil.org/wp-content/uploads/2023/02/Projectplan-Consortium-Versterkt-conflictoplossend-vermogen-1.pdf>; at the international level, the work of the Organisation for Economic Cooperation and Development (OECD) should be mentioned, with its Good Practice Principles for People-centred Justice of 2021: OECD, 'OECD Framework and Good Practice Principles for People-Centred Justice GOV/PGC(2021)26' (2021) <https://www.oecd.org/governance/global-roundtables-access-to-justice/good-practice-principles-for-people-centred-justice.pdf>; also to be mentioned are the activities of the World Justice Forum (among other initiatives): Robert Litsky, 'Marked Shift to People-Centered Justice at the World Justice Forum 2022', The Website of the World Justice Project, 29 August 2022 <https://worldjusticeproject.org/news/marked-shift-people-centered-justice-world-justice-forum-2022-0>.

in many states are insufficient to accommodate the justice needs of its citizens, responding, on average, to approximately 10% of such needs.[14] The OECD Framework and Good Practice Principles on People-Centred Justice of 2021 emphasize different policy improvements (called pillars) to achieve people-centered justice, encouraging the use of technology by governments and policymakers for better ('more equal and inclusive') access to justice.[15] These discussions offer us a fresh alternative to the three strands of literature identified by Van Loo in the way that they shift the focus of analysis from private justice providers (ADR institutions and professionals) and sovereign states – often seen as traditional regulators – onto the users of justice. They also fall within a relatively new academic discussion on the humanization of law, especially regarding the increasing role of technology in ensuring better justice outcomes for citizens and end users of private and public services.[16] In the context of this contribution, this strand of literature allows us to incorporate the interests and justice needs of platform users into the discussions on the regulatory paradigms behind the dispute resolution systems within online platforms, alongside the more traditional perspectives emphasizing top-down approaches to those discussions.

Two general conclusions stem from the brief literature review presented above. First, the function of dispute resolution – although currently largely understudied systematically in literature – is increasing within and outside online platforms, especially concerning the enforcement of terms, rights, and soft rules produced within online platforms that are also increasing in scope and that have relevance outside online platforms.[17] Second, different authors, whose works fall in different categories of the above-presented literature, assume different functions and regulatory models concerning dispute resolution within and beyond the platform economy. Let us now discuss the implications of these two observations for our current discussion.

1. The Increasing Function of Dispute Resolution within and beyond Online Platforms

Academic literature, especially in its thread on platform governance, points to the increasing number of new types of rules produced by online platforms and

[14] OECD (n 13) 2–3.

[15] OECD (n 13) 8.

[16] See, for example, Michiel Scheltema and Ivar Timmer, 'Putting Humans First: Digitisation of Government Services from the Citizen's Perspective' in Kai Jacob and others (eds) *Liquid Legal – Humanization and the Law* (Springer 2022) 175–193.

[17] This argument also underpins the study by Van Loo. See Van Loo (n 1). A similar argument was also made by Christoph Busch, 'The P2B Regulation (EU) 2019/1150: Towards a "Procedural Turn" in EU Platform Regulation? Editorial'(2020) 9(4) EuCML 134.

to the new types of activities of those platforms. These rules and activities can be categorized into three groups.[18] The first group refers to rules stemming from *terms and conditions of cross-border marketplaces* like e-Bay or Amazon, or other online platforms. This group seems to encompass the most traditional rules governing the online, cross-border transactions enabled through those platforms. The second group concerns the emerging role of online platforms such as the social media giants (eg, Facebook) in *shaping the fundamental rights of their users*, for example, the right to freedom of expression. This is done through the often-discretionary decisions of platforms regarding content moderation.[19] Finally, the third group of platform rules and activities, which largely overlaps with the second group, concerns the consequences of platforms' content moderation decisions for the economic viability of other platforms as a result of delisting or suspending accounts of business users by large online platforms. These categories of platforms' rules and activities – which, again, are more exemplary than exhaustive – demonstrate the increasing regulatory powers of online platforms and range from more traditional activities, such as formulating and incorporating terms and conditions into the contracts entered into by platform users for their commercial activities online, to new ones, such as the shaping of fundamental (human) rights of platform users and regulating the economic activity of other platforms within the digital platform economy. Consequently, online platforms have begun to assume increasing regulatory roles within and beyond the platform economy, and dispute resolution has begun to play an instrumental role in enforcing new types of rules generated by those platforms.

---

[18] The categories of rules produced by the platforms and their activities are by no means exhaustive. Rather, they serve to depict the increasing function of online platforms, often through dispute resolution means, at the enforcement level. Also, the term 'rules and activities' is understood broadly here, as terms and conditions of online platforms that become binding upon their incorporation into contracts (of adhesion) with the platform users; as legal rights, including fundamental rights of platform users, such as the right to freedom of expression; and also as private dynamics and norms produced as a consequence of a platform's decisions regarding content moderation, including their impact on the economic activities of platform users being businesses.

[19] Pietro Ortolani mentions that Facebook takes approximately 300,000 content moderation decisions per day. See Pietro Ortolani, 'The Resolution of Content Moderation Disputes under the Digital Services Act' (2023) 2 Giustizia Consensuale 533–573, with further references. The online version of the article is available on SSRN at <https://papers.ssrn.com/sol3/papers.cfm?abstract_id=4356598>. See also the discussion on the select policies of online platforms in the context of human rights standards, in Edoardo Celeste and others, *The Content Governance Dilemma. Digital Constitutionalism, Social Media and the Search for a Global Standard* (Palgrave Macmillan 2023), specifically chapter 5 'Platform Policies Versus Human Rights Standards' 93–129.

2. Indications Regarding Regulatory Models behind Dispute Resolution within Online Platforms

The second conclusion stemming from the literature review concerns different regulatory models assumed by different authors who study dispute resolution within online platforms. These regulatory models are crucial for explaining the exact role of dispute resolution within the platform economy, especially given its recently increasing role therein. Since the main goal of this chapter is to pursue a more systematic discussion of dispute resolution within online platforms, I briefly analyze here different regulatory models potentially applicable to dispute resolution within each strand of literature presented above to preliminarily map the most relevant regulatory paradigms for the broader systematic discussion on the increasing function of dispute resolution within the platform economy.

Returning to Van Loo's analysis, it is apparent that each strand of literature on dispute resolution within online platforms is quite distinct, advancing different, and sometimes even opposing, perspectives on the function of dispute resolution, especially vis-à-vis states.[20] A similar observation seems to be valid regarding the regulatory paradigms underlying those categories of literature; namely, each strand of literature presupposes a different regulatory paradigm.[21]

Because the first strand of literature draws parallels between online platforms and modern states and the third one contains critique and normative arguments for a better responsiveness of dispute resolution to the principles aiming to increase access to justice, we may presuppose that both categories of literature imply a specific form of *private-public regulation* on the side of online platforms. Private-public regulation can be understood as the coexistence of two regulatory regimes: (1) a private, or self-regulatory, regime on the side of online platforms corresponding to the private governance of the internet and (2) public regulation, stemming from democratic principles concerning the necessary separation of powers and rule-of-law standards following from these principles.[22] The concept of public regulation derives here from the democratic legitimacy of actions undertaken by state-sanctioned

---

[20] Van Loo (n 1) 832.

[21] Van Loo does not refer to regulatory models in his analysis. The analysis from this section is the analysis of the present author. It is important to stress, here again, that the analysis in question has an exploratory, general character. Further research into specific platforms needs to be conducted in the future to complement this analysis with concrete examples.

[22] On both concepts (public and private regulation), see Fabrizio Cafaggi and Andrea Renda, 'Public and Private Regulation Mapping the Labyrinth' (2012) 1 DovenschmidtQ 16–23; see also Russell W Mills, 'The Interaction of Private and Public Regulatory Governance: The Case of Association-Led Voluntary Aviation Safety Programs' (2016) 35(1) Pol&Soc 43–55.

institutions at the enforcement level, which – according to the literature under analysis – should be extended into private, online platforms due to their increasing quasi-public, regulatory functions.[23] Notably, the interplay between public and private regulation is often blurred, which begs further questions regarding the form of the dialogue between the public, state authorities, and online platforms and also its impact on the enforcement of terms, norms, and soft rules produced by online platforms somewhat in the shadow of the law.[24]

Mandatory mediation can serve as a relevant example of private-public regulation in the field of dispute resolution. While mediation is considered a voluntary and non-binding process – meaning that parties cannot be forced to settle their dispute through mediation – they can still be requested (eg, by a court) to attempt to resolve a dispute via mediation in certain situations, for example, if the dispute falls within the scope of disputes suitable for so-called *mandatory mediation* under domestic laws (usually because of its small value), and/or provided that parties' right to access to a court is not impeded.[25] Hence, mandatory mediation resembles private-public regulation with the parties, mediators, and mediation federations acting as private regulators shaping private mediation standards from the bottom up, and with public

---

[23] By regulatory functions, I mean here the public functions of online platforms falling within any of the three branches of governmental powers (be it the legislative, executive, or judicial branch). See Van Loo (n 1) 892–893; Mills (n 22) 44, with further references.

[24] Regarding the blurred interplay between private and public regulation, compare Mills' argument, which reads as follows: 'Despite the growing literature on private self-regulation mechanisms such as voluntary disclosure and self-audit programs, we know little about [the] interaction of private self-regulation or its effect on the ability of the public sector to develop similar governance structures.' Mills (n 22) 44.

[25] See the definition of mediation in art 3 (a) of the Mediation Directive: '"Mediation" means a structured process, however named or referred to, whereby two or more parties to a dispute attempt by themselves, on a voluntary basis, to reach an agreement on the settlement of their dispute with the assistance of a mediator. This process may be initiated by the parties or suggested or ordered by a court or prescribed by the law of a Member State. […]', Directive 2008/52/EC of the European Parliament and of the Council of 21 May 2008 on Certain Aspects of Mediation in Civil and Commercial Matters [2008] OJ L136/3. Recital 14 of the Mediation Directive specifies that mediation can also be compulsory 'or subject to incentives or sanctions provided that such legislation does not prevent parties from exercising their right of access to the judicial system.' This has also been confirmed in the case law of the Court of Justice of the EU. See CJEU 14 June 2017, C-75/16 *Livio Menini i Maria Antonia Rampanelli v Banco Popolare – Società Cooperativa, Menini i Rampanelli*, ECLI:EU:C:2017:457, paras 49 and 61; the P2B Regulation, in recital 40, includes quite a specific definition of voluntary mediation (as compared to other EU attempts to define mediation): '[…] mediation provided for in this Regulation should be a voluntary process in the sense that the parties are themselves in charge of the process and can start and terminate it at any time.'; for an overview of the approaches of Member States to mandatory mediation, see CH van Rhee, 'Mandatory Mediation Before Litigation in Civil and Commercial Matters: A European Perspective' (2021) 4(12) AJEE 7–24.

authorities, such as legislators and courts, sketching a broader, public regulatory framework for mediation, if any, and the enforcement of mediation settlements from the top down (if they are not voluntarily complied with by the disputants). This particular regime of private and public regulation of (mandatory) mediation seems to be directly recognized in the Mediation Directive, which states, in recital 14, that nothing 'in this Directive [should] prejudice existing self-regulating mediation systems in so far as these deal with aspects which are not covered by this Directive.'

The second strand of literature presented above tends to take the perspective of the *self-regulatory model* of dispute resolution. I draw this conclusion here because this body of literature focuses mainly on the economic efficiency of private dispute resolution in general and within online platforms in particular (where it discusses the application and potential adjustment needed for the efficient functioning of dispute resolution within online platforms, mostly those involved in e-commerce). Relevant discussions regarding regulatory models in business-to-consumer relationships stemming from e-commerce transactions have been conducted here by Maria Lorena Flórez Rojas,[26] who has explained the theory of self-regulation in the context of e-commerce platforms against the background of the concept of co-regulation, which seems comparable to the concept of private-public regulation analyzed above. In both self-regulation and co-regulation, private actors, such as businesses and consumers, can voluntarily set up their own standards, rules, and norms in the form of voluntary agreements or codes of conduct or practice (to mention a few).[27] The difference between self- and co-regulation lies in the level of the necessary regulatory involvement of the government, eg, through relevant legislation or at the enforcement level.[28]

The concept of self-regulation assumes that private actors themselves voluntarily produce 'self-regulatory instruments' and then monitor compliance and ensure their enforcement.[29] Flórez Rojas further distinguishes different forms of self-regulation that seem relevant for our current discussion, ie, tacitly-supported self-regulation, substitute self-regulation, conditioned self-regulation, and enforced self-regulation.[30] Tacitly-supported self-regulation means, as described by Flórez Rojas, the form of self-regulation where public support is visible only tacitly, through political support.[31] The substitute form of self-regulation concerns almost absolute self-regulatory powers of private actors, while public support is necessary only to safeguard the public inter-

---

[26] Maria Lorena Florez Rojas, 'Industry Self-Regulation Models in Dispute Resolution of E-Commerce B2C' (Law and Technology Master Program, Tilburg University 2015).

[27] See, in particular, Rojas (n 26) 29–32.

[28] Rojas (n 26) 31.

[29] Rojas (n 26) 39, with further references.

[30] Rojas (n 26) 40–41, with further references.

[31] Rojas (n 26) 40–41, with further references.

est.[32] Conditioned self-regulation is a form of self-regulation where private actors exercise their authority to produce private rules, which – in the end – are monitored and enforced by public actors.[33] Finally, enforced self-regulation denotes outsourcing, or in the words of Flórez Rojas, a 'subcontracting' of specific regulatory levels (ie, rules production, monitoring, and enforcement) to private actors by public authorities.[34] Regarding these self-regulatory models, the preliminary conclusion can be drawn that they mostly differ regarding the interplay between public and private actors at the level of rules monitoring and enforcement. For online platforms, this would involve the potential corresponding legislation (at national or EU levels) concerning the platform's dispute resolution systems and the options (if any) for a possible judicial review of the platform's dispute resolution procedures, which seems instrumental in applying the relevant self-regulatory model to their operations.

When speaking about self-regulatory models for e-commerce platforms, the concept of transnational private regulation (TPR) developed by Cafaggi also needs to be invoked, especially since those platforms operate globally.[35] TPR assumes the transfer of regulatory power from public to private actors and also from a national to a transnational level.[36] Dispute resolution's role is seen in TPR at the enforcement level, where it is recommended that different TPR regimes establish their own private dispute resolution schemes to strengthen private enforcement.[37] In principle, enforcement within TPR regimes is assumed by both private and public actors, such as private dispute resolution, courts, and/or administrative agencies.[38] The interplay between private and public actors is defined by, inter alia, different governance models applicable to specific TPRs that, in turn, determine the forms of a dia-

---

[32] Rojas (n 26) 40–41, with further references.

[33] Rojas (n 26) 40–41, with further references.

[34] Rojas (n 26) 41, with further references.

[35] Fabrizio Cafaggi, 'A Comparative Analysis of Transnational Private Regulation: Legitimacy, Quality, Effectiveness and Enforcement', EUI Working Paper LAW 2014/2015, 2014 <https://cadmus.eui.eu/handle/1814/33591>; Fabrizio Cafaggi, 'New Foundations of Transnational Private Regulation' (2010) EUI Working Paper RSCAS 2010/53 <https://cadmus.eui.eu/handle/1814/15284>; Fabrizio Cafaggi, *Comparative Report. A Comparative Analysis of Transnational Private Regulation: Legitimacy, Quality, Effectiveness and Enforcement* (2014), <https://www.eesc.europa.eu/sites/default/files/resources/docs/a-comparative-analysis-of-transnational-private-regulation-fcafaggi_12062014.pdf>.

[36] Barbara Warwas, 'The Application of Arbitration in Transnational Private Regulation: An Analytical Framework and Recommendations for Future Research' (2020) Zoomout 73 QIL 33, with further references to the work on TPR by Cafaggi.

[37] Warwas (n 36) 33 summarizing the recommendation in this regard by Cafaggi in Cafaggi 'Comparative Report (n 35) 102.

[38] Warwas (n 35) 34 summarizing the work by Cafaggi in this regard; on private enforcement of TPR through arbitration, see 47–49.

logue between private and public actors within those governance models.[39] Such a dialogue can take the forms of hybridization (where hard laws are applied to private actors and, vice versa, when private rules are applied to public actors), collaborative rulemaking (where rules are developed jointly by private and public actors), coordination (where rules are produced interdependently by private and public actors, each producing their own rules in the shadow of the other), and competition (where the rules are developed by private actors concerning the regulatory issue already regulated by public actors, often diminishing the legitimacy of such rules).[40] The concept of TPR seems quite relevant for the current discussion when it comes to the enforcement of platforms' rules and norms and also in relation to the various rights of platforms' users (be they economic or fundamental rights, among others). The scheme determining the interplay between dispute resolution systems developed by platforms and the regulatory requirements (if any) for those systems seems again instrumental in assessing the applicability of TPR to the platform's dispute resolution system in view of its increasing functions. I will turn to such analysis in the later part of this chapter.

Moving forward to the last and fourth strand of literature, which has at its core the interests of citizens in shaping relevant and effective justice models, the preliminary observation concerns the relevance that theories on *social regulation* have for this literature. Since it is hard to find one fitting theory here, I propose the potential theoretical (normative) framework based on pragmatism (specifically, John Dewey's approach), the theories of public utility, and the conceptions of decentralizing platform governance, the latter two having been summarized by Elettra Bietti.[41] Dewey's theory promotes a value-oriented social justice model as a form of democratic socialism.[42] The theories of public utility denote the concept of the internet as the public interest space, which implies some form of utility regulation on the side of platforms.[43] Finally, the conceptions promoting decentralization of platform governance through technical and social mechanisms support public, legislative attempts at such decentralization or bottom-up civic actions in this regard. An example of the former can be seen in the data mobility or interoperability measures in the US and in Europe (including the UK) that, in a very simplistic definition, help to increase data users' access to personal data stored by

---

39 Cafaggi, 'New Foundations of Transnational Private Regulation' (n 35), sections III and IV.

40 Cafaggi, 'New Foundations of Transnational Private Regulation' (n 35) 18.

41 Robert J Kent, 'Dewey and the Project of Critical Social Theory' (2000) 23(1/2) Social Thought and Research 1; Elettra Bietti, 'A Genealogy of Digital Platform Regulation' (2023) 7 GLTR 1, in particular 59–66.

42 Kent (n 41) 1.

43 Bietti (n 41) 59–60.

online platforms.[44] An example of the latter involves initiatives – such as the Platform Cooperativism Consortium – which see platform governance as a threat to democratic participation and which thus promote cooperative principles such as democratic ownership and governance.[45]

What all these theories and concepts have in common is the shift in the regulatory paradigm from market regulatory power to a more socially engaged form of regulation where individual citizen (or user-based) interests and values collectively constitute platform governance. However, these theories and conceptions still tend to somewhat identify private and public actors as being positioned on the opposing spectrum of democratic legitimacy, with public actors assuming oversight functions over private actors (digital platforms).[46] I propose here an alternative regulatory model, namely one of *multilevel regulation*, where all regulatory actors are treated equally, as opposed to embracing the more traditional hierarchical interdependence of these actors. The concept was first developed by Nupur Chowdhury and Ramses Wessel as the legal variant of the concept of multilevel governance.[47] Because it rejects hierarchical ordering in both governance and regulation, it offers us a relevant framework for accommodating different roles of private and public actors in the platform economy, roles that can be seen as complementary rather than competing. Additionally, in my previous work I proposed to expand the concept of multilevel regulation into the grassroots- and historical dispute resolution practices of early communities that existed before the modern state systems.[48] Extending this framework into the current analysis allows us to expand the theoretical framework proposed here even further, incorporating the roles of various social and civic initiatives, including those of citizens and platform users, into the new regulatory paradigm potentially applicable for the new functions of dispute resolution in the platform economy.

In sum, as seen from the brief analysis above, different strands of literature on dispute resolution within and beyond online platforms seem to be based on or advance different regulatory paradigms. The majority of the literature

---

[44] Bietti (n 41) 62–63, with further references, also to relevant legislation.

[45] 'Platform Cooperativism Consortium: Vision & Advantages', <https://platform.coop/about/vision-and-advantages/>, as referred to in Bietti (n 41) 63.

[46] See the examples enumerated by Bietti, such as the oversight role of the Federal Communications Commission over internet access, among others. Bietti (n 41) 59–60, with further references.

[47] Nupur Chowdhury and Ramses A Wessel, 'Conceptualising Multilevel Regulation in the EU: A Legal Translation of Multilevel Governance?' (2012) 18(3) Eur LJ 335; see also Andreas Follesdal, Ramses A Wessel, and Jan Wouters (eds), *Multilevel Regulation and the EU: The Interplay Between Global, European and National Normative Processes* (Brill Nijhoff 2008).

[48] Barbara Warwas, 'Returning to the Origins of Multilevel Regulation: The Role of Historical ADR Practices' (2023) 15(1) EJLS 127.

tends to emphasize the interplay between, on the one hand, private platforms that have certain regulatory powers (resembling public powers) over its users and, on the other, public actors equipped with traditional legislative, executive, and judicial powers that fall within the more classic understanding of democratic legitimacy. In this milieu of interaction, platforms and governments operate within the paradigm of private-public regulation, with private-public dialogue defining the checks and balances necessary for democratic governance of the platform economy, even if this dialogue is sometimes blurred. We also see the relevance of the theories on self-regulation and the theory of TPR at the global level, which is applicable to literature promoting the more autonomous role of dispute resolution within platforms due to its economic efficiency. Finally, the quite relevant paradigm that I propose to preliminarily adopt in this contribution concerns the social regulation paradigm that (as proposed) is based on multilevel regulation assuming that public and private actors have complementary roles in the regulation (and governance) of the digital platform economy. This paradigm also allows us to focus on a broader group of private, non-state actors in the platform economy, including citizens (platform users being natural persons). It is important to stress here, again, that more research needs to be conducted to test the application of this theory to (specific) online platforms, also in a more systematic manner. Below, I will preliminarily analyze the new solutions from the two EU regulations (P2B and DSA) concerning dispute resolution in the context of this newly proposed regulatory paradigm (social regulation) as well as in the more traditional ones (private-public regulation and self-regulation).

II. The New Provisions on Dispute Resolution within the EU Digital Market

In the section below, I analyze the new provisions on dispute resolution under the P2B and DSA Regulations.[49] The analysis concerns each Regulation separately, focusing on the following aspects: the dispute resolution means and a short explanation of them, the scope of application of the provisions, the types of disputes they cover, the function of dispute resolution, and enforcement with a focus on the interplay between private and public actors. The main goal of this analysis is to preliminarily assess the regulatory paradigm behind those provisions, given the discussion above, and to identify the im-

[49] The analysis is largely based on the legal commentary in Barbara Warwas, Digital Market. Digital Services Act. Digital Markets Act. Platform-to-business Regulation. Commentary, ed. Mateusz Grochowski (CH Beck 2023); comments on the articles on the internal complaint-handling system and mediation: arts 11–13 of Regulation 2019/1150; art 52 of Regulation 2022/1925; arts 19–21 and art 90 of Regulation 2022/2065.

plications of such a paradigm on the enforcement of rules and norms produced by online platforms.

1. P2B Regulation

The P2B Regulation sets forth two types of dispute resolution mechanisms: an internal complaint-handling system (art 11) and mediation (art 12). In the section below, I start with the internal complaint-handling system.

a) Internal complaint-handling system

Pursuant to art 11 of the P2B Regulation, providers of online intermediation services are obliged to adopt an *internal complaint-handling system*, which can also be outsourced to external dispute resolution providers as long as it meets the requirements of the Regulation.[50] The obligation is not applicable to providers of online intermediation services that constitute small enterprises unless they wish to set up the internal complaint-handling system voluntarily.[51] The internal complaint-handling system needs to follow certain procedural standards that the Regulation defines rather vaguely.[52] For example, art 11 requires that the system be 'easily accessible' and 'free of charge for business users' and 'shall ensure handling within a reasonable time frame.'[53] Furthermore, the system is required to follow the principles of transparency and equal treatment concerning 'equivalent situations, and treating complaints in a manner which is proportionate to their importance and complexity.'[54] Art 11(2) of the P2B Regulation also requires that the providers of online intermediation services 'duly consider complaints lodged and the follow-up which they may need to give to the complaint' so that the issue is addressed 'adequately.' The same provision requires a 'swift' and 'effective' processing of the complaints by the providers of online intermediation services and the necessary communication by them of the outcomes of the processes that should be drafted in a straightforward and easily accessible language. The latter obligation of (plain) communication is additionally strengthened by the obligation of transparency outlined in art 11(3) and (4) of

[50] P2B Regulation, recital 39 states that '[t]he use of the word "internal" should not be understood as preventing the delegation of an internal complaint-handling system to an external service provider or other corporate structure, as long as such a provider or other corporate structure has full authority and the ability to ensure compliance of the internal complaint-handling system with the requirements in this Regulation.' For a more detailed analysis of the meaning of the word "internal" in the internal complaint-handling system, see Warwas (n 49) 1246–1247.

[51] P2B Regulation, recital 38 and art 11(5).

[52] Busch (n 17) 134; similar observations are included in Warwas (n 49) 1247.

[53] P2B Regulation, art 11(1) para 2.

[54] P2B Regulation, art 11(1) para 2.

the P2B Regulation, according to which providers of online intermediation services (i) are expected to include all relevant information concerning the access to and the 'functioning of their internal complaint-handling system' in their terms and conditions,[55] and (ii) are to publish information on the 'functioning and effectiveness of their internal complaint-handling system'.[56]

Regarding the *scope of application*, the provisions on the internal complaint-handling system apply to online intermediation providers and online search engines within the meaning of art 1(1) and (2) of the P2B Regulation in their relations with business users and corporate website users.[57] The scope of disputes covered by art 11 concerns:

'(a) alleged non-compliance by that provider with any obligations laid down in this Regulation which affects the business user lodging the complaint ('the complainant');
(b) technological issues which relate directly to the provision of online intermediation services, and which affect the complainant;
(c) measures taken by, or behaviour of, that provider which relate directly to the provision of the online intermediation services, and which affect the complainant.'[58]

The *function* of the internal complaint-handling system is to provide business users with 'immediate, suitable and effective possibilities of redress'.[59] This function should be read in line with art 1(1) of the P2B Regulation, which defines the purpose of the Regulation on the whole as the necessary contribution to:

'[…] the proper functioning of the internal market by laying down rules to ensure that business users of online intermediation services and corporate website users in relation to online search engines are granted appropriate transparency, fairness and effective redress possibilities.'

Regarding *enforcement* and the interplay between the internal complaint-handling system and other forms of possible redress (including mediation and court proceedings), the Regulation does not make recourse of the complainants to the latter dependent on first having initiated an internal complaint. Recital 37 supports this option and states that

'[a]ny attempt to reach an agreement through the internal complaint-handling process does not affect the rights of providers of online intermediation services or business users to initiate judicial proceedings at any time during or after the internal complaint-handling process.'

---

55 P2B Regulation, art 11(3).

56 P2B Regulation, art 11(4).

57 Warwas (n 49) 1243–1244.

58 P2B Regulation, art 11(1)(a)–(c).

59 P2B Regulation, recital 37: 'In order to enable business users, including those whose use of the relevant online intermediation services might have been restricted, suspended or terminated, to have access to immediate, suitable and effective possibilities of redress, providers of online intermediation services should provide for an internal complaint-handling system.'

Moreover, recital 52 has emphasized that '[t]his Regulation seeks to ensure full respect for the right to an effective remedy and to a fair trial as laid down in Article 47 of the Charter of Fundamental Rights of the European Union […]'.

b) Mediation

Mediation is regulated in art 12 of the P2B Regulation. The P2B Regulation does not define mediation as such, which is in line with the policy of the Commission in this regard, as expressed in other acts of EU law regarding mediation and out-of-court dispute settlement.[60] Instead, the EU lawmakers focus on the role of mediators. In this vein, art 12(1) of the P2B Regulation establishes an obligation on the side of the providers of online intermediation services to include the names of at least two mediators in their terms and conditions from whom the parties to a dispute can choose in the event a dispute arises. Recital 40 of the P2B Regulation further specifies that those mediators can be public or private. What is more, according to recital 40, '[…] providers of online intermediation services and their business users should remain free to jointly identify any mediator of their choice after a dispute has arisen between them.'[61] This means that the parties are not bound by the names of mediators specified in the terms and conditions and are free to choose a different mediator for their dispute.[62] In practice, on the date of the publishing of the Report on the first preliminary review on the implementation of Regulation (EU) 2019/1150 on promoting fairness and transparency for business users of online intermediation services (ie 12 October 2023), 'only 25 of the 179 large and medium-sized online intermediation services under consideration provided the name of at least two mediators in their T&Cs [terms and conditions] for business users.'[63] Further, 35 other online intermediation service providers referred to a mediation organization rather than two mediators in their terms and conditions.[64]

Other relevant considerations concerning the definition of mediation under P2B involve the *requirements for mediators* under art 12(2) of the P2B Regulation. Because an in-depth analysis of the requirements to be met by mediators under the P2B Regulation falls outside the scope of this contribution, it is

---

[60] See Warwas (n 49) 1249–1261, particularly the comments on the definition of mediation at 1251–1252.

[61] P2B Regulation, recital 40.

[62] Warwas (n 49) 1251, with further references.

[63] 'Report from the Commission to the European Parliament, the Council and the European Economic and Social Committee on the application of Directive 2013/11/EU of the European Parliament and of the Council on alternative dispute resolution for consumer disputes and Regulation (EU) 524/2013 of the European Parliament and of the Council on online dispute resolution for consumer disputes' (COM/2019/425 final, 25 September 2019), online version, with further references.

[64] 'Report from the Commission to the European Parliament' (n 63).

here only relevant to mention that those mediators must: be impartial and independent, offer affordable mediation services for business users, provide mediation services in the relevant language of the terms and conditions applicable to the contractual relationship between the disputants that gave rise to a dispute, be easily accessible in person 'in the place of establishment or residence of the business user or remotely,' be able to provide mediation services 'without undue delay', and possess knowledge (in the words of the Regulation, 'a sufficient understanding') of 'general business-to-business commercial relations.'[65]

Notably, and as already mentioned above, mediation under the P2B Regulation follows the general principle of voluntariness, which means, in accord with recital 40, that '[...] mediation provided for in this Regulation should be a voluntary process in the sense that the parties are themselves in charge of the process and can start and terminate it at any time.'[66] This does not mean that the parties cannot be obliged to try to pursue mediation in good faith, the principle prescribed in art 12(3) of the P2B Regulation. This provision sets forth the scheme resembling mandatory mediation, as already explained above.[67]

Regarding the *scope of application*, the provisions on mediation should apply to online intermediation service providers that fall within the scope of the application of the Regulation itself, except for small enterprises.[68] Regarding the category of disputes falling within the scope of art 12 of the P2B Regulation, they concern

> 'any disputes between the provider and the business user arising in relation to the provision of the online intermediation services concerned, including complaints that could not be resolved by means of the internal complaint-handling system referred to in Article 11.'

Hence, mediation can be used to address (among others) the issues that have emerged in the context of the complaint-handling system, and it can be initiated irrespective of whether such issues had previously been resolved through such a system under art 11 of the P2B Regulation.[69]

Regarding the *function of the mediation provisions* set out in the P2B Regulation, recital 40 points to the potential of mediation to offer satisfactory dispute resolution for the providers of online intermediation services and their business users – without reliance on courts, where proceedings 'can be lengthy and costly.' The function of mediation is, therefore, to increase the economic efficiency of dispute resolution within the digital platform economy.[70]

---

[65] P2B Regulation, art 12(2)(a)–(f).
[66] See *supra* n 25.
[67] See section I.2.
[68] Warwas (n 49) 1250.
[69] See P2B Regulation, art 12(1) and Warwas (n 49) 1253, with further references.
[70] A similar observation can be found in Warwas (n 49) 1250, with further references.

Regarding *enforcement*, mediation, similar to the internal complaint-handling system, is one of the few forms of redress available to business users of the providers of online intermediation services (with judicial proceedings being possible at any stage of mediation).[71] Also, the provisions on mediation provide for a very visible interplay between private and public actors (including private and public mediators, providers of online intermediation services, Member States, and the European Commission, among others), especially when it comes to further development of the mediation infrastructure specific to the digital market. This is specified in art 13 of the P2B Regulation, which requires a direct collaboration initiated by the European Commission between the Commission itself and the Member States to set up specialized mediation organizations, which should include mediators with specialized knowledge in the field of the digital platform economy.[72] Such steps, as stated in recital 43, should increase the confidence that users within the platform economy have in mediation. This is, however, still a work in progress. The reports by the Commission in this regard demonstrate that such specialized mediation organizations have not yet been developed.[73] It is important to add here, also, that at the point when mediation settlements are not voluntarily complied with by the parties, they will need to be enforced in courts, which adds an additional public actor to the network of private-public actors potentially involved in the enforcement of dispute resolution under the P2B Regulation.

2. *Digital Services Act*

The DSA provides for two forms of dispute resolution. The first one concerns the internal complaint-handling system under art 20, while the second one involves out-of-court dispute settlement under art 21.

a) *The Internal Complaint-Handling System*

Art 20 of the DSA establishes an obligation on the side of the providers of online platforms to set up an internal complaint-handling system. This system needs to be 'effective', enabling the complainants to submit the complaint 'electronically and free of charge'.[74] Additionally, '[p]roviders of online platforms shall ensure that their internal complaint-handling systems are easy to access, user-friendly and enable and facilitate the submission of sufficiently precise and adequately substantiated complaints.'[75] According to art 20(4)

---

[71] P2B Regulation, art 12(5).

[72] Warwas (n 49) 1261–1262.

[73] 'Report from the Commission to the European Parliament' (n 63), online version.

[74] DSA, art 20(1).

[75] DSA, art 20(3).

of the DSA, the complaints should be addressed 'in a timely, non-discriminatory, diligent and non-arbitrary manner.' Art 20(6) further specifies that the complaints cannot be handled only through automated means as the qualified staff needs to supervise the making of the follow-up decisions. Those procedural requirements stemming from DSA, art 20 have been criticized by some commentators as being quite vague despite the Regulation's promise to offer a 'procedural turn' in platform governance.[76]

Regarding the *scope of application*, art 20 applies to the providers of online platforms within the meaning of art 3(i) of the DSA, except for micro and small enterprises.[77] The complainants can be natural persons or organizations representing complainants, such as consumer organizations.[78] The complaints can be submitted by the recipients of the services regardless of whether or not they had a contractual relationship with the providers of online platforms.[79]

Regarding the category of *disputes* that fall within the scope of application of art 20, they concern the decisions of online platforms regarding content moderation. Hence, art 20 can be used in reaction to the platform's decisions concerning potentially illegal content after an individual or an entity has submitted an unsuccessful notice under art 16 of the DSA or in response to the platform's decisions with regard to potential 'restrictions' that users of the platform have suffered under art 17(1).[80] art 20 of the DSA further enumerates potential examples of such decisions as:

> '(a) decisions whether or not to remove or disable access to or restrict visibility of the information; (b) decisions whether or not to suspend or terminate the provision of the service, in whole or in part, to the recipients; (c) decisions whether or not to suspend or terminate the recipients' account; (d) decisions whether or not to suspend, terminate or otherwise restrict the ability to monetise information provided by the recipients.'[81]

Regarding the *function* of the internal complaint-handling system under the DSA, it is twofold. On the one hand, and from a more general perspective, art 20 (as well as art 21) aims to limit the current unrestricted autonomy of online platforms that allows them to accumulate all powers over its users, including judicial powers. This is done by those articles requiring that online platforms provide certain procedural guarantees. On the other hand, the goal of the provisions in art 20 of the DSA is to enable '[r]ecipients of the service [...] to easily and effectively contest certain decisions of providers of online plat-

[76] Ortolani (n 19) 12; Busch (n 17) 133–134.

[77] On the exception, see DSA, art 19. For an in-depth analysis of DSA, art 20, see Warwas (n 49) 245–251, in particular 245–246.

[78] See DSA, art 86(2).

[79] Warwas (n 49) 249, with further references.

[80] Ortolani (n 19) 12.

[81] DSA, art 20(1)(a)–(d).

forms concerning the illegality of content or its incompatibility with the terms and conditions that negatively affect them.'[82] This also gives certain room for online platforms to analyze their prior decisions on content moderation before they reach the out-of-court dispute settlement or court proceedings.[83]

Regarding *enforcement*, as seen above, the internal complaint-handling system exists in parallel to art 21 and potential court proceedings; hence, the recipients can choose their preferred procedural path.[84]

b) *Out-of-Court Dispute Settlement*

Art 21 of the DSA establishes that recipients of online platform services have a right of recourse to 'any out-of-court dispute settlement body' certified in line with the provisions of the DSA. The DSA does not define the term out-of-court dispute settlement body, which is similar to the Commission's approach to mediation and other dispute resolution means under EU law. Rather, the DSA focuses on minimum requirements to be met by those bodies in order to receive the certification from the 'Digital Services Coordinator of the Member State where the out-of-court dispute settlement body is established.'[85] Although an in-depth analysis of those requirements falls outside the scope of this analysis, it is worthwhile to enumerate them here. The requirements concern: impartiality and independence (including financial independence), the 'necessary expertise', remuneration independent from the outcome of the procedure, easily accessible procedure through electronic means, the ability to settle disputes 'in a swift, efficient and cost-effective manner and in at least one of the official languages of the institutions of the Union', and 'clear and fair rules of procedure that are easily and publicly accessible, and that comply with applicable law […].'[86] These requirements constitute the basis for certification by the relevant Digital Services Coordinator for a period of five years.[87] The list of the certified out-of-court dispute settlement bodies is published by the European Commission following notification by Digital Services Coordinators.[88]

Regarding the *scope of application* and the category of disputes, DSA, art 21 entitles any '[r]ecipients of the service, including individuals or entities that have submitted notices addressed by the decisions referred to in Article 20(1)' to choose a certified body to resolve their dispute 'relating to those decisions, including complaints that have not been resolved by means of the

[82] DSA, recital 58. See also Warwas (n 49) 248, with further references.
[83] Warwas (n 49) 248, with further references to Pietro Ortolani.
[84] DSA, recital 59.
[85] DSA, art 21(3) in accordance with DSA, art 21(1).
[86] DSA, art 21(3)(a)–(f).
[87] DSA, art 21(3).
[88] DSA, art 21(8).

internal complaint-handling system referred to in that Article.' According to Pietro Ortolani, those disputes may concern both platform decisions concerning illegal content and decisions regarding the content that is contrary to a platform's terms and conditions.[89]

When it comes to the *function* of out-of-court dispute settlement under the DSA, at issue is the need to offer recipients of the platform's services and other parties entitled to rely on art 21 of the DSA a means of redress against the platform's decisions concerning content moderation. Out-of-court dispute settlement is seen here as a procedurally efficient and cost-effective mechanism of dispute settlement that can prove relevant and useful in the context of the activities of online platforms. This is in line with the Commission's general understanding of alternative dispute resolution, which promotes its use within the EU due to its purported economic efficiency.[90]

The discussion regarding *enforcement* seems quite interesting in the context of art 21 of the DSA. This is so because of the involvement of a very broad network of private and public actors at the level of enforcement, including out-of-court dispute settlement bodies, online platforms, courts (to which disputes can be referred at any stage of the proceedings),[91] Digital Services Coordinators (who are responsible for certification of the out-of-court dispute settlement bodies),[92] the Member States (which may also establish out-of-court dispute settlement bodies and support the activities of such bodies),[93] and the European Commission (which maintains the list of certified out-of-court dispute settlement bodies).[94] While at first glance, we could assume here a 'typical' form of private-public regulation, especially given the fact that the decisions of out-of-court dispute settlement bodies are in principle not binding upon the parties, a deeper analysis may suggest different conclusions. Notably, the parties to a dispute may themselves decide that the decision issued by the out-of-court dispute settlement body is binding, which changes the perspective and legal relevance of the activities of such a body.[95] All of this keeps the discussion on the potential regulatory paradigm applicable to the dispute resolution provisions under the DSA quite open.

---

[89] Ortolani (n 19) 16; similarly in Warwas (n 49) 256.

[90] See Warwas (n 49) 255.

[91] DSA, art 21(1) para 3 and recital 59. See also DSA, art 90, which provides for the possibility of issuing a representative action in the context of the DSA under Directive 2020/1828 of 25 November 2020 on representative actions for the protection of the collective interests of consumers and repealing Directive 2009/22/EC.

[92] See the already mentioned DSA, art 21(3).

[93] DSA, art 21(6).

[94] See the already mentioned DSA, art 21(8).

[95] Warwas (n 49) 257, with further references.

3. *Preliminary analysis in view of the research questions*

Let me now return to the two research questions posed at the beginning of this chapter. First, what are the systematic regulatory goals of the EU regulations on dispute resolution within online platforms? Second, what regulatory paradigm do those regulations imply regarding the enforcement of different types of rules and regulations produced by online platforms?

Regarding the first question, we see from the above analysis that the main purpose of both the P2B Regulation and the DSA was to set certain limitations on the private judicial activities of online platforms so as to limit their absolute regulatory powers in this regard. The intention was to do so through minimum procedural requirements regarding dispute resolution proceedings within online platforms. That said, and as seen above from the arguments of scholars such as Christopher Busch and Pietro Ortolani, those procedural requirements still remain very general. Hence, it is quite difficult to identify any systematic regulatory goals behind those regulations at this stage.

Second, when it comes to the impact of the regulatory environment on the rules, norms, and standards increasingly produced by the platforms, the one-size-fits-all regulatory paradigm also does not come to the fore at first glance. For example, on the one hand, a specific form of interplay between private and public actors at the level of enforcement (such as a form of mandatory mediation under art 12 of the P2B Regulation) and the particular relationship between Digital Services Coordinators and the out-of-court dispute settlement bodies at the certification level under art 21 of the DSA may suggest that the rule of *private-public regulation* should be applied to the dispute resolution means under both the P2B Regulation and the DSA. On the other hand, however, the fact that the parties may exercise their private powers within the out-of-court dispute settlement under art 21 and decide that the decision of the out-of-court dispute settlement bodies will eventually become binding upon them shifts the hierarchical relationship between private and public actors at the enforcement level quite significantly. This brings us closer to the discussion on both the *decentralization of platform governance* referred to by Elettra Bietti and the *multilevel regulation* discussed by Nupur Chowdhury and Ramses Wessel.[96] In this light, in the section below, I list the main conclusions stemming from this contribution, and I propose a few lines of research to be conducted in the future to answer the research questions posed in this chapter in a more systematic manner.

[96] Bietti (n 41) and Chowdhury and Wessel (n 47).

III. Conclusions

In this chapter, I have tried to spotlight the following trends concerning dispute resolution within the digital platform economy: First, the role of dispute resolution – although rather underestimated in the literature – is increasing. This concerns the increasing regulatory role of online platforms (1) concerning the shaping of the terms and conditions of cross-border marketplaces, which in turn affect the legal situation of the users of those platforms, (2) in shaping the fundamental rights of their users (eg, freedom of expression), and (3) in determining the economic situation of platform users through the activities of online platforms in the field of content moderation. Platforms having autonomy over dispute resolution allows them to not only produce rules, norms, and standards in the above context, but also to control their enforcement. Second, the analysis of platform activities is often shaped by the regulatory paradigm applied by scholars who analyze those activities (which often differs depending on the regulatory perspective). Here, I have proposed to look into new conceptions and regulatory theories such as that of people-centered justice, multilevel regulation, and decentralization of platform governance to search for a more up-to-date regulatory paradigm capable of incorporating the rights of users of the platform into the analysis. Finally, after having analyzed the dispute resolution provisions under the P2B Regulation and the DSA, I have suggested that some of those provisions could be applicable to those new theories; however, more systematic research is needed to test this hypothesis.

This brings me to my proposals for future research. Many academic discussions to date oscillate around similar paradigms concerning the roles and functions of private and public actors in the regulatory landscape, which often start from the principles of democratic legitimacy 'reserved' for public actors sanctioned by the modern state systems. Although valid and important, those discussions often position private and public actors at competing levels, with the private dispute settlement systems being seen as a threat to democratically legitimate public enforcement. In view of those discussions, a new regulatory paradigm is needed concerning dispute resolution within the context of the digital platform economy. Hence, I propose to further expand the discussion started in this contribution on the potential applicability of more daring regulatory theories on online platforms (including that of people-centered justice, multilevel regulation, and decentralization of platform governance). Those conceptions and theories should be analyzed in a more systematic manner by studying more concrete solutions for the application of the P2B Regulation and the DSA in the Member States and by investigating the developing practice of internal complaint-handling systems, mediation, and out-of-court dispute resolution bodies in relation to the various expanding activities of online platforms.

Part 3

Enforcing Platforms Rules – Domestic Perspectives

Enforcing Platform Rights – The Italian Case Law

Dianora Poletti and Federica Casarosa

I. Introduction

Defined comprehensively, online platforms have changed how citizens communicate, access knowledge and information, and buy or sell both goods or services. This change has also strongly affected the legal framework under which these behaviors have been regulated, on the one hand requiring the legislature to revise or adopt new rules and provisions[1] and on the other hand requiring the courts to interpret existing – sometimes technologically outdated – rules in an evolutive way.[2] This process has involved the participation of several ac-

[1] At European level, see the Directives and Regulations adopted in the last five years: Regulation (EU) 2019/1150 of the European Parliament and of the Council of 20 June 2019 on promoting fairness and transparency for business users of online intermediation services [2019] OJ L186/57 (P2B Regulation); Directive (EU) 2019/770 of the European Parliament and of the Council of 20 May 2019 on certain aspects concerning contracts for the supply of digital content and digital services [2019] OJ L136/1; Directive (EU) 2019/771 of the European Parliament and of the Council of 20 May 2019 on certain aspects concerning contracts for the sale of goods, amending Regulation (EU) 2017/2394 and Directive 2009/22/EC, and repealing Directive 1999/44/EC [2019] OJ L136/28; Regulation (EU) 2022/1925 of the European Parliament and of the Council of 14 September 2022 on contestable and fair markets in the digital sector and amending Directives (EU) 2019/1937 and (EU) 2020/1828 (Digital Markets Act) [2022] OJ L265/1 (DMA); Regulation (EU) 2022/2065 of the European Parliament and of the Council of 19 October 2022 on a Single Market For Digital Services and amending Directive 2000/31/EC (Digital Services Act) [2022] OJ L277/1 (DSA).

tors at national and European levels; moreover, given the wide range of activities that online platforms can carry out, it has affected several areas of law, ranging from consumer protection to media law to fundamental rights protection.

The contribution will not aim to address the overall process regarding online platforms. Instead, it will provide insights from the Italian legal context, showing the crucial role of courts and regulatory authorities in applying the provisions on liability of online intermediaries and highlighting the specific case of unfair commercial practices in online platforms.

While in the beginning Italian legislators were trailing after the choices made by European Union bodies, Italian jurisprudence has been very responsive to the changing social and economic framework, being the first to acknowledge the evolution of the information society structure where the role of the platforms was moving from one of mere intermediary to being an active party in online contractual exchanges. Since 2010, the judges have begun to evaluate whether or not the hosting providers should be qualified as passive or active providers, identifying criteria that interpreted and developed guidelines already articulated by the Court of Justice of the EU.[3] Since then, the cases addressing the role of platforms have progressively defined the criteria for distinguishing between passive intermediaries, in a strict sense, and active ones, as well as the liability regime that is applicable in both cases.

Yet there are other issues that Italian courts have analyzed. First, a limited set of cases have defined the role of platforms, in particular social networking ones, through the lens of contract law. Another increasingly relevant body of case law has emerged from the application of consumer protection rules by the National Competition and Market Authority (*Autorità Garante per la concorrenza e il mercato* – AGCM) and, through judicial review, by administrative courts. The AGCM is the regulatory authority in charge of verifying compliance with competition rules and consumer protection rules, including rules on unfair commercial practices and unfair contract terms. An analysis of the cases shows the impact that these decisions may have on the conduct of online platforms.

The present contribution will start with a short analysis of the interplay between European and national policy and legislation addressing online platforms (II); then the enforcement mechanisms for violations will be presented, distinguishing between the proceedings before civil courts and administrative

[2] Evangelia Psychogiopoulou and Federica Casarosa, 'Social Media before Domestic and European Courts' in Evangelia Psychogiopoulou and Federica Casarosa (eds), *Social Media, Fundamental Rights and Courts* (Routledge 2023).

[3] For a historical analysis, see Ilaria Montagnani, *Internet, contenuti illeciti e responsabilità degli intermediari* (Egea 2018); for a recent analysis of the courts' decisions as regards social media, see Federica Casarosa and Maria Concetta Causarano, 'Social Media before Higher Courts in Italy' in Evangelia Psychogiopoulou and Federica Casarosa (eds), *Social Media, Fundamental Rights and Courts* (Routledge 2023).

authorities (III). The subsequent analysis will focus on the most relevant decisions issued by civil and administrative courts.

II. The Interplay between European and Italian Policies Regarding Online Platforms

When looking at the evolution of the legal framework applicable to online platforms, we may differentiate between four phases characterized by an intertwining connection between the role of platforms in the marketplace and the formalization of this role in legal terms. Accordingly, the four phases may be labelled in the following way: first, platforms as mere intermediaries; second, the shift towards a platform economy; third, platform society; and fourth, platform coexistence. Each stage has posed challenges that the European bodies have attempted addressed in hard and soft law interventions.[4] This progression is well defined at the European level, and each stage represents an evolution from the previous one. At the national level, the level of interest and awareness required a more extended gestation period, initially only trailing after the European regulations and then showing little initiative to legislate areas not covered by European rules independently.

The first phase dates back to the 1990s and proceeds until the first decade of 2000. It is now perceived as the 'prehistoric' age for platforms, which were still defined as gateways for accessing online space. At that time, platforms were mere intermediaries, while users were in charge of providing content. Internet service providers (ISP), defined in the Directive on Electronic Commerce (ECD),[5] were, at most, providers of virtual space used to create a personal blog or a website open to other users' comments or serving as a virtual shop, only presenting the available offers.[6] These examples are a far cry from the rich and complex interaction offered by today's platforms.

The legislation, particularly the already mentioned ECD, aimed at removing barriers to cross-border online services and ensuring the free movement of information society services between Member States, providing not only standard rules for the establishment of ISPs and the provision of e-commerce

[4] Dianora Poletti, 'The regulatory framework for current technological challenges: some methodological considerations' in Giusella Finocchiaro, Luigi Balestra and Marina Timoteo (eds), *Major Legal Trends in the Digital Economy – The Approach of the EU, the US and China* (Il Mulino 2022) 231.

[5] Directive 2000/31/EC of the European Parliament and of the Council of 8 June 2000 on certain legal aspects of information society services, in particular electronic commerce, in the Internal Market ('Directive on electronic commerce') [2000] OJ L178/1 (ECD).

[6] ECD, art 2(a) referred to information society service providers (ISSP), defining them as 'any service normally provided for remuneration, at a distance, by electronic means and at the individual request of a recipient of services'.

services but also the liability regime for intermediaries operating online in the EU. This legislation was the point of reference for the growth and flourishing of ISPs, thanks to the fundamental principle of exemption from liability for the transmitted or hosted content. This so-called safe-harbor principle was also supported by the absence of general oversight obligations and was thereby intended to create a neutral environment in which platforms could thrive.[7] As the first cases reached the Court of Justice of the European Union, the role of ISPs started to be questioned: the L'Oreal and Luis Vuitton cases[8] tried to identify the boundaries of the concept of a passive hosting provider to apply the exemption of liability, pursuant to recitals 22 and 23 ECD.

During this period, Italy was still taking its first steps in online commerce, and the importance of this sector was still limited. As a result, Italian policymakers did not devote sufficient attention to this topic and followed the lead of the EU. This is probably why Italian legislators implemented the ECD by merely copying and pasting the original version into Legislative Decree no 70 of 9 April 2003.

The second phase can be found in the decade between 2010 and 2020. In those years, platforms had already modified their structure and services to move from being providers of mere storage services to providers of additional and complex services in which the information uploaded by users becomes an integral part of the business model. However, the idea of a European market able to compete with the US market as put forward by the ECD still needed to be accomplished. The legal provisions to reduce the barriers to digital market access for European small and medium-sized enterprises did not achieve the expected results. At the same time, these provisions have allowed the flourishing of US platforms that have become internet giants, with millions of users and a market that has almost reached the level of moligopoly.[9]

In this phase, a crucial role was played by the Commission and its interventions in regulating the internal digital market. The Communication 'Strategy for a Digital Single Market in Europe'[10] was followed by the Commis-

---

[7] Stefano Bocchini, *La responsabilità civile degli intermediari del commercio elettronico* (ESI 2003); Giulio Ponzanelli, 'Verso un diritto uniforme per la responsabilità degli internet service provider' in Salvatore Sica and Pasquale Stanzione (eds), *Commercio elettronico e categorie civilistiche* (Giuffré 2002) 87.

[8] See CJEU 23 March 2010, joined cases C-236/08 to C-238/08, *Google France SARL and Google Inc. v Louis Vuitton Malletier SA*, ECLI:EU:C:2010:159; and CJEU 12 July 2011, C-324/09, *L'Oréal SA and Others v eBay International AG and Others*, ECLI:EU:C:2011:474.

[9] Nicolas Petit, *Big Tech and the Digital Economy: The Moligopoly Scenario* (OUP 2020).

[10] Communication from the Commission to the European Parliament, the Council, the European Economic and Social Committee and the Committee of the Regions, A Digital Single Market Strategy for Europe, Brussels, 6 May 2015, COM/2015/0192 final.

sion Communication 'Countering illegal content online. Towards greater accountability of online platforms'.[11] The latter addressed the measures to tackle the increasing amount of online illegal content, considering the consequences of the fundamental right to freedom of expression and information. Thereafter, the Communication 'Online platforms and the digital single market: opportunities and challenges for Europe'[12] explicitly states that '[t]he platform economy offers great opportunities for European start-ups to innovate and presents, also for established market players, the possibility to develop new business models, products and services' and paves the way for the European data strategy.

This was the phase in which the sharing economy began gaining momentum and online platforms became parties in discussion with the European institutions, their being called upon to collaborate in combating illegal activities committed online by users. Such collaboration implies that the platforms become online gatekeepers monitoring internet activities. As a result, we are, at least for specific sectors, moving beyond a need for platform oversight obligations. This was the outcome of both soft and hard law interventions: worth mentioning, as an example of soft law, is the Code of Conduct on Hate Speech drafted by the European Commission in collaboration with Facebook, Twitter, YouTube and Microsoft in May 2016;[13] while as examples of hard law one can point to Directive 2017/541 on combating terrorism,[14] as well as the proposal for a Regulation on European Production and Preservation Orders.[15]

---

[11] Communication from the Commission to the European Parliament, the Council, the European Economic and Social Committee and the Committee of the Regions, Tackling Illegal Content Online – Towards an enhanced responsibility of online platforms, Brussels, 28 September 2017, COM/2017/555 final.

[12] Communication from the Commission to the European Parliament, the Council, the European Economic and Social Committee and the Committee of the Regions, Online Platforms and the Digital Single Market – Opportunities and Challenges for Europe, Brussels, 25 May 2016, COM/2016/288 final.

[13] See <https://commission.europa.eu/strategy-and-policy/policies/justice-and-fundamental-rights/combatting-discrimination/racism-and-xenophobia/eu-code-conduct-countering-illegal-hate-speech-online_en>. On the role of the code of conduct, see Federica Casarosa, 'When the Algorithm Is Not Fully Reliable: The Collaboration between Technology and Humans in the Fight against Hate Speech' in Hans-W Micklitz et al. (eds), *Constitutional Challenges in the Algorithmic Society* (CUP 2021) 298.

[14] Directive (EU) 2017/541 of the European Parliament and of the Council of 15 March 2017 on combating terrorism and replacing Council Framework Decision 2002/475/JHA and amending Council Decision 2005/671/JHA [2017] OJ L88/6.

[15] The Proposal for a Regulation on European Production and Preservation Orders for electronic evidence in criminal matters (COM/2018/225 final) required five years of negotiation at the European level and resulted in Regulation (EU) 2023/1543 of the European Parliament and of the Council on European Production Orders and European Preservation Orders for electronic evidence in criminal proceedings and for the execution of custodial sentences following criminal proceedings [2023] OJ L191/118, only in July 2023.

Yet the monitoring function carried out by platforms implies that they retain their intermediary function. The so-called Good Samaritan rule was still applicable and so important that the Digital Services Act also continued to allow online platforms to search for content without jeopardizing their neutral position vis-à-vis the content uploaded.

This occurs also when online platforms rapidly increase their power through the self-regulation established by the terms of services that regulate and monitor the conduct of their users. The increasing number of users and the amount of data flowing on the internet represents the fuel of online platforms, which are increasingly pursuing data to exploit their economic values and to personalize offers and advertisements to their users.[16]

In this period, the Italian parliament also presented two legislative acts addressing some specific features of the sharing economy. Both proposals regulate online platforms as intermediaries situated between users who would like to share space and time resources and goods or services.[17] It is interesting to note that, in both documents, the approach adopted was to create an authorization regime based, in one case, on a 'corporate policy document' that would have to be verified by the AGCM and, in the other case, on inclusion in a national register for online sharing platforms, managed, again, by the AGCM.[18] However, none of the proposals were adopted.

The third and fourth phases almost overlapped and ran for shorter periods and again saw the Italian policy shadowing the European one. The beginning of the third phase coincided with the launch of the European Data Strategy,[19] which was a harbinger of a different approach towards online platforms. First, greater accountability was required for online platforms, as exemplified by the Directive on copyright in the digital market,[20] where liability is envisaged for online content-sharing service providers in respect of unauthorized acts of

---

[16] Dianora Poletti, 'Gli intermediari dei dati' in Arnaldo Morace Pinelli (ed), *La circolazione dei dati personali. Persona, contratto e mercato* (Pacini 2023) 106.

[17] See Law Proposal 3564, 27 January 2016 on 'Disciplina delle piattaforme digitali per la condivisione di beni e servizi e disposizioni per la promozione dell'economia della condivisione' (Regulation of digital platforms for sharing goods and services and provisions for the promotion of the sharing economy), <www.camera.it/leg17/126?idDocumento=3564>; and the Law Proposal 2268, 3 March 2016, on 'Disposizioni in materia di sharing economy' (Regulation on sharing economy), <https://www.senato.it/service/PDF/PDFServer/DF/321410.pdf>.

[18] Guido D'Ippolito, 'Sharing Economy: L'esperienza Italiana Della XVII Legislatura Alla Luce Degli Orientamenti Europei' [2018] Medialaws 298.

[19] Communication from the Commission to the European Parliament, the Council, the European Economic and Social Committee and the Committee of the Regions, A European strategy for data, Brussels, 19 February 2020, COM/2020/66 final.

[20] Directive (EU) 2019/790 of the European Parliament and of the Council of 17 April 2019 on Copyright and Related Rights in the Digital Single Market and Amending Directives 96/9/EC and 2001/29/EC [2019] OJ L130/92 (DSM Copyright Directive).

communication to the public. Another example is the P2B Regulation, which essentially extends certain consumer rights, primarily transparency, to professionals who contract with the platform. The most important acts, however, are the Digital Services Act, which aims to strengthen the EU's single market and update the scope of liability for service providers, and the Digital Markets Act, which seeks to limit the powers of large platforms (the so-called very large platforms)[21] in general so as to curb their bargaining strength and market power.

The fourth phase is the current one: platform coexistence. This is the phase where the European Data Strategy aims to regulate large platforms and correspondingly incentivize small and medium-sized European platforms and build a market in which platforms can have different roles. The EU's intentions are clear: (a) grow the data-driven economy by drafting uniform rules; (b) create a 'made in EU' governance based on respect for fundamental rights and the values of European culture, which will make the European digital space safer and more attractive to investors from abroad. The digital economy is now entirely based on data. It requires legislation that safeguards the free circulation of data but, at the same time, respects the fundamental rights of the EU.[22]

III. Italian Case Law on Online Platforms

1. Hosting Platform Providers: Distinguishing between an Active and Passive Role

The challenges emerging in the application of ISP liability in respect of unlawful content available online is reflected in the rich interpretative work elaborated by the Italian courts. The point of reference is the national legislation implementing the ECD, namely Legislative Decree no 70 of 9 April 2003. Arts 14, 15, 16, and 17 provide for the regulatory framework defining ISP liability, distinguishing between mere conduit, caching, and hosting. Such cases of liability exemption must be considered exceptions vis-à-vis the general system of tort liability; consequently, the cases included in Legislative Decree 70/2003 must be considered predetermined by law and subject to strict interpretation. The exemptions of liability are all based on the premise that the provider does not interfere with the content transmitted or hosted; in other words, the exemptions assume total neutrality vis-à-vis content uploaded onto the internet by third parties. Then, art 17 provides for the absence of a general monitoring obligation, excluding a general obligation to supervise the content an ISP

21 DSA, art 33(1).
22 Poletti (n 16).

transmits or stores and excluding a general obligation to actively search for facts or circumstances indicating the presence of unlawful content.

The ISP is obliged (a) to inform without delay the judicial authority or the administrative authority having supervisory functions of allegedly unlawful activities or information concerning a recipient of its services; (b) to communicate without delay, upon request of the competent authorities, information in its possession that allows the identification of the recipient of its services with which it has data storage agreements in order to identify and prevent unlawful activities.

Italian courts have adapted the interpretation of this legislative framework based on the rapid evolution of the activities of online platforms, as described in the second phase above. Several decisions have discussed the distinction between active and passive hosting providers. The first case relating to this distinction was the decision of the Tribunal of Milan in 2011, where the concept of a dynamic hosting provider was sketched out: the provider carries out activities that no longer allow it to be qualified as a mere intermediary. Although the court of appeal overturned the decision,[23] other tribunals attempted to define what would constitute an active hosting provider to solve similar cases.[24] Yet in some cases, the courts' evaluations were conflicting as, for instance, when the same ISP, Tripadvisor, was categorized as a passive hosting provider in one decision and as an active one in another.[25]

The criteria identified by the case law were then clarified in Supreme Court decision no 7708/2019, where the Court listed a set of 'interference indicators' that can shift the position of the hosting provider from a role that is merely technical, automated, and passive to an active role.[26] The interfer-

[23] See Court of Appeal Milan, 7 January 2015, no 29, with a comment by Michele Iaselli, 'Caso Yahoo! Video: la Corte di Appello di Milano non vede responsabilità nell'operato dell'Internet Provider' [2016] Riv. Dir. Ind. 166ff.

[24] Tribunal Rome 27 April 2016, no 8437, with a comment by Emilio Tosi, 'Contrasti giurisprudenziali in materia di responsabilità civile degli hosting provider – passivi e attivi – tra tipizzazione normativa e interpretazione evolutiva applicata alle nuove figure soggettive dei motori di ricerca, social network e aggregatori di contenuti' [2017] Riv. Dir. Ind. 3ff; Court of Appeal Rome 29 April 2017, no 2833 [2018] AIDA 627ff; Tribunal Turin 24 January 2018, no 342 [2018] AIDA 796ff; Tribunal Florence 26 February 2018, [2018] AIDA 825ff; Tribunal Milan, 12 April 2018 [2019] Giur. annotata dir. ind. (1) 296ff; Tribunal Rome 10 January 2019, no 693 [2019] AIDA 766ff.

[25] See the different evaluations of the Tribunal of Venice 24 February 2015 and the Tribunal Grosseto 2016, no 46, with a comment by Lavinia Vizzoni, 'Recensioni non genuine su Tripadvisor: quali responsabilità?' [2018] Responsabilita' Civile e Previdenza 706.

[26] Court of Cassation 19 March 2019, no 7709, sect. I, with a comment by Emilio Tosi, 'La disciplina applicabile all'hosting provider per la pubblicazione di contenuti digitali protetti dal diritto d'autore, tra speciale irresponsabilità dell'ISP passivo e comune responsabilità dell'ISP attivo, alla luce di Cassazione 7708/2019 e 7709/2019' [2019] Riv. Dir. Ind. 226. See also Eleonora Rosati, *Italian Supreme Court clarifies availability of safe*

ence indicators are the following activities: filters, selection, indexing, organizing, cataloguing, aggregation, evaluation, usage, modification, extraction, and promotion. The list is not exhaustive, and it is up to the court to verify if and which activities are carried out in the specific case. For instance, the activity of promotion can be found when there is a connection between content uploaded by users and advertising messages (with revenue to be earned by the service provider). In contrast, aggregation and evaluation can be found in the case of a recommendation system that is automatically provided based on the user's previous activity. To reach this decision, the Supreme Court reviewed the case law of the CJEU, referring to the cases of *Coöperatieve Vereniging SNB-REACT U.A. v Deepak Mehta*[27] and *Stichting Brein v Ziggo BV and XS4All Internet BV*,[28] where the CJEU acknowledged the possibility that the provider could be held liable for copyright infringement. Additionally, the Supreme Court made reference to the Communication on illegal online content, pointing to the part affirming that the safe harbor applies only to hosting providers that do not play an 'active role'. The Supreme Court evaluated the current European framework, which still lacks an effective conceptual system based on defined criteria, such as the ones listed above.

The criteria were applied to the role played by the Yahoo! platform, resulting in a classification as a passive or neutral intermediary since the platform was only providing a hosting service for content (in particular videos) uploaded by users without carrying out any processing or manipulation of data, despite the use of advanced technologies. Having framed the figure of Yahoo! as a passive hosting provider, the Court went further by stating that there is no exemption from liability if there was knowledge of the unlawful activity without an immediate reaction to take down the content. Therefore, it is essential to identify the moment and the means through which the provider 'becomes aware'. The Court resolved the different approaches adopted by lower courts, affirming that a simple communication regarding the unlawful content provided by the rightsholder is sufficient: it is not necessary for the notice to include the indication of the relevant URLs; a simple indication of the title of the work should allow the provider to identify the content.[29] Moreover, the Court added that the notice received by the provider may also

---

harbours, content of notice-and-takedown requests, and stay-down obligations, available at <http://ipkitten.blogspot.com/2019/03/italian-supreme-court-clarifies.html>.

[27] CJEU 7 August 2018, C-521/17, *Coöperatieve Vereniging SNB-REACT U.A. v Deepak Mehta*, ECLI:EU:C:2018:639.

[28] CJEU 14 June 2017, C-610/15, *Stichting Brein v Ziggo BV and XS4All Internet BV*, ECLI:EU:C:2017:45.

[29] Note that the Supreme Court clarifies that a simple indication is sufficient in those cases where the title of work consists of 'words combined in an original way, so that they can be distinguished from common language'. The additional information, such as a URL, is crucial only when it is 'indispensable' for identifying the content online.

impose an obligation to prevent the re-uploading of the same infringing content. This does not impose on the hosting provider a general monitoring obligation – which would be contrary to art 17 Legislative Decree 70/2003 – and is in line with the case law of the CJEU.[30]

Following this Supreme Court decision, the lower courts have adopted the interference indicators as elements of their evaluation, adding some interesting clarifications. In particular, the Tribunal of Rome affirmed that the status of being an active or passive hosting provider is not a general classification of the overall activity of the ISP, as the latter can perform active and passive functions. Therefore, it is up to the court to ascertain the provider's behavior with regards to the data transmitted or uploaded in concrete terms.[31] In another decision, the Rome tribunal addressed the 'awareness' element needed to trigger the platform's reaction. The court affirmed that the hosting provider will generally be classified as active and will be presumed to have knowledge of the illegal content it hosts, even when it has not received notice from the injured party. Consequently, it is up to the active hosting provider to prove that it does not have actual knowledge of the infringing content.[32] Finally, in a more recent decision, the Supreme Court held that an active hosting provider cannot benefit from the exemption of liability provided by art 16 Legislative Decree 70/2003 and confirmed that the ISP is liable when the following conditions are jointly met:

(a) it has legal knowledge of the unlawful content, through notice by either the rightsholder or a third party;
(b) the unlawfulness of the content is reasonably ascertainable (resulting in gross negligence);
(c) it had the opportunity to take helpful action, as it was made sufficiently and specifically aware of the unlawful content to be removed.[33]

2. *Hosting platforms and contract law rules*

Although less numerous than the previous strand of jurisprudence, a few civil law cases have addressed the application of a platform's terms and conditions through the lens of contract law. The cases focus primarily on the interplay between contractual autonomy and the limitations on a user's freedom of expression on social networks.

---

30 The Supreme Court refers in its decision to the already mentioned *L'Oréal* case (n 8) as well as to the most recent CJEU ruling of 27 March 2014, C-314/12, *UPC Telekabel Wien GmbH v Constantin Film Verleih GmbH and Wega Filmproduktionsgesellschaft mbH*, ECLI:EU:C:2014:192.

31 Tribunal Rome 12 July 2019, no 14757 [2020] AIDA 791ff.

32 Tribunal Rome 2 October 2019, no 18727 [2020] AIDA 795ff.

33 Court of Cassation 13 December 2021, no 39763, sect I [2022] AIDA 792ff.

Apart from one exception,[34] the approaches adopted by the lower courts have been similar: the social networking platform and the users are parties to a contractual agreement that entails reciprocal obligations. In particular, the user should comply with the standards adopted by the platform; a violation of these standards is a breach of contract that results in the suspension or termination of the account. These cases add, however, an interesting dimension as the platform's standards may interfere with the ability of users to exercise their freedom of speech, with the consequence that the platform assumes the role of censor in respect of online political discourse.

The decision of the Tribunal of Rome clarifies this tension.[35] The case focused on a claim against the suspension of the profile of an extreme right-wing political association (Forza Nuova) from Facebook. The suspension was justified because the political association promoted content and disseminated information that incited hatred through the social platform. Such conduct was deemed to be contrary to community standards by the social network. Then, the political association brought a claim against the platform's decision. The court's decision affirmed the contractual nature of the relationship between the social platform and its users, allowing the platform to react, consistent with the contractual clauses agreed by the users, if a violation occurs. According to the court, a different approach would be contrary to the principle of contractual autonomy. That being said, the courts addressed the content disseminated through the social platform, affirming that it constituted incitement to hatred and that the provider had a legal duty to terminate the contract. The court supported its argument with reference to ECtHR jurisprudence and through the interpretation of hate speech as an abuse of right, thus a violation of art 17 ECHR; the content disseminated by the political association cannot be protected as freedom of expression as the latter could otherwise be used for purposes contrary to the letter and the spirit of the ECHR.

This line of reasoning was then followed by other courts,[36] with the caveat that although the platform is not deemed part of the public sphere, the relationship between the platform and the users still needs to be balanced.

---

[34] Tribunal Rome 12 December 2019 [2020] Diritto dell'Informazione e dell'Informatica (1) 104ff.

[35] Tribunal Rome (sect Human rights and immigration) 24 February 2020, [2020] Diritto dell'Informazione e dell'Informatica (3) 552ff.

[36] Tribunal Siena 19 January 2020, no 2968, [2020] Riv. Dir. Internet, available at <https://dirittodiinternet.it/gira-la-ruota-casapound-siena-prevale-profilo-privatistico-ed-profilo-rimane-disattivato-tribunale-siena-19-gennaio-2020/>, accessed 10 September 2024, in which the court was called upon to decide an appeal brought by a CasaPound activist who complained about the deletion of his Facebook profile due to the dissemination of messages deemed to have dangerous and defamatory content; Tribunal Trieste 27 November 2020, no 2032 [2021] Diritto di Internet (1) 93ff; Tribunal Varese 2 August 2022, no 1181 [2022] Diritto e Giustizia, available at <https://www.dirittoegiustizia.it/#/docu

3. Hosting platforms and unfair commercial practices

Another interesting strand of cases that has emerged in respect of the role of online platforms in digital markets relates to the application of the Unfair Commercial Practices Directive (UCPD).[37] Although civil courts should arguably be the fora in which consumers bring claims against the commercial conduct of online platforms, here the leading players are the AGCM and, consequently, the administrative courts that judicially review the regulatory authority's decisions.

The Italian legislation implementing the UCPD followed the same objective of the Directive prohibiting commercial conduct that could affect consumers' freedom of choice by direct or indirect manipulation.[38] In particular, provisions identifying types of misleading and aggressive commercial practices were included in arts 21–23 and 24–26 of the Consumer Code, respectively.[39] Accordingly, the enforcement regime involves civil courts, in the case of individual claims, and the national market authority, the AGCM.[40] In cases involving the latter entity, pursuant to art 27 Consumer Code, the AGCM has the power to stop the unfair conduct and to eliminate its effects, as well as the power to sanction the traders engaging in prohibited practices even when these practices do not have an immediate impact on contractual relationships.[41]

---

mentDetail/10040815>, accessed 10 September 2024; Tribunal Milan 19 July 2021, [2021] Diritto dell'Informazione e dell'Informatica (3) 490. See Giulio Enea Vigevani, 'Dal 'caso Casapound' del 2019 alla 'sentenza Casapound' del 2022: piattaforme digitali, libertà d'espressione e odio on line nella giurisprudenza italiana' [2023] Medialaws 152.

[37] Directive 2005/29/EC of the European Parliament and of the Council of 11 May 2005 concerning unfair business-to-consumer commercial practices in the internal market and amending Council Directive 84/450/EEC, Directives 97/7/EC, 98/27/EC and 2002/65/EC of the European Parliament and of the Council and Regulation (EC) 2006/2004 of the European Parliament and of the Council ('Unfair Commercial Practices Directive') [2005] OJ L149/22 (UPCD)

[38] Note that this objective was approached as market regulation: the prohibition of unfair commercial practices protects both consumers and also competitors, as well as the market in general. See Sara Cacucci, *Pratiche commerciali scorrette e disciplina dell'attività negoziale* (Cacucci 2012); Anna Beckers, 'The regulation of market communication and market behaviour: Corporate social responsibility and the Directives on Unfair Commercial Practices and Unfair Contract Terms' (2017) 54(2) CML Rev 475; Stephen Weaterhill and Ulf Bernitz, *The Regulation of Unfair Commercial Practices under EC Directive 2005/29 – New rules and new techniques* (Hart 2007).

[39] Legislative Decree 2 August 2007, no 146 implemented the UCPD, introducing new articles in the existing Consumer Code, adopted by Legislative Decree 6 September 2005, no 206.

[40] See the policy choices adopted by the other EU Member States in the Commission's 'First Report on the application of Directive 2005/29/EC ('Unfair Commercial Practices Directive')', COM/2013/139 final.

It is important to note that an ISP is classified as a trader under art 18(1)(b) Consumer Code,[42] which defines the latter as 'any natural or legal person who […] is acting for purposes relating to his trade, business, craft or profession and anyone acting in the name of or on behalf of a trader'. Accordingly, the ISP must comply with the standards of professional diligence identified in the same legislation (pursuant to art 20).[43] As a result, if the ISP does not adhere to these standards,[44] and the conduct is capable of distorting the consumer's economic behavior, then the online platform can be held liable for unfair commercial practices.

When looking at the cases decided by the AGCM and eventually by administrative courts, two trends emerge and show how the interpretation of the UCPD provisions may impact the conduct of online platforms.

a) Platform adopting unfair commercial practices.

In some cases, the analysis of the ACGM focused on the conduct of the digital platform regarding the services provided by the latter to the consumers; if such conduct was deemed unfair, the AGCM could sanction the digital platform.

The first example involves a Lithuanian ISP providing a platform used by consumers as a forum for C2C exchanges. The platform was subject to two different proceedings before the AGCM that addressed two different commercial practices, deemed unfair in both cases.[45]

In the first proceeding, the AGCM analyzed, after receiving several notices from consumers, the platform's activity, particularly the promotional claim regarding its being free of cost for users. The results of the investigations led the regulatory authority to affirm that consumers were misled by the commercial claim: the service provided by the platform was free of charge only for those who sold their goods on it, while the consumers who wished to buy goods were subject to an additional fee. Consumers were made aware of this cost only at the end of the online purchase procedure, as the commission fee

[41] Giovanni De Cristofaro, *Pratiche commerciali scorrette e codice del consumo*, (Giappichelli 2008); Giovanni De Cristofaro, 'Le pratiche commerciali scorrette nei rapporti tra professionisti e consumatori: il d.lgs. 146 del 2 agosto 2007, attuativo della direttiva 2005/29/CE' [2007] Studium iuris 1188; Massimo Libertini, 'Le prime pronunce dei giudici amministrativi in materia di pratiche commerciali scorrette' [2009] Giur. comm. 886ss.

[42] Note that the provision included in the Consumer Code follows exactly the definition included in UCPD, art 2(b).

[43] The professional standard of diligence is defined in Consumer Code, art 18(1)(h) as the 'average degree of specific skill and care that consumers reasonably expect from a professional towards them with respect to the general principles of fairness and good faith in the professional's field of activity'.

[44] Obviously, the conduct can also be qualified as a misleading or an aggressive practice that may fall into the black or grey list defined by the UCPD.

[45] AGCM 20 July 2021, no 29788; and AGCM 25 October 2022, no 30355.

was then added. Thus, the commercial practice was qualified as misleading, considering that the consumer did not receive 'from the first contact – all the information useful for a commercial decision'. The AGCM also stressed that the availability of such information on another webpage of the online platform was not sufficient to make the consumer aware of the cost. As a result of the AGCM's decision, the promotional claim of the platform has been modified, and it currently does not include any reference to the gratuitousness of the service for users.

The second proceeding initiated ex officio by the AGCM addressed another commercial practice, namely a 'buyer protection fee'. The platform added this cost as a final cost for the purchaser, ranging between 3% and 8% of the price of goods purchased. In this case, the AGCM also deemed the commercial practice misleading as the platform did not provide any information to the buyer regarding the criteria upon which such additional fee was calculated.[46]

Another case decided recently by the AGCM sanctioned a well-known social networking platform for an unfair commercial practice.[47] This is the first ruling that reached the Consiglio di Stato (Supreme Administrative Court), and it allowed the Court to identify the connection between the service, advertised as 'free' by the social networking platform, and the collection of users' personal data. The fact that the platform could access and exploit personal data was deemed as a counter-performance in the contractual agreement between the platform and the registered user.[48] The AGCM found the conduct to be a misleading practice, as the platform did not inform the consumer sufficiently and thoroughly about the personal data that was processed to personalize the service and for personalized advertising: the acceptance of terms and conditions at the moment of registration did not allow the user to become sufficiently informed about the collection and processing of personal data for

---

[46] Elisa Simionato, 'Vinted: sanzione dell'AGCM da 1,5 milioni per pratiche commerciali scorrette', *Ius in Itinere* (2 December 2022), <https://www.iusinitinere.it/vinted-sanzione-dellagcm-da-15-milioni-per-pratiche-commerciali-scorrette-43612> accessed 3 February 2023.

[47] AGCM 29 November 2018, no 27432. Note that the social networking platform failed to comply with the order requiring it to eliminate the unfair practice; after a second investigation, the decision was appealed before the Tribunale Amministrativo Regionale Roma-Lazio, 10 January 2020, no 261 and was heard later by the Consiglio di Stato (Supreme Administrative Court) 29 March 2021, no 2631.

[48] Claudia Irti, *Consenso 'negoziato' e circolazione dei dati personali* (Giappichelli 2021) 173; Giuseppe Cassano, 'Si può fare commercio di dati personali?' [2021] Diritto dell'Internet; Simone Franca, 'L'intreccio fra disciplina delle pratiche commerciali scorrette e normativa in tema di protezione dei dati personali: il caso Facebook approda al Consiglio di Stato' [2021] Rivista della regolazione dei mercati 365; Antonella Di Cerbo, 'Il corrispettivo dei servizi digitali: i dati personali' (2021) 2 EJPLT, available at <www.ejplt.tatodpr.eu> accessed 10 September 2024; Alberto De Franceschi, 'Italian Consumer Law after the Transposition of Directives (EU) 2019/770 and 2019/771' [2022] EuCML 72.

unspecified purposes. According to the data protection legislation, such data processing can be lawful only in the event of informed consent for specifically identified purposes.[49] Interestingly, the reasoning of the initial AGCM decision, which later landed before the Supreme Administrative Court, considered the economic value of personal data and recognized that the data was a proper subject of unfair commercial practices legislation since it was the object of the transaction that involved the platform and the user.[50]

b) Unfair commercial practices carried out on the digital platform

Another strand of cases the AGCM has decided upon involves misleading or aggressive conduct performed by third parties, ie traders selling goods or services on the platform.

Several cases involved the selling of COVID-19 test kits and other parasanitary products (such as filter masks) on intermediary platforms. In most cases, the AGCM affirmed that the commercial claims appeared likely to mislead the recipients into believing it possible to avoid COVID-19 infection by using the masks and self-diagnosing the virus through use of (unauthorized) home-test kits. Such conduct was, therefore, contrary to professional diligence and liable to distort to an appreciable extent the economic conduct of the average consumer as regards the product, inducing him to make commercial decisions that he would not otherwise have made.[51] The authority highlighted that the traders were also able to significantly increase the price of certain products, exploiting the vulnerability of consumers during the health crisis.

It essential to observe that the AGCM did not attribute the unfair commercial conduct to the platform itself. However, it affirmed that the digital platform should still be obliged to meet the standard of professional diligence, pursuant to Consumer Code, art 20, and thus monitor and eventually prevent unfair practices. In one case, the authority sanctioned the digital platform for such a lack of control over third-party conduct.

This approach conflicts with the exemption of liability applicable under art 16 Legislative Decree 70/2003, described above. Suppose the online platform is classified as a hosting provider that does not interfere with the user's activities (ie it is a passive hosting provider). In that case, it has no general obligation to monitor the content transmitted or stored, nor does it have a general obligation to actively seek facts or circumstances indicating the pres-

[49] See, in particular, Supreme Administrative Court 29 March 2021, No. 2631, para 23.

[50] See, more generally, Sebastian Lohsse, Reiner Schulze and Dirk Staudenmayer (eds), *Data as Counter-Performance – Contract Law 2.0?* (Hart/Nomos 2020); Alberto De Franceschi, *La circolazione dei dati personali tra privacy e contratto* (ESI 2021).

[51] AGCM February 2020, PS11705; AGCM March 2020, PS11716–PS11717; AGCM 17 March 2020, no 28/173; AGCM 27 March 2020, no 28207; AGCM April 2020, PS11734; AGCM April 2020, PS11732; AGCM April 2020, PS11722.

ence of illegal activities. However, the decision of the Supreme Administrative Court, no 3851/2021, addressing the appeal against a decision of the AGCM, resolved this conundrum, affirming the compatibility of the unfair commercial practice and the exemption of liability for hosting providers.[52] The Supreme Administrative Court declared that the position of a trader, according to the definition provided by the legislation on unfair commercial practices, and the position of a hosting provider, according to the definition provided by the legislation on electronic commerce, are not in conflict. The two items of legislation must be interpreted such that application of the professional standards requirements does not impose additional obligations on the hosting provider. According to the Court, there should be a case-by-case analysis of the involvement of the digital platform in the commercial practice, and only where the hosting provider is deemed to be involved in such commercial practice would it be permissible to hold the platform liable for its failure to control the misconduct of the third party.

The interpretation of the Council of State shows the shift from a regime of general exemption of liability, provided by the ECD, in the direction of one increasing the responsibility of the platforms vis-à-vis the need to protect consumers and, in more general terms, weaker parties.[53]

The shift acknowledged in the Italian jurisprudence is also supported by recent European legislative developments, particularly the Digital Services Act.[54] Although keeping the same structure and liability regime for digital platforms as provided in the previous ECD, DSA, art 6(3) includes a specific exception to the scope of application of the liability regime for hosting providers, affirming that it does not apply

> 'with respect to the liability under consumer protection law of online platforms that allow consumers to conclude distance contracts with traders, where such an online platform presents the specific item of information or otherwise enables the specific transaction at issue in a way that would lead an average consumer to believe that the information, or the product or service that is the object of the transaction, is provided either by the online platform itself or by a recipient of the service who is acting under its authority or control.'

This provision, though convoluted, seems to imply that whenever the consumer believes (or is led to believe) that the platform or its auxiliaries provide the goods or services, the platform's liability is not excluded. It will be up to the platform to demonstrate that it has no 'authority or control' over the other traders.

---

[52] Council of State 18 May 2021, no 3851.

[53] Laura Guffanti Pesenti, 'Note in tema di piattaforme digitali e pratiche commerciali scorrette' (2021) 6 JUS-online 17.

[54] Note that academic literature had already articulated the need to define 'some sort of 'secondary liability' of the platform provider'. See Christoph Busch et al., 'The Rise of the Platform Economy: A New Challenge for EU Consumer Law?' (2016) 5(1) EuCML 3.

Regulating the Digital Revolution

France's Blueprint for Platform Governance

Sara Migliorini and Constance Bonzé

I. Introduction

Digital platforms have become essential to our daily lives and to the global economy. Social media platforms have enhanced global communication and interactions, allowed the instant dissemination of news and information, and have offered various opportunities for business promotion, educational growth, creative expression, community building, and political and social activism. The development of digital labor platforms has opened up new areas of the economy, meeting needs and creating jobs. As recognized by France's High Administrative Court (*Conseil d'Etat*),[1] digital platforms can effectively combat territorial and social divide by delivering goods and services more efficiently, faster, and in a more personalized way. Platform economies have also emerged in response to the economic crisis by allowing an 'on-demand' labor market to flourish, based on the optimization of assets that were not fully exploited until then. Some self-employed workers have found within platforms a renewed economic, social, and cultural model which

[1] Conseil d'Etat, 'Puissance publique et plateformes numériques: accompagner l'ubérisation?', Annual Study, 2017, at 21.

provides a way for them to increase their income with more independence. French courts have also recognized social media platforms as an essential tool for participation and as a part of citizens' democratic life.[2]

Yet the practices of platforms are raising specific new regulatory questions across many sectors. While France has chosen to support the development of the platform economy, it has also enacted binding rules to ensure transparency, fairness, and content moderation. These developments are particularly relevant in light of the coming into force of the Digital Services Act (DSA).[3] Additionally, social media platforms have been at the center of two different debates, which for their part have led to legislative and jurisprudential developments: the presence of unfair terms in the social media agreements between providers and users, and the framework for freedom of expression on social networks. In parallel, the conditions of platform workers have also raised concerns. Finally, as elsewhere, also in France platforms have cut into worker's rights and rely mainly on the 'gig economy' model, with their labor force being comprised almost entirely of self-employed individuals. Although this model responds to some workers' need for flexibility and autonomy, a growing number of organizations and public authorities have raised concerns regarding the precarious employment situation of platform workers, the existence of inequalities, and the lack of opportunities to grow and develop under the platform model,[4] thus triggering reactions from lawmakers and courts.

This chapter explores the extent to which the French legal order has granted protection, or even enforceability, to the rules of platforms, while also giving account of instances in which the executive branch, the legislature, or the courts have overruled them. In so doing, we will discuss the limits of platforms' autonomy under French law and the grounds used to limit their power; we will also reflect upon the policy options against the background of the *acquis* and emerging EU law tailoring platforms.

The sections of this chapter first examine the approach of French legislators and French courts towards unfair terms in contracts concluded between the providers of social networking services and their users (II). The second section discusses obligations of fairness and transparency and the regulation

---

[2] See decision no 2009-580 DC of 10 June 2009, *«Hadopi I»*.

[3] Regulation (EU) 2022/2065 of the European Parliament and of the Council of 19 October 2022 on a Single Market For Digital Services and amending Directive 2000/31/EC (Digital Services Act) [2022] OJ L277/1 (DSA).

[4] See, for instance, reports from the French Council for Economic Analysis (CAE) and from the French Directorate for Research, Studies and Statistics (DARES): Nicolas Colin, Augustin Landier, Pierre Mohnen and Anne Perrot, 'Économie numérique', Note du CAE n° 26, octobre 2015; Dorothée Ast, 'En trente ans, forte progression de l'emploi dans les métiers qualifiés et dans certains métiers peu qualifiés de services', Dares Analyses n° 028 2015.

of hate speech (III). Finally, workers' rights and social protection are analyzed in the context of online platforms (IV).

II. Unfair Contract Terms and Data Protection

Along with the increasing use of social media in France, the French Commission on Unfair Terms (*la Commission des clauses abusives*, attached to the Ministry for Consumer Affairs) raised the alarm regarding the presence of unfair terms within the contracts concluded between providers of social networking service and users.[5] Consumer associations brought collective redress actions that have given French courts the possibility to strike down terms included in social media terms of services where such terms are unlawful in light of the French Consumer Code and the French Data Protection Act.[6]

1. *Unfair Contract Terms in French Consumer Law*

In line with the Unfair Contract Terms Directive (UCTD),[7] in a contract concluded between professionals and consumers, terms are unfair under French law if they have the object or effect of creating, to the detriment of the consumer, a significant imbalance between the rights and obligations of the parties to the contract.[8] The French Commission on Unfair Terms published a recommendation on contracts for the provision of social network services in 2014[9] and subsequently, in 2023, a recommendation on online marketplaces for the sale of goods.[10] The Commission is an independent body made up of

[5] Recommandation n° 2014-02 relative aux contrats proposés par les fournisseurs de services de réseaux sociaux.

[6] Loi n° 78-17 du 6 janvier 1978 relative à l'informatique, aux fichiers et aux libertés ('La loi Informatique et Libertés'). The law was updated on 1 June 2019, to align with the General Data Protection Regulation (GDPR).

[7] Council Directive 93/13/EEC of 5 April 1993 on unfair terms in consumer contracts [1993] OJ L95/29 (UCTD), art 3.

[8] French Consumer Code, art L212-1.

[9] Recommandation n° 2014-02 relative aux contrats proposés par les fournisseurs de services de réseaux sociaux, available in French at <https://www.clauses-abusives.fr/recommandation/contrats-de-fourniture-de-services-de-reseaux-sociaux-nouveau/>.

[10] Recommandation n° 23-01 de la Commission des clauses abusives sur les places de marché en ligne de vente de biens, available in French at <https://www.clauses-abusives.fr/recommandation/places-de-marche-en-ligne-de-vente-de-biens/>. Since the transposition of Directive (EU) 2019/2161 of the European Parliament and of the Council of 27 November 2019 amending Council Directive 93/13/EEC and Directives 98/6/EC, 2005/29/EC and 2011/83/EU of the European Parliament and of the Council as regards the better enforcement and modernisation of Union consumer protection rules [2019] OJ L328/7 (Omnibus Directive), online marketplace platforms are defined under the introductory article, para 14, of the French Consumer Code, where it states that an online marketplace is 'a ser-

judges, experts in contract law, and representatives of consumer and professionals. The opinions and recommendations of the Commission are not binding. However, they are often followed by professionals and can serve as a reference for judges when assessing whether a clause inserted in a contract between a professional and a consumer is unfair.

The 2014 recommendation highlighted that agreements between social media and users are to be qualified as contracts and, moreover, as consumer contracts presenting an asymmetry of information between the parties.[11] The Commission carried out an examination of model agreements proposed by professional social networking service providers to their consumer or non-professional co-contractors and identified 46 types of unfair terms under art L212-1 of the French Consumer Code. In the 2023 recommendation, the analysis of 64 online marketplace contracts for the sale of goods offered to consumers throughout France revealed 69 unfair terms in the model contracts usually offered by professionals to consumers.[12] Terms identified as unfair were grouped under different categories, including contract readability and wording, formation of the contract, parties' obligations, protection of personal data, contract performance, and dispute resolution.

Identified issues relating to contract readability and wording included how the terms were drafted or presented to the consumer, their language, and cross-references.[13] Issues related to formation concerned consent, such as the use of implicit acceptance clauses.[14] When discussing the obligations of parties, the Commission on Unfair Terms reasoned that most agreements between social media providers and their users include a term stating that the services offered are free of charge. Consequently, the user is 'led to believe that the social media service is devoid of any consideration on their part'. However, the Commission pointed out that, while the user does not provide any monetary consideration, 'the data, information and content they provide, whether consciously or not, when using the social network, constitute a consideration, which can be analyzed as a kind of remuneration or price', which the social media provider can and does monetize. In the Commission's view, the drafting ambiguity of such a clause puts consumers at a disadvantage, insofar as the clause does not clearly explain the pricing of the service; therefore, it should be considered abusive under art L132-1(7) of the Consumer Code.

Other terms of standard social media agreements were found to raise concerns about the categorization of personal data, the processing of personal

vice using software, including a website, part of a website or an application, operated by a professional or on his behalf, which enables consumers to conclude distance contracts with other professionals or consumers'.

[11] Recommandation n°2014-02, recital 5.

[12] Recommandation n°23-01, 95–101.

[13] Recommandation n°2014-02, 1–7.

[14] Recommandation n°2014-02, 8–13.

data, and the retention of content after account deletion.[15] Contract performance terms that were qualified as unfair included clauses relating to unilateral modifications to the site or to the general terms and conditions of use.[16] Finally, dispute resolution clauses that were qualified as unfair included clauses regarding evidence and choice-of-law clauses.[17] Choice-of-law clauses were identified by the Commission as leading consumers to believe that they did not benefit from the mandatory provisions of French law in cases where they were more protective than those of the foreign law referred to in the choice-of-law clause.[18]

2. *French Courts Strike Down Contractual Clauses Inserted by Social Media Providers*

French courts have applied the domestic transposition of the Unfair Contract Terms Directive extensively so as to strike down clauses found in the general terms of services of platforms such as Facebook and Twitter, concurring with the views of the Commission on Unfair Terms reported above. In 2018 and 2019, the Paris Court of First Instance (Tribunal de Grande Instance de Paris, TGI) issued rulings in three important cases regarding allegedly unfair contract terms included in Twitter, Google, and Facebook contracts with French-based users. In these cases, the TGI had to adjudicate the legality of several terms and conditions of use, including clauses on the user's presumption of liability and the service provider's exoneration from responsibility, on confidentiality and data collection, and on choice-of-court and choice-of-law clauses. It is interesting to note that the three cases were 'sister' cases brought by the same consumer association and largely overlapped in terms of the claims raised.

a) *Application of French consumer law despite the gratuitous nature of the social media service*

In *UFC Que Choisir v Twitter*,[19] the claimant (a consumer association) contended that some of the clauses included in Twitter's general terms of sale were unfair under French consumer law (including provisions transposing EU-relevant texts), namely the choice-of-court agreement in favor of San Francisco County courts, the choice-of-law agreement in favor of California law, and the clause referencing the rules on the legal capacity of natural persons of the United States. The TGI looked at whether French consumer law

[15] Recommandation n°2014-02, 14–31; Recommandation n°23-01, 30–33.

[16] Recommandation n°2014-02, 32–40; Recommandation n°23-01, 53 and 80.

[17] Recommandation n°2014-02, 41–46; Recommandation n°23-01, 23–25.

[18] Recommandation n°2014-02, 46.

[19] TGI de Paris 7 August 2018, RG 14/07300, *UFC Que Choisir v Twitter*.

was applicable to Twitter's contract. In the TGI's view, although a Twitter account is free of charge, the contract between Twitter and the user is not gratuitous.[20] Consideration for the service is found in the personal data that the user communicates to Twitter, which uses such data for different purposes. Therefore, the TGI found that a contract for the provision of social network services, such as the one that links French users to the Twitter company, is a consumer contract, subject to the provisions of the French Consumer Code, including the rules on unfair terms, which cannot be waived by the parties. As a result, the TGI held that French Twitter users are entitled to the protection afforded to them by French consumer law.[21]

In the case *UFC Que Choisir v Facebook*,[22] the TGI came to the same conclusion because Facebook collects and markets data deposited free of charge by users when they access the platform, and Facebook benefits from its activity and acts for commercial purposes,[23] which thus makes Facebook a 'professional' within the meaning of the introductory article of the French Consumer Code, which defines a professional as any natural or legal person, public or private, acting for purposes within the scope of its commercial, industrial, craft, liberal or agricultural activity, including when acting in the name or on behalf of another professional.[24] The same reasoning was applied in *UFC Que Choisir v Google.*[25]

b) The user's presumption of liability and the service provider's exoneration from responsibility

French courts struck down clauses prescribing a presumption of liability attaching to the user and an exoneration of any responsibility on the part of the service provider, particularly in light of the French Consumer Code and the French Data Protection Act.[26] Art 121 of the French Data Protection Act provides that the data controller is required to take all necessary precautions, with regard for the nature of the data and the risks presented by its processing, to protect the security of the data and, in particular, to prevent it from being distorted, damaged, or accessed by unauthorized third parties. In *UFC Que Choisir v Twitter,* the TGI ruled that art 121 of the French Data Protection Act renders unlawful a clause prescribing that the user, in all cases and

---

[20] *UFC Que Choisir v Twitter* (n 19) II.A.

[21] *UFC Que Choisir v Twitter* (n 19) II.A.

[22] TGI de Paris 9 April 2019, RG 14/07298, *UFC Que Choisir v Facebook.*

[23] *UFC Que Choisir v Facebook* (n 22) I.B.1.b.

[24] French Consumer Code, introductory article.

[25] TGI de Paris 12 February 2019, RG 14/07224, *UFC Que Choisir v Google,* III.

[26] Loi n° 78-17 du 6 janvier 1978 relative à l'informatique, aux fichiers et aux libertés ('La loi Informatique et Libertés'). The law was updated on 1 June 2019, to align with the General Data Protection Regulation (GDPR).

without any reminder of the operator's own obligations, is presumed responsible for the consequences of the use of their account, even when done by an unauthorized third party.[27]

Under art L221-15 of the French Consumer Code, the professional is automatically liable to the consumer for the proper performance of the obligations arising from a distance contract, whether these obligations are performed by the professional who concluded the contract or by other service providers. However, the professional may be exonerated from all or part of their liability by proving that the non-performance or poor performance of the contract is attributable either to the consumer, to the unforeseeable and insurmountable act of a third party to the contract, or to a case of force majeure. In *UFC Que Choisir v Google*, the TGI noted that the liability clause in the contract had the effect of excluding the responsibility of the service provider in all cases of malfunction of the services provided to the consumer and of eliminating the consumer's right to compensation in the event of the professional's breach of any of its obligations. The TGI ruled that the clause was unlawful under art L221-15 of the French Consumer Code.[28] In *UFC Que Choisir v Facebook*, the TGI followed the same reasoning and struck down limitation of liability clauses, relying on both the French Data Protection Act and art L221-15 of the French Consumer Code.[29]

c) *Data collection*

Under the French Data Protection Act, personal data must be processed lawfully, fairly, and transparently with regard to the data subject.[30] It must be collected for specified, explicit, and legitimate purposes and not further processed in a way incompatible with those purposes.[31] Personal data must also be adequate, relevant, and, with regard to the purposes for which it is processed, limited to what is necessary.[32] Additionally, the person from whom personal data is collected must be informed by the data controller of the identity of the data controller (and, where applicable, of its representative), of the purpose of the data processing, and of the recipients or categories of recipients of the data.[33]

In *UFC Que Choisir v Twitter*, the TGI noted that the contract clauses provided that the elements of content 'provided by the user', including personal data, could be seen by other users as well as on services and websites provid-

---

27 *UFC Que Choisir v Twitter* (n 19) III.A.3.a.

28 *UFC Que Choisir v Google* (n 25) VII.2.s.

29 *UFC Que Choisir v Facebook* (n 22) II.A.9.b.

30 French Data Protection Act, art 4.1.

31 French Data Protection Act, art 4.2.

32 French Data Protection Act, art 4.3.

33 French Data Protection Act, art 116.

ed by third parties, but the clauses did not inform the user of the specific data collected, the purpose of the collection of data, or the specific recipients of the data.[34] The TGI consequently ruled that the clauses in question were unlawful in light of the French Data Protection Act.[35] Following similar reasoning and under the same articles of the French Data Protection Act, in *UFC Que Choisir v Google* the TGI ruled that the service provider failed to inform the user precisely of the collection of information stored on the devices used to connect to the social network, of the presumed consent to the collection of personal data – thus preventing the user from withholding such consent – and of the purpose of such processing.[36]

d) Choice-of-court and choice-of-law clauses

In *UFC Que Choisir v Twitter*, the TGI applied the French rules on unfair contract terms in assessing the legality of Twitter's terms of sale, and in particular the choice-of-court and choice-of-law agreements. The TGI held that such clauses have the effect of subjecting Twitter's contract to the jurisdiction and law of a non-EU State, therefore stripping French Twitter users of the protection granted by UCTD.[37] The TGI declared the above-mentioned clauses null and void under art L212-1 of the French Consumer Code and UCTD.[38]

Similarly in *UFC Que Choisir v Facebook*,[39] the court ruled that the choice-of-court agreement in favor of San Francisco courts and the choice-of-law agreement in favor of California law had the effect of subjecting Facebook's general terms to the jurisdiction and law of a non-EU State, therefore stripping French Facebook users of the protection granted by UCTD. The TGI likewise declared the above-mentioned clauses null and void under art L212-1 of the French Consumer Code and UCTD.[40]

Twitter appealed the TGI's decision in *UFC Que Choisir v Twitter*, but the Paris Court of Appeal upheld the TGI's ruling on 14 April 2023.[41]

III. Transparency, Fairness, and the Fight Against Illegal Content

France has chosen to support the development of new forms of economic activity, all the while requiring transparency and fairness from platforms.

---

[34] *UFC Que Choisir v Twitter* (n 19) III.A.3.b.
[35] *UFC Que Choisir v Twitter* (n 19) III.A.3.b.
[36] *UFC Que Choisir v Google* (n 25) VIII.1.f.
[37] *UFC Que Choisir v Twitter* (n 19) III.22.5 and III.22.6.
[38] *UFC Que Choisir v Twitter* (n 19) III.22.5 and III.22.6.
[39] *UFC Que Choisir v Facebook* (n 22).
[40] *UFC Que Choisir v Facebook* (n 22) II.A.18.c and II.A.18.d.
[41] Cour d'appel de Paris14 April 2023, RG 19/09244, *UFC Que Choisir v Twitter*.

This dual-goal process has, however, not been without its setbacks. Finding the right balance between regulating online platforms and protecting fundamental rights, while at the same time fostering economic growth, is still a work in progress in France, as demonstrated by the Constitutional Council's striking down of the French Online Hate Speech Law.[42] The section below reviews that decision as well as how these national developments align with the Digital Services Act (DSA).

1. *Obligations of Transparency and Fairness*

Concerns over the impact of digital platforms led the French legislators to endeavor to implement a regulatory framework in order to strengthen the protection of individuals in the digital society and guarantee digital access for all. In 2016, the Law for a Digital Republic was implemented to promote the circulation of data and knowledge through an opening up of public and general interest data, the creation of a public data service, and free access to public research literature.[43] The same Law also contains provisions regulating obligations of transparency for social media platforms.

Firstly, the Law introduced art L111-7 in the French Consumer Code, according to which an online platform operator is

> 'any natural or legal person offering, on a professional basis, whether or not in return for payment, an online public communication service based on (1) the classification or referencing, by means of computer algorithms, of content, goods or services offered or placed online by third parties; (2) or the bringing together of several parties with a view to the sale of a good, the provision of a service or the exchange or sharing of content, goods or services'.

Secondly, based on the Law for a Digital Republic, decrees were adopted to strengthen the transparency and fairness obligations that digital platforms must meet. These decrees were the result of extensive consultation within the National Consumer Council (*Conseil National de la Consommation*, CNC) and with business representatives from the sectors concerned. Platforms that promote content, goods, or services offered by third parties, such as search engines, or social networks, now have to specify the referencing and ranking criteria they use.[44] This information must be directly and easily accessible from all pages of the site. The following information must be included: (1) the conditions for listing and delisting content and offers of goods and services, in particular the rules applicable to listing and the obligations that must be complied with in order to be delisted; (2) default ranking criteria for

---

[42] Conseil Constitutionnel, décision n° 2020-801 DC du 18 juin 2020.

[43] Loi n° 2016-1321 du 7 octobre 2016 pour une République digitale («loi Lemaire»), Journal officiel de la République française, n° 235, 8 octobre 2016.

[44] Décret n° 2017-1434 du 29 septembre 2017 relatif aux obligations d'information des opérateurs de plateformes numériques.

content and offers of goods and services as well as their main parameters; (3) where applicable, the existence of a link or remuneration between the platform operator and the listed providers, insofar as this link or remuneration has an influence on the listing or ranking of the content, goods, or services offered or placed online.[45] Another decree adopted in connection with application of the Law for a Digital Republic requires sites publishing consumer reviews to specify whether they have been verified and the methodology that was used.[46] Ultimately, the goal is for consumers to have access to clearer, more objective, and more transparent information.

With the upcoming entry into force of the DSA, France appears to be already prepared on the transparency front, and arguably some of the new obligations introduced EU-wide by the DSA already find corresponding provisions in the French legal order. For example, the DSA highlights that a core part of an online platform's business is the manner in which information is prioritized and presented on the platform, for instance via algorithm ranking and prioritizing information.[47] As such, and in alignment with the French decree n° 2017-1434, providers of online platforms must set out in their terms and conditions, in plain and intelligible language, the main parameters used in their recommended systems.[48]

2. *Content Moderation and Hate Speech*

The increasing use of social media led to concerns regarding online hate speech and criminal content. In May 2020, the French parliament adopted the Online Hate Speech Law, designed to combat various forms of online hate speech, terrorist speech, and child pornography.[49] The law was heavily inspired by the German Network Enforcement Act, adopted in June 2017, which subjects social media providers to fines of up to 50 million euros if they fail to remove 'obviously illegal' speech within 24 hours of it being reported.[50] Under the Online Hate Speech Law, online platform operators who 'offered an online public communication service based on bringing together several parties with a view to sharing public content' were required, in the general interest of respect for human dignity, to remove or make inacces-

[45] French Consumer Code, art D111-7.

[46] Décret n° 2017-1435 du 29 septembre 2017 relatif à la fixation d'un seuil de connexions à partir duquel les opérateurs de plateformes en ligne élaborent et diffusent des bonnes pratiques pour renforcer la loyauté, la clarté et la transparence des informations transmises aux consommateurs, Décret n° 2017-1436 du 29 septembre 2017 relatif aux obligations d'information relatives aux avis en ligne de consommateurs.

[47] DSA, recital 70.

[48] Cf DSA, art 27.

[49] Loi visant à lutter contre les contenus haineux sur internet, 18 mai 2020 ('loi Avia').

[50] Gesetz zur Verbesserung der Rechtsdurchsetzung in sozialen Netzwerken (Network Enforcement Act, NetzDG) vom 1. September 2017.

sible, within 24 hours of notification by one or more persons, forms of online hate speech.[51] Failure to comply with the obligation was punishable by a fine of 250,000 euros.[52]

Various political groups and free speech advocates expressed concerns and objections over the content of the law, which was challenged before the French Constitutional Council (*Conseil Constitutionnel*, the court in charge of judicial review under France's Constitution). The Constitutional Council ultimately struck down most of the provisions of the Online Hate Speech Law.[53] The Constitutional Council noted that the obligation to remove content was imposed on the operator as soon as a person had notified it of unlawful content. The obligation was not subject to the prior intervention of a judge nor to any other condition. It was therefore up to the social media platform to examine all content reported by users – however numerous such requests might be – in order to avoid the risk of being penalized.[54] It was also up to the social media platform to examine the content, even in instances in which it may have been of a technical nature, or subject to specific rules, such as those covering traditional media.[55] The Constitutional Council also noted that the 24-hour timeframe was particularly short.[56]

In addition, the Council also struck down the provisions that concerned taking down content related to terrorism and child pornography. A French decree from 2015 had already required internet service providers and social media platforms, within 24 hours of receiving a government order, to take down content that violated either art 421-2-5 of the French Criminal Code (which criminalizes content promoting or justifying terrorist acts) or art 227-23 of the same code (which criminalizes child pornography).[57] The French Online Hate Speech law, however, went further and imposed on social media platforms an obligation to remove such content within one hour.[58] That provision was struck down by the Constitutional Council, which ruled that the one-hour time limit infringed freedom of expression and communication in a way that was not appropriate, necessary, and proportionate to the aim pursued.[59]

This decision was not the end of the discussion surrounding the issue of the prompt removal of web pages containing or disseminating illegal content.

[51] Former art 6-2 of the French Online Hate Speech Law.

[52] Former art 1-12 of the French Online Hate Speech Law.

[53] Conseil Constitutionnel, décision n° 2020-801 DC du 18 juin 2020.

[54] Conseil Constitutionnel, décision n° 2020-801 DC du 18 juin 2020 at 14.

[55] Conseil Constitutionnel, décision n° 2020-801 DC du 18 juin 2020 at 15.

[56] Conseil Constitutionnel, décision n° 2020-801 DC du 18 juin 2020 at 16.

[57] Décret n° 2015-125 du 5 février 2015 relatif au blocage des sites provoquant à des actes de terrorisme ou en faisant l'apologie et des sites diffusant des images et représentations de mineurs à caractère pornographique, JORF n° 0031 du 6 février 2015.

[58] Former art 1 of the French Online Hate Speech Law.

[59] Conseil Constitutionnel, décision n° 2020-801 DC du 18 juin 2020 at 9.

On 5 July 2023, a French bill on 'securing and regulating digital space' was passed unanimously by the Senate and is now being examined by the National Assembly.[60] The bill's tabling was prompted by the recent initiatives at both EU (the DSA) and national level (parliamentary work on the exposure of minors to pornographic content, and the report on digital sovereignty).[61] It also follows recent national efforts to regulate the activities of influencers. Under the bill, failure by hosting service providers to remove pornographic images within 24 hours of receipt of the removal request is punishable by one year's imprisonment and a fine of 250,000 euros.[62] The DSA addresses the removal of illegal content from platforms, in particular child pornography, and requires service providers to 'act expeditiously' to remove or to disable access to the illegal content upon being informed or becoming aware of such content.[63] The DSA does not provide for a time limit but instead refers as an example to the 24-hour time limit laid out in the 2016 Code of conduct on countering illegal hate speech online.[64]

IV. Workers' Rights and Social Protection

With the rapid increase in the number of self-employed individuals performing work in a digital setting in France, the issue of their status and protection became a topic of discussion at the governmental and parliamentary levels. Recent legislative developments have been strengthening and recognizing specific rights for self-employed workers on platforms, while French courts have been reclassifying the legal relationship between self-employed workers and digital platforms.

1. *Digital Platform Workers' Rights Under French Law*

The French Law on the Modernization of the Economy (LME) of 4 August 2008 created the micro-entrepreneur status to enable any individual, whether a student, employee, jobseeker or pensioner, to operate a craft, commercial, or

60 Projet de loi n°1514, adopté par le Sénat visant à sécuriser et réguler l'espace numérique. The legislative process can be followed here: <https://www.senat.fr/dossier-legislatif/pjl22-593.html>.

61 Assemblée Nationale, Rapport d'information n°4299 sur le thème « Bâtir et promouvoir une souveraineté numérique nationale et européenne », 29 juin 2021.

62 Projet de loi n°1514, art 3.15.

63 DSA, art 6.1.

64 DSA, recital 87. The Code of conduct on countering illegal hate speech online was signed on 31 May 2016 by the Commission and Google (YouTube), Facebook, Twitter, Microsoft hosted consumer services (eg, Xbox gaming services or LinkedIn), Instagram, Google+, Dailymotion, Snap, and Jeuxvideo.com.

self-employed business on an individual basis.[65] The combined effect of the LME along with the increasing availability and use of the internet and smartphones, the emergence of specific urban needs, and the growing search for new sources of income led to the rapid development of digital labor platforms. As an example, the number of self-employed workers registered in France in the transport and delivery sectors increased by 80.6% between 2017 and 2018.[66]

The law of 8 August 2016,[67] imposed obligations on platforms to partly contribute to workers' insurance covering risks of accidents at work[68] and to workers' training costs.[69] The 2016 law also recognizes the rights of platform workers to strike and to form a trade union.[70] The law of 24 December 2019[71] recognizes the rights of platform workers to access all data concerning their own activities within the platform.[72] The law of 23 December 2021 allows platforms to offer their workers collective complementary social health protection.[73]

The French legislators have also been focusing on structuring social dialogue between employee representatives and platform representatives in order to rebalance contractual relationships in the platform sector and to reconcile social and economic performance. The ordinance of 21 April 2021 provides for the appointment of organizations representing workers in the car-sharing and vehicle delivery sectors.[74] The ordinance of 6 April 2022 lays down the procedures for representing platform organizations at sectoral level and also the rules for social dialogue.[75]

The obligations of mobility platforms have been strengthened in order to consolidate the guarantees of independence for platform workers. For example, the law of 24 December 2019 requires platforms facilitating services related to mobility, such as Uber, to inform workers of the distance they will

---

[65] La loi n° 2008-776 du 4 août 2008 de modernisation de l'économie (LME).

[66] Catherine Fournier, Michel Forissier and Frédérique Puissat, 'Travailleurs des plateformes: au-delà de la question du statut, quelles protections ?', Rapport d'information de la commission des Affaires sociales du Sénat, n°452, mai 2020.

[67] Loi n° 2016-1088 du 8 août 2016 relative au travail, à la modernisation du dialogue social et à la sécurisation des parcours professionnels.

[68] French Labour Code, art L7342-2.

[69] French Labour Code, art L7342-3.

[70] French Labour Code, art L7342-5 and art L7342-6.

[71] Loi n° 2019-1428 du 24 décembre 2019 d'orientation des mobilités.

[72] French Labour Code, art L7342-7.

[73] Loi n° 2021-1754 du 23 décembre 2021 de financement de la sécurité sociale pour 2022, art 105.

[74] Ordonnance n° 2021-484 du 21 avril 2021 relative aux modalités de représentation des travailleurs indépendants recourant pour leur activité aux plateformes et aux conditions d'exercice de cette représentation.

[75] Ordonnance n° 2022-492 du 6 avril 2022 renforçant l'autonomie des travailleurs indépendants des plateformes de mobilité, portant organisation du dialogue social de secteur et complétant les missions de l'Autorité des relations sociales des plateformes d'emploi.

be expected to cover as service providers and the guaranteed minimum price they will receive.[76] It also establishes the right of workers to choose their working hours and periods of inactivity and to go offline and be inaccessible during their non-working hours; it additionally prevents platforms from terminating the contract if a worker exercises such rights.[77]

2. *The Classification of Self-employed Platform Workers as Employees*

Rules regulating the relationship between platforms and workers – rules created privately and unilaterally by platforms – largely run counter to French labor law, which has led the Cour de Cassation to intervene in several cases. The Cour de Cassation announced a first ruling on the status of digital platform workers in the *Take Eat Easy* case,[78] where the contract binding a bicycle delivery rider to a digital platform was classified as an employment contract. A second decision (the *Uber* case) on a similar issue seemed to indicate a jurisprudential trend in favor of protecting platform economy workers.[79] However a third case (*Le Cab*) served to mitigate the French courts' approach and established that the reclassification of self-employed platform workers as employees would not be systematic.[80]

In the *Take Eat Easy* case, the company, Take Eat Easy, used a web platform and an application to connect partner restaurants, customers ordering meals through the platform, and self-employed bicycle delivery riders. A rider applied to the company and took the necessary steps to register as a self-employed contractor and entered into a contract for the provision of services with the company. The rider then applied to the Labor Court to have his contract reclassified as an employment contract. In its decision, the Cour de Cassation referred to art L8221-6 of the French Labor Code, which establishes a presumption of non-salaried status for persons registered as self-employed contractors.[81] In the same judgment, the Cour de Cassation also applied an established French standard to platform workers in order to assess the nature of their contractual relationship with platforms. Under French law, the existence of an employment relationship depends neither on the will expressed by the parties nor on the name they have given to their agreement, but on the de facto conditions under which the worker's activity is carried out. A contract of employment exists where work is performed under the authority of an employer who has the power to give orders and instructions, to monitor their

[76] French Transport Code, art L1326-2.

[77] French Transport Code, art L1326-4.

[78] Cass. Soc. 28 November 2018, n° 17-20.079.

[79] Cass. Soc. 4 March 2020, n° 19-13.316.

[80] Cass. Soc. 13 April 2022, n° 20-14.870.

[81] Cass. Soc. 28 November 2018, n°17-20.079 at §1.

execution, and to sanction the failings of the employer's subordinate.[82] This assessment is carried out by French courts based on the evidence and on a case-by-case basis. In the immediate case, the Court noted that the platform application was equipped with a geolocation system, enabling the company to track the driver's position in real time and to record the total number of kilometers travelled; the court observed as well that Take Eat Easy had the power to impose penalties on the driver. In light of these elements, the Court ruled that the company exercised a power of direction and control over the performance of the service that was characteristic of a relationship of subordination, and the Court concluded that the contract was indeed an employment contract under art L8221-6 of the French Labor Code.[83]

In the *Uber* case, Uber had permanently deactivated the Uber account of a driver, depriving him of the possibility of receiving new booking requests. The driver brought an action before the labor court (*conseil de prud'hommes*) to challenge the terms of the termination, which he considered akin to unfair dismissal. The driver argued that his relationship with Uber should be reclassified as an employment relationship, and he claimed compensation and back-pay. The labor court held that the contract was commercial in nature, relying on art L8221-6 of the French Labor Code, which establishes a presumption of non-salaried status for persons registered with the *Registre du Commerce et des Sociétés*, as was the case for the driver.[84] The driver appealed this decision. The case went up to the Cour de Cassation, which observed that the driver had to follow Uber's instructions, did not set his own fares, was not free to organize his schedule, was not in a position to build his own clientele, was monitored via a geolocation system, and was subject to sanctions (in particular, the driver was subject to a rating system that could result in the loss of access to the Uber application).[85] In light of these elements, the Court ruled that the body of evidence was sufficient to characterize the relationship as one of employment and to conclude that the status of the driver as a self-employed worker was fictitious.[86] Consequently, the worker was entitled to payment of a sum equal to six months' salary for undeclared work (French Labor Code, arts L8221-5 and L8223-1).

In the *Le Cab* case, the Cour de Cassation analyzed the relationship between drivers and the digital platform 'Le Cab', operated by a company that concludes vehicle hire and membership contracts with these drivers.[87] Initially, the Paris Court of Appeal applied the Cour de Cassation's approach

---

[82] Cass. Soc. 28 November 2018, n°17-20.079, at §3. See also Cass. Soc. 13 November 1996, n° 94-13187, Bull. V n° 386, *Société générale*.

[83] Cass. Soc. 13 November 1996, n° 94-13187, Bull. V n° 386, *Société générale* at §4.

[84] Conseil de Prud'hommes de Paris 28 June 2018, RG n° 17/04674.

[85] Cass. Soc. 4 March 2020, n° 19-13.316, § 10–14.

[86] Cass. Soc. 4 March 2020, n° 19-13.316, at § 15.

[87] Cass. Soc. 13 April 2022, n° 20-14.870.

adopted in the *Take Eat Easy* and the *Uber* cases and analyzed whether, under the evidence at hand, an employment relationship could be identified, overturning the legal presumption of non-employment of individuals registered as self-employed under art L8221-6 of the French Labor Code.[88] The Court of Appeal found that a series of factors supported the identification of a contract of employment, such as drivers' lack of freedom in choosing their vehicle, the possibility for the company to geolocate drivers in real time, so as to be able to allocate journeys, and the company's permanent control over a driver's activity, with the company setting the cost of the journeys, issuing invoices in the name and on behalf of drivers, having the ability to adjust the price of a journey upward or downward depending on the timetable, and having the power to impose penalties as determined by the system allowing passengers to rate drivers. However, on a subsequent appeal on points of law, the Cour de Cassation found that those grounds were insufficient to identify a contract of employment, as there was no evidence that the company sent the driver instructions on how to carry out the work, nor was there any evidence suggesting the company had the power to monitor compliance with these instructions or to impose penalties for non-compliance.[89]

While puzzling, the *Le Cab* decision stands as a reminder that the existence of a legal relationship of employment is based on the evidence presented and is assessed on a case-by-case basis; consequently, the absence of some factors – such as the ones in the case at hand – may be sufficient to confirm the presumption of self-employment. More generally, the body of jurisprudence highlights all the legal uncertainties that still remain surrounding the relationship between self-employed workers and digital platforms.

V. Conclusion

As in other jurisdictions, in France there co-exist two opposites trends regarding the enforcement of platform rules. On the one hand, platforms have been recognized as essential to the exercise of basic freedoms and rights. The French Constitutional Court and the highest administrative court (*Conseil d'Etat*) have recognized the potential of platforms to effectively contribute to the exercise of freedom of speech, including during elections and with respect to public participation by citizens, as well as to reduce territorial inequalities and the social divide. In regard to this first trend, platforms are an indispensable tool for the democratic, social, and economic life of citizens and are granted relative autonomy when it comes to setting the 'rules of the game'.

[88] Cour d'appel de Paris 29 January 2020, n° 18/10059.

[89] Cass. Soc. 13 April 2022, n° 20-14.870, at § 10.

On the other hand, France's executive, legislative, and judicial branches have also heavily intervened in the regulation of platforms, overriding platforms' rules and requiring adherence to certain laws and regulations. The highest court in civil and criminal matters (the Cour de Cassation) has extensively applied the domestic transposition of the Unfair Contract Terms Directive in striking down clauses in the general terms of services of platforms such as Facebook and Twitter. It has also intervened in favor of the protection of vulnerable platform's workers, reclassifying them as employees entitled to French labor rights.

France has chosen to support the development of digital platforms, all the while requiring transparency, fairness, and content moderation. The legislative process to regulate digital platforms has been gradual and complex. Some setbacks have been experienced, as illustrated by the Constitutional Council striking down the Online Hate Speech Law in 2020. In that respect, recent developments at EU level, with the Digital Services Act, have been welcomed in France, and there have been renewed national legislative efforts to combat the online dissemination of illegal content.

Private Law Regulation of Online Platforms in the Netherlands

Eric Tjong Tjin Tai, Paul Verbruggen and Ruşen Öncü

Many online platforms are designed to facilitate transactions between buyers and sellers of goods and providers and recipients of services. To that end, platforms establish and enforce their own rules, policies, and mechanisms. However, how they (can) go about that is regulated by law. In this Chapter, we assess the scope for establishing and enforcing platform rules through the means of private law in the Netherlands. Under Dutch private law, the enforcement by platforms of their rules can simply be accomplished with ordinary means of contract law, combined with the de facto power mechanisms at the disposal of platforms (eg control over payments, management of review and reputational instruments, exclusion from participation/membership, termination of contract). However, these means are subject to review by courts whenever platform participants, via either individual or collective actions, contest the actions of the platform. In this Chapter, we describe and critically assess the current state of Dutch law by (i) providing an overview of the relevant legal framework in the area of private law; and (ii) reviewing the case law concerning the private law regulation of online platform contracts, rules, and activities. Accordingly, we will discuss how online platform regulation is affected by the default or mandatory rules applicable to specific contracts (eg agency, brokerage, and services more generally), general terms and conditions, unfair commercial practices, precontractual information duties, and e-commerce. We will not be concerned with case law in the domains of administrative law, competition law, criminal law, labor law or tax law. The resulting assessment charts the scope for online platforms to set their own rules and policies for transactions regarding goods and services in the Netherlands.

I. Introduction

Online platforms play an increasingly important role in society and commerce. They may directly offer goods and services to both businesses and consumers (eg social media, streaming platforms, search engines). Alternatively, they may act as intermediaries, facilitating transactions between platform participants, again both businesses and consumers (eg online marketplaces, sharing or booking platforms, app stores). Either way, the relationships they entertain with their participants, and the relationships between the platform participants, are regulated by means of standardized private rules. While this body of private regulation forms the private constitution of online platforms, it is subject to external regulation. That (meta-)regulation is based on legal rules, both from the public and private law domain.

In this Chapter, we discuss the relationship between the private, internal rules created by online platforms to regulate the interactions with platform participants and the regulatory controls that private law employs in the Netherlands. We start our analysis by discussing the general mechanisms available in Dutch private law to review and enforce platform private rule-making and enforcement activities (sections II and III). Such mechanisms operate within the framework of general rules of contract law, including good faith (sections IV and V), as well as more specific (regulated) forms of contract, for example brokerage or intermediary agreements (sections VI and VII). The harmonized European Union (EU) rules on data protection, pre-contractual information duties, and on immunities for civil liability also affect the content of the rules online platforms employ to design and deliver their services (sections VIII and IX). As the EU rules governing online platforms are covered elsewhere in this book, we will engage with these rules only as far as their interpretation and application in Dutch law is concerned.

II. Enforcing Internal Organizational Rules in Dutch Law

Business organizations and other cooperative undertakings typically establish rules to arrange their internal structure, tasks, and affairs. Such rules go by various names, depending on the relationship, the sector of business, the form of legal personality, and so forth. In the Netherlands, these are called *statuten* (bylaws), *reglement* (regulation), beleid (*policy*), *richtlijnen* (guidelines), *algemene voorwaarden* (general terms and conditions), and so on. Rules within incorporated bodies are principally the subject of corporate law, which we shall not discuss here. Our focus is on rules that have effect outside incorporated bodies, namely the rules that online platforms spell out to control the organization of the platform and its services, as well as the conduct of platform participants. While the platform itself is an incorporated body, its activities and business operations are not. Moreover, the participants interacting on the platform are not employees or shareholders, and neither do they constitute internal entities of the platform.

The typical structure of a platform is as follows. The platform develops an internet website and application ('app'), which is powered by a backend server. The platform enables interaction between the participants ('users', 'members', 'customers') via its services; indeed, this interaction is the *raison d'être* of the platform. There are various kinds of platforms, depending on the role and purpose of the platform. We will discuss these in section VI, after setting out the general approach of Dutch law. Participants can only join the platform as a seller or buyer of products (either goods or services) by entering into a contract with the platform. Upon contracting with the platform, they typically also agree – on a take-it-or-leave-it basis – to a standardized set of general terms and conditions the platform uses to regulate the interaction with the platform and amongst the participants.[1] The contract itself need not be a contract for monetary benefit (consideration). Under Dutch law, the mere acceptance of terms and conditions suffices to produce an enforceable contractual relationship that, in the case of platforms, implies rights and obligations for both parties – a so-called 'reciprocal agreement' (*wederkerige overeenkomst*).[2]

---

[1] See eg TFE Tjong Tjin Tai, 'Platformen als uitdaging voor het privaatrecht' (2018) 149(7214) Weekblad voor Privaatrecht, Notariaat en Registratie 835; R Koolhoven, 'De deeleconomie' in EH Hondius and V Mak (eds), *Handboek Consumentenrecht* (5th edn, Uitgeverij Paris 2020);V Mak, 'Contracteren in de platformeconomie' (2021) 2 Maandblad voor Vermogensrecht 57.

[2] DCC, art 6:261.

III. Enforcement by the Platform and State Review

As a party to the contract, the platform itself is the primary enforcer of its internal rules. Dutch law presumes that parties first and foremost manage their own affairs. Dutch contract law offers various instruments to contracting parties to manage the contractual relationship extrajudicially, that is, without recourse to the civil courts. These include instruments of nullification (*buitengerechtelijke vernietiging*),[3] suspension of performance (*opschorting*),[4] and termination (*buitengerechtelijke ontbinding*) of contracts.[5] Dutch contract law also enables contracting parties to define and design private remedies, sanction (escalation) policies, and review or dispute settlement mechanisms.[6]

If a participant refuses to accept the platform's standpoint on their legal positions, the platform will typically restrict, suspend, or terminate the provision of its services to the participant involved. This means, for example, that they may block the visibility of user ratings,[7] delist a participant, or delist certain goods or services a participant has on offer. Alternatively, they may withhold access to ('freeze') funds acquired on the platform, such as user credit at Airbnb or eBay. Ultimately, the participant may be banned from the platform, losing all the data stored on the platform under the participant profile. These private remedies and sanctions are all iterations of the traditional remedies of suspension of performance and (partial) termination of contract.

If the platform needs other means of enforcement besides the aforementioned ones, or if the platform wants to make sure that it is correct as to its interpretation of its legal position, the platform needs to go to court. It can petition the court for a specific remedy for breach of contract (*wanprestatie*), or it can ask for a declaration of rights based on that breach. Conversely, a participant may claim that the platform acted in breach of contract when using some of its enforcement mechanisms. Alternatively, participants may

---

[3] DCC, art 3:49 in conjunction with art 3:50.

[4] DCC, arts 3:52 and 6:262.

[5] DCC, art 6:267(1).

[6] For example, Booking.com offers a 'Dispute resolution center' for disputes between business users offering accommodation on its platform with customers renting such accommodation. Booking.com is a limited liability company ('besloten vennootschap' – 'B.V.') incorporated in the Netherlands with its head office in Amsterdam. See Partner dispute: Resolution center (booking.com). Booking.com also uses an out-of-court mediation procedure to remediate conflicts it has with its accommodation partners. See Booking.com B.V., Mediation Protocol (2020) <https://partner.booking.com/sites/default/files/2020-06/booking.com_mediation_protocol_30june2020.pdf>.

[7] The parameters under which such ratings may exist are regulated under art 5 of Regulation (EU) 2019/1150 of the European Parliament and of the Council of 20 June 2019 on promoting fairness and transparency for business users of online intermediation services [2019] OJ L186/57 (P2B Regulation).

bring a claim in tort law if the platform has wrongfully harmed their protected interests preceding or during the time of their participation on the platform. Here, the violation of statutory rules on consumer rights (eg information duties, unfair commercial practices), privacy, and personal data by the platform can constitute grounds for damages claims sounding in negligence (*onrechtmatige daad*).

In all of these situations, the court will essentially have to assess whether the platform rules are valid and, if so, whether they have been applied in a legally 'permissible' manner. Either way, the validity of the platform rules will be examined.[8] This is the principal way in which judicial enforcement (and review) of platform rules occurs in the Netherlands. Alternatively, representative organizations, such as the Dutch Consumer Association (*Consumentenbond*) or other non-profit organizations having the statutory goal of representing public interests (eg privacy, personal data protection, and mental health), can, by way of collective action, petition the civil court to assess the validity of the rules in the abstract.[9] Public enforcement agencies, such as the Authority for Consumers and Markets (*Autoriteit Consument & Markt*) and the Data Protection Authority (*Autoriteit Persoonsgegevens*), may also step in. Our focus here is on private litigants, however.[10]

IV. Content of the Rules in General, Including State Influence

The content of platform rules is primarily governed by the principle of party autonomy. The platform is free to propose platform rules, and parties are free to accept or refuse these as conditions of their contractual relationship. In the latter case, the party cannot participate in the platform because the platform rules are offered on a take-it-or-leave-it basis. This consequence of a refusal to accept the contracting terms equally follows from the principle of freedom of contract.

The freedom of contract is limited by both general (default) rules of contract law and specific (mandatory) rules, some of which have been adopted to

---

[8] We disregard the issue as to whether the courts need to examine the validity of platform rules or platform operations on their own motion. Such *ex officio* judicial enforcement of mandatory rules of EU consumer protection law is frequently required in cases of default proceedings (*absentia* cases) for debt collection to ensure the full and effective application of EU law.

[9] See DCC, art 3:305a. On the conditions governing collective actions in the Netherlands, see in detail: Ianika N Tzankova and Xandra E Kramer, 'From Injunction and Settlement to Action: Collective Redress and Funding in the Netherlands' in Alan Uzelac and Stefaan Voet (eds), *Class Actions in Europe* (Springer 2021).

[10] For an analysis of enforcement actions taken by the Authority for Consumers and Markets: JW Rutgers and W Sauter, 'Voorwaarden van platformen: Mededingings- en contractenrecht' (2022) 70(4) SEW – Tijdschrift voor Europees en economisch recht 188.

implement EU Directives and Regulations. The general contract law rules will be discussed in section V, below. Mandatory rules following from European legislative instruments typically limit or prohibit the use of certain (general) terms and conditions. In that way, these rules frequently form of the basis of the validity assessment civil courts undertake in relation to the private platform rules.[11] This is illustrated by the preliminary reference case of *VKI/Amazon*. The case concerned the choice-of-law clause in Amazon's general terms and conditions, which according to the Court of Justice of the EU (CJEU) were subject to the fairness and transparency tests of the Unfair Contract Terms Directive.[12] After this decision, online platforms – also those operating in the Netherlands – have amended their terms and conditions to meet the requirements set out by the CJEU.

However, mandatory rules may also impose positive obligations on platforms to establish new rules. This is the case where platforms have (precontractual) information duties. For example, an online marketplace is required to disclose to consumers before they enter into a distance contract with a third party via the platform: (i) whether this party is a business ('trader') or a consumer; (ii) that the EU consumer law acquis does not apply whenever a contract is concluded with a third party who is consumer; and (iii) how the contracting obligations vis-à-vis the consumer are shared between the platform and the third-party.[13] In order to comply with these mandatory rules, the online marketplace regulates in its platform rules the way in which the third party offering products via the platform is to disclose information to potential buyers.[14] Additional examples are the rules that platforms have inserted in their terms and conditions on respecting and safeguarding intellectual property (IP) rights.[15]

---

[11] This is illustrated by the preliminary reference in *Verein für Konsumenteninformation v Amazon EU Sarl* (Case C-191/15). The case concerned the choice-of-law clause in Amazon's general terms and conditions, which according to the CJEU did not meet the fairness test of the Unfair Contract Terms Directive. After this decision, platforms have amended their terms and conditions to meet the requirements set out by the CJEU. For further discussion, see: JW Rutgers, *Cowboys en consumenten. Algemene voorwaarden in een digitale wereld* (Inaugural address, Vrije Universiteit Amsterdam 2017).

[12] CJEU 28 July 2016, C-191/15 *Verein für Konsumenteninformation v Amazon EU Sarl*, ECLI :EU:C:2016:612, paras 67–71; Council Directive 93/13/EEC of 5 April 1993 on unfair terms in consumer contracts [1993] OJ L95/29 (UCTD).

[13] See DCC, art 6:230m(3), implementing art 6a of the Consumer Rights Directive (Directive 2011/83/EU as amended by Directive 2019/2161/EU). See also the case of *Tiketa* (CJEU 24 February 2022, C-536/20, ECLI:EU:C:2022:112).

[14] See, for example: arts 2 (on 'Identity of the Trader') and 4(3) (on 'The Offer') of the general terms and conditions for sales by third-party sellers of bol.com: <https://www.bol.com/nl/nl/tc/voorwaarden-koper-verkoper-zakelijk/>. This information disclosure aligns with the obligations online intermediary platforms have under arts 30 and 31 of the Digital Services Act.

[15] See for example <https://www.bol.com/nl/nl/tc/notice-and-take-down-procedure/>.

While IP right owners have the principal responsibility in enforcing these rights, platforms play a facilitative role in protecting these rights whenever, for example, counterfeit products or copyright-protected content is illegally offered via their services. Damages claims directed at platforms, as mediated by the E-Commerce Directive and the Digital Services Act,[16] have incentivized platforms to undertake pro-active and preventative measures, including notice and take-down procedures (see in detail section IX, below).[17]

The content of the platform rules may also be influenced through the mechanism of contractual interpretation and/or the operation of good faith (*redelijkheid en billijkheid*). All contracts governed by Dutch law are subject to good faith (DCC, art 6:248). What good faith entails is determined, inter alia, by reference to generally accepted principles of law, the current normative opinions about the law ('levende rechtsovertuigingen') in the Netherlands, and the societal and private interests involved in the case at hand.[18] In this way, participants may find that certain conduct is not allowed on the platform, even though it was not explicitly prohibited in the terms and conditions.[19] Importantly, fundamental rights such as those articulated by the European Convention on Human Rights and the EU Charter of Fundamental Rights, are also part of the generally accepted legal principles determining the meaning of good faith. Accordingly, these rights may also, albeit indirectly, weigh in on the content of platform rules.[20]

What is more, the good faith categories of 'generally accepted principles' and 'current normative opinions about the law' enable civil courts to also consider industry practice and private regulation as relevant in determining the content of platform rules. For instance, the broader understanding in in-

---

[16] Directive 2000/31/EC of the European Parliament and of the Council of 8 June 2000 on certain legal aspects of information society services, in particular electronic commerce, in the Internal Market ('Directive on electronic commerce') [2000] OJ L178/1; Regulation (EU) 2022/2065 of the European Parliament and of the Council of 19 October 2022 on a Single Market for Digital Services and amending Directive 2000/31/EC (Digital Services Act) [2022] OJ L277/1 (DSA).

[17] Regarding counterfeit products, at present 33 online platforms have committed to taking such measures under an EU Memorandum of Understanding. See <https://single-market-economy.ec.europa.eu/industry/strategy/intellectual-property/enforcement-intellectual-property-rights/memorandum-understanding-sale-counterfeit-goods-internet_en>.

[18] DCC, art 3:12. The list is not exhaustive: WHM Reehuis and EE Slob, *Parlementaire geschiedenis van het nieuwe Burgerlijk Wetboek, Invoering Boeken 3, 5 en 6: Boek 3, Vermogensrecht in het algemeen* (Kluwer 1990) 1035.

[19] See Dutch Supreme Court 19 October 2007, C06/123HR *Vodafone/ETC*, ECLI:NL:HR:2007:BA7024 (concerning the inappropriate use of contracted telecommunications services).

[20] See for example: District Court Amsterdam 13 October 2020, *Stichting Virus Waarheid/Facebook*, ECLI:NL:RBAMS:2020:4966. For further discussion, see section VII.1, below.

dustry or society that social media platforms should moderate content could ultimately cause the internal rules of these platforms to be interpreted as containing an implicit clause that gives a platform the right to moderate and remove content, even where that was not explicitly mentioned in the internal rules. However, it should be noted that this is not the usual way in which such changes occur. Firstly, platforms usually rely on explicit terms, and they add new clauses by simply changing their terms and conditions and offering participants the option to exit the platform if they do not want to accept the revised platform rules. Secondly, a change in the understanding of industry or society usually influences platforms rules by way of newly adopted laws or via self- or co-regulatory mechanisms. The neo-corporatist sentiment is strong in the Netherlands, and therefore the government will typically invite societal stakeholders to offer opinions and develop 'voluntary' private initiatives within the sector. This can be further strengthened by parliamentary discussions, proposed legislation, and the like. Experiences with product safety regulation[21] and social media moderation[22] serve as examples here. If a sector governs itself adequately, the state is unlikely to intervene.

V. General Rules of Dutch Contract Law

Dutch contract law starts from the principle of *pacta sunt servanda*. Like most civil law systems, the violation of any term of the contract constitutes a breach, which in principle entitles the other party to a remedy. There is no distinction between representations, warranties, and other contract terms in Dutch law. The principal remedies are available *de lege* and do not need specific contractual clauses to be relied on. These remedies are specific performance (*nakoming*), damages (*schadevergoeding*), and termination (*ontbinding*). Additionally, suspension of performance (*opschorting*), nullification (*vernietiging*), or denunciation in case of long-term contracts (*opzegging*) may be invoked.

[21] Soon after the adoption of the European Product Safety Pledge in 2018, the Netherlands Authority for Food and Product Safety initiated talks with the leading online marketplaces in the Netherlands. In 2019, it adopted collaborative protocols with these platforms. See <https://zoek.officielebekendmakingen.nl/blg-892721.pdf> (regarding marktplaats.nl) <https://www.tweedekamer.nl/downloads/document?id=2019D30503> (regarding bol.com). These co-regulatory arrangements are evaluated on a yearly basis and, if needed, reviewed. For further discussion, see: Paul Verbruggen, 'Online platformen en onveilige producten' (2020) 5 Tijdschrift voor Consumentenrecht en handelspraktijken 255, 260.

[22] See the 'Project Online Content Moderatie' (PrOCoM), coordinated and financed by the Dutch Ministry of Justice and Security in 2022. The project seeks to develop a public-private framework in which citizens, government officials, and the IT sector may act to effectively moderate illegal online content. See for details <https://hetccv.nl/app/uploads/2023/08/20221108_Projectplan_PrOCoM.pdf>.

Control over the enforcement of contractual rules occurs in several ways. First, the validity of the contract as a whole is governed by *bonos mores*, public policy, and mandatory statutory law, as well as by defects of consent. Second, the validity of specific contract terms (including general terms and conditions) is addressed by the rules on unfair terms (*algemene voorwaarden*, DCC, arts 6:231-6:247) and more generally by the principle of good faith (*redelijkheid en billijkheid*). This principle permeates the entirety of the Dutch law of obligations. As per DCC, art 6:2(1), all individuals are required to behave according to good faith. More particularly, good faith determines how parties to a contract should behave vis-à-vis each other (DCC, art 6:248(1)). Accordingly, this principle guides the interpretation of the contract, both its terms and its blanks (gap-filling), and the applicability of terms. With regard to this latter point, the principle of good faith can prohibit the application of specific clauses (the *derogerende werking van redelijkheid en billijkheid*).[23] While this limiting function of good faith may appear extreme, it is only applied restrictively. The courts generally favor interventions as regards only a specific application, instead of an outright ruling that a clause is completely contrary to good faith.[24] In this way, the limiting function of good faith has effects very similar to the general prohibition on abuse of right that is recognized in many civil law jurisdictions.[25]

Finally, good faith may also restrict the application of specific remedies in contractual relations. Unless the DCC determines otherwise,[26] there is no priority among the remedies that parties can invoke. Consequently, the promisee (*schuldenaar*) may choose which remedy to rely on. The mere breach is sufficient to create a right to specific performance (*nakoming*). The only exceptions are impossibility and disproportionality.[27] For damages, it suffices that the breach can be attributed to the promisor and that it caused damage (DCC, art 6:75). Limitations on the scope of damages are legal causation

---

[23] DCC, arts 6:2(2) and 6:248(2).

[24] Dutch Supreme Court 9 January 1998, 16488 (C96/306) *Kinderdagverblijf Snoopy*, ECLI:NL:HR:1998:ZC2540. For platforms, see *Stichting Virus Waarheid* (n 20), in which the specific application of Facebook's community guidelines was reviewed (*in casu* the removal of a post by the claimant) and not the guidelines themselves.

[25] In French law this exists as a general principle; in German law, see BGB, § 226. In Dutch law there is the general rule of DCC, art 3:13. On the functions of good faith and its relationship with the doctrine of abuse of rights, see: Martijn W Hesselink, 'The concept of good faith' in Arthur S Hartkamp and others (eds), *Towards a European Civil Code* (Kluwer Law International 2011).

[26] An example is consumer sales law (DCC, art 7:21), in which a specific hierarchy of remedies is set out, following the (old) Consumer Sales Directive (Directive 1999/44/EC of the European Parliament and of the Council of 25 May 1999 on certain aspects of the sale of consumer goods and associated guarantees [1999] OJ L171/12).

[27] Dutch Supreme Court 5 January 2001, C99/115HR *Multi Vastgoed/Nethou*, ECLI:NL:HR:2001:AA9311; DCC, art 3:13 (*misbruik van recht, abus de droit*).

(*toerekening naar redelijkheid*, DCC, art 6:98), contributory negligence (*eigen schuld,* DCC, art 6:101), and mitigation (*matiging*, DCC, art 6:109), just to name a few controlling devices. For termination (*ontbinding*), there is the restriction that the breach must have been sufficiently serious to warrant termination (DCC, art 6:265).

VI. Specific Contracts in Dutch Contract Law

When determining the legal rules for platforms, the approach that Dutch civil courts take – in line with most civil law systems – is to attempt to classify the platform-participant relationship as one of the specific (or 'nominate') contracts in the DCC.[28] Insofar as that relationship qualifies as a specific contract, the relevant rules apply with priority over or – if expressly determined – in conjunction with the general rules of contract law. Specific contract law rules typically involve a mix of mandatory and default rules. While the first type of rules is aimed at protecting a 'weaker' party in the contractual relationship, the second intends to facilitate simple specific contracts by providing fair default rules on particular issues that reflect what parties would probably agree on had they turned their minds to those issues.

Dutch law has the following specific contracts that are relevant for platforms:[29]

- Sale (*koop*), including consumer sale (*consumentenkoop*)
- Service contracts in general (*opdracht*). This nominate contract is subdivided into:
  - Mandate (*lastgeving*)
  - Brokerage and intermediary agreements (*bemiddeling*)
  - Commercial agency (*agentuur*)
  - Labor contracts (*arbeidsovereenkomst*)

The relevance of these contracts becomes clear when we look at the principal types of online platforms that presently exist. We can distinguish between, at least, four types:

[28] See also: Eric Tjong Tjin Tai, 'Platformen als uitdaging voor het privaatrecht' (2018) 149(7214) Weekblad voor Privaatrecht, Notariaat en Registratie 835; Eric Tjong Tjin Tai and Jaap van Slooten, 'Platformarbeid en privaatrecht' in Mike Houwerzijl, Saskia Montebovi and Nuna Zekic (eds), *Platformisering, algoritmisering en sociale bescherming* (Wolters Kluwer 2021); MY Schaub, 'Het juridische kader voor online ondernemen in vogelvlucht' [2022] (2) Ondernemingsrecht 43.

[29] We only discuss contracts specifically relevant for platforms in their function as platforms; we will not discuss all possible contracts where the platform is the primary service provider for the client, since that would be tantamount to a comprehensive course on Dutch contract law. For instance, we will not discuss transport contracts in relation to Uber.

1. Platforms as Primary Service Providers

The platform is strongly involved in providing a primary service, to such an extent that it must be classified as providing the service itself. The prime example is Uber, which is frequently characterized as a taxi company employing drivers.[30] The same considerations emerge around food delivery apps, such as Deliveroo, Just Eat Takeaway, Uber Eats, and Wolt.[31] We will not discuss these kinds of platforms. Many of our remarks that follow also apply to such platforms; however, as these entities are the principal service provider and the employer, additional rules apply (in particular labor law and tax regulations). Addressing these matters would overcomplicate the issues (and our analysis). As far as online marketplaces such as Amazon are concerned, these platforms may also be viewed as primary service providers when they offer the product themselves via their own marketplace and not through third-party traders. In that case, the rules of (consumer) sale apply.

2. Platforms as Intermediaries

In this type, platforms facilitate the conclusion of contracts between platform participants, who may either be 'traders' or 'consumers'. A key example is Airbnb, as well as Amazon, Booking.com, crypto.com, eBay, Etsy, LightintheBox, Rakuten, Temu, and many other quality intermediary platforms. These platforms typically earn revenue by asking a fee or commission for each contract, service, order, or transaction completed through the platform services. Taking into account the source of revenue these platforms have, the nominate contract that is likely to apply in Dutch law is that of intermediary/brokerage or, possibly, commercial agency. Using the terminology of the DCC, this is the contract governing the vertical relation between the platform and participant (the 'client') who offers his goods or services via the platform, rather than the individual contract that is concluded after the client transacted via the platform with another participant (the 'third party').[32] The contract that the platform has in relation to this buyer can also be brokerage. This may lead to discussions regarding a conflict of interests. We will turn to that issue in section VII.

---

[30] See eg *Uber BV and others v Aslam and others* [2021] UKSC 5, [90]-[102].

[31] In the Netherlands, the Dutch Supreme Court ruled that Deliveroo riders qualify as employees. See Dutch Supreme Court 4 March 2023, C99/115HR *Deliveroo*, ECLI:NL:HR:2023:443, NJ 2024/35. Based on this ruling, the Court of Appeal of Amsterdam is considering to submit pre-judicial question to the Dutch Supreme Court regarding the classification of Uber drivers. See Court of Appeal of Amsterdam 3 October 2023, 200.300.335/01 *Uber BV/FNV*, ECLI:NL:GHAMS:2023:2220. In the case of the *Helpling* – an intermediary platform for contracts with a person to do household chores – the District Court of Amsterdam ruled again, classifying the persons offering their help on this platform as employees of the platform. See District Court Amsterdam 1 July 2019, 7299840 CV EXPL 18-23708 *FNV/Helpling*, ECLI:NL:RBAMS:20194546.

3. Social Media Platforms

This type of platform offers all participants the possibility to publish and read communicative expressions. This can be done for profit, but also for free (ie without payment of a sum of money). The platform typically makes money from advertisements, but possibly also by providing access to personal data. Key examples include Facebook, Reddit, TikTok, X (formerly Twitter), and YouTube. It is also possible that the platform asks the participants for a fee. The contract that would typically govern the relationships involved in this type of platform is a service contract (DCC, art 7:400). Dutch law recognizes a general service contract for any kind of service, provided there is some manner of remuneration where the service provider is acting in his or her profession or trade (DCC, art 7:405) or provided there is recovery of expenses (DCC, art 7:406). While the latter will not apply to the case of online platforms, the former may since the collection and processing of consumers' personal data can be seen as a manner of remuneration for platform services.[33] If the service is provided without any monetary payment, the assumption is that there is no actual contractual relationship but rather an informal relationship without obligations, in line with volunteer work.[34]

4. Cooperative Platforms

Platforms belonging to this type are focused principally on some kind of cooperative venture, such as helping each other out in solving programming issues (Stackoverflow) or general questions (Quora) or developing software (GitHub). These platforms typically do not ask a fee from the participants and do not pay individuals who answer questions, but it does happen that some individuals are paid for answering questions. Revenue may be generated by online advertisements. Furthermore, platforms may generate revenue simply by data collection, which supposedly may be of value in the longer term. In the short term, they may not make a profit and may simply be kept afloat by an influx of investor capital. With this fourth type of platform there also is no clear classification of the contracts involved, although if a participant is paid for providing answers, these activities may enable the classification of a service contract.

---

[32] Note that 'third party' is the term used in DCC, art 7:425 to distinguish between intermediaries and their clients. In the context of online platforms, third parties are not genuine third parties to the platform as they will also be participants on the platform.

[33] See art 3(1) of Directive (EU) 2019/770 of the European Parliament and of the Council of 20 May 2019 on certain aspects concerning contracts for the supply of digital content and digital services [2019] OJ L136/1.

[34] Eric Tjong Tjin Tai, 'Aansprakelijkheid jegens vrijwilligers' (2022) 152(7361) Weekblad voor Privaatrecht, Notariaat en Registratie 148.

VII. Review of Platform Rules through Contract Law

Now that we have set out the framework governing platforms, we can discuss the specifics of how Dutch contract law reviews platform rules. We will discuss several examples and instances of case law in relation to the types of platforms identified above. As noted, we will not discuss the application of contract law rules to platforms that are primary service providers (Type A). After all, this type of platform is subject to the same rules as any other provider of that same service. For the three remaining categories (Types B, C, and D) a more detailed analysis is required.

1. *Unfair Terms*

As a general rule, the general terms and conditions of a platform will determine the content of the contract between the platform and participants (section 4). However, the content is subject to review by courts applying either good faith (section 5) or specific instruments, including the doctrine of unfair terms. In Dutch law, this doctrine is implemented in the rules on 'general conditions' (*algemene voorwaarden*, DCC, arts 6:231–6:247), which contain an implementation of the Unfair Contract Terms Directive. These rules are not specific to platforms. The principal material test asks whether the general terms and conditions are 'unreasonably burdensome' (*onredelijk bezwarend*, DCC, art 6:233(a)).[35] This test is, amongst other means, operationalized through lists of terms that are held to be unreasonable (black list, DCC, art 6:236) and presumed to be unreasonable (grey list, DCC, art 237). These rules protect consumers in particular, but they may also have indicative value for professionals and corporations (particularly small and medium-sized enterprises).[36] If the court considers a term unreasonably burdensome, the term is voidable as a general rule (DCC, art 6:233). However, influenced by the burgeoning case law of the CJEU on the *ex officio* application of the Unfair Contract Terms Directive, the Dutch Supreme Court has held that courts, on their own motion, need to avoid general terms and conditions that are unreasonably burdensome in business-to-consumer relationships.[37] This sanction is equivalent to what art 6(1) of the Directive requires of Member States.

How do the rules on 'general conditions' apply to online platforms? It should be noted at the outset that these rules have a clear restriction: they can only prohibit terms and conditions that are unreasonable in general. The rules

[35] See in detail MBM Loos, *Algemene voorwaarden* (4th edn, Boom juridisch 2024) 167ff.

[36] The leading case is Dutch Supreme Court 8 September 2023, 22/02716 *Hibma Zuivel*, ECLI:NL:HR:2023:1197. See in detail Loos (n 35) 414–422.

[37] Dutch Supreme Court 13 September 2013, 12/00395 *Heesakkers/Voets*, ECLI:NL:HR:2013:691, NJ 2014/274.

do not cover the specific application of general conditions vis-à-vis an individual platform participant. For this reason, the general principle of good faith (DCC, art 6:248) is far more important as an instrument for judicial review when it comes to platforms. It is this principle that allows for the protection of a platform participant against the unreasonable application of a term that is not in itself unfair.[38]

An example of the assessment of the private regulation of a social media platform (Type C) is the case of *Stichting Virus Waarheid/Facebook*.[39] In this case, Facebook had removed a post of the claimant based on the platform's community guidelines. The claimant, a non-profit organization that was very critical of the COVID-19 measures taken by the Dutch government, considered the removal to violate ECHR, art 10 (freedom of expression). The District Court of Amsterdam correctly held that the removal could not be reviewed directly based on this fundamental right, due to the lack of a direct horizontal effect. Instead, the right could be used as a proxy to determine the standard of good faith (DCC, art 6:248) or wrongful act (*onrechtmatige daad*, DCC, art 6:162) in the specific case. Here, the claim failed because the claimant did not sufficiently make clear why Facebook had violated this right. The discretionary power of the platform to determine its own policies is high and, in this specific instance, the threshold for unfairness or wrongfulness was even higher, given that Facebook developed the policy after the European Commission had urged it to do so.[40]

A similar case concerns LinkedIn, which had cancelled the account of a Dutch Member of Parliament for repeated posts in violation of the platform's COVID-19 policy.[41] Here, the District Court of North Holland held that LinkedIn was wrong to do so. While the legal framework was the same – indirect assessment of art 10 ECHR through the open norm of good faith (DCC, art 6:248) – the outcome was different. In contrast to other major platforms, LinkedIn had not further elaborated its COVID-19 policy and had not explained why earlier posts of the Member of Parliament were in violation of its rules. The District Court also took into consideration that the account is a long-term contract which can be cancelled by the platform, but the decision to cancel is open to judicial review according to the norms of DCC, art 6:248. As a result, LinkedIn did not 'behave sufficiently carefully'.[42] The District

[38] See the main text corresponding to notes 22–23.

[39] *Stichting Virus Waarheid* (n 20). In a similar vein, see District Court Rotterdam 29 October 2021, C/10/622391/KG ZA 21-622 *X/Facebook*, ECLI:NL:RBROT:2021:10459.

[40] *Stichting Virus Waarheid* (n 20) para 4.24.

[41] District Court North Holland 6 October 2021, C/15/319230/KG ZA 21-432 *Kamerlid/LinkedIn*, ECLI:NL:RBNHO:2021:8539.

[42] *Kamerlid* (n 41) paras 4.20–4.24.

Court ordered LinkedIn to reinstate the account, but it did not order the platform to republish the posts, as they contained false information.

The two cases show the typical review on the basis of DCC, art 6: 248. Courts tend to stress a reasonable and predictable application of rules. The proportionality of the platform measures and the severity of the consequences for the participant involved is also relevant (note the difference between the cancellation of an account and the removal of posts). These cases also indicate that the Dutch rules on unfair terms and conditions are mostly irrelevant as these only deal with traditional issues, not with issues that are important on platforms, such as freedom of expression, non-discrimination, and other public interests.

Finally, we note that there has not been any case law addressing the relationship between professional participants (business, traders, influencers) and online social media platforms. We assume this is the case because those situations are outside the scope of consumer law, as a result of which the normal rules for jurisdiction apply and such cases probably need to be litigated abroad, particularly in Ireland (where most platforms are incorporated in the EU). Likewise, no case law has emerged regarding the unfairness of general terms and conditions used by intermediary platforms (Type B) vis-à-vis business participants. The Platform-to-Business (P2B) Regulation (Regulation (EU) 2019/1150) introduced new rules regarding such terms.[43] Art 3 of the Regulation requires, inter alia, that the terms must be drafted in plain and intelligible language, must be easily available to business users at all stages of the commercial relationship, and must set out the ground for any corrective measures the platform can take against the business. Based on art 3(3), violating these mandatory rules leads to the nullity of the terms used. To our knowledge, no case law has emerged in the Netherlands based on these rules for general terms and conditions.

2. *Specific Contracts*

Regarding the rules on specific (nominate) contracts, the main contract is the service contract (*overeenkomst van opdracht*, DCC, art 7:400).[44] The three

---

[43] For an analysis under Dutch law, see: JHM Spanjaard, 'Online tussenhandelaren: transparantie en eerlijkheid als geboden' (2021) 1 Contracteren 3; V Mak, 'Contracteren in de platformeconomie' (2021) 2 Maandblad voor Vermogensrecht 57.

[44] TFE Tjong Tjin Tai, *Mr. C. Asser's handleiding tot beoefening van het Nederlands burgerlijk recht: bijzondere overeenkomsten. Opdracht, inclusief de geneeskundige behandelingsovereenkomst en de reisovereenkomst* vol 7-IV, (4th edn, Wolters Kluwer 2022); TFE Tjong Tjin Tai, 'Services, Including Services of General Interest' in CW Twigg-Flessner (ed), *Research Handbook on EU Consumer and Contract Law* (Edward Elgar 2016); TFE Tjong Tjin Tai, 'Service Contracts in the Dutch Civil Code' in Reinhard Zimmerman (ed), *Service Contracts* (Mohr Siebeck 2010).

categories of platforms involved (Types B, C, and D) can be classified primarily as providing services, besides undertaking other specific obligations. Service contracts are restricted regarding their content in several ways.

First of all, the service provider (*opdrachtnemer,* platform) owes a general duty of care or diligence towards the principal (*opdrachtgever*, participants) based on DCC, art 7:401.[45] This duty of care can be restricted given the nature of the service and reasonable limitations inherent in the service or contract, but it cannot be completely contracted out. This general duty implies efforts to realize the main aim of the contracted service, precautionary measures, the duty to warn and to inform, and post-contractual obligations. Even in the absence of specific contractual terms, the platform will therefore be held to reasonable obligations flowing from the nature of the platform service. Conversely, this implies that the platform cannot restrict its actual obligations too severely, as that would be contrary to its general duty of care.

There are specific rules regarding instructions (DCC, art 7:402), the right to demand account of the performance of the service (DCC, art 7:403), and fees (DCC, art 7:405), but these give way to more specific rules, which typically can be found in platform conditions and regulations. Alternatively, the specific rules on service contracts are not relevant given the mass-character of platforms, which does not allow that the principal (the participant) give individual instructions to the service provider (the platform) or that the latter gives account to the former regarding the performance of its services.

Some rules are mandatory law insofar as the principal is a consumer.[46] These include rules that provide the consumer the right to cancel the contract without notice (DCC, art 7:408) and that restrict the right of the principal to impose a fine (DCC, art 7:411). These rules are to be interpreted in such a way that consumers can cancel without notice, but they may need to pay for reasonable costs that have been incurred before cancellation, typically corresponding to a period of time deemed reasonable in relation to the subject matter of the contact at issue.[47] A platform term that deviates from these rules is null and void.

For a mandate contract (*lastgeving*, DCC, art 7:414), there are rules applying to conflict of interests (DCC, art 7:416-418) that can apply also to services in general (DCC, art 7:424 and the general rules of Dutch contract law). The particular interpretation of the rules is subject to some discussion, but the

[45] Note that it is possible, depending on the kind of platform, that a participant is also a service provider vis-à-vis the platform.

[46] DCC, art 7:413.

[47] This can be deduced from Dutch Supreme Court 10 February 2023, 21/04816, ECLI:NL:HR:2023:198, where the period was one month, related to the provision of child care. See also: art 6:237(k) DCC, which allows subscription contracts for longer than a year provided the consumer, after one year, has the right to cancel with notice of at most one month.

thrust of these rules appears to be that a conflict of interests is prohibited unless the principal, upon being informed about the specific conflict, accepts it nevertheless.[48] In some instances, these rules could restrict platforms that are both intermediary and primary service providers, like Amazon or its Dutch counterpart Bol.com.

3. *Specific Service Contracts: Intermediary Contracts*

The DCC also includes rules on specific service contracts: mandate, intermediaries/brokerage, and commercial agency (the last thing being a subset of brokerage). Intermediary contracts/contracts of brokerage are of greatest practical importance to online platforms (Types B, C, D) and will be discussed in some detail below. For mandate, the rules on conflicts of interests have been indicated above. Commercial agency can, according to the letter of the law, be applicable to intermediary platforms, but it would lead to the platform being protected from actions of its members,[49] hence, these rules are unlikely to lead to additional review on behalf of members. We will therefore not discuss them.

The Dutch Supreme Court has now ruled twice on classification of the contractual relations intermediary platforms (Category B) entertain with 'clients' and 'third parties' who purchase the products offered for sale via their platforms. The first case is that of *Booking.com*.[50] This case revolves around the question of whether Booking.com – a limited liability company incorporated in the Netherlands and based in Amsterdam – is required to participate in the sectoral pension fund for travel agents based on Dutch pension regulations. Participation in that fund depends on whether a company can be considered as brokering or intermediating ('bemiddelen') the conclusion of contracts related to 'travel', including contracts for transport, accommodation, and package travel. The subdistrict court judge (*kantonrechter*) and the court of appeal held for Booking.com, finding that an online platform did not broker such contracts. The Supreme Court overturned the decision of the court of appeal. It held that since the pension regulations did not define the term brokering, the question of whether Booking.com brokers contracts needs to be assessed based on the nominate contract law rules of intermediation (DCC, art 7:425). This article reads as follows:

---

48 Tjong Tjin Tai, *Asser's handleiding* (n 44) nos 231–243.

49 These rules were set up to protect weaker commercial agents against strong principals, see Tjong Tjin Tai, *Asser's handleiding* (n 44) no 320 and the Commercial Agency Directive, Council Directive 86/653/EEC of 18 December 1986 on the coordination of the laws of the Member States relating to self-employed commercial agents[1986] OJ L382/17.

50 Dutch Supreme Court 9 April 2021, 19/04002 *Booking.com*, ECLI:NL:HR:2021:527, NJ 2021/206, annotated by TFE Tjong Tjin Tai.

'An intermediary agreement is a service provision agreement under which one of the parties, ("the intermediary") has engaged himself towards the other party ("the client") to work on payment of a fee (remuneration) as an intermediary in arranging one or more contracts to be concluded by his client with third persons.'[51]

The Supreme Court clarified this description by holding that the intermediary offers services that are conducive to concluding a contract between the client and the third party. Not required is that the intermediary itself concludes a contract to the benefit of the client; it is sufficient that its activities contribute to the conclusion of such a contract. While the Supreme Court stressed that the classification of a contract concluded between the client and third parties (travelers) for travel services via Booking.com needs to be assessed individually, taking into account all relevant facts and circumstances, its ruling offered important general insights into the classification question. First, it considered that if the intermediary requests a fee whenever a contract is concluded between the client and the third party, this points to intermediation.[52] Second, the nature, scope, and intensity of the intermediary's activities may vary, but to speak of intermediation these activities need not entail much.[53] Given that the case at hand did not concern a specific contract, the analysis of the Supreme Court is more general, essentially assessing whether the business model of Booking.com would amount to intermediation. On this point, it reasoned that the company: (i) runs a booking platform for travel accommodations; (ii) allows third parties to book accommodations as aided by the functionalities of the platform; (iii) runs the administrative backend of the booking process; and (iv) receives a commission from the client after the third party has booked the accommodation or a related service of the client via the platform. The Supreme Court held that the facts compelled the conclusion that Booking.com is an intermediary for the purposes of Dutch pension regulations.

The classification of platform services as constituting a brokerage or intermediary contract under the DCC does not entail much, however. The nominate contract is discussed in just three articles in the DCC, all iterations of the general principle of good faith. The first (quoted above) describes the contract, the second concerns remuneration (DCC, art 7:426), and the third declares applicable the rules regarding conflicts of interest in a nominate contract of mandate (DCC, art 7:427 in conjunction with arts 7:417–418). These rules also concern the 'serving of two masters'. One rule (DCC, art 7:417(4)) specifically prohibits the intermediary from claiming payment for his services from the buyer or a lessee of real estate property. This rule cannot be contracted out and also applies even if the intermediary does not

---

[51] Translation from <http://www.dutchcivillaw.com/legislation/dcctitle7777.htm>.

[52] *Booking.com* (n 50) para 4.1.5.

[53] *Booking.com* (n 50) para 4.1.6.

receive remuneration from the seller or lessor of the property. The background to the mandatory rule, which applies only to residential buildings, is protection of consumers on the housing market.[54]

The question of whether the services of Booking.com complied with the prohibition of DCC, art 7:417(4) was not addressed by the Dutch Supreme Court. Soon after, however, that question, along with a number of other issues, was put to the Supreme Court in a national preliminary reference procedure related to Airbnb. This intermediary platform allows individuals to rent short- and long-term homestays for holidays and business trips from other individuals. Lessors and lessees can either be businesses or consumers. Airbnb charges a service fee to both the lessor and lessee. The District Court of Amsterdam ruled in 2020 that Airbnb's charging policy violated the prohibition of DCC, art 7:417(4).[55] As a consequence, a number of collective action vehicles were established to recover the payment of the service fees charged to lessees in the Netherlands. A total of 200 civil lawsuits in the Netherlands were concerned with this question, underpinning the need for guidance from the Dutch Supreme Court.

A number of these lawsuits were before the subdistrict court judge (*kantonrechter*) of Rotterdam, who decided to submit several preliminary questions to the Supreme Court. The first question was whether Airbnb serves as a broker for lease contracts. That question was answered in the affirmative. Relying on its ruling in *Booking.com*, the Supreme Court held, for the purposes of Dutch private law (and not pension regulations), that Airbnb enables the conclusion of lease contracts, receives remuneration for that service, and that parties to the contract can only meet each other through the platform.[56] The second question concerned the applicability of DCC, art 7:417(4). After reviewing the parliamentary discussions and the nature of the rule, the Supreme Court found that the prohibition in question applies only to long-term leases of living space and not to leases for purposes other than residential use (ie holiday vacations and business trips). As a result, Airbnb was not prohibited from charging fees from both the lessor and lessee for brokering transactions via its platform.

As Airbnb did not violate any mandatory rules, the Supreme Court did not answer the questions the *kantonrechter* had raised as regards the validity of the involved intermediary contract (nullity and nullification) and the prescription of claims (*verjaring*). It did, however, answer the question of whether Airbnb's contract terms requiring payment of service charges by the consum-

---

[54] Dutch Supreme Court 16 October 2015, 15/00688 *Duinzigt/Tacq*, ECLI:NL:HR:2015:3099, NJ 2016/108, annotated by TFE Tjong Tjin Tai.

[55] District Court Amsterdam 9 March 2020, ECLI:NL:RBAMS:2020:1477, NJ 2021/51.

[56] Dutch Supreme Court 19 November 2021, 21/00168 *Airbnb*, ECLI:NL:HR:2021:1725, NJ 2021/396, annotated by TFE Tjong Tjin Tai.

er violate the mandatory rules regarding unfair terms (*algemene voorwaarden*, DCC, arts 6:231–247) and whether the platform engaged in unfair commercial practices. Regarding the first question, the Supreme Court considered that, since the amount of the service fees depends on the actual acceptance of a booking proposition, the consumer will have individually negotiated this term of the contract. This ruling came despite the fact that these fees are calculated automatically by Airbnb. Moreover, art 4(2) of the Unfair Contract Terms Directive and the case law of the CJEU dictates that a national court is not to assess the validity of general terms and conditions governing the main subject matter of the contract, nor those regarding the adequacy of the price and remuneration. The exception to this rule, namely that the terms are not set in plain and intelligible language, does not apply, the Supreme Court found. After all, the service fees are clearly specified in Airbnb's booking proposition. It is for that same reason that the Court also considered that Airbnb does not engage in unfair commercial practices (DCC, art 6:193a)[57] to the extent that it charges consumers service fees when they book an accommodation via the platform. As regards those transactions, Airbnb is transparent about the renumeration required, the total fees due for a booking, and that it is intermediating for both the lessor and the consumer-lessee.

VIII. Other Grounds for Reviewing Platform Contracts, Rules, and Activities

The validity of platform rules and activities may also be assessed based on a combination of the laws regarding data protection and pre-contractual information duties. One example is the decision of the District Court of Amsterdam in the case of *Data Privacy Stichting/Facebook*.[58] In this case, a third-party-funded, non-profit organization called Data Privacy Stichting petitioned the court, by way of a collective action, to assess the validity of Facebook's use of personal data under the Dutch implementation legislation of the Personal Data Directive (Directive 96/46/EC, PDD) and the General Data Protection Regulation (Regulation (EU) 2016/679, GDPR) for the period be-

[57] Implementing art 5(2) of the Unfair Commercial Practices Directive (Directive 2005/29/EC of the European Parliament and of the Council of 11 May 2005 concerning unfair business-to-consumer commercial practices in the internal market and amending Council Directive 84/450/EEC, Directives 97/7/EC, 98/27/EC and 2002/65/EC of the European Parliament and of the Council and Regulation (EC) 2006/2004 of the European Parliament and of the Council ('Unfair Commercial Practices Directive') [2005] OJ L 149/22 (UCPD)).

[58] District Court Amsterdam 15 March 2023, C/13/683377/HA ZA 20-468, ECLI:NL:RBAMS:2023:1407, TvC 2023/5, 196, annotated by DJH Op Heij; JOR 2023/225, annotated by DA van der Kooij and JG Reus.

tween 1 April 2010 and 1 January 2020. The collective action vehicle[59] claimed that Facebook had not correctly informed its users about the ways in which their personal data would be processed, amongst other things for the development of applications of third parties (eg games) and online (behavioral) advertising. In a very extensive ruling, the District Court of Amsterdam found that Facebook had indeed violated several principles and rules in the PDD and GDPR. That finding was in line with that of the decision of the Dutch Data Protection Authority in 2017.[60] The authority did not impose any sanction, however. In this civil lawsuit, the collective action vehicle sought to secure a damages award (inter alia based on GDPR, arts 82 and 83) to recover the material and immaterial damage the violation of the data protection rules allegedly caused to those represented by the collective action vehicle.

For the purposes of this Chapter, it is important to note that the District Court of Amsterdam also found the failure on the part of Facebook to correctly inform platform participants about the use of personal data for advertising purposes to constitute an omission of essential information in terms of DCC, art 6:193d (corresponding to UCPD, art 7). The average consumer-participant needs that material information, the District Court reasoned, to make an informed transactional decision. The court went on to state that, without it, individuals are likely to have taken a transactional decision that they would not have taken otherwise.[61] The consideration that Facebook violated mandatory data protection rules and engaged in an unfair commercial practice triggers the question of whether the platform is liable for any of the material and immaterial damage these violations caused. While the case of *Österreichische Post* sets out rules for the recovery of such damages, the merely unpleasant feelings a violation of the GPDR triggers is not sufficient to award damages. As far as unfair commercial practices are concerned, only damage caused directly by such practices is recoverable (DCC, art 6:193j(2)).[62] These conditions limit the chances of recovering the harm suffered by Facebook users. In response to the decision of the Amsterdam court, on 1 August 2023 Facebook changed its platform rules and now explicitly asks for permission to conduct

---

[59] A collective action vehicle is a specific legal entity established for the purpose of bringing and managing a collective damages claim.

[60] Data Protection Authority, Report with final conclusions z2014-009292, 21 February 2017.

[61] District Court Amsterdam 30 June 2021, C/13/683377/HA ZA 20-468, ECLI:NL:RBAMS:2021:3307, para 7.17.

[62] L Tigelaar and C Pavillon, 'De bewijslastomkering bij oneerlijke handelspraktijken: Een jurisprudentie-onderzoek naar de toepassing van art 6:193j lid 1 en 2 BW' (2021) 4 Tijdschrift voor Consumentenrecht & handelspraktijken 204. For an application of the strict causation element in the context of online platforms, see District Court Gelderland 22 November 2023, C/05/411051/HZ ZA 22-324, ECLI:NL:RBGEL:2023:6324 (*Crypto.com*).

data processing for advertising purposes. As such, it also follows the CJEU ruling in *Meta Platforms/Bundeskartellamt* of 4 July 2023.[63]

Another collective action procedure before the District Court of Amsterdam also intends to have social media platform rules reviewed based on a combination of data protection and pre-contractual information duties. This (joined) procedure is against TikTok and has been brought by three different claim vehicles, each funded by commercial third parties and jointly representing some 180,000 platform users, both minors and adults. The procedure, which is not yet at the stage of trial at the time of writing, is essentially about the validity of TikTok's rules and platform activities in light of EU rules on data protection, audiovisual media services, and consumer protection. Regarding the latter group of rules, the vehicles claim that national implementation rules regarding the Consumer Rights Directive, the Unfair Commercial Practice Directive, and the Unfair Contract Terms Directive have been violated. The District Court issued an interim judgment in October 2023, setting out various standards of admissibility, the applicable law under the Rome I Regulation, and the so-called 'exclusive representative'.[64] In January 2024, it issued another interim judgment finding all three vehicles admissible in their claims and appointing vehicles as the lead plaintiffs (*exclusieve belangenbehartiger*, Dutch Code of Civil Procedure, art 1018e) for the minors and adults represented in the case. It is expected that this case will trigger questions similar to the *Facebook* case regarding the (mis)use of personal data, consumer and minor protection, and follow-on damages claims.

IX. Influence of Liability Exemptions

We discuss lastly the EU rules on immunity from civil liability for online platforms. The E-Commerce Directive (ECD) has been the principal source of regulation regarding this matter.[65] Dutch courts assess this immunity either prior to or upon establishing that an unlawful act under tort law standards exists. Case law shows that claims against online platforms, frequently initiated by claim vehicles,[66] can affect the content of the rules online platforms

---

[63] CJEU 4 July 2023, C-252/21 *Meta Platforms and Others,* ECLI:EU:2022:704.

[64] District Court Amsterdam 25 October 2023, C/13/702849/HA ZA 21-526, ECLI:NL:RBAMS:2023:6694, JOR 2023/294, annotated by TMC Arons.

[65] Directive 2000/31/EC of the European Parliament and of the Council of 8 June 2000 on certain legal aspects of information society services, in particular electronic commerce, in the Internal Market ('Directive on electronic commerce') [2000] OJ L178/1 (ECD).

[66] This is made possible through the Directive on representative actions. See Annex I, point (6), Directive (EU) 2020/1828 of the European Parliament and of the Council of 25 November 2020 on representative actions for the protection of the collective interests of consumers and repealing Directive 2009/22/EC [2020] OJ L409/1.

employ to design and deliver their services.[67] As most platforms discussed here qualify as 'hosts', the liability exemption set out in art 14 ECD is most important for our discussion. Art 6 of the Digital Services Act (DSA) has replaced art 14 ECD.[68] However, the conditions governing the liability exemption for hosts have remained essentially the same.[69] In line with both ECD, art 14 and DSA, art 6, DCC, art 6:196c(4) stipulates that hosts are not liable for information that is stored at the request of a recipient of the service under a number of conditions.

1. The Classification of Online Platforms: 'Active' and 'Passive' Hosts

In order for online platforms to successfully invoke DCC, art 6:196c(4), the online platform first and foremost must qualify as a host. A host is defined as a person providing a service of the information society, as set out in DCC, art 3:15d(3),[70] that consists of the storage of information provided by a recipient of the service.[71] The CJEU has consistently ruled that online platforms can benefit from this exemption only when they do not play an active role with regard to the stored information.[72] This means that when the operator of an online marketplace stores offers of products for sale on its server, sets the terms of its service, is remunerated for that service, and provides general information to its customers, such actions cannot have the effect of preclud-

---

[67] For an example in which a hosting provider implemented a new, faster notice and takedown procedure during the course of proceedings initiated against the provider, see: Dutch Supreme Court 27 January 2023, 17/01135 *Stichting Brein/NSE*, ECLI:NL:HR:2023:94, paras 2.2 and 3.6.3. For an example in which a hosting provider changed their terms and conditions as a result of a liability claim, see: District Court Amsterdam 16 February 2022, C/13/680916/HA ZA 20-284 *Stichting Stop Online Shaming/X*, ECLI:NL:RBAMS:2022:557, para 3.7.

[68] Art 89(1) and (2) Regulation (EU) 2022/2065 of the European Parliament and of the Council of 19 October 2022 on a Single Market for Digital Services and amending Directive 2000/31/EC (Digital Services Act) [2022] OJ L277/1 (DSA).

[69] A minor adjustment concerns DSA, art 6(3), which adds that the liability exemption does not apply under certain conditions where an online platform is intermediating between consumers and traders. For further discussion of this provision and its implications for Dutch law, see Martien Schaub, 'Oude, nieuwe en toekomstige verplichtingen voor online marktplaatsen' (2022) 6 TvC 254. For the potential relevance of the DSA framework in relation to two cases involving notice and takedown procedures, see notes 86-87.

[70] The definition of information society services follows from ECD, art 2(a), referring to art 1(2) of Directive 98/34/EC as amended by Directive 98/48/EC, which was repealed by art 1(1), point (b), Directive 2015/1535.

[71] The definition of a host follows from ECD, art 14(1).

[72] CJEU 23 March 2010, C-236/08 to C-238/08 *Google France and Google*, ECLI:EU:C:2010:159, paras 114 and 120; CJEU 12 July 2011, C-324/09 *L'Oréal/eBay*, ECLI:EU:C:2011:474, para 113; CJEU 22 June 2021, C-682/18 and C-683/18 *Youtube/Cyando*, ECLI:EU:C:2021:503, para 106. See also ECD, recital 42.

ing its eligibility for the liability exemptions as provided for by the ECD.[73] In line with the CJEU, the Court of Appeal Leeuwarden and the District Court of The Hague held that intermediaries providing information about the formatting of advertisements – through general guidelines – does not mean they can be precluded from the exemption on the ground that they play an active role.[74] Moreover, in *Google France and Google*, the implementation of technological measures aimed at detecting infringing content did not de facto lead to the conclusion that the online platform was playing an active role and had knowledge of infringing content.[75]

Therefore, additional circumstances are required to establish that an online platform is playing an active role with regard to activities on its platform. What these additional circumstances are has yet to be specified. No general standards in Dutch case law exist with regards to the question of whether an online platform qualifies as an active or passive host. For instance, the District Court of The Hague concluded that the use of preventive screenings by Facebook when placing ads does not result in Facebook playing an active role.[76] However, concerning the very same role of Facebook as a regulator of digital advertising space, the District Court of Amsterdam considered the platform as performing an active role whenever it facilitates ads, generates revenue from that practice, and retains control over the ads through its advertising policy.[77] What is apparent is that different courts take a different stance on the role of an online platform, considering the specifics of the case.

2. *Absence of 'Knowledge' as a Condition for Exemption*

The host is not liable (a) when it does not know of the unlawful activities or information or (b) in the context of a damages claim, when it cannot be reasonably expected to have known of the illegal activities or information. When it has such knowledge or when it should have had such knowledge, the online

[73] *L'Oréal* (n 72) para 115.

[74] Court of Appeal Leeuwarden 22 May 2012, 107.001.948/01 *Stokke/Marktplaats*, ECLI:NL:GHLEE:2012:BW6296, paras 5.4–5.5; District Court The Hague 17 March 2021, C/09/579872/HA ZA 19-954 *Tommy Hilfiger/Facebook*, ECLI:NL:RBDHA:2021:2422, paras 4.24.7 and 4.24.9; District Court The Hague 30 August 2023, C/09/622304/HA ZA 21-1105 *Audi/Fruugo*, ECLI:NL:RBDHA:2023:12679, para 4.27.

[75] *Google France and Google* (n 72) para 109. For Dutch case law where this is taken into consideration, see: *Audi* (n 74) para 4.10; Court of Appeal 26 March 2024, 200.316.164/01 *X/Google*, ECLI:NL:GHAMS:2024:767, para 4.4.5.

[76] In drawing this conclusion, the Court also refers to *Stokke/Marktplaats* (n 74). *Tommy Hilfiger* (n 74) para 4.24.7.

[77] The District Court of Amsterdam concluded that the policy being carried out through a largely automated process does not lead to Facebook having a passive role. District Court Amsterdam 11 November 2019, C/13/665397/KG ZA 19-455 MDvH/MB *X/Facebook*, ECLI:NL:RBAMS:2019:8415, paras 4.14–4.15.

platform must promptly remove the unlawful information or disable access to it.[78] Therefore, while online platforms may qualify as hosts, the mere qualification as a host alone does not exempt them from liability. Even when qualification as a host follows, the platform is still obligated to remove unlawful information when knowledge of it arises.[79]

The element of 'knowledge' can be satisfied in two ways. Firstly, knowledge can exist when the intermediary undertakes voluntary investigations and, by doing so, uncovers illegal activities or illegal information.[80] Secondly, knowledge can exist if the intermediary receives a notification that is sufficiently precise and adequately substantiated.[81] A mere notification requesting removal does not suffice. The accuracy of the notification should not be in question; this is established if the notification appears to originate from a court or if the reported activities or information are manifestly unlawful.[82] As affirmed by Dutch case law,[83] and in line with case law of the CJEU, the knowledge criterion is not satisfied by the hosting provider being – in a general sense – aware of illegal activities or illegal information on its platform.[84] Additionally, it should be noted that the knowledge the online platform has or should have regarding the illegality of information as a result of a notification or its own investigations does not in itself lead to the conclusion that it performed an active role.[85]

Case law shows that the element of 'knowledge' is not a matter of great contention in the Netherlands. In short, knowledge (or 'awareness') of manifestly unlawful activities or information obliges the intermediary to act expeditiously to remove or disable access to the information. Neither the ECD nor the CJEU specify how fast online platforms must respond in order to act expeditiously. The Court of Appeal of Amsterdam considered, in general, that the time span between notification and removal must be reasonable for the market in question.[86] Dutch courts generally take the position that whenever an intermediary has an effective notice and takedown procedure, this will, in principle,

[78] Knowledge can reasonably be assumed to have existed when a diligent economic operator should have identified the illegality in question. *L'Oréal* (n 72) para 120.

[79] See eg: District Court of Amsterdam 23 December 2009, 444877 – KG ZA 09-2617, ECLI:NL:RBAMS:2009:BK7383.

[80] *L'Oréal* (n 72) para 122.

[81] *L'Oréal* (n 72) para 122; *Youtube/Cyando* (n 72) para 115.

[82] Explanatory memorandum on DCC, art 6:196c, TK (House of Representatives) 2001/02, 28197, no 3, 49. See eg: District Court Zeeland-West-Brabant 4 February 2020, C/02/379134/KG ZA 20-626 *Griebling/Google Ireland*, ECLI:NL:RBZWB:2020:6923.

[83] See eg: *X/Google* (n 75); *Stichting Brein/NSE* (n 67) para 3.5.4.

[84] *Youtube/Cyando* (n 72) para 111.

[85] ECD, recital 40. See also: *Stokke/Marktplaats* (n 74) para 5.5.

[86] Court of Appeal of Amsterdam 19 August 2014, 200.097.924-01 *News-Service Europe/Stichting Brein*, ECLI:NL:GHAMS:2014:3435, para 3.7.1.

satisfy the requirement of expeditious corrective action.[87] What effectiveness consists of, however, is not entirely clear. Here, the Dutch courts consider the policies implemented by online platforms. For instance, the District Court of The Hague made clear that the knowledge criterion could be satisfied even where an online platform made no mention of a notice and takedown procedure on its website.[88] Another example of this relates to the judgment of the Court of Appeal of Amsterdam concerning fraudulent bitcoin advertisements. The fact that fraudulent bitcoin advertisements were deleted shortly after being reported also meant that identical or highly similar advertisements posted at a later point in time should have been identified as well. Google should have designed its content moderation systems in such a way that this was achieved. As this was not done, and as it had not been established by Google that it was unreasonable to expect it to have done so – in its capacity as a diligent economic operator – the exemption claim failed.[89] Thus, the liability exemptions, the criteria therein, and the interpretation of Dutch courts influence the way hosting providers design and give effect to their policies.

3. *Court Injunctions*

DCC, art 6:196c(5) states that the applicability of the liability exemption does not prevent courts from imposing a prohibitive or affirmative injunction on online platforms.[90] The petitions that platform participants or third parties submit to the court can broadly be sorted into three categories: (1) injunctions to provide the personal information of a participant allegedly engaging in illegal activities or sharing illegal information; (2) injunctions to remove or to disable access to illegal information and; (3) injunctions to adopt measures to

---

[87] *News-Service Europe* (n 86) para 3.4.10. See additionally: Court of Appeal 's-Hertogenbosch 5 October 2015, HD 200.155.105_01 *X/Google*, ECLI:NL:GHSHE:2015:3904, para 3.12. While there is no harmonized notice and takedown mechanism in the Netherlands, it should be noted there is a Notice-And-Takedown Code of Conduct (2018). However, case law does not clarify whether the condition under art 6:196c(4), section b, is met if the platform complies with the Code of Conduct. Under DSA, recital 104, more clearance is given on this, as it is set out that the mere fact of participating in and implementing a code of conduct should not in itself create a presumption of compliance with the regulation.

[88] *Audi* (n 74) para 4.32. Thus, the effectiveness of notice and takedown policies is not tied to the clearance online platforms provide on their internal procedures. It should be noted that a question that arises is whether this case would have been assessed the same had DSA, art 16 been applicable at time of the proceedings, as this provision requires the putting in place of easy to access and user-friendly notice and action mechanisms.

[89] *X/Google* (n 75) para 4.4.11.

[90] Under the ECD this follows from art 14(3) and recital 45. The Court of Justice confirms this by stating that the liability exemptions do not concern the conditions under which judicial remedies for civil liability may be exercised against a service provider. CJEU 11 September 2014, C-291/13 *Papasavvas v O Fileleftheros Dimosia Etairia Ltd.*, ECLI:EU:C:2014:2209, para 53.

prevent illegal activities or the sharing of illegal information in the future. According to established EU case law, these petitions oftentimes require the striking of a fair balance between various rights and interests involved.[91] The adopted measures taken by the courts must align with the principles of proportionality and subsidiarity.[92] The measures are governed by national law, but the EU law principles of equivalence and effectiveness must be taken into account.[93]

While the applicability of the liability exemption for a host does not, in principle, prevent courts from imposing injunctions on online platforms, Dutch case law shows that the applicability of art 6:196c(4) DCC affects the nature of the injunction imposed by courts. The case of *Tommy Hilfiger/Facebook* illustrates this point.[94] This case, which concerns fake advertisements posted on Facebook and Instagram for Tommy Hilfiger clothing, was tried before the Amsterdam and The Hague District Courts. In interim proceedings, the court in Amsterdam concluded that Facebook, due to its active role, could be compelled to implement filters in order to prevent the systematic infringement of intellectual property rights.[95] Conversely, the court in The Hague held that Facebook was playing a passive role and thus a less far-reaching filter was ordered.[96] Irrespective of the classification as a

---

[91] Whether freedom of speech, privacy, intellectual property rights, or protection of reputation. See in this regard: CJEU 29 January 2008, C-275/06 *Promusicae*, ECLI:EU:C:2008:54, paras 65–68.

[92] This is mentioned regarding the measure of disabling access to information. Explanatory memorandum on Article 6:196c DCC, TK (House of Representatives) 2001/02, 28197, no 3, 65. The fairness and proportionality of the measures adopted are also mentioned in *L'Oréal/eBay*, but here it is stated that these objectives arise from Directive 2004/48/EC of the European Parliament and of the Council of 29 April 2004 on the enforcement of intellectual property rights [2004] OJ L 157/45. See: *L'Oréal* (n 72) para 139. In later case law the requirements of proportionality and subsidiarity are again related to measures regarding intellectual property rights. CJEU 24 November 2011, C-70/10 *Scarlet Extended,* ECLI:EU:C:2011:771, paras 36–40; CJEU 16 February 2012, C-360/10 *SABAM/Netlog,* ECLI:EU:C:2012:85. In Dutch case law these principles are taken into account in the assessment of petitions submitted by platform participants or third parties. See for example: District Court Amsterdam 21 February 2023, C/13/726811/KG ZA 22-1049, ECLI:NL:RBAMS:2023:954, para 4.7; District Court The Hague 31 July 2023, C-09-648247-KG ZA 23-441 *X/Meta*, ECLI:NL:RBDHA:2023:11254, para 5.10.

[93] *Papasavvas* (n 90) para 53.

[94] Regarding preventive measures for infringing information, the European Court of Justice concludes that these may be imposed regardless of the role the online platform plays concerning the information that is stored. *L'Oréal* (n 72) paras 122 and 134.

[95] District Court Amsterdam 21 December 2018, C/13/656859 *Tommy Hilfiger/Facebook*, ECLI:NL:RBAMS:2018:9362, para 4.10.

[96] *Tommy Hilfiger* (n 74).

host, the platform was ordered to provide the personal information of the alleged infringer in both cases.[97]

Furthermore, when the intermediary platform is deemed to have knowledge of the transmission/sharing of manifestly unlawful information, it acts wrongfully (*onrechtmatige daad,* DCC, art 6:162) if it only provides the personal information of the person sharing the information (the 'infringer').[98] The platform may also act wrongfully if it refuses to provide the personal information of the infringer, even when the information at issue is not manifestly unlawful.[99] Regarding a court order to remove or disable access to information, the information must be illegal. Prior knowledge of the illegal information is not required.[100] Additionally, the sufficiently concrete threat of future illegal activities can justify the imposition of a court injunction.[101] The injunction must not, however, unreasonably obstruct the online platform from operating its business. For instance, a filter must be suitable for automated monitoring.[102] According to ECD, art 15, Member States cannot oblige providers to monitor information which they transmit or store, nor can they impose a general obligation to actively seek facts or circumstances indicating illegal activity. While this article has not been transposed into the Dutch legal order,[103] the prohibition has been recognized in case law.[104]

[97] This follows from the conditions set out in *Lycos/Pessers* relating to the circumstances under which a hosting provider has the duty to provide personal information of a participant allegedly engaging in illegal activities or sharing illegal information. According to established case law of the CJEU (*Promusicae* (n 91)), fundamental rights are balanced against one another. Dutch Supreme Court 25 November 2005, C04/234HR *Lycos/Pessers*, ECLI:NL:HR:2005:AU4019.

[98] District Court 's-Gravenhage 5 January 2007, 276747/KG ZA 06-1417 *BREIN/KPN*, ECLI:NL:RBSGR:2007:AZ5678, para 4.15.

[99] *Lycos* (n 97) paras 5.2.2 and 5.3.4.

[100] This differs from DCC, art 6:196c(4). See for example: District Court Oost-Brabant 2 May 2014, C-01-272969 – KG ZA 13-881 *X/Google*, ECLI:NL:RBOBR:2014:5774.

[101] For a case where a filter was imposed, see: *Tommy Hilfiger* (n 95) para 4.10.

[102] *Tommy Hilfiger* (n 74) para 4.45.

[103] The reason for this being that such a monitoring obligation for service providers does not exist within the Dutch legal order. Explanatory memorandum on Article 6:196c DCC, TK (House of Representatives) 2001/02, 28197, no 3, 27.

[104] See for example: *Tommy Hilfiger* (n 74); *News-Service Europe* (n 86); Dutch Supreme Court 7 June 2019, 17/01135 *NSE/BREIN*, ECLI:NL:HR:2019:849. It should be noted that online platforms that do not qualify as a host, due to their active role with regard to the information stored, are not able to derive any rights from ECD, art 15. District Court Utrecht 22 October 2019, 250077/HA ZA 08-1124, ECLI:NL:RBUTR:2009:BJ6008, para 4.45.

X. Conclusion

This Chapter has set out the scope for online platforms to establish and enforce their own rules, policies, and mechanisms vis-à-vis platform participants and third parties under Dutch private law. That scope is wide, yet it is not unlimited. The principles of party autonomy and freedom of contract grant a platform the power to adopt its own rules and procedures and to enforce these in the contractual relationships it entertains with its participants as well as in the relationships amongst the participants. However, this contractual basis for the private constitution of platforms is subject to regulation under a variety of principles and (mandatory) rules in contract law. As our assessment demonstrates, judicial validity assessments of platform rules based on good faith provide an important instrument through which individual participants can seek protection against platform measures, including the removal of content and the banning of participants.

Further checks against the contractual powers that online platforms may exercise against their participants are offered by specific contracts, of which intermediary contracts/contracts of brokerage are most important for intermediary platforms. Collective actions brought by consumers and other public-interest organizations against platforms to assess the validity of internal rules have lately become prominent avenues of litigation. Here, EU laws on data protection, minor protection, and consumer protection serve as a baseline for litigation. Whenever a breach of these laws is established, follow-up questions regarding private law remedies (damages, termination) and sanctions (nullity, nullification) are triggered. Finally, the exposure of online platforms to extra-contractual liability proves a source of private law regulation of these platforms. As shown by the analysis of the Dutch case law on the matter, such exposure – which is mediated by the conditions for immunity from liability under the rules of the ECD and DSA – may affect platform rules, requiring the amendment of existing rules or the adoption of new ones. Accordingly, many of the limitations that Dutch private law imposes on online platforms follow from the judicial interpretation and application of pre-existing rules of private law.

Liability of Online Marketplaces

The Portuguese Solution for the Sale of Consumer Goods

Joana Campos Carvalho[*]

I. Introduction

Online platforms can be defined as hosting services that, at the request of a recipient of the service, store and disseminate information to the public.[1] Online platforms include, among others, social networks, such as Instagram or Linkedin, massively multiplayer online games, such as World of Warcraft, and online marketplaces, which constitute the focus of this paper. Online marketplaces are a subcategory inside the greater category of online platforms and can be defined as services 'using software, including a website, part of a website or an application, operated by or on behalf of a trader which allow consumers to conclude distance contracts with other traders or consumers'.[2]

---

[*] All internet links were last accessed on 9 September 2024.

[1] Regulation (EU) 2022/2065 of the European Parliament and of the Council of 19 October 2022 on a Single Market for Digital Services and amending Directive 2000/31/EC (Digital Services Act) [2022] OJ L277/1 (DSA), art 3(i). The full definition clarifies that entities that fulfil these criteria are considered online platforms 'unless that activity is a minor and purely ancillary feature of another service or a minor functionality of the principal service and, for objective and technical reasons, cannot be used without that other service, and the integration of the feature or functionality into the other service is not a means to circumvent the applicability of this Regulation'.

[2] Directive 2005/29/EC of the European Parliament and of the Council of 11 May 2005 concerning unfair business-to-consumer commercial practices in the internal market and amending Council Directive 84/450/EEC, Directives 97/7/EC, 98/27/EC and 2002/65/EC

The business model of online marketplaces is based on a triangularity. Three contracts are concluded in order for the user to have access to the good or service: (i) the contract between the marketplace operator and the supplier; (ii) the contract between the marketplace operator and the customer; (iii) the main contract. This main contract, which is the one that allows access to the good or service, is concluded directly between the supplier and the customer (usually a sales contract, provision of services, lease, etc). Bearing in mind that the principle of relativity of contracts is a fundamental principle of private law and that the marketplace operator is not a party to the main contract, the straightforward conclusion would be that the marketplace operator is never liable for problems that occur which relate to main contract. However, closer observation shows that these entities usually occupy a very relevant role in the transaction, thus having a significant impact on customer trust, and that the focus cannot be solely on the main contract and its parties but must rather take in the whole triangle and the different dynamics it entails.

This issue has been significantly debated in Europe. The work of the ELI Model Rules on Online Platforms research group, especially art 20, is a good example of this discussion and the attempts to achieve balanced solutions. It sets forth the joint liability of supplier and platform operator in cases of predominant influence, thus acknowledging the need to address and regulate the role of the platform operator in the contractual dynamic.[3]

In Portugal, the topic of the contractual liability of online marketplaces was addressed in the consumer sales law adopted in 2021 (Decree-Law 84/2021), which transposes Directives 2019/770 and 2019/771.[4] Art 44 of Decree-Law 84/2021 will be the main focus of the paper as it entails an attempt at regulating the matter of contractual liability, departing from a purely bilateral approach and focusing instead on the entire triangular dynamic.

This approach, namely the focus on the entire network instead of on single contracts, recognizes online platforms as private regulators of social and economic issues, acknowledging that they control and thus are able to regulate the communities of their users.

---

of the European Parliament and of the Council and Regulation (EC) 2006/2004 of the European Parliament and of the Council ('Unfair Commercial Practices Directive') [2005] OJ L149/22 (UCPD), as amended by Directive (EU) 2019/2161, art 2(n).

[3] European Law Institute, *Model Rules on Online Platforms*, 2019, available at <https://www.europeanlawinstitute.eu/projects-publications/completed-projects/online-platforms/>.

[4] Directive (EU) 2019/770 of the European Parliament and of the Council of 20 May 2019 on certain aspects concerning contracts for the supply of digital content and digital services [2019] OJ L136/1; Directive (EU) 2019/771 of the European Parliament and of the Council of 20 May 2019 on certain aspects concerning contracts for the sale of goods, amending Regulation (EU) 2017/2394 and Directive 2009/22/EC, and repealing Directive 1999/44/EC [2019] OJ L136/28

By approving a rule that makes online marketplaces liable for the conformity of goods that are supplied by a user of the marketplace, Portugal is limiting the possibility of platforms to set the terms of their relationship with users, in that such a rule limits their possibility to establish contractual terms that exempt them from this type of liability.[5]

However, in addition to that, this rule also encourages platforms to further self-regulate. By making the platform responsible for the conformity (and therefore the quality) of the goods and services supplied, the State is incentivizing platforms to regulate the market, because achieving high standards of quality in the marketplace lowers their risk of being held liable and thus of incurring financial losses.

We will firstly explore the influence of EU law on the Portuguese solution. Then we will lay out the Portuguese regime and the requirements for the liability of the marketplace operator, indicating the parallels with the ELI Model Rules. Finally, we present some critical remarks regarding the adopted solution.

II. Liability of Online Marketplaces: The Portuguese Solution for the Sale of Goods and the Supply of Digital Content and Services

1. The Influence of EU Law

Directive (EU) 2019/770 regulates certain aspects of contracts for the supply of digital content and services. In turn, Directive (EU) 2019/771 regulates certain aspects of contracts for the sale of goods, amends Regulation (EU) 2017/2394 and Directive 2009/22/EC, and repeals Directive 1999/44/EC, which until now regulated the sale of consumer goods. These two Directives were transposed into the Portuguese legal system through Decree-Law 84/2021, of 18 October 2021, which regulates consumer rights in the sale of goods and the supply of digital content and services, revoking Decree-Law 67/2003, which previously regulated the sale of consumer goods in Portugal. These Directives do not regulate the activity of online marketplaces. However, they include two relevant recitals that were decisive during the Portuguese legislative procedure. It is interesting to note that these recitals include the

[5] These contract terms are very common. See, for instance, Booking.com's general terms: A3.-1 'When you book an accommodation, flight or attraction, Booking.com B.V. provides and is responsible for the Platform – but not the Travel Experience itself' and A4.-4 'We're not a party to the terms between you and the Service Provider. The Service Provider is solely responsible for the Travel Experience', available at <https://www.booking.com/content/terms>.

only references made in the Directives to online platforms; there are no rules relating to this topic.

Recital 23 of Directive 2019/771 reads as follows:

> 'Platform providers could be considered to be sellers under this Directive if they act for purposes relating to their own business and as the direct contractual partner of the consumer for the sale of goods. Member States should remain free to extend the application of this Directive to platform providers that do not fulfil the requirements for being considered a seller under this Directive'.

The content of recital 18 of Directive 2019/770 is identical, except for the term 'sellers' that is replaced by 'traders' and the phrase 'sale of goods' which is replaced by 'supply of digital content or a digital service'.[6]

It is possible to divide the recital and to distinguish two parts. The first part, corresponding to the first sentence, clarifies the cases in which the regime of the Directives applies to platform operators. Directive 2019/771 applies where operators are considered to be sellers and Directive 2019/770 where they are qualified as traders. The recitals further clarify that this is the case where the operators (i) act for purposes related to their own business and (ii) act as a direct contractual partner of the consumer. The first requirement does not raise many doubts, and it is verified whenever the operator pursues, with the platform, commercial and profit-making objectives. Regarding the second requirement, where the consumer is legitimately convinced that he is entering into a contract with the operator of the platform, the latter is his contractual partner even if the operator wishes to hide behind another legal construction. This recital clarifies that operators that sell or provide services on the platform alongside other suppliers are considered to be sellers or professionals regarding their own products (eg Amazon). It also clarifies that operators claiming to be mere intermediaries, but acting as direct contractual partners, such as Uber or Farfetch, are also considered sellers or professionals. The second part of the recitals grants the Member States the possibility to extend the Directive's scope of application. Member States are free to decide upon the application of the Directives' regime to operators who are not considered to be sellers or professionals.[7] However, this freedom is not absolute. The criteria defined by national laws for considering the regime of the Directive applicable to platform operators have to respect European law, such as

---

[6] On these recitals, Esther Arroyo Amayuelas, 'El derecho de las plataformas en la Unión Europea' in Esther Arroyo Amayuelas and others, *Servicios en plataforma Estrategias regulatorias* (Marcial Pons 2021) 51.

[7] Karin Sein and Gerald Spindler, 'The new directive on contracts for the supply of digital content and digital services – Scope of application and trader's obligation to supply – Part 1' (2019) 15(3) ERCL 257, 261.

arts 6 and 8 of the Digital Services Act[8] (corresponding to the still in force arts 14 and 15 of the E-Commerce Directive[9]), and, we would add, also the principles of national law. It was based on the second part of the recitals that Portuguese legislators included a rule on the platform operators' liability in Decree-Law 84/2021.

2. *Decree-Law 84/2021*

Decree-Law 84/2021 of 18 October 2021 (DL 84/2021) regulates consumer rights in the sale of goods and the supply of digital content and services, transposing Directives (EU) 2019/771 and (EU) 2019/770. The act applies only to consumer relations, ie relations between a trader and a consumer.[10] Furthermore, it applies only to contracts of sale and other contracts for the supply of tangible things, such as works and leases, and also to contracts for the supply of digital content and services (art 3).[11] Therefore, only certain online marketplaces will be covered by this regime. For example, contracts concluded on Amazon or Vinted are covered. The case of Airbnb is debatable. The contract concluded between the guest and the host is a mixed contract that has lease elements. Thus, this regime may apply when an issue related to that part of the contract is at stake.

DL 84/2021 includes a rule that provides for the joint and several liability of the operator of the online market (art 44).[12] This is an innovative solution and, to date, unique in the European context.[13]

---

[8] Regulation (EU) 2022/2065 of the European Parliament and of the Council of 19 October 2022 on a Single Market for Digital Services and amending Directive 2000/31/EC (Digital Services Act) [2022] OJ L277/1 (DSA).

[9] Directive 2000/31/EC of the European Parliament and of the Council of 8 June 2000 on certain legal aspects of information society services, in particular electronic commerce, in the Internal Market ('Directive on electronic commerce') [2000] OJ L178/1.

[10] On the concept of consumer, Geraint Howells, Christian Twigg-Flesner and Thomas Wilhelmsson, *Rethinking EU Consumer Law* (Routledge 2018) 25.

[11] On the decree's scope of application, Jorge Morais Carvalho, 'Decreto-Lei n.º 84/2021, de 18 de outubro – Apresentação geral', *Diretivas 2019/770 e 2019/771 e Decreto-Lei nº 84/2021* (Almedina 2022) 51; David Falcão, 'Análise à nova lei das garantias – DL 84/2021, de 18 de outubro' (2021) III, IV Revista da Ordem dos Advogados 493, 496; Jorge Morais Carvalho, *Compra e venda e fornecimento de conteúdos e serviços digitais: Anotação ao Decreto-Lei n.º 84/2021, de 18 de outubro* (Almedina 2021) 24; Sandra Passinhas, 'O novo regime da compra e venda de bens de consumo – exegese do novo regime legal' [2021] Revista de direito comercial 1463, 1468.

[12] Mafalda Miranda Barbosa, 'Responsabilidade civil das plataformas digitais' (2022) 4 Revista de direito da responsabilidade 791, 795, argues that this solution seems to be in line with the *Wathelet* judgment (CJEU 9 November 2016, C-149/15, ECLI:EU:C:2016:840). It seems to us that this article and the judgment deal with different issues. The Wathelet judgment aims to solve a situation where the intermediary behaves as a party – the court having ruled that there is liability because the customer has become convinced

a) Requirements for the liability of the online marketplace's operator

Art 44(1) DL 84/2021 states that

> 'the online marketplace provider who, acting for purposes related to its activity, is the contractual partner of the supplier [...] is jointly and severally liable, vis-à-vis the consumer, for the lack of conformity under the terms of the present decree-law.'

The first requirement is that the operator acts for purposes related to its activity, which is the case whenever its activity concerns the operation or use of the platform. The second requirement for liability is that the platform operator is a contractual partner of the supplier. It is difficult to understand the purpose of using this expression in the law. A contractual partner of the supplier is someone who has entered into a contract with the supplier. When analyzing the triangular structure of contracts concluded through online marketplaces, a contract is always concluded between the supplier and the platform operator. To that extent, the operator is always a contractual partner of the supplier.

---

that the intermediary is a party. This matter is referred to in the first part of recital 23 of Directive 2019/771 and recital 18 of Directive 2019/770. The solution in art 44 concerns situations where the customer knows that his counterparty is not the marketplace operator. Liability is based on the circumstance that the operator, although not being a party and not presenting itself as such, exercises control over the contract.

[13] In Brazil, for instance, the question arises differently, since the concept of supplier in the Consumer Protection Code (art 3) is interpreted quite broadly, including, in addition to the producer, any person who, exercising a professional activity, participates in the supply chain until the good or service reaches the end recipient. Therefore, as a rule, the online marketplace is also qualified as supplier, and there are several case law decisions that confirm this understanding. All suppliers (seller, producer, online marketplace, etc.) are jointly and severally liable for defects in the product or service (art 18), which means that in Brazil the marketplace may be liable according to the general terms of the Consumer Protection Code (Claudia Lima Marques, *Contratos no Código de Defesa do Consumidor* (9th edn, Revista dos Tribunais 2019) RB-2.2; Bruno Miragem, *Curso de direito do consumidor* (Revista dos Tribunais 2020) RB-1.58; Alvimar Virgílio de Almeida, *Defesa do consumidor na economia compartilhada: a questão da responsabilidade civil* (Pontifícia Universidade Católica de São Paulo 2019) 116; Claudia Lima Marques, 'A nova noção de fornecedor no consumo compartilhado: Um estudo sobre as correlações do pluralismo contratual e o acesso ao consumo' (2017) 111 Revista de Direito do Consumidor 247, 256; 261; Bruno Miragem, 'Novo paradigma tecnológico, mercado de consumo digital e o direito do consumidor' (2019) 125 Revista de Direito do Consumidor 17, 26, admits that this conclusion may depend on 'the way in which the organiser of the platform acts'. Fernanda Manuela Goebel and Analice Achaefer de Moura, 'A possibilidade de responsabilização da plataforma de economia compartilhamento Airbnb' (2022) 13(1) Revista de Direito Faculdade Dom Alberto 18, 30.; Guilherme Mucelin, *Conexão online e hiperconfiança* (Revista dos Tribunais 2020) RB-2.1; Davi Pinheiro de Morais, *O marketplace: análise da relação de consumo em prol do fornecedor e a responsabilidade civil das intermediadoras de produtos e serviços* (Faculdade Baiana de Direito) 44–46.

The purpose of the law is not, however, to hold online marketplace operators liable in all cases. This is made clear in art 44(2), which clarifies that the operator of the online marketplace is considered to be the contractual partner of the trader only whenever it exercises a predominant influence on the conclusion of the contract. From the reading of both rules, it appears that the law refers to a contractual partner not in a technical/legal sense, but rather in the sense of partnership in business,[14] of two people who come together to achieve a certain objective – in this case to conclude a contract with the client.

It would have been preferable to avoid this expression (which adds nothing and proves to be inaccurate) by directly specifying, in para 1, that the second requirement is the exercise of predominant influence by the operator in the conclusion of the contract. The use of the expression predominant influence reflects the approach adopted in art 20 of the ELI Model Rules on Online Platforms (Model Rules).[15]

b) Comparison between the ELI Model Rules and the Portuguese solution

The legislative procedure leading to the adoption of the Portuguese regime was not very transparent.[16] No preparatory works were made publicly available, which makes it difficult to determine the reasoning behind art 44 DL 84/2021. Nevertheless, the terminology used, especially the reference to predominant influence, makes it clear that the Portuguese law finds its inspiration in the Model Rules. Despite that, the Portuguese legislators have also taken some decisions that distance the Portuguese solution from the Model Rules.

---

[14] Barbosa (n 12) 797, speaks of the operator as a 'business partner of the party providing the good or service'.

[15] European Law Institute (n 3). Christoph Busch, 'Europäische Modellregeln für Online-Vermittlungsplattformen' in Peter Rott and Klaus Tonner (eds.), *Online-Vermittlungsplattformen in der Rechtspraxis* (Nomos Praxis 2018). Critical of the solution of art 20, Fabian Vilgertshofer, *Online-Plattformen und vertragliche Haftung* (CH Beck 2019) 69, as he believes that its adoption, particularly in German law, would imply a breach in the system, thus resulting in a deviation from (i) the rules of interpretation of legal statements, in that it is clear that the operator is not a party, and (ii) the principle of relativity of contracts. Also Andreas Engert, 'Digitale Plattformen' (2018) 218 AcP 304, 316, believes that the solution of the Model Rules is not appropriate as it calls into question the principle of private autonomy without justification. It is up to online marketplaces to choose to the extent to which they want to be liable, with the knowledge that their business model relies heavily on the trust of users and that they therefore cannot, strategically speaking, totally remove themselves from problems. However, that should be their choice.

[16] Jorge Morais Carvalho, 'Portugal' in Alberto De Franceschi and Reiner Schulze (eds), *Harmonizing Digital Contract Law – The Impact of EU Directives 2019/770 and 2019/771 and the Regulation of Online Platforms* (Nomos 2023) 527, criticizes the fact that 'the entire process took place in the secrecy of the offices, without the necessary public discussion of the solutions enshrined in the legal regime'.

Firstly, the liability of art 20 of the Model Rules stems from trust on the consumer side.[17] Liability exists when the client can reasonably rely on a certain scenario, ie when the platform operator's actions lead him to believe in a certain design of reality.[18] The logic of the solution is the following: if I made someone (reasonably) believe that they would have certain rights by the way I behaved, then I must be liable for it. If the operator creates the trust in the customer that he forms a unity with the supplier, that both are closely linked, then he must answer as if that unity really existed. Under Portuguese law, the trust element is missing: there is liability when there is predominant influence, and it is not necessary to know whether the counterparty trusted in the existence of that predominant influence. The intention is not to match the consequences with what the reality appeared to be; rather, the objective is that the platform operator be liable when it effectively exercises control.[19]

Secondly, the Portuguese law refers to a predominant influence over the contract and not over the supplier. In practice, the result will be the same, since the criteria in para 2 for determining the existence of predominant influence over the contract are similar to those in the Model Rules for determining the existence of predominant influence over the supplier. However, in terms of the logic of the solution and its theoretical underpinning, the regimes are distinct. The predominant influence on the supplier encapsulates the idea that there is a factual approximation to a situation of a single legal person or a close collaborative relationship that motivates the liability of the operator.[20] Just as a legal person is liable for the acts of its organs or employees, the platform operator is liable when the way it behaves towards suppliers resembles a hierarchical relationship within a single legal entity. The predominant influence over the contract, on the other hand, referred to by Portuguese law does not refer to a

[17] Vilgertshofer (n 15) 68; Research Group on the Law of Digital Services, 'Discussion Draft of a Directive on Online Intermediary Platforms' (2016) 5(4) EuCML 164, 165.

[18] Klaus Tonner, 'Verbraucherschutz in der Plattform-Ökonomie' (2017) 32(5) VuR 161, 162.

[19] Nataliia Filatova-Bilous, 'Once again platform liability: on the edge of the 'Uber' and 'Airbnb' cases' (2021) 10(2) Internet Policy Review – Journal on Internet Regulation 1, 12, refers to an objective approach (although she does not specifically speak about Portuguese law), which is opposed to the subjective approach followed, for example, in the ELI Model Rules.

[20] Juliette Sénéchal, 'L'opérateur de plateforme en ligne, régulateur économique par fourniture de prestations de services interpersonnelles – Un phénomène complexe à saisir selon trois approches de droit économique transversales et complémentaires' in Juliette Sénéchal and Sophie Stalla-Bourdillon (eds), *Rôle et responsabilité des opérateurs de plateforme en ligne: aproche(s) transversale(s) ou aproches sectorielles?* (IRJS Éditions 2018) 8, points out that the concept of predominant influence enables online marketplace providers to move from being mere intermediaries to being responsible for the supplier's compliance with its obligations.

factual unit – a team – on the supplier's side, but to a situation in which someone interferes in the contract concluded between two other people.

Thirdly, both solutions rely on the concept of predominant influence.[21] However, in the Model Rules the concept of predominant influence appears as a type concept and under Portuguese Law it is constructed as a classificatory concept.[22] In the Model Rules there is a list of criteria to help assess the existence of predominant influence, but this list is merely exemplary. The analysis is always a general one: the various characteristics that can be observed (ultimately by a court) lead to the conclusion that there is or that there isn't control over the supplier. In some cases, more characteristics are present, in others less, but with greater intensity. The conclusion is always the result of that global analysis. art 20-2 Model rules includes a set of criteria that can be taken into account when assessing the existence of predominant influence. However, those criteria are only indicative and do not exclude other criteria that the enforcer may consider relevant in the specific case. The assessment is up to the enforcer of the standard, who has to look at reality as a whole to conclude whether, in that particular case, the client could rely on the existence of a predominant influence. Portuguese law, by using the adverb 'namely',[23] points to a completely different type of analysis. It is enough that one of the listed characteristics is verified for there to be a predominant influence. This is a classificatory concept and not a type concept. There is no fluidity in the analysis, but a rigidity that we feel is not in line with the diverse and complex nature of platforms.

[21] Felix Maultzsch, 'Contractual liability of online platform operators: European proposals and established principles' (2018) 14, 3 ERCL 209, 227, expresses his opposition to this liability solution, arguing that making a person liable for the obligations of another merely because he exercises a predominant influence over him is contrary to the logic of contract law.

[22] On type and classificatory concepts, Karl Larenz, *Methodenlehre der Rechtswissenschaft* (Springer 1991) 307. Both serve to describe and identify a given reality. However, the classificatory concept uses the enunciation of a set of characteristics or qualities that must be present in the object. There are a certain number of elements in the classificatory concept and they are all necessary. If one of these characteristics or qualities is missing, the object must be considered excluded from the concept. The type concept, on the other hand, does not need to be rigid or exhaustive. It is possible for a finished object not to have all the qualities that make up the type concept and still be included in it. Marie Jull Sørensen, 'Intermediary platforms – The contractual legal framework' (2018) 1 NJCL 63, 90; Maultzsch (n 11) 222. Busch (n 15) 161, speaks of a 'mobile system', which allows for adjustment to the specific case.

[23] 'For the purposes of [art 44(1)], the online marketplace provider is a contractual partner of the professional whenever it exercises a predominant influence over the conclusion of the contract, which will occur *namely* in the following situations [...]' (art 44(2) DL 84/2021, emphasis added).

Art 44(3) adds that

'Without prejudice to the preceding provisions, any facts that lead the consumer to rely on the online marketplace provider having a predominant influence over the professional providing the good, digital content or digital service may be considered for the purpose of determining the existence of a predominant influence over the conclusion of the contract'.

This provision allows for facts other than those identified in para 2 to be considered in concluding that predominant influence exists. It removes some of the rigidity from the analysis since it gives the enforcer freedom to conclude that predominant influence exists in other cases not foreseen in the law. However, the rigidity remains in the opposite direction: whenever one of the law's criteria is met there is predominant influence, with no room for consideration of the specific case. Furthermore, the rule contained in art 44(3) comes close to the solution of the model law in the two points where art 44(2) departs from it. On the one hand, it is a liability based on trust – on a performance that led the consumer to believe in a certain scenario. On the other hand, it is determined that there is predominant influence over the contract when there is predominant influence over the supplier.

In short, the Portuguese solution is constructed as follows: there is liability of the operator of the online market for breach of the main contract in two situations. On the one hand, there is liability when the market operator has predominant influence over the contract. This happens in the five situations provided for in the sub paras of art 44(2) DL 84/2021. The rule is constructed on the basis of a classificatory concept, whereby the enforcer of the law is limited to verifying whether any of the sub paras is fulfilled. It is sufficient if one of the subparas is fulfilled for there to be predominant influence and, therefore, liability of the operator. The enforcer of the law is not able to assess the concrete case as a whole. On the other hand, there is liability when any facts occur that are likely to give rise to the consumer's confidence that the operator has a predominant influence over the professional. This rule is based on an indeterminate concept, which requires the enforcer to conduct an overall analysis in order to conclude whether, in that specific case, there is predominant influence.

c) The criteria of article 44(2)

Art 44(2) DL 84/2021 lists the situations in which predominant influence over the contract is deemed to exist.

The concept of predominant influence points to the recognition of online platforms – or in this case online marketplaces – as entities that exercise regulatory power on the market. It departs from a purely contractual approach that, based on the principle of relativity, concludes that the platform, because it is not a party to the supplier-consumer contract, is entirely removed from any problems arising from that relationship. The concept of predominant influence acknowledges the importance of self-regulation, enforced by online platforms on their users, on the design of all relationships formed on the platform.

There are four paragraphs under art 44(2), which correspond to five distinct situations.

Firstly, there is predominant influence when the contract is concluded exclusively through the means made available by the online marketplace provider (subpara a). These cases correspond to those where the platform is constructed in such a way that the contract is necessarily concluded in that digital space. For example, on Amazon the contract is concluded through the platform's software. The customer adds the products to the cart and checks out, thus accepting the contractual proposal that the supplier has issued through the website. More debatable would be the situation of platforms that provide a messaging service through which the parties can conclude the contract. There are some cases where the customers use the messaging service and others where they do not. There are situations where people exchange contacts and continue negotiations off the platform, and there are situations where people arrange to meet through the platform and only conclude the contract in person, for example because the buyer wants to see the condition of the item first. We argue that this paragraph has to be understood as being restricted to cases where the architecture obliges the contract to be concluded within the platform. It is not sufficient that the platform allows for the conclusion of the contract. It is necessary that it requires the conclusion through the means made available there. Where there is the option of using the platform to conclude the contract, an additional service is offered to users. Where the contract is necessarily concluded through the platform, there is a situation of control over the relationship that the parties establish through the platform.

Secondly, there is predominant influence when payment is made exclusively through means made available by the online marketplace provider (subpara b). This point should also be understood as meaning that it covers platforms whose architecture implies that payments take place via the platform. The existence of a payment possibility via the platform, by contrast, is not sufficient. The processing of payments through the platform is associated with a control over the financial side of the contract and the fulfilment itself. Platform operators that process payments occupy a guarantor role that gives them great power especially over suppliers. They receive the payment from customers and withhold it until the suppliers comply. This allows them to exert pressure on the supplier and leaves the supplier in a position of dependence.

Thirdly, there is predominant influence where 'the terms of the contract concluded with the consumer are essentially determined by the online marketplace provider' (subpara c). This criterion is intended to cover platforms which determine a significant part of the terms of contracts concluded between the consumer and the supplier. They usually do so by including general contract terms in their contracts with users. For example, on Airbnb, the standard terms and conditions in the contract with the host read: 'Any terms or conditions you include in any supplementary agreement with Guests must: (i) be consistent with these Terms, our Policies, and the information provided in your Advertisement' (point 5.2). And in those terms relating to the contract entered into with the guest it reads: 'The cancellation policy and all other rules, standards, policies or requirements identified in the Advertisement or during the Booking form part of your contract with the Host' (points 2.2 and 3.1).

Fourthly, the law autonomizes the determination of one of the contractual clauses – that of the price – by establishing that there is predominant influence when the price to be paid by the consumer is likely to be influenced by the platform operator (subpara c). Note that it is not necessary for the price to be determined by the platform operator; it is sufficient for it to influence that determination. It is not easy to determine when the operator influences the price. The mere fact of using a given platform will influence the price, as the supplier will probably analyze the prices charged on the platform for products similar to its own in order to set the price. Some platforms provide tools to perform this analysis. For example, Airbnb has a tool that allows hosts to 'quickly access a map that shows the average prices of places like yours'.[24] We would argue that this type of tool is not enough to conclude that the platform influences the price, since the spirit of freedom of the provider remains. There is influence on price only when there is a concerted strategy on the part of the platform, which, although it does not set the price, imposes certain criteria or makes access to certain benefits dependent on compliance with price rules. These paragraphs serve to define when there is control over the platform operator, and it is in this light that they must be interpreted.

Finally, there is predominant influence when the advertising associated with the platform is focused on the online marketplace provider rather than the professionals (subpara d). This point has to be understood as referring to the image that the platform operator communicates through its marketing. Does the platform present itself as a unit, where the customer's trust is directed exclusively to the platform operator? This is the case with Amazon, which conveys the message that on the platform the customer has access to everything and in a fast and secure way thanks to the Amazon system. Or does the platform want to present itself as an entity that groups and manages suppliers that have their own identity? This point in particular demonstrates that the nature of the analysis is rarely conducive to binary answers of yes or no. As far as marketing is concerned, there is a continuum in which the various platforms are positioned between the axes of 'totally platform-focused' and 'totally supplier-focused', and it is doubtful that any of them are at the extremes.

---

[24] <https://www.airbnb.co.uk/resources/hosting-homes/a/new-pricing-tool-compares-similar-listings-nearby-583>.

d) *Consequences of the existence of predominant influence over the contract*

Art 44(1) DL 84/2021 provides that the operator of the online market is jointly and severally liable to the consumer, pursuant to the decree-law. Joint and several liability is the source of joint and several obligations. As regards these obligations, the two debtors – the supplier and the market operator – are liable for full performance, pursuant to art 512 of the Portuguese Civil Code, which means that the consumer can demand compliance from either of the debtors.[25] The question may be raised as to whether this rule only determines the existence of an obligation of the market operator to indemnify the consumer, since this is the obligation that arises in the sphere of the debtor when there is civil liability. However, the rule determines that the operator is liable under the terms of DL 84/2021. This regime establishes that the non-fulfilment of the contract, specifically the non-conformity of the goods with the contract, gives rise to various distinct rights within the legal sphere of the consumer – repair, replacement, price reduction, or termination of the contract – although the consumer may not always be able to choose between them all at the outset (art 15 DL 84/2021).

The consumer appears to be able to exercise these rights against the platform operator under the same terms that would apply against the seller. However, the obligations corresponding to these rights are intended for the party to the contract who provides the goods to the consumer, so a cautious interpretation is needed. The activity of the operator of the online marketplace, although it may be very significant in the context of the conclusion of the contract, should not be confused with the activity of the supplier. The operator does not have the same products as the supplier to replace the defective good and may not have the expertise within its business structure to repair the good. For this reason, the refusal referred to in art 15-3 – 'the trader may refuse to remedy the lack of conformity of the goods if repair or replacement is impossible or would impose costs that would be disproportionate' – must be assessed taking into account these particularities.

As for the other two rights, they can only logically be enforced against the counterparty.[26] The consumer may not demand the termination of the contract from someone who is not party to the contract. He may demand payment in the amount corresponding to the price he has paid or a part of that price, but this will be by way of damages. The marketplace operator cannot return the price paid, as it does not belong to him, even if it has received it in practice.

---

[25] António Menezes Cordeiro, *Tratado de direito civil português, II, Tomo I* (Almedina 2009) 719.

[26] For example, in the context of product liability, these two rights are not available to the buyer precisely for this reason: Luís Menezes Leitão, 'O novo regime da venda de bens de consumo' (2005) II Estudos do Instituto de Direito do Consumo 37, 63.

e) *The limit of article 6 of the Digital Services Act*

The permission that is granted to Member States to hold operators of online marketplaces liable under the regime of Directives 2019/770 and 2019/771 must be understood in the overall context of European law. Specifically, the provision of Portuguese law must be read in conjunction with art 6 of the Digital Services Act (corresponding to the still in force art 14 of the E-Commerce Directive), which sets forth that where an information society service is provided that consists of the storage of information provided by a recipient of the service, Member States are to ensure that the service provider is not liable for the information stored at the request of a recipient of the service, provided that the conditions listed in the Regulation's subparagraphs are met. It follows that even if an online marketplace is covered by art 44 DL 84/2021, it will not be held liable if it falls within the scope of protection of art 6 of the Digital Services Act.

f) *Right of redress*

Art 46 DL 84/2021 provides that

> 'an online marketplace provider who, pursuant to Articles 44 and 45, becomes liable to the consumer because of misleading statements by the trader or the trader's failure to perform the contract shall have the right to be indemnified by the trader under the general terms'.[27]

It follows that the responsibility of the operator is only a means of protecting consumers, since it will be easier for consumers to obtain compensation, but the economic effects of the breach are kept on the supplier's side. The only case where the marketplace operator bears the economic burden is the case of insolvency of the supplier. In this case, the marketplace operator may not be able to recover what it has spent on resolving the consumer's problem.

In short, the solution of DL 84/2021 implies a twofold protection of the consumer: (i) it gives the consumer more choice, allowing him to decide between resorting to the supplier, to the marketplace operator, or to both and to thereby determine which of the two is capable of providing a faster or more satisfactory response; (ii) it protects him from the possible insolvency of the supplier, passing this risk on to the operator.

---

[27] On the general terms of the right of redress in Portugal, Rui Pinto Duarte, 'O direito de regresso do vendedor final na venda para consumo' (2001) II(4) Themis – Revista da Faculdade de Direito da UNL 173, 186; Paulo Mota Pinto, 'Conformidade e garantias na venda de bens de consumo: A directiva 1999/44/CE e o direito português' (2000) 2 Estudos de direito do consumidor 197, 280.

3. *Critical Remarks on the Portuguese Solution*

The business model of platforms has been recognized as beneficial to society.[28] Furthermore, online marketplaces are not all the same. Rather, it is a business model that is adopted by very different companies of very different sizes. To give a few examples, Airbnb will vary significantly form Vinted, and Amazon will differ greatly from national marketplaces for the peer-to-peer sales of goods. Moreover, the revenue structure itself varies greatly, with some companies taking a substantial share of the provider's profit margin and others a small share or nothing at all, basing their profits only on third-party advertising hosted on the site. It follows that regulation should be cautious, ensuring that the necessary interests are protected, without, however, calling into question the business model as a whole. Furthermore, a solution that treats all online marketplaces as equal is hardly adequate.[29] And that is precisely what the Portuguese law does – adopt a unitary solution to a problem that has different aspects. Virtually all online marketplaces meet at least one of the undemanding subparagraphs of art 44 DL 84/2021, which means that virtually all online marketplaces are liable under this rule.[30] Even compared to the solution in the ELI Model Rules, the Portuguese solution goes further. Although the Portuguese act uses the same term 'predominant influence', it does so with a different content. Used as a classificatory concept in the Portuguese act and as a type concept in the Model Rules, the term will cover a

---

[28] This has been recognized in several European Union documents. See, eg, Regulation (EU) 2019/1150 of the European Parliament and of the Council of 20 June 2019 on promoting fairness and transparency for business users of online intermediation services [2019] OJ L186/57 (P2B Regulation), recital 1: 'Online intermediation services are key enablers of entrepreneurship and new business models, trade and innovation, which can also improve consumer welfare […] They offer access to new markets and commercial opportunities allowing undertakings to exploit the benefits of the internal market. They allow consumers in the Union to exploit those benefits, in particular by increasing their choice of goods and services, as well as by contributing to offering competitive pricing online'. Maultzsch (n 11) 212, speaks of potential for innovation and added value; Vanessa Mak, 'Private Law Perspectives on Platform Services. Airbnb: Home Rentals between AYOR and NIMBY' (2016) 5(1) EuCML 19, 25.

[29] The path of differentiation is the one followed in the European Union after the approval of the Digital Services Act, as it distinguishes between online platforms and very large online platforms, with the latter being those with more than 45 million users (art. 25). Maria Romana Allegri, 'Il futuro digitale dell'Unione europea: nuove categorie di intermediari digitali, nuove forme di responsabilità' (2021) 2 Rivista Italiana di Informatica e Diritto 7, 16.

[30] Such a solution may have the effect of favouring larger online marketplaces to the detriment of smaller ones, as the former are better able to cope with increased operating costs. Ricardo Pazos Castro, 'Uber, Airbnb y la llamada "influencia decisiva" de las plataformas digitales' (2020) 31 IDP – Revista d'Internet, dret i política 1, 10.

much larger number of situations under Portuguese law.[31] More than that, the *raison d'être* behind the Model Rules concept is lost. The idea there is to guarantee that the operator will be liable for the (bad) performance of the supplier if he creates the expectation that he controls the supplier – because the client believed that the marketplace operator would have a say in that performance. The Portuguese solution has the advantage of being innovative and will certainly serve as an example to be discussed in other European countries. However, if it is widely (and consistently) applied, it may have the unwanted side effect of harming Portuguese consumers because it will mean the end of some national marketplaces which do not have the financial capacity to assume the obligations imposed on them,[32] and it may lead some foreign marketplaces to stop operating in Portugal because the potential economic benefits offered by the Portuguese market do not outweigh the risks.[33]

Furthermore, we would argue that the solution is contrary to European law.[34] The European Commission's Communication on online platforms[35] states that any regulation 'must be conducive to furthering sustainable development and scaling-up of the platform business model in Europe', since platforms 'play a prominent role in the creation of 'digital value' that underpins future economic growth in the EU and consequently are of major importance to the effective functioning of the digital single market'.[36] As this document

---

[31] Sørensen (n 22) 90, criticizes the choice of a standard concept in the model law on account of its more debatable application, which creates uncertainty.

[32] Research group on the Law of Digital Services (n 17) 165: 'a heavy-handed regulatory approach creates the risk of stifling innovation and creativity'. Luca Belli and Cristiana Sappa, 'The intermediary conundrum – Cyber-regulators, cyber-police or both?' (2017) 8(3) JIPITEC 183, 192, talk about the risk of a less eclectic market.

[33] For instance, the Research group on the Law of Digital Services (n 17) 164, argued that if it was felt that platforms needed to be regulated, this should take place at European level to avoid imposing obstacles to the development of the single market. There is also the possibility that the solution will not be applied in practice because consumers are unaware of its existence. Addressing a reduced awareness of their rights among Portuguese consumers, António Pinto Monteiro, Sandra Passinhas and Maria Raquel Guimarães, 'Enforcement and Effectiveness of Consumer Law in Portugal: Filling the Gap between the Law on the Books and the Law in Action' in Hans Micklitz and Geneviève Saumier (eds), *Enforcement and Effectiveness of Consumer Law* (Springer 2018) 476.

[34] The Research group on the Law of Digital Services (n 17) 165, notes the European Commission's cautious approach to this issue, seeking solutions that strike a balance between market regulation and innovation.

[35] European Commission, 'Online Platforms and the Digital Single Market Opportunities and Challenges for Europe', COM/2016/288 final (Communication from the Commission to the European Parliament, the Council, the European Economic and Social Committee and the Committee of the Regions).

[36] Page 5 of the Communication. On the relevance placed on the idea of a digital single market, Dariusz Adamski, 'Lost on the digital platform: Europe's legal travails with the digital single market' (2018) 55 CML Rev 719, 721.

includes the guidelines on this issue, it is in its light that one should interpret the permission included in the recitals of Directives 2019/770 and 2019/771.[37] In this sense, Member States may extend the application of the Directives to platform operators, but they must do so in a way that ensures a balanced solution that does not lead to the end of the viability of the business model of online marketplaces, in particular smaller ones. Going back to the principles of private law, this solution also seems to call into question the principle of private autonomy, without sufficient reason.[38]

We do not argue that online marketplace operators can always hide behind triangularity. There are cases where they should be considered parties to the contract because they give this impression to the user, and operators are also liable for a breach of the main contract insofar as they assume this obligation (eg Amazon's A-to-z guarantee)[39]. However, we argue that it should be possible to use a business model that is based on the separation of three contracts, and on the separation of responsibilities, provided that the user is aware of this separation.[40]

It is also true that the Portuguese solution does not place the final burden on the marketplace operator. The marketplace operator is primarily responsible and may exercise a right of redress against the supplier. However, even this position of being responsible in the first place represents a significant burden that a small company may not be able to bear.

---

[37] Christian Twigg-Flesner, 'From REFIT to a rethink: Time for fundamental EU consumer law reform?' (2017) 6(5) EuCML 185, 189, argues that European consumer law should increasingly become a set of principles guiding the legislative output of the Member States.

[38] With regard to the solution of the ELI Model Rules, Maultzsch (n 11) 230, argues that '[t]here are no compelling reasons for such a restriction of freedom of contract'. *A fortiori* he would defend this in Portuguese law where the solution is even more demanding for operators. The author argues that 'liberal contract law should not prescribe mandatory and therefore necessarily 'rough' responsibilities solely on the basis that one of the parties has superior risk control from an objective point of view. Rather, it leaves room for more apt individual contractual solutions'. Also, Damjan Možina, 'Retail business, platform services and information duties' (2016) 5(1) EuCML 25, 29, argues that any measures to maintain customer confidence should be left to regulation by the market.

[39] Available at: <https://www.amazon.com/gp/help/customer/display.html?nodeId=GQ37ZCNECJKTFYQV>.

[40] In economic terms, the platform-based business model has advantages, David S Evans, 'Some empirical aspects of multi-sided platform industries' (2003) 2, 3 RNE 191, 192: a platform increases 'social surplus when three necessary conditions are true: (1) there are distinct groups of customers; (2) a member of one group benefits from having his demand coordinated with one or more members of another group; and (3) an intermediary can facilitate that coordination more efficiently than bi-lateral relationships between the members of the group'.

We maintain that the solution would be more balanced if it were closer to the solution of the Model Rules, whereby marketplace operators who create the expectation that they have a predominant influence over suppliers are held liable.[41] Alternatively, if one wishes to maintain the more comprehensive solution of the Portuguese act, it might be more balanced to make a differentiation according to the size (and financial capacity) of the company,[42] following, for example, the distinction proposed in the Digital Services Act between online platforms and very large online platforms[43] and imposing liability only on the latter.

III. Conclusions

Art 44 DL 84/2021 sets forth that an online marketplace operator exercising predominant influence over the contract is jointly and severally liable with the supplier to the consumer for the lack of conformity of the subject matter with the contract. The Portuguese solution, which is pioneering in the European context, draws inspiration from the ELI model law but covers a much wider range of online marketplaces. The term 'predominant influence' is used as a type concept in the Model Rules and as a classificatory concept in the Portuguese law, which results in a rigidity that is not in line with the variety of business models existing among platforms.

We argue that the Portuguese solution is contrary to EU law, insofar as it may jeopardize the business model of platforms, at least for smaller platforms, which goes against the European goals. The permission to extend the application of Directives 2019/770 and 2019/771 to platform operators must

---

[41] On the ELI Model Rules Research Group's concern for this balance, Christoph Busch, Gerhard Dannemann and Hans Schulte-Nölke, 'Ein neues Vertrags- und Verbraucherrecht für online-Plattformen im digitalen Binnenmarkt? – Diskussionsentwurf für eine mögliche EU-Richtlinie' (2016) MMR 787, 788. Taking the contrary position, Maultzsch (n 11) 235, maintains that a solution such as that of the Model Rules should be accepted only in C2C relationships, ie situations where the main contract is concluded between two private individuals. Jorge Tomillo Urbina, 'Los consumidores ante las plataformas de intermediacion online: Algunas reflexiones' (2021) 27 LEX – Revista de la Facultad de Derecho y Ciencia Politica 97, 127, and Gemma Rubio Gimeno, 'Responsabilidad de las plataformas de economía colaborativa y responsabilidad del proveedor del servicio' in Gemma Rubio Gimeno and Antonio Orti Vallejo (eds), *Propuestas de regulación de las plataformas de economía colaborativa: perspectivas general y sectoriales* (Aranzadi 2019) 133, also argue that the supplier should be held liable in C2C cases. This is a situation that is not covered by DL 84/2021, which applies only to B2C relationships. Engert (n 15) 316, is completely opposed to the solution of the Model Rules.

[42] Busch, Dannemann and Schulte-Nölke (n 41) 671, argue that the model law solution allows for this differentiation.

[43] DSA, art 25.

be read in the light of, among other texts, the European Commission's Communication on digital platforms.

We conclude that the solution would be more balanced if it were closer to the solution of the ELI Model Rules, in which liability is imposed only on marketplace operators who create the expectation that they exercise predominant influence over suppliers. Alternatively, if the more comprehensive solution of Portuguese approach is to be maintained, it might be more balanced to differentiate according to the size (and financial capacity) of the companies, following, for example, the distinction proposed in the Digital Services Act between online platforms and very large online platforms, with liability of this nature imposed only on the latter.

Contributors

Friederike Bahl
Permanent Fellow at the Hamburg Colloquium for Social Theory; Associate Editor for the Sociology of Industry and Labour at 'Soziopolis'

Constance Bonzé
Researcher for the Centre for Comparative Law at the British Institute of International and Comparative Law, London

Joana Campos Carvalho
Assistant Professor at NOVA School of Law, Lisbon; Researcher at CEDIS – Research & Development Centre on Law and Society and the NOVA Consumer Lab

Marta Cantero Gamito
Professor of Information Technology Law at the University of Tartu; Research Fellow at the Florence School of Transnational Governance

Federica Casarosa
Research Affiliate at Scuola Superiore Sant'Anna, Pisa; Professor at the European University Institute, Florence

Pietro Dunn
Public Servant for the Italian Ministry of Justice

Costanza Di Francesco Maesa
Marie Sklodowska-Curie Postdoctoral Fellow, University of Siena, Department of Business and Law, and University of São Paulo, Department of Law

Giovanni De Gregorio
PLMJ Chair in Law and Technology at the Católica Global School of Law, Universidade Católica Portuguesa, Lisbon

Mateusz Grochowski
Associate Professor of Law, Tulane University School of Law; Affiliated Fellow at the Yale Information Society Project; Corresponding Fellow at the Yale Center for the Study of Private Law

Johannes Ipsen
Research Assistant and Doctoral Candidate at Leuphana University Lüneburg

Katarzyna Łakomiec
Assistant Professor, Institute of Law Studies Polish Academy of Sciences; Humboldt Research Fellow, Max Planck Institute for Comparative Public Law and International Law

Hans-W Micklitz
Part-time Professor at the European University Institute, Florence

Sara Migliorini
Assistant Professor of Global Legal Studies, University of Macau

Ruşen Öncü
PhD Candidate at Tilburg University, Tilburg Law School

Dianora Poletti († 2024)
Former Full Professor of Private Law, University of Pisa; Judge at the Supreme Court of Cassation, Rome

Claudia Schubert
Professor for Civil Law, Labour Law, Company Law and Comparative Law at the Faculty of Law, University of Hamburg; Member of the Association Committee of the Association of German Labour Courts

Eric Tjong Tjin Tai
Full Professor of Private Law at Tilburg University, Tilburg Law School

Paul Verbruggen
Full Professor of Private Law at Tilburg University, Tilburg Law School

Barbara Warwas
Lector (Professor of Applied Sciences) in Multilevel Regulation at The Hague University of Applied Sciences